GCE A2 Level

A2 Level for Edexcel

Health & Social Care

Series editor: Neil Moonie

www.heinemann.co.uk
✓ Free online support
✓ Useful weblinks
✓ 24 hour online ordering

01865 888058

Heinemann Educational Publishers
Halley Court, Jordan Hill, Oxford OX2 8EJ
Part of Harcourt Education

Heinemann is the registered trademark of Harcourt Education Limited

First published 2006
10 09 08 07 06
10 9 8 7 6 5 4 3 2

British Library Cataloguing in Publication Data is available
from the British Library on request.

10-digit ISBN: 0 435 35294 6
13-digit ISBN: 978 0 435352 94 3

Edited by Diane Chandler
Typeset and illustrated by Tek Art
Original illustrations © Harcourt Education Limited, 2006
Cover design by Peter Stratton
Printed and bound in China through Phoenix Offset
Cover photo: © Getty Images/Photodisc

Websites
Please note that the examples of websites suggested in this book were up to date at the time
of writing. It is essential for tutors to preview each site before using it to ensure that the URL
is still accurate and the content is appropriate. We suggest that tutors bookmark useful sites
and consider enabling students to access them through the school or college intranet.

Tel: 01865 888058   www.heinemann.co.uk

Endorsement
This high-quality material is endorsed by Edexcel and has been through a rigorous quality
assurance programme to ensure that it is a suitable companion to the specification for both
learners and teachers. This does not mean that its contents will be used verbatim when
setting examinations nor is it to be read as being the official specification – a copy of which is
available at www.edexcel.org.uk

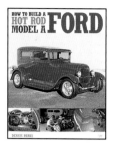
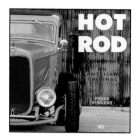
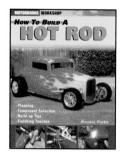

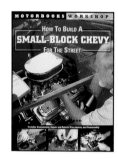

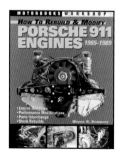
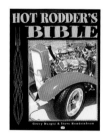
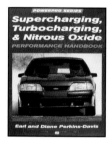

Contents

Acknowledgements

Unit 7

The following organisations and individuals contributed towards this chapter:

The London Borough of Sutton
Sutton and Merton Primary Care Trust
Epsom and St Helier University Hospital Trust
Sutton and Merton Bereavement Service
Age Concern
The Carers Centre Sutton
The Stroke Association

Unit 10

Dee Spencer-Perkins would like to thank Gail Lincoln for her advice and practical support.

Unit 11

The following organisations assisted with this chapter:
The London Borough of Sutton
Sutton and Merton Primary Care Trust
Epsom and St Helier University Hospital Trust

Introduction

This book has been written to support students who are studying for the GCE A2 Edexcel award. The book is designed to support the six A2 Units of the award:

Unit 7 Meeting individual needs (externally assessed)
Unit 8 Promoting health and well-being (internally assessed)
Unit 9 Investigating disease (internally assessed)
Unit 10 Using and understanding research (internally assessed)
Unit 11 Social issues and welfare needs (internally assessed)
Unit 12 Understanding human behaviour (externally assessed)

This book has been organised to cover each of these units in detail. Headings are designed to make it easy to follow the content of each unit and to find the information needed to support achievement. As well as providing information each unit is designed to stimulate the development of the thinking skills needed to achieve an advanced award.

Assessment

Each unit will be assessed by coursework or by an external test set and marked by Edexcel. Detailed guidance for coursework assessment and external test requirements can be found in the unit specifications and at Edexcel's website at www.edexcel.org.uk. This book has been designed to support students to achieve high grades as set out in Edexcel's guidance available during 2005.

Special features of this book

Throughout the text there are a number of features that are designed to encourage reflection and to help students make links between theory and practice. In particular this book has been designed to encourage a depth of learning and understanding and to encourage students to go beyond a surface level of understanding characterised by a reliance on memorising and describing issues.

The special features of this book include:

What if?

What if?

Thought provoking questions or dilemmas are presented in order to encourage reflective thinking. Sometimes these questions might provide a basis for reflection involving discussion with others.

Did you know?

Did you know?

Interesting facts or snippets of information are included to encourage reflective thinking.

Try it out

Try it out

Practical activities or tasks that might be undertaken by individuals or groups are suggested. These activities may encourage a deeper level of exploration and understanding.

SCENARIO

Scenario

We have used this term in place of the more traditional term 'case study' because the idea of people being perceived as 'cases' does not fit easily with the notion of empowerment – a key value highlighted by government policy and by Edexcel standards. Scenarios are presented throughout the units to help explain the significance of theoretical ideas to Health, Social Care and Early Years settings.

Consider this

Consider this

Each author has designed a 'consider this' feature at the end of each section of each unit. Each 'consider this' involves a brief scenario followed by a series of questions. The first easy questions ask students to simply identify issues. The next questions ask students to go into greater depth and analyse issues using theory. These questions are designed to challenge thinking skills to go beyond a simple memory for information. Finally there are questions that ask for an in-depth understanding of issues. At this level the questions require students to access a wide range of learning in order to make an appropriate judgement or evaluation about an issue. The ability to evaluate is a 'thinking skill' that will contribute towards the achievement of high grades at Advanced level.

Key concept

Key concept

Because the authors believe that the development of analytic and evaluative skills requires the ability to use concepts, the authors have identified key concepts and offered a brief explanation of how these terms might be used.

Section summary

Schematic diagrams, tables or other systems for providing an overview of theoretical content are used at the end of sections in order to help clarify the theory in each section.

Assessment guidance

At the end of each unit there is a 'how you will be assessed' section that provides either sample test material for externally assessed units or outline guidance and ideas designed to help students achieve the highest grades when preparing internally assessed coursework.

Unit test

Internally assessed units also feature 10 questions that can be used as a learning check for the content of that unit.

Glossary

This book contains a useful glossary to provide fast reference for key terms and concepts used within the units.

References

There is a full list of references used within each unit together with useful websites at the end of each unit.

Author details

Beryl Stretch, former Head of Health and Social Care in a large College of Further Education. Currently part of the senior examining board for Edexcel, GCE and GCSE Health and Social Care. Former external and internal verifier for VCE, GNVQ, NVQ programmes and Examiner for GCSE human biology. Contributor to several best-selling textbooks on health and social care at all levels.

David Herne moved from teaching into health education in a local authority, then went on to become the policy lead for health in a metropolitan authority before moving in to the NHS to manage a health promotion service. David is currently a Specialist in Public Health working in the fields of sexual health, alcohol and substance use for a large Lancashire Primary Care Trust and tutor for the Open University on the level 1 'Understanding Health and Social Care' course and previously on the level 3 'Promoting Health, Skills, Perspectives and Practice'. David has been a contributor to several previous Heinemann texts, including those for BTEC, GCE AS level and AVCE courses.

Dee Spencer-Perkins, began her social services career in research, moving on to become a trainer and then a training manager. She is a Chartered Member of the Chartered Institute of Personnel and Development, and now works as an independent trainer, consultant and writer specialising in language and communication. Dee also has a keen interest in disability issues.

Neil Moonie, former Deputy Director of the Department of Social Services, Health and Education in a College of Further and Higher Education. Chartered Psychologist, part-time lecturer and contributor to a wide range of textbooks and learning resources in the field of health and social care. Editor of Heinemann's GNVQ Intermediate and Advanced textbooks on health and social care since 1993 and editor of the 2000 Standards AVCE textbook.

Sylvia Aslangul has been involved with health and social care all her working life. She has a nursing background and she then moved into teaching vocational and degree courses in Further and Higher Education. She is an Associate Lecturer in Health with the Open University. She was an External Verifier for Health and Social Care courses for Edexcel for 15 years. She has been editor and contributor to a range of textbooks on health and social care. Sylvia represents the voluntary sector on health and care committees that organise and develop services in her local area.

Meeting individual needs

This unit covers the following sections:

7.1. Structure and provision of services

7.2 Meeting individual needs

7.3 Practitioner roles

7.4 Quality assurance and regulation

Introduction

Unit 7

Every health and social care practitioner needs to understand how health and social care services are provided within the UK. The care planning process involves both practitioners and service users. Services should be organised to meet individual needs of service users and their carers. A range of practitioners are involved in delivering health and social care, and this unit shows how these groups work together.

Services need to be regulated in order to protect both the service provider and the service user, and the issue of regulation and accountability is also covered in this unit.

How you will be assessed

The unit is externally assessed through a written examination. This unit will be assessed using a synoptic test exploring knowledge of this unit together with understanding of core health and social care issues covered in previous units, that is units 1, 2, and 3. There is a practice test at the end of the chapter.

7.1 Structure and provision of services

This section covers the organisation of health and social care services, and how central and local government fund and plan services. It covers how these services are organised at the time of writing, but further changes are expected in the future. Legislation and policy directives from central government state how health and care providers should organise their services, and these directives are constantly changing.

With the development and reorganisation of national and local statutory services, many of the departments in health and social care overlap.

For example, local social services include housing departments, and children's services link with education and health.

Health and social services have been traditionally provided by three sectors:

* the public (statutory) sector
* the private sector
* the voluntary sector.

Sometimes the private and voluntary sectors are called the independent sector. Informal care is also essential to the provision of care, so we could say that there are four sectors of care (see Figure 7.1).

The public (or statutory) sector

This sector includes the National Health Service (NHS), which provides services in hospitals and in the community. The NHS was set up in the UK in 1948, and is paid for through taxation and National Insurance contributions. For most services it is free at the point of delivery. In other words most of the services received are free. Some services are charged for, for example dental services, prescriptions and eye tests. People who have low incomes, or who have particular health conditions, or who are in particular age groups are exempt from these charges.

Funding of the NHS

The NHS budget for England and Wales is planned to reach £105.6 billion by 2007–08. Central taxation and National Insurance contributions provide 95 per cent of the funding, while patient charges account for only 2 per cent funding. Many NHS buildings and administrative systems are old and with the new patient initiatives, such as new booking systems for hospital appointments, much of the government's budget will go on new national IT systems, new buildings and equipment.

The NHS: legislation and policy since 1990

NHS and Community Care Act (1990)
The NHS and Community Care Act of 1990 developed from two White Papers. *Working for Patients* (1989) was concerned with the future organisation of the health service, and *Caring for People* (1989), was concerned with the provision of care in the community. As a result of the 1990 Act several changes took place:

* social services took the lead role for community care services in England and Wales
* social services and social work departments had to produce community care plans for their area

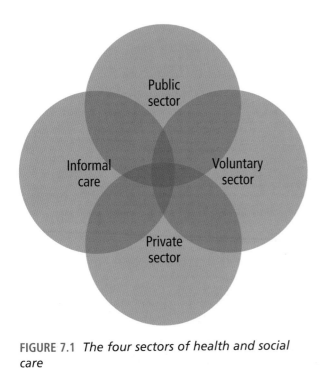

FIGURE 7.1 *The four sectors of health and social care*

* the Department of Social Security stopped paying board and lodging for people in residential homes

* care managers were appointed by social services to assess people's needs, if they were eligible for a service, and also to arrange services to meet those needs if resources were available.

Instead of services being provided mainly by the statutory health and social care services, after the 1990 Act services were commissioned by social services from a range of agencies, including private and voluntary agencies. This approach is called the mixed economy of care.

Following the 1990 Act, registration and inspection units were set up separately from the local authority to inspect residential services provided by the council and services provided by the private and voluntary sector.

Key concept

Mixed economy of care: the provision of care from a range of service providers. The Conservative government of the 1980s felt that introducing competition between service providers would increase the cost-effectiveness and quality of services. Instead of most services being provided by the local social services, these services would be commissioned from the private or voluntary sector, and social services would provide services to clients who had complex needs.

Providers of services: these could be NHS Trust hospitals, private agencies or the voluntary sector.

Commissioners of services: these could be Primary Care Groups – later to become Primary Care Trusts (PCTs) – and social services departments.

With the NHS and Community Care Act, hospitals were able to arrange contracts with private agencies, particularly for catering and cleaning, instead of employing people directly to do this work. Private agencies compete for contracts and hospitals choose cost-effective services.

What if?

If you were going to buy a new mobile phone, would cost be the main factor or are there other factors that you would consider to be important? Is buying the cheapest always a good idea? Can you think of any problems that might arise if a highly price-sensitive market develops in the area of care?

Since 1990 there has been a great deal of legislation affecting the provision of health and social care services. Some of the key changes are described below.

The New NHS: modern, dependable

The White Paper *The New NHS* (1997) set out the government's plans to modernise the NHS over the following ten years. GPs were organised into Primary Care Groups (PCGs) responsible to the local health authority, and local social services began to work more closely with their partners in health. The doctor–patient relationship was seen as an important way of building confidence in the health service.

The Health Act 1999

This Act reformed primary care, allowing the creation of Primary Care Trusts, and requiring all hospital trusts to improve their services. The Act also allowed the introduction of:

* walk-in high street health centres

* increased use of day surgery in health centres

* health checks and advice sessions in new clinics

* one-stop shops – varied health care services at one site

* wider partnerships, encouraging GPs to team up with pharmacists, counsellors and dentists to provide a range of services from one site.

The NHS Plan 2000

This ten-year NHS Plan set out a vision of a health service designed around the patient. The targets include the following:

* 7,000 extra beds in hospitals and intermediate care

* over 100 new hospitals

* clean wards overseen by modern matrons and providing better hospital food

* modern IT systems in every hospital and GP surgery

* 7,500 more consultants and 2,000 more GPs

* 20,000 more nurses and therapists

* child care support for NHS staff with 100 on-site nurseries.

As a result of these changes, waiting times for treatment should be reduced and long waits in accident and emergency departments ended. For more details on the NHS Plan see www.nhs.uk/nhsplan.

There is also an NHS Plan for Scotland, available on www.show.scot.nhs.uk/sehd/onh/onh-00htm. The NHS Plan for Wales, published in 2001, can be accessed on www.wales.gov.uk/healthplanonline.

The core principles of the NHS

The NHS will:

* provide a universal service for all, based on clinical need, not the ability to pay

* provide a comprehensive range of services

* organise its services around the needs and preferences of individual patients, their families and their carers

* respond to the different needs of different populations

* work continually to improve quality services and to minimise errors

* support and value its staff

* devote public funds for health care solely to NHS patients

* work together with others to provide a seamless service

* help to keep people healthy and work to reduce inequalities

* respect the confidentiality of individual patients and provide open access to information about services, treatment and performance.

How does the NHS work?

Parliament passes legislation for the health service in England and Wales. Scotland and Northern Ireland are responsible for the health service in their regions. The Secretary of State for Health is a member of the Cabinet and has overall responsibility for the work of the Department of Health. He or she works directly with a group of ministers for health.

The Department of Health

The role of the Department of Health is to support the government to improve the health and well-being of the population, and to improve standards of public health.

The Department of Health also sets national standards for the NHS, for example the National Service Frameworks (NSFs). NSFs have been developed for services, including those for mental health, for older people, for diabetes, and for children. NSFs set standards and targets and health and social care organisations have to show how they are meeting these targets.

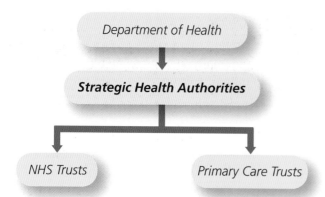

```
Department of Health
        │
        ▼
Strategic Health Authorities
        │
   ┌────┴────┐
   ▼         ▼
NHS Trusts   Primary Care Trusts
```

FIGURE 7.2 *Key organisations in the NHS*

Structure of the NHS

The NHS is divided up into several sectors. (See Figure 7.2.)

Strategic health authorities

There are 28 strategic health authorities in England, each responsible for the health of the population in their area. They develop strategies for health services and manage the NHS Trusts in their area.

Special health authorities

These are specialist bodies which are part of the NHS; ambulance services and the NHS Direct service are examples. They are accountable to the Department of Health and have to produce an annual report.

Secondary services

Secondary services are provided in or by hospitals, which are NHS Trusts. Trusts were created in 1991 under NHS reforms to provide hospital care, mental health care and specialist services. Some NHS Trusts act as regional centres for specialist services, such as spinal or cancer treatment. NHS Trusts are self-governing bodies with their own board of directors. They receive their funding from the Department of Health and also from Primary Care Trusts (PCTs) which send patients to them – both as in-patients and as out-patients.

Secondary care is also provided by NHS Foundation Trusts. These were set up in 2004 following the Health and Social Care (Community Health and Standards) Act 2003. Foundation Trusts are independent public interest organisations, and are free from central government control. They are controlled locally through a board of governors. All Foundation Trusts had to demonstrate a high standard of service and apply to become trusts

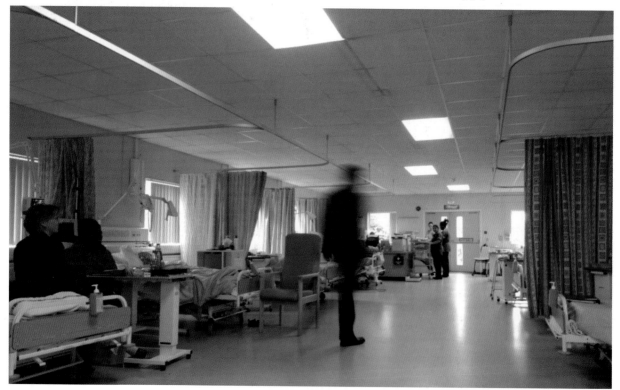

FIGURE 7.3 *A hospital ward*

before the government granted them Foundation status. At the moment only a few hospitals in England have Foundation status, mainly in London (e.g. Guys and St Thomas') or in the case of specialist hospitals such as the Royal Marsden Hospital which specialises in the treatment of cancer. The government proposes that all hospitals should aim to achieve Foundation status in the future.

Primary care services

Since 1999, Primary Care Trusts (PCTs) have developed to provide a range of services in the community. Their role is to assess and meet local health needs. At the moment PCTs control 75 per cent of the entire NHS budget and they commission services from hospitals and other health care providers such as NHS Direct.

Key concept

Primary care: **this relates to all the care that takes place in the community and not in the hospital setting.**

Primary care services are provided by GPs, dentists, pharmacists and opticians, as well as community staff attached to GP surgeries or clinics, such as practice nurses, district nurses and community health care assistants. Practices are developing more specialist services as it is hoped that more people will be treated in the community and in primary care, rather than in hospital, because people prefer to be treated near their own homes and to see the same nurse or doctor each visit. This also reduces the pressure on local acute hospitals. Examples of special services offered at GP practices include hypertension clinics (for people with high blood pressure), asthma clinics and diabetic clinics. Many of these clinics are led by nurses who have had specialist training.

FIGURE 7.4 *A GP working with his patients*

ADULTS AND OLDER PEOPLE	BABIES AND YOUNG CHILDREN	PEOPLE WITH MENTAL HEALTH PROBLEMS
Hospital care – Out-patient	Maternity services	Group therapy
In-patient	Dental care	Drop-in day centre
Mental health – Community Services (CPN)	Physiotherapy	Secondary care – In-patient care
Hospital	Hospital services – Out-patient	Out-patient care
Health promotion – Smoking	In-patient	Community Mental Health Team (CMHT)
Obesity	Child psychology	Therapists – Music
Alcohol	Speech therapy	Art
Sexual health	Eye services	Day hospital
Drug team	Primary health services – GPs	Behavioural psychologists
Specialist services – Stroke	Practice nurses	Psychotherapists
Diagnostic tests – X-rays	School nurses	Primary care – GPs
Blood tests	Health visitors	CPN
Intermediate care (jointly with social services)	Child Protection Service (jointly with education and social services)	Counselling
Occupational therapy		
Physiotherapy		
Primary health care – District nurses		
GPs		
Practice nurses		
Pharmacists		
Dentists		
Podiatry		
Rehabilitation		
Family planning		

TABLE 7.1 *Services provided by the NHS to a range of client groups*

FIGURE 7.5 *NHS Direct services*

Intermediate care services

Primary Care Trusts work closely with local authority social services departments, and this partnership has increased greatly in recent years. In some areas, plans are being developed to integrate health and social care services for certain groups – such as older people – or for particular services such as intermediate care. Intermediate care services are provided jointly by local PCTs and local authority social services departments, to support people who have been discharged from hospital but still need assistance. The service also reduces hospital admissions by putting health and care services in place so that people can be cared for in their own home.

SCENARIO

Beatrice

Beatrice is 80 years old and lives on her own. She has diabetes, arthritis and a heart condition. Very often she forgets to check her blood levels and adjust her insulin dose. This has resulted in Beatrice falling into a comatose state, to be found, fortunately, by her daughter when she visited. Her daughter phoned for an ambulance to take her mother to the local hospital and be admitted. With **intermediate care** services in place, her daughter (or Beatrice herself) would be given the number of the local intermediate care service. A nurse would visit and test Beatrice's blood and urine, adjust the insulin and advise Beatrice how to look after herself. If the intermediate care team assessed Beatrice and decided that she needed to be referred to hospital, this would be done. This approach means that Beatrice can stay at home and does not have the trauma of being admitted to hospital. It also means that scarce beds at the hospital are kept for acute emergencies.

Further developments in the NHS

Walk-in centres

These have been set up in large towns to reduce the pressure on hospital Accident and Emergency departments. They are open from 7 am to 11 pm every day and are a nurse-led service. Most people attending these centres have minor complaints, and they are usually given advice and treatment.

NHS Direct

NHS Direct provides a nurse-led 24-hour, seven-days-a-week telephone service. It is a special health authority (see page 6) and provides an annual report on its activities. PCTs commission the service from their local NHS Direct centre.

NHS Direct offers service users information about health services in their local area, and gives medical advice (see Figure 7.5). It has a website (www.nhsdirect.nhs.uk) which offers advice and guidance. There is also a new NHS Direct interactive service on digital satellite TV.

Calls to NHS Direct are charged at local rate, and all calls are recorded. The nurse who takes the call will assess the problem and advise on treatment. If it is something serious, the caller will be advised to see his or her local doctor or to go to hospital. If the problem is very serious, the nurse can call an ambulance on the caller's behalf.

Out-of-hours services

GPs now have new contracts so they are not obliged to provide a 24-hour service. PCTs have taken on responsibility for providing health care out of normal surgery times (see Figure 7.6). Patients who need this service phone a local number and are assessed on the phone. If there is a clinical need, a duty doctor will phone back within 20 minutes and assess the situation. If required, the patient will attend a local centre to be seen within an hour. Some patients may receive a home visit.

National plans are being developed to provide a one-stop emergency telephone number that will link with health and social care services.

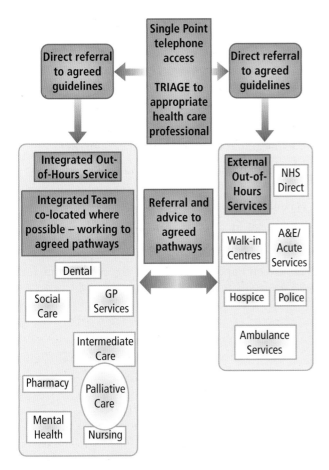

FIGURE 7.6 *A model of out-of-hours care*

Social services

Successive Acts of Parliament have made central and local government in England and Wales responsible for the provision of the wide range of social services. The main services provided by local councils are personal social services, education and housing. This section will discuss personal social services.

Parliament sets out the powers and responsibilities of local councils. Councils have a **duty** to keep certain records, for example they have to keep a register of sick and chronically disabled people who are in their area. They also have a **duty** to provide accommodation for certain groups such as people with mental health problems who have been discharged from hospital. Councils also have **powers** to decide what level of service they will provide and the charges they will make for their services. Social services are monitored on performance and

spending by central government and by the Commission for Social Care Inspection. Some services related to education and children, such as child minding and nursery school provision, are monitored by the Office for Standards in Education (OFSTED) (see section 7.4).

Funding of social services

Central government funds local councils through the Standard Spending Assessment (SSA) formula. The amount of money given to local councils is based on the population profile of the area and includes factors such as the number of older people and single parents in the area, as well as types of housing, ethnic groupings and population density. Apart from the SSA, local councils raise funds from the local council tax and from fees and charges for their services.

The local council provides social care services to those who are assessed as being in need. However, many services provided by the council are means tested (i.e. people who apply for social services have their income assessed as well as their needs), and some payment is usually required.

Social services provide care 24 hours a day, seven days a week, and there is a duty social worker on call for emergencies at all times.

Social services provide a range of services to a range of client groups, but changes in policy have led to social services becoming purchasers of services rather than providing them directly themselves (see Table 7.2). Voluntary organisations and private agencies provide services such as personal care, adoption and fostering services, but the local authority retains responsibility for ensuring that the services are of a high quality.

The 1998 White Paper, *Modernising Social Services*, set out the programme for change in the social services. Staff were to be trained and standards of care would be improved. A national register of care staff was to be set up. Protection of vulnerable client groups, such as older people, people with learning disabilities, people with mental health problems, and children, was seen as a key issue. All staff had to receive training on protection issues related to abuse. This was in response to news stories of abuse by social services staff of people from a range of client groups. The White Paper also called for closer working between health and social care services, with joint funding of projects and joint budgets. These areas are still developing.

In March 2005 the Green Paper *Independence, Well-being and Choice* was published. This was a consultation paper setting out proposals for the future direction of social care for all adults in England. It is expected that the rest of the UK will develop similar proposals. The emphasis in the Green Paper is on:

* helping people remain in their own homes and giving them greater control and choice over the way their needs are met

* encouraging adult social services to work with a range of partners, including PCTs and the private and voluntary sector, in order to provide services that are cost-effective and meet the needs of a diverse community

* making sure no one is marginalised in society – social inclusion must underpin all services

* ensuring services are of high quality and delivered by a well-trained work force or by informal carers who are themselves supported

* ensuring technology is used to support people, especially related to housing (see below)

* ensuring that people with greatest needs should receive the support and protection they need

* ensuring that vulnerable people are supported and risks to them assessed.

This Green Paper puts forward the programme for social services for the next 10 to 15 years.

OLDER PEOPLE	PEOPLE WITH DISABILITIES	BABIES AND YOUNG CHILDREN
Residential care	Supported housing	Emergency social worker support
Social worker support	Direct payments advice	Family centres
Information and advice	Domiciliary care	Liaison with education and health services (Sure Start)
Domiciliary care	Equipment	
Needs assessment	Home adaptation	Child protection
Financial assessment	Respite care	Support for children with disabilities
Transport	Specialist social worker support	Family support
Day care	Transport	Fostering and adoption services
Equipment		Specialist social worker
Supported/sheltered housing		

TABLE 7.2 *Social services provided to different client groups*

The use of technology to allow people to stay in their own homes

The increasing use of technology to support people with specific needs is a good example of the kind of change suggested in the Green Paper. Through the provision of equipment and making adaptations to their homes, people can remain in their own homes. New technology has been developed that may help clients with a range of different needs – see the scenario below for an example of the use of assistive technology.

> ### Key concept
>
> *Assistive technology:* the use of people and technology to provide remote assistance to service users and carers.

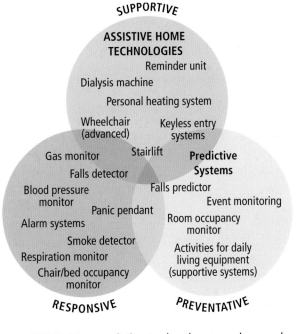

FIGURE 7.7 *How assistive technology can be used to promote independence*

SCENARIO

Assistive technology

The local social services and the Alzheimer's Society are working together in a London borough with 40 older people who are suffering from the early stages of dementia, to see if assistive technology (see Figure 7.7) will help these clients remain in their own homes. There is an IT link between each home and social services that gives off an alarm if the person is in danger. Sensors and monitors are used to detect falls, to remind people to take their medication, and to identify whether people are active or inactive. Environmental monitoring includes high or low temperature detection, water flooding, smoke and gas detection.

What if?

What are the potential benefits for:

a) clients?

b) social and health services in the use of this approach?

Can you think of any potential problems?

The independent sector

The work of independent providers (private and voluntary organisations) has become increasingly important since the 1990 NHS and Community Care Act. As we have already seen, social services buy services from a range of organisations, including the private and voluntary sector.

Voluntary sector

Voluntary organisations were often set up to look after the interests of a particular client group – such as older people (e.g. Age Concern), children (e.g. National Children's Home), or people with learning disabilities (e.g. Mencap). These voluntary organisations acted as pressure groups and tried to influence government policy. Now many of these organisations depend on the money earned from the services they provide for social services. Many of the larger organisations operate at a national level where they represent their particular client group and provide information through leaflets, websites and brochures. Local branches are responsible for providing a range of services, and they are also represented on local health and social care committees.

PEOPLE IN HOSPITAL	OLDER PEOPLE IN THE COMMUNITY	BABIES/CHILDREN IN THE COMMUNITY	PEOPLE WITH LEARNING DISABILITIES AND THEIR CARERS
Discharge support	Meals on Wheels	Parenting groups	Holidays
Counselling	Hairdressing	Playgroups	Support groups
Visiting	Gardening	Toddlers clubs	Day centres
Hospital care services	Shopping	Homestart – support for parents	Respite care
Bereavement services	Transport	Family support groups (NCH, NSPCC)	Baby sitting
Canteen for patients and visitors	Befriending	National Childbirth Trust (NCT)	Holiday play schemes
Hospital shop	Advocacy		Leisure clubs
'Friends' of the hospital	Day centres		Therapies – Art – Music – Reflexology
	Lunch clubs		
	Exercise classes		After-school clubs

TABLE 7.3 *The range of services provided by the voluntary sector to different client groups*

SCENARIO

Age Concern

Age Concern acts as a lobbyist for older people, and also provides a range of services paid for by social services or by the NHS. In one London borough, Age Concern offers services including the following:

* information and advice on benefits, housing and other issues

* the Ageing Well Project assists people to prevent accidents in the home and promotes healthy living and exercise

* the Healthy Living Project offers healthy meals in a café, exercise classes and advice on health

* a home security service, which provides smoke alarms and security locks and chains, as well as testing electric blankets

* a hospital discharge scheme, which supports people who have left hospital and need help with shopping and confidence-building

* an advocacy scheme to support older people.

Try it out

Contact your local Age Concern office to look at their annual report. This will show the range of services they offer and how they are funded.

Perhaps your teacher could invite someone from the voluntary sector to your college to talk about the work they do in the community.

All voluntary organisations depend on volunteers who give their time freely. However voluntary organisations also employ professionals who raise funding, negotiate contracts with health and social care services, and co-ordinate services (see Table 7.3). All voluntary organisations produce an annual report in which they show how the

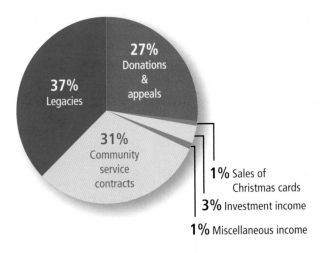

27% Donations & appeals

37% Legacies

31% Community service contracts

1% Sales of Christmas cards

3% Investment income

1% Miscellaneous income

FIGURE 7.8 *Funding of the Stroke Association of England and Wales 2004–05*

organisation is funded for the year. Much of the funding is through income paid by the statutory sector for services provided (see Figure 7.8).

Try it out

Look at Figure 7.11 and describe the pattern you see. Where does most of the funding come from?

The private sector

The private sector now contributes a great deal towards health and social care services.

* Many residential homes previously owned by social services have been sold to private companies or individuals, and social services commission places for their clients from the private sector.

* Private residential homes cater for groups such as older people, people with learning disabilities, and people with mental health problems.

* Home help and home care services that were previously provided directly by council staff are now provided by private agencies.

Private health care is also increasing in importance. Some people have private health insurance provided by their employers, and many others use their savings to pay for private health care either in hospitals or in the community. Many dentists are now private contractors. The government has indicated that more use of the private sector may be made in the future. Private hospitals may be commissioned by NHS Trusts to perform operations in order to reduce waiting lists.

Try it out

Contact a private hospital and find out the range of services it provides. Compare the services it offers with those at the local NHS hospital.

Informal carers

According to the 2001 census, there are 5.2 million carers in England and Wales. In this census, for the first time, people were asked whether they provided unpaid care for a family member or friend and for how many hours. Of the 5.2 million carers identified, over a million provided more than 50 hours of care a week.

Carers

What do we mean by a carer? Many people think it only refers to paid carers, and this is why it is difficult to identify the real number of informal unpaid carers. Previous figures have estimated that there are six million unpaid carers. Carers look after a range of people: it may be someone with a physical or mental illness or disability, or someone who needs support because of age-related difficulties.

Parent carers

This refers to someone who is the parent of a disabled child. Many parents do not see themselves as carers, just as parents. This could be a problem, as they may not be aware of the various carers' allowances and support available.

Young carers

These are people under the age of 18 who have caring responsibilities for another family member who is disabled or unwell from either mental or physical illness. The Department for Education and Skills now takes responsibility for young carers – in the past, many young carers were not identified and did not have the support they needed in order to be successful in their studies and to deal with bullying. In one London centre, the youngest carer was six years old.

FIGURE 7.9 *A young carer*

What if?

If you knew a young carer who was being bullied, how could you help her cope?

In a study called *Too Much to Take On* (1999), 20 young carers' groups were questioned about caring and bullying. Forty-four per cent of the carers that responded were aged 11 to 13. This can be a difficult age for young carers, as they are changing schools and making new friends while coping with their caring responsibilities. Of the young carers in this study, 35 per cent were 10 or under, which means they were coping with a lot of responsibility at a very young age.

More girls than boys take on the caring role: 60 per cent in the study were female and 40 per cent were male. Sixteen per cent of the young carers were the primary carer – the only person providing care.

Young carers who are the primary carer are more likely to care for someone with a physical disability (32 per cent) or a mental health problem (37 per cent). Nearly half of the young carers in the study were looking after their mother (26 per cent were primary carers). Of the boys, 49 per cent were caring for their mother, and of the girls 18 per cent were caring for their father. In situations where a daughter is caring for her father or a son is caring for his mother, the carer may feel under stress if they have to carry out personal tasks such as bathing or dressing.

These are some of the things the young carers in the study did in their caring role:

* cooking
* cleaning
* shopping
* providing emotional support
* washing, dressing and toileting (this could include changing incontinence pads)
* caring for younger siblings.

Most young carers share responsibility with another adult.

Carers who work outside the home

Many older carers also do full-time work, and studies have shown that many carers have to leave work or work part-time in order to fulfil their caring role. This affects their opportunities to contribute to pensions (including the state pension). The Carers (Equal Opportunities) Bill will also help carers (including young carers) access work and training opportunities. From 2006 the rights of working carers will be formally recognised and they will be entitled to flexible working which will help safeguard pension rights which have been affected by their caring role.

Updates to recent legislation in health and social care

Many changes in legislation in health and social care relate to vulnerable groups in society such as children and those with mental health problems.

The Children Act (1989)

This important piece of legislation stated that services must be provided for those children assessed as being in need. Social services could provide these services directly, work in partnership with voluntary organisations, or purchase services from independent or private sector agencies. Children who are assessed as being in need will be eligible for the following services:

* day care for children under five and not at school

* care and supervised activities outside school hours and during school holidays

* accommodation if required, if children are lost, abandoned or without a carer who can provide accommodation.

Social services must also provide:

* assessment of needs

* an emergency service 24 hours a day, 365 days a year.

In spite of many strategies related to children, including the Early Years Development and Childcare Partnerships which developed Sure Start programmes after 2001, it was felt that additional changes were needed if the health of children and young people was to improve. As part of the changes recommended by various reports, social services departments have now separated children's services from other social services. Figure 7.10 shows the organisation of a children's social services department.

Every Child Matters

The Green Paper *Every Child Matters*, published in September 2003, was a consultation document in which young people and their families, professionals and those working with children were asked for their views. The response showed that the aims of children's services should be to

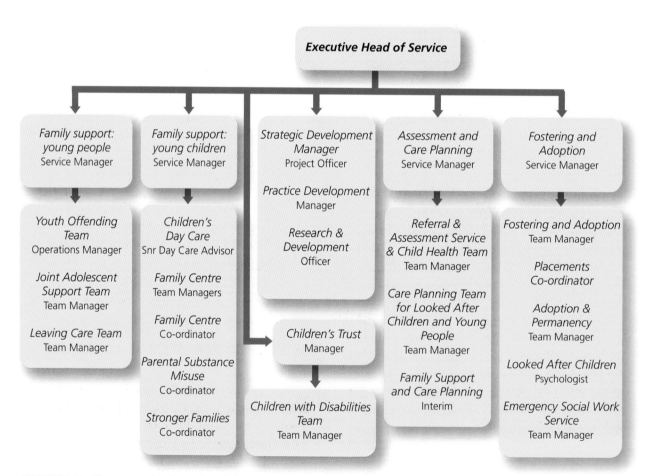

FIGURE 7.10 *The organisation of a children's social services department*

minimise risks for all children, and support them to:

* be healthy

* stay safe

* enjoy and achieve

* make a positive contribution

* achieve economic well-being.

These proposals fed into the Children Act (2004).

The Children Act (2004)

The Children Act (2004) sets out a new framework for children's services, building on the five aims of the Green Paper. The Act shifted the emphasis from intervention to prevention, and encouraged services to work together more effectively. This means that local authorities take the lead in developing children's services, but ensure involvement of a wide range of agencies, including the private and voluntary sector. Parents and carers are included on the committees that develop the local plans. In some areas pilot Children's Trusts have already been established, and representatives from education, health, social services and community organisations are included on the strategy boards. Children's Trusts are a way of bringing together all professional groups who look after children. This is seen as a more effective way of meeting the needs of vulnerable children who could be at risk.

More information about Children's Trusts is available on www.everychildmatters.gov.uk. The National Service Framework for Children, Young People and Maternity Services (2004) links into the Children Act (2004) and includes everyone delivering services to children and young people. The NSF sets standards for the first time for children's health and social care. These standards promote high-quality care, women- and child-centred services and personalised care that meet the needs of parents, children and their families. There are 11 standards in all. The website www.dh.gov.uk/childrensnsf has the standards in detail.

The Mental Health Act (1983)

The Mental Health Act (1983) lays down the rules for compulsory admission to hospital if a person with mental illness poses a risk to the health and safety of themselves or others. The hospital is expected to follow the mental health code of practice. Members of the Mental Health Commission regularly visit the hospital where patients are detained under the Act and they offer all patients (including voluntary patients) a chance to meet with them and discuss their care.

The Draft Mental Health Bill (2002 and 2004)

A Draft Mental Health Bill was introduced in 2002, as it was felt that certain patients with a mental illness were still in the community, where they could cause harm either to themselves or to others. This Bill re-examined the process by which patients are detained in hospital. There has been a great deal of discussion over the contents of this Draft Bill. There were two main areas of concern.

* Mental illness was defined as any disability or disorder of the mind which results in an impairment or loss of functioning. Critics, including supporters and carers of people with mental health problems, were concerned that this broad definition would mean that more people would be detained against their will.

* People with a mental health problem and living in the community will be subject to a community order and expected to take their medication, and they will be closely supervised. Critics feel this is unworkable, as it is difficult to ensure patients take their medication, and this would place a burden on carers who are already stressed by caring.

Because of the problems in implementing the Bill, the legislation has been delayed. As a result of the comments made, a new Draft Mental Health Bill was published in September 2004. Changes included:

* a definition of mental disorder to stress that the effect of the disorder (e.g. violent behaviour) rather than the diagnosis is important

* the Health Care Commission will have a role in monitoring mental health services

* a period of hospital assessment will be required before treatment in the community

* patients can refuse ECT (electro-convulsive therapy) if they retain the mental capacity to make an informed decision.

The delay to the implementation of the Bill is due to the additional staff needed if the proposals go ahead. An additional 900 members of staff will be required, including 130 psychiatrists.

Many of the anxieties raised about the new Bill were related to the Human Rights Act (1998) as some of the proposals seem to infringe people's rights. See this page for more information on the Human Rights Act.

The Disability Discrimination Act (1995)

This Act is designed to prevent discrimination against people with disabilities, and covers employment, access to education and transport, housing and obtaining goods and services. Under the Act, further duties on companies providing goods and services came into force in 2004 when service providers had to make 'reasonable' changes to their premises so that disabled people had access. Examples of changes required included:

* additional disabled car parking spaces in hotels and leisure centres

* grab rails in toilets

* ground floor rooms for clients using the services (e.g. in a solicitor's office)

* stair lifts in premises without a lift.

Some premises may not be adaptable. For example, a dentist who has a practice on the first floor may not be able to provide a ground floor room, and the provision of a lift or stair lift may not be possible. There has been quite a lot of debate about what constitutes 'reasonable' adaptation.

The Human Rights Act (1998)

The Human Rights Act (1998) is an important document which has major implications for people working in health and social care. The Act makes it unlawful for a public authority (including the NHS) to act in a way that is incompatible with any rights agreed under the terms of the European Convention. The aim of the Act is to achieve a fair balance between the public interest and the individual's rights. The main human rights which are most relevant to working in care are as follows:

* Article 2: everyone's right to life shall be protected by law.

* Article 3: no one should be subjected to inhuman or degrading treatment or punishment.

* Article 5: everyone has the right to liberty and security of person.

* Article 6: everyone is entitled to a fair and public hearing in the determination of a person's civil rights and obligations, or of any criminal charge brought against them. Everyone is entitled to a fair and public hearing within a reasonable time by an independent and impartial tribunal established by law.

* Article 8: everyone has a right to respect for their private and family life, their home and their correspondence.

* Article 9: everyone has the right of freedom of thought, conscience and religion.

* Article 10: everyone has the right to freedom of expression.

* Article 11: everyone has the right to freedom of peaceful assembly and to a freedom of association with others, including the right to form and join trade unions for the protection of their interests.

* Article 12: men and women of marriageable age have the right to marry and found a family according to the national laws governing the exercise of this right.

* Article 14: the enjoyment of the rights and freedoms set forth in this convention shall be secured without discrimination on any grounds such as sex, race, colour, language, religion, political or other opinion, national or social origin.

Clearly, the Human Rights Act overlaps other legislation such as the Race Relations Act (1995) and the Disability Discrimination Act (1995).

More detail on the Human Rights Act is available on www.homeoffice.gov.uk/hract.

The Human Rights Act does not allow people to bring a case against an organisation that is not a public authority. The Act has changed how the courts interpret and develop the existing law; examples of this include older people using the Human Rights Act against a council who wished to close their residential home, and cases being brought under the Act to prevent sterilisation of men and women with learning disabilities. The Human Rights Act has also had an impact on informed consent issues.

Did you know?

Between 1987 and 1999, 50 women with learning disabilities were sterilised on the grounds of the operations being in their best interest to avoid the trauma of pregnancy or because constant surveillance would reduce their freedom and quality of life.

What if?

Look at the following examples and decide which article of the Act is relevant to each. What might be the implications of the Act for the way service users should be treated?

1. Mixed psychiatric wards where female patients have been at risk of rape or attack by male patients.

2. Denial of fertility treatment to disabled women.

3. Placing of children of disabled parents in care instead of providing appropriate support.

4. Disabled people subjected to treatment without consent.

5. Refusal of treatment on grounds of life expectancy, impairment or quality of life.

6. Opening of post, staff having keys to people's rooms, listening to residents' phone calls.

7. Denial of freedom to come and go from a residential home.

8. Denial of appropriate cultural facilities or food.

9. Withdrawal of treatment from PVS patients (those in a persistent vegetative state).

10. Detentions under the Mental Health Act (especially if there are long delays before a review tribunal).

Human rights

Look at the following case studies. Which article of the Human Rights Act is relevant? And what are the responsibilities of the caring staff?

Ben

Ben is 41. He has a learning disability. Ben likes swimming, meeting his friends in the club and using computers. He has gone to day centres on and off for 20 years. His parents are getting old and he is worried about the future. He wants to learn how to live on his own or with his friends. He knows that to do this he needs a job, to help him pay his bills and look after his mum and dad. At school and college he has passed training courses in cooking, basic skills and computing.

At his day centre, Ben helps the staff by answering the phone and working in the reception area. He does this three times a week and he wants to get paid for the work he does. His job is busy and can be stressful in the mornings, when people go out to their activities, and in the evening when they return. Ben often tells the bus drivers which person should get on which bus and what time they are expected home.

At lunch time when they are short-staffed, Ben is expected to answer the phones and take charge of the reception area. Ben enjoys his job but would like recognition and pay for it.

What are the issues here?

Kevin

Kevin is 32. He lives in a group home for people with learning disabilities. His girlfriend, Joanne, lives in another house run by the same charity, and they meet at the day centre. Kevin is not allowed to have his girlfriend visit. He has told the staff he would like her to visit him and would like private time with her in his bedroom, but the staff refuse his request. They also open and read his letters and correspondence.

Summary of Section 7.1

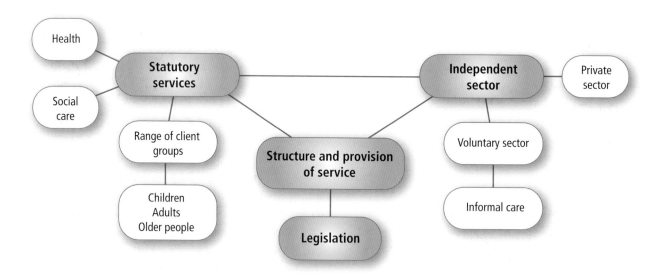

Elizabeth

You have a neighbour, Elizabeth, who is in her eighties and has been in hospital following a fall in which she fractured her hip. Elizabeth lives alone, her only daughter lives 100 miles away and only sees her mother occasionally.

1. What services may be involved in her discharge from hospital to home?
2. What health and social care workers may be involved in her care?
3. Will Elizabeth pay for the services she receives from social services? From the NHS?
4. On her discharge home, Elizabeth will need equipment to ensure her independence at home. Who will provide equipment such as hand rails, a commode, and crutches?
5. Elizabeth needs help with shopping and cleaning. Who might provide this?
6. Promoting independence and supporting people to remain in their own homes is a key aspect of policy. Evaluate this approach. What problems may arise in enabling Elizabeth to remain in her home?

FIGURE 7.11 *Elizabeth in hospital after her fall*

7.2 Meeting individual needs

This section covers how providers of health and social care services organise services to meet the individual's unique needs. There are three important aspects that are covered in this section:

* the process of care planning

* the care planning cycle

* assessment of service provision; identifying needs, monitoring and reviewing of care plans and the importance of involving service users and carers in the process.

The process of care planning

Care plans may be developed by one professional such as a nurse or by a multi-disciplinary team.

Care plan: a procedure set up to outline and record a course of care, treatment or therapy between professional workers and service users and their carers.

They can also be developed by the service users themselves working with the appropriate health and social care professionals.

Care planning should be needs-led, and should benefit the service user's health and well-being. If there is a carer, their needs should also be included in the care planning.

Care planning based on the needs of the individual was seen as a cornerstone of the NHS and Community Care Act (1990). However, with increasing demands on the service (partly caused by the increasing numbers of older people in the population), social services have had to develop criteria which determine who will receive care services and how these will be delivered.

In 2003, the Department of Health produced a document called *Fair Access to Care Services: Guidance on Eligibility Criteria for Adult Social Care*. Councils should assess an individual's needs and decide which needs are most important (see Figure 7.12). An assessment should be made of the risks that may occur for the person if care is not provided. Councils should focus on those in greatest immediate, or longer, term need. The idea behind the guidance is that there should be a more consistent approach to needs assessment in all parts of England and Wales, as until these new proposals, different councils operated different systems when assessing need. For example, if you had two relatives living in different parts of the country with the same levels of disability, you could find they were offered different levels of service. A relative in one part of the country might pay nothing for services, whereas a relative living elsewhere might be means tested.

The process of care planning in the community

With the development of closer working between health and social care in the community, care planning has become more streamlined. With the development of IT systems, many care

Q	No need	Critical		Substantial	Moderate	Low	
1		Life is/will be threatened.					
2		Significant health problems have/will develop.					
3		There is/will be immediate little choice about vital aspects of the immediate environment.		Is/will be only partial choice and control over the immediate environment.			
4		Serious abuse/neglect has/will occur.		Abuse or neglect has occurred/will occurred.			
5		Is/will be an inability to carry out vital personal care or domestic routines.		Is/will be an inability to carry out the majority of personal care and domestic routines.	Is/will be an inability to carry out several personal care or domestic routines.	Is/will be an inability to carry out one or two personal care or domestic tasks.	
6		Vital involvement in work, education or learning will not be sustained.		Involvement in many aspects of work education or learning cannot/will not be sustained.	Involvement in several aspects of work, education or learning cannot/will not be sustained.	Involvement in one or two aspects of work, education or learning cannot/will not be sustained.	
7		Vital social support systems and relationships cannot/will not be sustained.		The majority of social support systems and relationships cannot/will not be sustained.	Several social supports systems and relationships cannot/will not be sustained.	One or two social support systems and relationships cannot/will not be sustained.	
8		Vital family and other social roles and responsibilities cannot/will not be undertaken.		The majority of family and other social roles and responsibilities cannot/will not be undertaken.	Several family and other social roles and relationships cannot/will not be undertaken.	One or two family and other social roles and responsibilities cannot/will not be sustained.	

FIGURE 7.12 *The FACS (Fair Access to Care Services) approach*

assessments are sent by email to different practitioners involved in a person's care. It is hoped that by developing multi-disciplinary working, the service user will not have to continually respond to the same questions. Professionals will also benefit from this approach as they will be supported as part of a team and they will also be kept up to date with the service user's progress.

Assessment

Assessment of need is the cornerstone of care planning as it lies at the heart of effective service delivery for a range of health and social care provision. Assessment should be carried out so that service users and their carers can:

* gain a better understanding of their situation

* identify the options that are available for managing their own lives

* set the aims and goals that should be achieved through the care plan

* understand the basis on which decisions are reached.

Key concept

Assessment: the method used to determine the different needs of a client, patient or service user. The term 'assessment' is used in a variety of ways, explained in more detail in this section.

Assessment should be co-ordinated and integrated across all the agencies relevant to the service user. Assessment should be shared among professionals, with the informed consent of the client, so that health and social care workers do not repeat assessments.

The initial assessment would be done by the professional who has first contact with the client or patient. This could be a nurse or a social worker. Other specialist assessments (e.g. by an occupational therapist) may be included at a later stage. At every stage of the assessment, the individual's and the carer's views should be included.

The care plan cycle in social care
Referral for assessment of need

In social services there has been an increase in joint working with the local PCT so that a person coming for assessment may be referred for health services to the PCT. In some areas the point of referral is through a single point of access, usually by telephone, and the referral may be made by a health or social care professional or by the user or carer. An example of the approach is shown in Figure 7.13 (page 26).

Core details

These details are the basic information about the person. They should be sent to every professional working with the client – usually using IT, so that the client does not have to repeat the same information. Core details include the client's name, address, date of birth, marital status, ethnicity, significant contacts, health details, disability registration, and housing information.

Assessment of need

With more joined-up working between health and social care, a key worker (sometimes called the lead professional), either a health worker or a worker from social services, would assess the needs of the service user, usually visiting them at their home, in hospital if they are about to be discharged, or in a rehabilitation unit. Although the guidance focuses on the service user, carers should also be involved in the assessment process. The eligibility criteria for service is graded into four bands, which describe the seriousness of the risk to independence or other effects if needs are not addressed. The bands are as follows:

* *critical*: when life is or will be threatened, or serious abuse or neglect has occurred or may occur, or serious health problems have developed

* *substantial*: this band covers less critical factors, but there is still a substantial risk to the person if care is not delivered

* *moderate* and *low*: these bands have a lower level of risk.

The full details of FACS (Fair Access to Care Services) are available on www.doh.gov.uk/seg/facs.

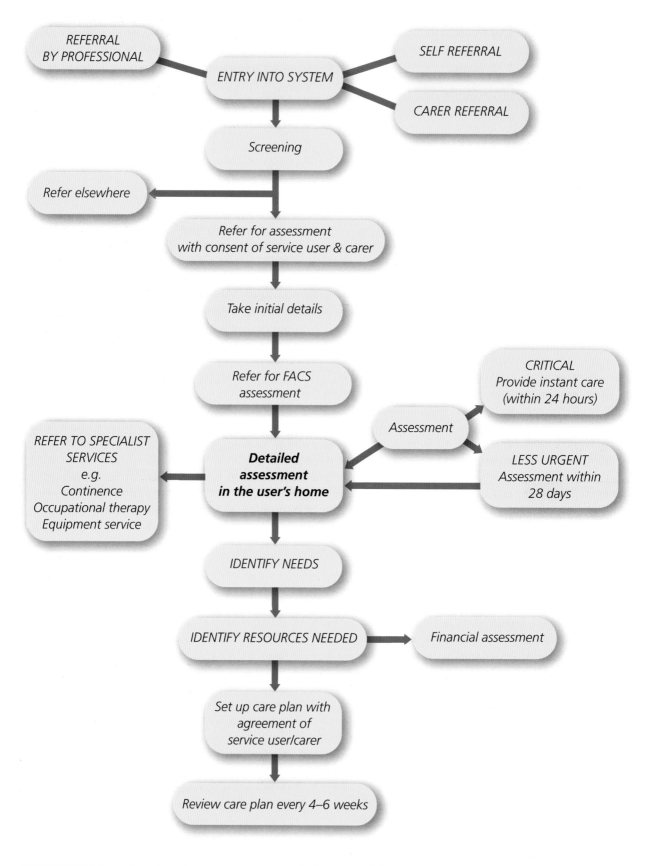

FIGURE 7.13 *The referral and assessment approach in one social service's department*

Subsequent stages of the care plan cycle

Once the assessment of need has been carried out, the process continues. The whole care plan cycle includes:

* *referral for assessment*

* *assessment of need*

* *deciding eligibility for service*: does the client fit social services criteria?

* *drawing up a care plan*: who will do what and when (may include targets)

* *identifying services that will be provided*: the service user and/or their carer should have contact details of everyone involved in their care

* *review of the care plan and service provision*: this may take place three months after the start of the care plan, or it may be less frequent depending on the situation. If there is a sudden change in the health or mobility of the service user, reviews may be more frequent.

Figure 7.14 is an example of a care plan for a patient who has had a knee replacement. In all stages of the process of care planning, service users and carers should participate.

The service user is central to the care planning process. However, in some cases the service user may be unable to understand the process, and they may need the help of an advocate.

> **Key concept**
>
> *Advocate*: a person who speaks out on behalf of patients or clients. Advocates can be professional workers, family members or volunteers.

Care planning has to take account of the diversity of the individual related to culture, language, intellectual ability, and mobility. Councils should be aware of the rights of service users and have regard for the Sex Discrimination Act (1975), the Disability Discrimination Act (1995), the Human Rights Act (1998) and the Race Relations (Amendment) Act (2000).

Name: Florence Ashley

D.O.B: 1.1.22

Date of Assessment: 13.6.06

Targets	How can targets be met	Action to be taken	Whose commitment	Review date
To improve mobility	Attend weekly physio at local hospital. Review equipment provision in home and order additional aids if needed	Arrange transport and book appointment O.T. to visit home	Debbie Smith community physio (lead professional) Mary Jones O.T. assistant	13.7.06 13.7.06
To maintain wound care	Home visit by district nurse to monitor wound	co-ordinate DN visits	Debbie Smith lead professional Sara Barker DN	20.6.06
To maintain good circulation	To encourage mobility. to change compression stockings	visits by H.C.A 4 times a week	Pam Ball H.C.A.	20.6.06

FIGURE 7.14 *Care plan of a service user with a knee replacement*

Types of assessment

Assessment is a term used in many contexts in health and social care. Some of the common types of assessment follow.

Financial assessment

Most social services departments make a charge for services provided after a care assessment, but this is subject to a financial assessment (or means test). The charging policy is set locally, so it will vary according to region. However, with Fair Access to Care Services (FACS) it is hoped that national guidelines will soon be in place so that people will be assessed in a similar way, no matter where they live. In all cases, the person being assessed for care has to complete a financial assessment.

Carers' assessment (Carers' and Disabled Children's Act 2000)

Carers who provide a substantial amount of care now have a right to have a needs assessment themselves. Social services may provide a break for the carer or respite care for the person they care for.

Care programme approach (CPA) assessment

Under the National Service Framework (NSF) for Mental Health, people with mental illness are now assessed using the CPA approach. This includes an assessment of the carer's needs, as well as a very detailed assessment of the service user's mental condition and suggestions for treatment. The CPA assessment should be reviewed at least once a year.

Family assessment

In the case of a child with special needs, the assessment should look at the whole family when considering the provision of appropriate services.

Young carer's assessment

Under the terms of the Carers' and Disabled Children's Act (1990) and the Carers' Recognition and Services Act (1995), people under 18 who provide care to adult family members are entitled to an assessment of their needs.

Occupational therapy (OT) assessment

This looks at the physical needs of a person and how to support them in their own home so that they can retain independence (see Figure 7.15).

Stairs	Yes	No	Describe, listing any concerns
None			
Into Home			
To Bathroom			
To Toilet			
To Bedroom			
To Kitchen			
Stair Rails			
Garden to Pavement			
Heating			
Central Heating			
Gas Fires			
Solid Fuel			
Able to Use Safely			
Adequate			
No Heating			
Eligible for Grant			
Do fires need checking?			
Toilet/Bathroom			
Upstairs Toilet			
Downstairs Toilet			
Outside Toilet			
Commode			
Bathroom			
Bath Aids			
General			
Can manage oven			
Can manage microwave			
Does oven need checking?			
Are there smoke alarms?			

FIGURE 7.15 *An OT assessment*

Risk assessment

All service providers – such as social services, home care agencies or voluntary organisations – have a legal responsibility to do a risk assessment before they provide services in order to protect the health and safety of their staff. If services are to be provided in a service user's own home, certain things will be included in a risk assessment (see Figure 7.16):

* layout and location of the home
* any overprotective dogs
* any risks associated with having to move the person who has care needs.

Carers and the service manager will discuss possible risks and how to deal with them. All social care assessments cover a range of needs and risks (see Figure 7.16).

Summary of identified assessment needs and risks	
Needs:	Health and Well-being (incl Mental Health)
	Personal and Domestic Care Routines
	Housing and Personal Safety
	Spiritual and Cultural Needs
	Social Support and Relationships (incl other roles and responsibilities)
	Finances
	Leisure, Education and Employment
	Transport

FIGURE 7.16 *Range of needs covered in a social care assessment*

Look at the following examples and decide which assessment applies (there could be several relevant assessments).

1. Daisy is nine years old and lives with her family. She has spina bifida. As she is getting heavier her mother is finding it difficult to lift her in and out of the car, in and out of the bath and around the house. Daisy uses a wheelchair most of the time.

2. John (36) has schizophrenia. His elderly parents look after him and are feeling very tired.

3. Jane (70) is a former head teacher. She lives on her own. She has arthritis and is finding it increasingly difficult to manage. She has a state pension and a teacher's pension.

Further issues related to care planning

Direct payments

In the Fair Access to Care Services document, the government urges councils to encourage the use of direct payments whenever possible. In this scheme, the council decides what services are required and how much they will cost. This sum will be made available to the client and they can buy the services from private agencies or individuals.

Advantages of direct payments

The client decides which services they will have and when. For example, they could ask a care worker to come at particular times of the day to attend to their needs, rather than not knowing when a care worker supplied by the council will come to their house. Direct payments are seen to empower the client.

Disadvantages of direct payments

Some clients would not want to take the responsibility of organising their care and paying for it. Some clients would not understand the process.

Up to the present time most people using direct payments have tended to be younger adults, and you may have seen advertisements for people requiring personal care in the local press.

Care planning in health care

Care planning in social care is often about supporting clients whose needs are long-term. As time goes by, the care plan will be reviewed on a regular basis and additional needs may develop due to increasing age, disability or lack of mobility. However, in care planning in the acute setting of a hospital the care plan may go through the following seven stages:

1. Recognition of a problem

2. Initial assessment and investigation

3. Assessment and planning

4. Implementation and review

5. Leads to a period of rehabilitation

6. Leads to separation (rehabilitation is judged to be complete)

7. Disengagement (treatment is complete).

SCENARIO

Tony

Look at the following case study and identify the seven stages in Tony's care cycle.

Tony is 50. He has suffered from severe osteoarthritis after a sports injury to his knee when playing football. He is finding it difficult to walk far or manage stairs, and he has had to change to an automatic car as he cannot manage using the clutch pedal. He is in a great deal of pain. He goes to see his GP who looks at his knee and sends him for an X-ray. The X-ray confirms that Tony has severe arthritis in his knee joint and the doctor also notices that he has muscle wastage in his thigh muscle. He refers Tony to the consultant orthopaedic surgeon who examines Tony and decides he needs a total knee replacement. He is put on the waiting list, and meanwhile he attends physiotherapy for exercises to improve his muscles.

After six months, Tony enters hospital and has his operation. Only 24 hours later Tony is walking with a zimmer frame and starting physiotherapy. He has painkillers for the pain and other drugs to reduce the danger of deep vein thrombosis. After six days Tony is discharged from hospital to his home. The occupational therapist has advised him to use a 'helping hand' to pick things up from the floor and use a high bar stool in the kitchen. For three weeks Tony manages on crutches, and then he is able to walk with a stick. He continues to do his exercises to strengthen his leg.

After six weeks he sees the consultant again. He starts driving again and goes back to work eight weeks after the surgery. The pain is getting better and he can do more and more each week. He sees the consultant six months after the operation and he is discharged from hospital. He is now able to lead a normal life and do most of the activities he has always enjoyed in the past.

FIGURE 7.17 *Tony on his crutches*

Children's issues related to assessment in the community

As we have seen earlier, services for children in health and social care are often managed differently. This is because they are seen as particularly vulnerable, and also because their needs may change rapidly. With increased integration between health and social care services and education, multi-agency working is more likely.

A child will be assigned a key worker who could be from health, social services or education. The chart (Figure 7.18) shows how different agencies work together to ensure that the needs of children are met through using a common assessment approach. Specialist assessments may also be used in more complicated cases.

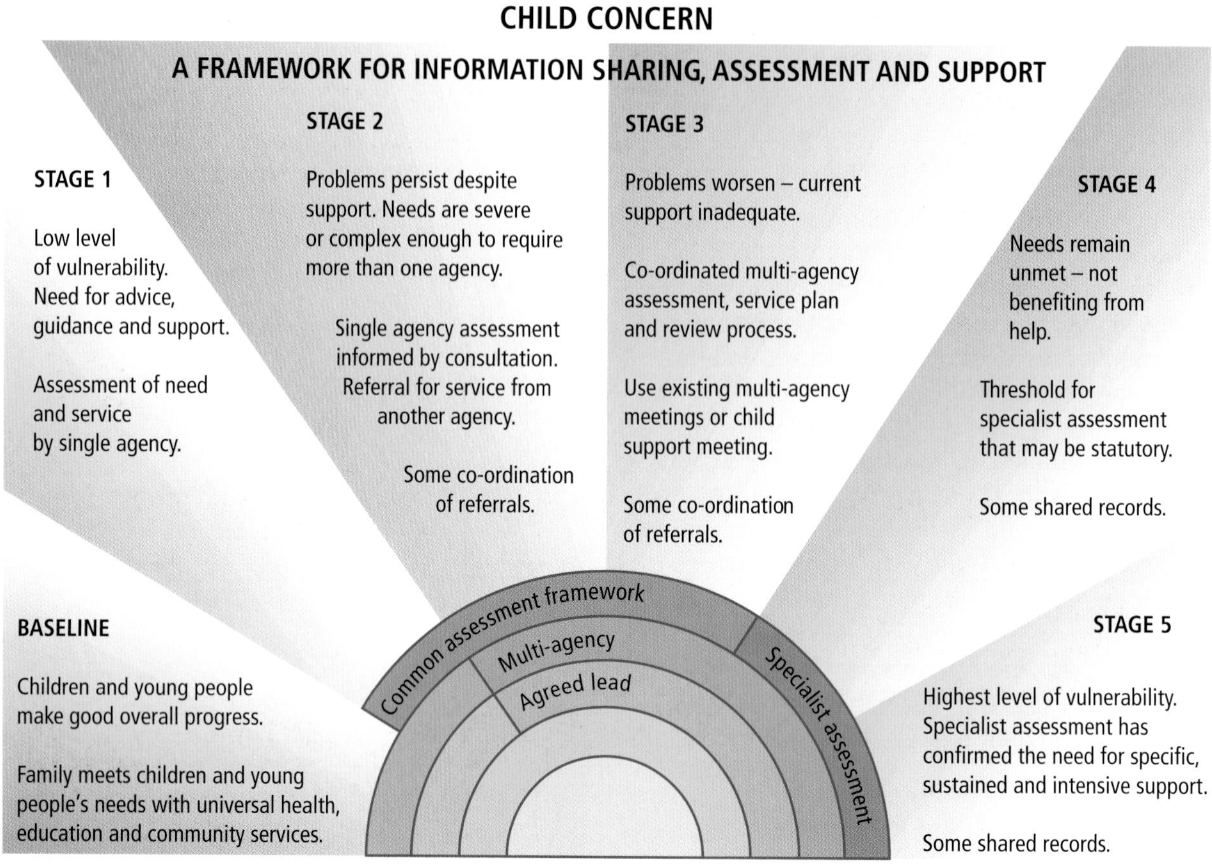

CHILD CONCERN

A FRAMEWORK FOR INFORMATION SHARING, ASSESSMENT AND SUPPORT

STAGE 1

Low level
of vulnerability.
Need for advice,
guidance and support.

Assessment of need
and service
by single agency.

STAGE 2

Problems persist despite
support. Needs are severe
or complex enough to require
more than one agency.

Single agency assessment
informed by consultation.
Referral for service from
another agency.

Some co-ordination
of referrals.

STAGE 3

Problems worsen – current
support inadequate.

Co-ordinated multi-agency
assessment, service plan
and review process.

Use existing multi-agency
meetings or child
support meeting.

Some co-ordination
of referrals.

STAGE 4

Needs remain
unmet – not
benefiting from
help.

Threshold for
specialist assessment
that may be statutory.

Some shared records.

BASELINE

Children and young people
make good overall progress.

Family meets children and young
people's needs with universal health,
education and community services.

Common assessment framework

Multi-agency

Agreed lead

Specialist assessment

STAGE 5

Highest level of vulnerability.
Specialist assessment has
confirmed the need for specific,
sustained and intensive support.

Some shared records.

FIGURE 7.18 *Assessment and review of children*

Resource issues in service provision

Resource allocation is part of the assessment process. Although the Community Care Act advocates a needs-based approach, with the increased demand for services (partly because of the increasing life expectancy of clients) there is pressure on resources. Resources include staff as well as equipment and provision for other therapies, such as speech therapy and physiotherapy.

The FACS approach limits resources by categorising clients by the different levels of support needed. Sometimes age may be used as a means of restricting resource provision. In one London area, children over seven are not referred for speech therapy. In health services there is such a shortage of child psychiatrists and psychologists that children may not be referred to the local Child and Adolescent Mental Health Team (CAMHT) unless they are suicidal.

Risks

Risks can include safety issues for the client or for other people. For example, a risk assessment on someone with a mental health problem will assess the level of risk the person presents to themselves (for example, self-harm) as well as to others. In a care assessment for someone with dementia, it may be decided that the risks involved in the person remaining in their own home are too high, and they will need to be cared for in a residential setting. In an organisation, risk assessments may include health and safety issues in the workplace and also financial risk. Two examples of financial risk assessments are:

✳ A new surgical centre is opened that provides hip and knee replacements. The funding paid by the NHS for each operation does not fully cover the costs, so the centre will either have to cut costs to stay in business or find another way of covering the additional costs.

* Many private care homes have been closed as the fees charged are higher than the local social services will pay for, and relatives cannot pay the additional cost.

Confidentiality issues

Confidentiality refers to the need to keep private any information provided by the client in the course of treatment or in the provision of a service. With the development of email systems transferring personal data about clients between health and social care services, confidentiality has become a key issue. Care workers have to insert a password to access confidential data, but concerns have been raised by patients' groups about confidentiality. In some cases a client may not wish her family to know her personal details – and this could include her main carer. It is important that care workers respect the wishes of their clients about who has access to their personal details.

The Data Protection Act (1998) protects information on computer-based records. All data held on computer records should be:

* accurate and up-to-date

* obtained fairly and lawfully

* used only for a specified lawful purpose

* kept confidential

* available for scrutiny.

Models and theories relevant to care plans

There are several models and theories relevant to care plans that you need to know about.

Normalisation

The normalisation model was developed in Scandinavia in the 1970s. The model was based on the view that people should fit in with society rather than that society should accept people with learning disabilities as they are.

The Jay Committee was set up in 1979 in the UK to discuss the care of people with learning disabilities, and the service principles of the Committee show the influence of normalisation.

The following is a direct quotation from the Jay Committee; it includes some outdated terms (e.g. 'mentally handicapped') and attitudes.

1. Mentally handicapped people should use normal services where possible.

2. Existing networks of support should be strengthened by professional services.

3. Specialised services for handicapped people should only be provided if they are likely to meet additional needs that cannot be met by general services.

4. Someone needs to intercede on the behalf of mentally handicapped people in obtaining services.

Key concept

Normalisation: the model that takes the view that people with any disability should 'fit in' with society.

Try it out

The term 'mental handicap' is no longer used nowadays. People with learning disabilities are termed to have 'special needs'. By changing the name of a group of service users, the idea was that these groups would not be marginalised or labelled in any way.

Does the name change to 'special needs' remove the stigma of disability? What do you think?

Criticisms of the normalisation model

In this unit we have discussed the importance of assessing the needs of clients and service users and planning how these needs can be met. With the normalisation model there seems to be an assumption that everyone in the category of 'mental handicap' is the same, therefore the 'one size fits all' approach is taken. If we are going to improve professional practice we need to assess people's needs on an individual basis, whatever their disability or condition.

Changing the name of a model of care does not change people's attitudes or remove stigma and discrimination.

Empowerment

Empowerment means giving people power and treating them not as passive receivers of health and social care services, but as active participants in the care planning process and in decision-making. Patients and clients need to be given access to information so that they can make an informed choice. Empowering a group may be easier to achieve than empowering isolated individuals.

FIGURE 7.19 *Advocacy in progress*

Advocacy

Advocacy developed as a result of changes in policy, particularly related to the closure of long-stay hospitals in the 1980s, when people with learning disabilities were discharged into the community. Closure of large mental hospitals was another factor as advocates for people with mental distress were needed. Recently, advocacy (see Figure 7.19) has become a more generalised approach covering a range of issues and a range of client groups.

Advocacy is:

* supporting people to speak for themselves

* being on the person's side when they want to say something

* helping people to understand their rights and making sure these are respected

* providing information and support so that choices can be made and problems resolved, for example ensuring that the person is able to give informed consent to an operation.

There are different types of advocacy.

* *Self-advocacy:* speaking up for oneself. This approach is linked to people with learning disabilities and mental health problems.

* *Citizen advocacy*: a one-to-one relationship between a volunteer spokesperson and the client.

SCENARIO

User and carer group

A group of older people formed a user and carer group. They had been dissatisfied with the levels of care they had experienced in the community. They were supported by a worker from Age Concern. They had training on aspects of committee work and the organisation of health and social care services. Members of this group represent older people on a range of committees and participate in discussions and decisions about the organisation of care in their area. As a group they are recognised by the service providers in their area. They also support each other.

Key concept

Empowerment: the way in which health and social care professionals encourage clients to make decisions and take control over their lives. Empowerment continues to be a useful approach both for service users and carers and for service providers.

* *Peer advocacy:* this may involve a person who has experienced a service supporting a client who is using the service.
* *Professional advocacy:* professional advocates are paid and they are formally supervised, trained, supported and monitored.
* *Crisis advocacy:* this could be undertaken by a volunteer or a paid advocate, to deal with a one-off crisis.
* *Parent/carer advocacy:* where the service user is either a child or is an adult who has had a head injury that has affected their mental capacity to contribute to care planning and consent.

Key concept

Advocacy: a process whereby a worker, carer or volunteer speaks or acts on behalf of a client or patient to ensure they receive the service they require and are entitled to.

SCENARIO
Advocacy

Advocacy Partners is a registered charity based in South London and Surrey. It provides advocacy for people with learning and physical disabilities as well as older people. The charity was set up in 1981 and it was the first independent advocacy scheme in Britain. In the annual report the director writes about how the organisation supports people to make the changes they want. This is done by:

* making time, getting to know the person's preferences, views and needs
* listening closely to what the person is saying
* taking the person's side
* being person-centred, concentrating on the person as an individual
* being clear about what we can do; there are some things that cannot be changed or cannot be achieved and it is important that the client isn't given false hope or promises
* making available a range of advocacy approaches, both long- and short-term.

Consider this

Here are some examples of the work this organisation has done recently. Look at them carefully and discuss the benefits of advocacy for Edwina and Alex. How might things have turned out for them if advocacy had not been available?

SCENARIO
Edwina

Edwina, an older woman, could no longer use her bathroom due to the effects of severe arthritis. Social services felt unable to make the necessary changes, but instead offered to provide staff to take her from her home to have a bath. Edwina valued her independence and privacy. Her advocate helped her to challenge the decision and she now has a new 'wet room'. Edwina is really pleased and feels safe and independent.

Social services have also been saved the continued cost of a support service.

SCENARIO
Alex

Alex, a man in his 40s with severe learning disabilities, was diagnosed with a life-threatening illness. His consultant concluded that Alex should not have the necessary surgery, as due to his disability his quality of life would remain poor. Shona, Alex's advocate, worked closely with his support staff and the consultant. Eventually she was able to persuade the consultant that if Alex was able to express himself he would explain the many things he enjoyed and that made his life pleasurable despite his illness. Surgery was carried out and Alex has made a full recovery.

Networking

Networks are informal links that are made within and between different groups, which could be in the same organisation or in different organisations. Networks help people share information and give each other emotional and practical support. In a hospital or other health or social care organisation, networks can develop between or within departments. This may be a more effective way of spreading information than through formal communication such as committee meetings and newsletters. Networks can help people achieve a sense of belonging, which is important when many people can feel socially isolated. Networks can also help create positive practical outcomes – for example, by helping each other and sharing experiences, carers could contribute more actively to proposed care plans.

Many self-help groups in the community could be seen as a form of network. For example, a user and carer group was formed which consisted of relatives caring for people with early dementia and some of the clients themselves. A new day unit was being built for dementia patients and this group contributed to the planning and organisation of the centre. The professionals realised the group had useful knowledge, and they raised issues that hadn't occurred to the planners.

Summary of Section 7.2

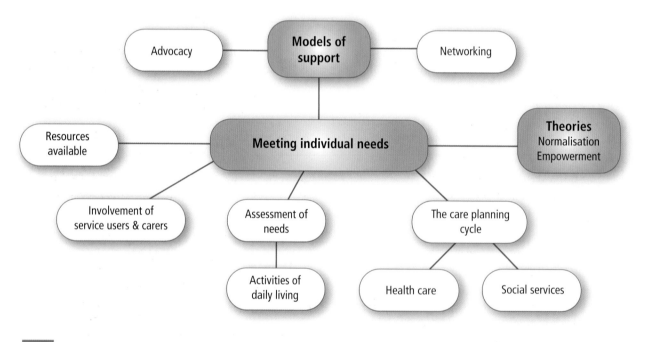

Consider this

You visit a residential home for people with learning disabilities. There are twelve people in the home between the ages of 19 and 35 – eight women and four men. During the day the clients go to education classes or on work placements. The home manager meets frequently with the residents to discuss outings and holidays. Relatives and friends are encouraged to visit. Several residents go out on their own or with a friend to the library, shopping or to the pub. They all have their own bank accounts. Frank, a newly arrived resident, has little verbal communication so the local advocacy group has found a volunteer advocate who will help him express his views and wishes. Each resident has an individual care plan that is regularly updated. In the most recent inspection report, concerns were expressed about health and safety issues as one of the residents likes to smoke.

1. If you were the manager of the home, how would you ensure that clients' needs were being met?

2. How could you promote a risk-free environment in the home for the clients?

3. How could you promote further independence for this group? How would you balance risk and promote independence?

4. Evaluate the role of advocacy when supporting clients with learning disabilities.

FIGURE 7.20 *Residential care for young adults with learning disabilities*

7.3 Practitioner roles

In this section we look at how organisational cultures can affect the work of the practitioner in providing services, and how a positive care environment can safeguard and promote a service user's rights. There is a range of professional roles in health and social care organisations. Although multi-disciplinary working is becoming established, different professions have different training, functions and approaches.

In Primary Care Trusts (PCTs) there may be a multi-disciplinary team consisting of nurses, doctors, physiotherapists, occupational therapists and health care assistants. PCTs are increasingly working with their colleagues in social services, so social workers are also part of the team. This is particularly the case when working in discharge planning from hospital. Under the **Community Care (Delayed Discharges) Act 2003**, the NHS must inform social services of any adult patients who are likely to need care on discharge. If social services do not put services in place, the council must pay the hospital £120 per day for each day the patient is occupying a bed after they should have been discharged. As a result of this legislation, discharge teams were set up that included practitioners from both the NHS and social services.

Each organisation has its own culture and this may cause problems when health and social care groups have to work together. A firmly held professional culture can affect caring in a negative way, if professionals are not prepared to be flexible and put the needs of the service user first.

Organisational culture

Organisational culture could be defined as the way of life for a particular group of professionals and may include:

* technical or professional language used

* a dress code (or absence of dress code)

* methods of communication used

* ways in which clients are approached

* the range of clearly defined roles within the organisation.

The culture could be based on a qualification that everyone has achieved (such as RGN or Social Work Diploma) and the training they have had.

Developing an organisational culture

The culture of an organisation can be developed through additional training for all staff, shared aims, and the formal and informal interactions between workers. Team-building events are often seen as a way of developing a positive culture in an organisation.

Organisational culture: the values, beliefs and norms of a specific organisation which shape the ways in which individual members achieve the aims of the whole group.

When staff are appointed to posts in any organisation – hospital, council or private residential homes – they will have a period of induction when they will be informed about what is expected of them in their post. The induction programme in a residential home will include:

✱ health and safety

✱ manual handling (safe lifting procedures)

✱ policies of the home related to complaints, confidentiality and discrimination.

People working within organisations usually have clearly defined roles, as shown in the organisation chart of a children's social services department (Figure 7.10, page 18).

Barriers to joint working

In the NSF (National Service Framework) for Older People, nurses and social care workers had to develop a single assessment process. Until recently, people were assessed separately for their health and social care needs and for their entitlement to benefits and what they should pay towards their care. Social care workers assessed people on their income, and nurses assessed clinical need.

This was confusing for older people as they saw so many different people and had to answer the same questions many times. However, nurses did not wish to do financial assessment and did not want to be trained to do this. This was a real problem, as the focus on assessing need should have been on the service user, not on the culture of the staff.

In some regions a single assessment process has been developed, but in others a financial assessment is done by a finance officer from the council. In some ways the idea of a professional culture can actually affect caring in a negative way. According to government policy guidelines, health and social care services will be working together in all communities by 2006. It is therefore important that these new organisations develop a culture that includes everyone. One method of developing a culture in an organisation is to encourage everyone to feel part of the organisation's development, and that requires effective communication.

Effective communication

With the development of IT systems, many health and social care organisations have their own website and also their own intranet. In a PCT, everyone working for the trust will have their own email address, and communication also takes place through regular team or departmental meetings. Departments may have team events and training events to provide a way of communicating changes in working practice.

Because so many changes are taking place in health and social care, effective communication of these changes is essential so that people feel part of the process. If changes to working practices are proposed, staff who will be affected should be offered an opportunity to comment on these proposals, ensuring communication is a two-way process between staff and managers and not just 'top down' from managers.

Effective communication between different professionals caring for the same clients is also the key to effective care. Patients may have hand-held records that are kept at home and completed by each professional involved in their care. The use of faxes and emails is also increasing. Patients' records, test results and X-rays can now be sent electronically between organisations and this should improve patient care. In 2003, the Department of Health issued good practice guidelines under which patients who had been seen by a consultant in hospital should be sent a copy of the letter that was sent to their GP about their care.

All health and care organisations have a communications policy, which is reviewed on a regular basis. In hospital and other NHS Trusts there is an identified person who is responsible for dealing with the media and issuing statements to the press if there are issues of public interest.

If you have already obtained a copy of an annual report from a health or social care organisation, you should find information about communication in the report.

What if?

> Imagine you are on the management group of a residential home for people with learning disabilities.
>
> What kind of mission statement would you produce?
>
> How might it differ from a mission statement you might develop for the following?
>
> * a voluntary group that provides support for single mothers
>
> * a day centre for older people.

Key concept

Effective communication: this is the process by which information is transmitted, received, understood and acted upon.

Mission statements

Many organisations have mission statements which state the aims and core values of the organisation and reflect the culture of the organisation. These may be displayed in the form of posters and leaflets and in written communication from the organisation, as well as in annual reports and staff handbooks.

Key concept

Mission statement: a formal statement of the aims and values of an organisation.

The following is the mission statement from a voluntary organisation that offers bereavement support.

> *'The Bereavement Service will provide, through carefully selected and trained volunteers, immediate practical and emotional support to bereaved people. It will give ongoing support or counselling for the relief of distress and sense of loss occasioned by such bereavement. It will also serve to educate and increase the awareness of the nature of grief and bereavement. The service will be freely available to those living in the borough who are affected by loss, regardless of race, colour, nationality, religion, gender, age, sexual orientation or physical disability.'*

Advantages and disadvantages of mission statements

Mission statements can help people working within an organisation to know and understand the organisation's aims. They can also help service users know what to expect from the service provided by the organisation. However, mission statements need to be reviewed on a regular basis to reflect possible changes to services.

Many NHS Trusts and social services departments no longer use mission statements but instead list the aims of the organisation linked to the plan for the coming year. It can be difficult to audit a mission statement and to establish how the organisation has performed in the previous year, whereas a plan can be monitored to see if targets have been met.

Roles in health and social care

Roles are attached to job descriptions and describe what the person does who is fulfilling that role. If a person leaves their job, the role will remain the same but someone else will fulfil it. If you look at an organisation chart you will see that the chart shows roles rather than names of individuals. It is important that people are clear about what their role is.

As we have seen in Figure 7.10, in social services there is a clear management structure with directors at the top and social care teams at the bottom. This is called a hierarchical bureaucratic structure. In a care home the team will be much smaller with a manager in charge and various workers with different levels of qualification. In a smaller organisation roles may not be as clearly defined as with staff sickness or shortage, workers may perform a variety of tasks.

In health and social care the roles of doctors, nurses and other workers are clearly defined and upheld by codes of conduct.

Every role within health and social care brings certain responsibilities with it, which the post holder needs to undertake in order to work effectively.

Key concept

Role: the expected pattern of behaviour associated with a particular position in society.

Try it out

Examine the following job description and identify the responsibilities that come with the role of Care Manager.

Job description

Care Manager (hospital service)
Report to: Senior Care Manager

Main purpose of the job

1. Assess the needs of individuals and their carers.
2. Together with the service users and carers, devise and implement care plans according to their needs.
3. Provide counselling and continuing support to users and carers when appropriate.
4. Monitor, review and evaluate services in order to ensure that they are provided effectively and in accordance with need.

Responsibilities and duties

1. Provide an assessment service to individuals, their carers and other agencies.
2. Initiate and co-ordinate care plans for and with individual service users and their carers, liaising with professional colleagues and representatives of voluntary and private agencies.
3. Supervise and support staff as agreed with the Care Manager.
4. Offer support, counselling and advice as required to service users and their carers.
5. Through the assessment and prioritisation of need, purchase appropriate services within the budgetary constraints.
6. Monitor the efficiency and effectiveness of care plans.
7. Review the needs of individual service users and their carers.
8. Identify and report needs not met and service shortfalls in the construction of care plans.
9. Maintain client records in accordance with council policy.
10. Respond to and, where possible, resolve complaints using the council's complaints policy.
11. Advise the manager on the quality and value for money of purchased services.
12. Participate in multi-disciplinary and inter-agency meetings and working groups and represent the department as required.

Look carefully at the job description and draw up a list of the skills required in this post.

What knowledge do you think a person would need to do this job?

What previous experience would be helpful in this job?

Accountability

In all statutory health and social care organisations, the board is responsible for internal control of the organisation. The chief executive on the board is responsible for maintaining a secure system that safeguards public funds and ensures that a quality service is provided at all times.

One of the areas of risk for health trusts at the moment is financial, and you may have seen articles in the press when hospital trusts have failed to balance the budgets and are in debt. In these cases the Strategic Health Authority may take over control, and the Department of Health through the Commission for Health Care Audit and Inspection (CHAI) will develop an action plan to assist the trust.

NHS Trusts are also accountable for the professional standards of service offered to patients in their care, and this is ensured through clinical governance systems (see section 7.4). The accountability of the board to patients and the public is ensured through the appointment of non-executive directors. These are lay people with particular expertise in finance, communication or other skills. If you read the annual report of a trust you will see the members of the board listed. One of the functions of the board is to adopt and maintain codes of conduct, accountability and openness, and non-executive members ensure that decisions are taken openly, rather than behind closed doors.

Key concept

Accountability: the requirement to justify and publicise an organisation's actions and decisions.

The chief executive of a PCT or a hospital trust is accountable to the Strategic Health Authority and to the Department of Health for the effective management of the organisation, including financial management. As part of the accountability process, professional workers are monitored internally by the organisation they work in and they are also externally regulated.

Regulation of professional groups

The **General Medical Council (GMC)** licenses doctors to practise medicine in the UK. Its role is to protect patients and to maintain the standards the public has a right to expect. It has four main functions:

* keeping an up-to-date register of qualified doctors

* developing good medical practice

* promoting high standards of medical education

* dealing with poorly performing doctors whose practice does not meet the standards required.

If a doctor is not meeting the standards required, the GMC acts to protect patients from harm; this may involve removing the doctor from the register so that they are unable to practise.

The **Nursing and Midwifery Council (NMC)** is an organisation set up by parliament to make sure nurses, midwives and health visitors provide high standards of care to their patients and clients. The NMC:

* maintains a register of qualified nurses, midwives and health visitors

* sets standards for education, practice and conduct

* provides advice for nurses, midwives and health visitors

* considers allegations of misconduct or unfitness to practise due to ill-health.

If nurses or health visitors are guilty of misconduct, the NMC can remove them from the register and they will be unable to practise.

The **General Social Care Council (GSCC)** was set up in 2001 under the Care Standards Act (2001). The GSCC is responsible for:

* developing the code of practice for social care workers

* keeping a register of social care professionals

* the training and education of social care workers.

(For more details see the website www.gscc.org.uk.)

Effective team building

Organisations recognise that one way of improving working in teams or multi-disciplinary working within an organisation is through team-building events. Many of the problems with working across organisations have been due to lack of knowledge about other professional groups. Many committees that develop health and social care services in an area have members drawn from the social services, health, and the voluntary sector. One approach used when trying to improve the way a team works together is to set them a task they have to complete. (See scenario below.)

> ### Key concept
>
> *Team building:* the development of the strengths of a group who work together so that they become more effective.

Barriers to organisational culture

In most NHS and social services, organisational development (OD) is the responsibility of a senior manager. OD is about encouraging the individual to have the same goals and values as that of the organisation. This is achieved through:

* the recruitment of people who have values that reflect those of the organisation

* induction programmes that help the individual feel part of the organisation

* review and appraisal schemes that help people feel their views and feelings are respected.

Barriers to the development of an organisational culture can be set up by people within an organisation if they do not agree with the culture of the organisation. Inappropriate recruitment and selection procedures can be the problem if people are recruited who do not agree with the aims and ethics of the organisation.

Other barriers can be caused by the organisation itself. Reorganisation of work and job roles can cause a great deal of anxiety among workers. At the moment there are so many changes to the ways in which nurses and social workers fulfil their roles, that this may affect staff morale. Managers need to ensure staff are informed about changes and allowed to express their views. Rapid staff turnover also affects the working culture and gives rise to a lack of stability and continuity. In this situation people may lose commitment to the organisation and to its goals.

SCENARIO

Action plan

A project was being developed around planning health and care services for the future for older people. Team members from health and social services and also from the voluntary sector who provide services and support for older people spent a day together to work out an action plan. Older people were also invited, to give their views on the services currently available and the changes they would like made. The morning was spent in small groups discussing what the problems were in the area, then some older people joined the groups and told members of their experiences. Each group developed a plan for future services that would meet the needs of the clients and service users, and would be affordable.

Many of the professionals had never met before and did not understand the issues faced by the different groups. Their contact with older people and older people's voluntary services had also been limited. At the end of the day an action plan had been drawn up for future service provision, which will be developed further.

Perhaps you have a part-time job.

Are you clear about what your role is?

Do you feel you have too much or not enough responsibility?

How could your experience of the job be improved?

How far is it your responsibility to contribute to the organisation through your own efforts?

How far is it the responsibility of the organisation (or your manager) to make you feel part of the working team?

What makes you feel happy about the job, or do you work just for the money?

Appropriate selection and recruitment

All organisations have a recruitment and selection policy and procedure in order to ensure that the most suitable person is appointed. In the application pack for a post, there will be the relevant information about the post and the organisation. You will also be asked to write a supporting statement; usually the statement needs to reflect the skills required in the job.

Look again at the job description of the hospital care manager (page 40).

If you wanted to apply for the post of hospital care manager what kind of information would you need to include in your supporting statement in order to be shortlisted? (Many competent people do not write an effective supporting statement that reflects the skills needed for the post. The supporting statement is used to draw up the shortlist, so this is very important.)

The advertising of the post is relevant.

How is the advertisement worded and where will it be placed – in a local or national publication?

What are the advantages and disadvantages of each?

Would you use the Internet to advertise?

Summary of Section 7.3

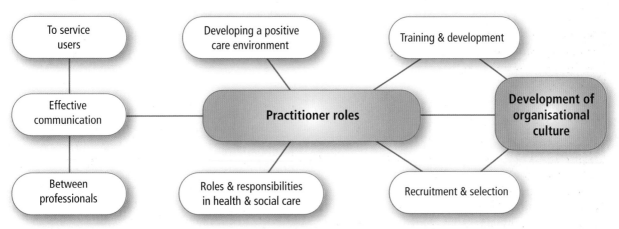

You visit a private home for older people with dementia. The owner of the home tells you he has problems recruiting and retaining staff. Most of the long-serving members of staff at the home have worked part-time for many years on particular shifts and they don't like change. A new manager has recently been appointed. She has achieved her NVQ Level 4 in Care Management and she is determined that all existing staff should update their training in health and safety, and undertake NVQ qualifications. The long-serving staff resent the new proposals. They feel they are competent and they don't need training. The manager decides to implement fortnightly team meetings and annual staff appraisal, and each member of staff will develop an individual learning plan.

As a start, the manager wants to arrange a team-building event.

1. Can you identify the barriers the manager faces in changing the attitudes of staff?

2. If you were organising a training programme at the home, how could you encourage staff to feel involved and committed?

3. How could the manager have an influence on the organisational culture of the home that would improve working practice and service delivery?

4. How would you evaluate improvements in working practice? How could you provide evidence that improvements have taken place?

7.4 Quality assurance and regulation

This section covers how quality is maintained in health and social care organisations. We have seen that the culture of an organisation can affect the quality of service provided to patients and clients. As we have also seen, organisations in health and social care have to be accountable to the public for the way they fulfil their roles. Press reports of poor provision, unfair treatment and neglect of vulnerable groups have led to improved services. The terms 'standards', 'governance' and 'quality control' are now commonplace in health and social care services.

The quality of delivery of services are increasingly being developed; for example, NSFs (National Service Frameworks) and national targets are being set by government for health and social care.

Key concept

Standard: the level and quality of service or performance conforms to a recognised ideal model.

Governance: this is the organisation and delivery of services so that they meet the standards required by the inspection bodies.

Quality control: the systems that are put in place by health and social care organisations to ensure that services are of a high quality.

SCENARIO

Lack of service

Many complaints received by a local PCT were about access to chiropody services. There was a shortage of chiropodists (or podiatrists) and this meant long waiting lists. In an area with a high proportion of older people with foot problems there was no toenail cutting service. The problem was highlighted by a letter to the local paper and the OSC decided to investigate podiatry services in the area. As a result the local Age Concern provided a toenail cutting service and health care assistants are being trained to cut nails. Podiatry assistants are also being trained to do more skilled work so that fully-trained podiatrists can concentrate on more advanced treatments.

The role of the local overview and scrutiny committee (OSC) is to monitor the quality of service provision in the NHS in their area. If there are concerns raised about the provision of certain services the OSC has the power to investigate and to encourage the development of a quality service. Although OSCs do not fund the service they are an important aspect of quality control.

Quality assurance and regulation in the NHS

One of the key aims of the NHS Plan is 'to improve quality services' and to reduce errors. The model for delivering quality services is set out in the **1998 Department of Health paper *A First Class Service: Quality in the New NHS*.**

The Healthcare Commission

The Healthcare Commission was set up under the Health and Social Care (Community Health and Standard) Act 2003 and is known in legislation by its full name, the Commission for Healthcare Audit and Inspection (CHAI). The Commission came into being on 1 April 2004 and has the general function of encouraging improvement in the provision of health care by and for NHS bodies in England and Wales. The Commission has taken over many of the functions previously undertaken by the Commission for Health Improvement (CHI) and the National Care Standards Commission (both CHI and the NCSC ceased to exist on 31 March 2004). The Healthcare Commission also took over the work of the Mental Health Act Commission (MHAC) and the work of the Audit Commission, looking at the cost-effectiveness of the NHS.

The key aims of the Healthcare Commission are to monitor:

* availability of, access to, quality and effectiveness of health care
* economy and efficiency of the provision of health care
* availability and quality of information provided to the public about health care

* safeguarding and promotion of the rights and welfare of children, and the effectiveness of measures to do so.

The main statutory functions of the commission include:

* carrying out reviews and investigations into the provision of health care and the arrangements to promote and protect public health, including studies aimed at improving economy, efficiency and effectiveness in the NHS
* promoting the co-ordination of reviews undertaken by other bodies
* publishing information about the state of health care across the NHS and the independent sector, including the results of national clinical audits
* reviewing the quality of data relating to health and health care.

This new body will cover many areas related to quality in the NHS. It will work in partnership with the Audit Commission and the Commission for Social Care Inspection. In addition to all these functions the Healthcare Commission has to ensure that all NHS organisations comply with the Human Rights Act and the Race Relations (Amendment) Act. There are details of the Healthcare Commission on its website www.healthcarecommission.org.uk.

Internal monitoring in the NHS

Every NHS organisation has its own system for monitoring performance and service delivery. Every NHS Trust has to report annually on the quality of service it provides and the arrangements it makes to deal with complaints and risk management.

> **Try it out**
>
> If you obtain the annual report from your local NHS Trust, it will include a section on performance monitoring. There are regular public meetings of the board of the local trusts and if you attend one of these and look at the papers available at the meeting you will get a good idea of what the trust is doing to improve performance.

Monitoring of performance in the NHS since 2003

Commission for Patient and Public Involvement in Health (CPPIH)

This was set up to work at national, regional and local levels in England to monitor the NHS and to involve the public in decision-making about the provision of health services. This is done through setting up Patient and Public Involvement Forums (PPI forums).

Every NHS Trust in England has a forum and its members are often ex-patients of the trust who can contribute their experience.

Patient and Public Involvement Forums

The terminology for these tends to differ. Some trusts refer to them as Patients' Forums, others refer to them as Public Forums, which can be confusing. They are independent organisations that operate at a local level and they have the powers to inspect all premises used by NHS patients, including those in the private sector. They consider the quality of services from the patient's viewpoint. If there is a planned change to service, the PPI forums will be involved in the consultation process. PPI forums hold several public meetings a year, which should be advertised in the local newspapers. If you attend one of these you will be able to see what work the PPI forum does as you will have access to their annual report and action plan for the following year.

Overview and Scrutiny Committees (OSCs)

The Health and Social Care Act (2001) gave new powers to overview and scrutiny committees in local councils who have social service responsibilities. OSCs can review and scrutinise all matters related to the planning, provision and operation of health services in the area covered by the council. In many areas there is a close working relationship between the OSC and the PPI forums, as forums can refer issues of concern to the OSC. It is possible to attend an OSC meeting, as they are held in public, but members of the public are not able to contribute to the meeting. However, there are often interesting items on the agenda about services in the area which will help you understand how the local NHS services operate.

SCENARIO
MRSA

In an acute hospital in South East England, concern was expressed by members of the public, the local press, members of the trust's PPI forum and the local OSC about the high levels of MRSA in the hospital. The trust has a duty to provide information about the infection rates and as a result of the concern raised, an action plan was produced by the infection control committee to show how they would reduce infection rates at the hospital. The infection control consultant came to meetings of the OSC and the PPI forum to explain the action plan, and that monitoring of the plan will be done by the OSC and the forum.

Try it out

The NHS and the services it provides are varied and complex. It is led by highly-trained professionals. Can you think of any problems that could arise for lay members on the OSC and the forum who do not have extensive medical knowledge?

Independent Complaints Advocacy Service (ICAS)

These advocacy services were also established under the Health and Social Care Act 2001. They are independent bodies who help patients pursue a complaint about a particular NHS service. They also offer information and advice and will act as advocate for the patient (e.g. write letters, attend meetings, and speak on their behalf). They also advise patients of the options open to them if they wish to complain. Citizens Advice Bureaux can tell people the location of their local ICAS.

Patients Advice and Liaison Services (PALS)

All trusts must have a PALS service which offers advice to patients. In a hospital the PALS office is usually near the main reception, and all patients using the trust should be advised of its existence. PALS try to resolve problems on the spot – this could be dealing with a complaint about cleaning on a ward, or about the quality of the food. PALS give information to patients, their carers, and their families about local health services. They also help people contact local support groups. They direct people to ICAS or the trust's own complaints service and they may refer issues of concern to the hospital management and to the PPI forum. PALS produce a leaflet telling people about their service, and these are usually easily available through the trust.

Auditing and identifying poor service provision within the NHS

Although the monitoring role of external independent bodies (such as the Healthcare Commission) is important, NHS organisations have to develop their own quality assurance systems. This is done through clinical governance systems.

Clinical governance is about:

* improving services for patients
* managing risks
* involving patients and the public.

In a PCT there is a wide range of services that have to be covered by clinical governance. These include services provided by GPs, dentists, pharmacists, community and intermediate care services. The director of clinical services within each PCT has overall responsibility for clinical governance, and there is also a head of clinical governance who is responsible for developing and implementing the clinical governance strategy on a daily basis. There is an annual clinical governance plan. For example, in one PCT the clinical governance team works with GP surgeries to identify areas in order to improve practice.

Record keeping, confidentiality, complaints and health and safety all come under clinical governance. Training staff and ensuring staff have the appropriate qualifications for the job

they do is also part of clinical governance. **NICE (the National Institute for Health and Clinical Excellence** – see their website http://www.nice.org.uk) issues directives on patient safety and the safety of procedures, as well as on drug use; the clinical governance team ensures that the PCT responds to these directives as well as to guidelines from the Department of Health.

Clinical governance is about identifying problems in practice and learning from them. In order to do this, health care workers (including doctors) have to feel that the trust they work for is supporting them and perhaps identifying training needs rather than blaming individuals. Examples of clinical governance issues recently dealt with by one PCT include:

1. poor practice in taking cervical smears

2. a TB outbreak caused by a health worker with TB

3. an unregistered nurse discovered practising in a GPs surgery.

The PCT aimed to deal with these issues so that quality of care was maintained and health workers did not feel threatened.

In example 1, the practice nurse identified as taking smears incorrectly was retrained and then supervised for a period of time.

In example 2, patients in contact with the health worker were immunised and a review was made of how health workers are assessed as being free from TB. As many GPs were not familiar with the signs and symptoms of TB, additional training for GPs on recognising TB was set up. BCG vaccines offering protection against TB were offered to all children between the ages of 10 and 14.

In example 3, all practices in the PCT had to review the procedure for checking registration documents to ensure that the qualifications were genuine. In this specific case the PCT notified the police and the unqualified nurse was charged and sentenced. Patients were also notified and offered advice.

From these examples it is clear that clinical governance in all health services is a key issue and can affect the well-being of patients and the quality of services.

Auditing services in the NHS

All NHS Trusts have to have a complaints system set up to record, monitor and review complaints. A manager at senior level is appointed to lead the process. Complaints are reported to the trust board four times a year and any significant patterns are monitored. As well as complaints monitoring, hospital trusts administer the UK In-patient Survey to everyone who has been an in-patient for at least one night. The survey is part of the monitoring process and is required by the Healthcare Commission. It consists of 68 questions and covers seven key areas. These are:

* emergency and planned admissions

* environment and facilities

* care and treatment, especially pain relief

* doctors and nurses

* adequacy of patient information

* discharge

* overall impression.

Here are some of the questions patients were asked in a recent survey:

1. After arriving at hospital, how long did you wait for admission to a room or a ward?

2. During your stay in hospital, did you ever share a room or bay with a member of the opposite sex?

3. How clean was the hospital room or ward that you were in?

4. How clean were the toilets and bathrooms that you used?

5. How would you rate the courtesy of the doctors?

In one trust the scores were 'good' for emergency care, and 'adequate' for nurses on duty and explanation of test results. However, the trust scored badly on information and communication, food, and the use of mixed sex wards. As a result of this survey the trust has drawn up a plan to improve these areas.

Surveys like this are a useful tool to identify areas of poor quality, but as with all research tools, you have to be aware of the sample size and the scoring system. In this survey 481 patients took part. This reflected a 61.6 per cent response rate, so about a third of patients did not complete or return the form. If there had been a 100 per cent response rate the results could have been different. As with all surveys there are problems with taking a representative sample.

The way questions are worded can present problems as people may not understand what is meant. If patients are given only the options of excellent, good, adequate or poor this may limit the usefulness of the survey. Patients' responses can be affected by a range of factors. They may feel if they say that services are 'poor' that this may affect the treatment they receive from staff. Different people have different ideas about what is a 'good meal' – this could refer to size or content or whether or not the food is hot, etc.

National Patients' Surveys take place every year. In 2004, the following National Patients' Surveys took place:

* children and young people survey

* ambulance trusts survey

* service users in mental health trusts survey.

The surveys are collated by the NHS Survey Advice Centre and are used for the performance ratings of trusts.

Involving service users in the NHS

Section 11 of the Health and Social Care Act (2001) places a duty on NHS Trusts to make arrangements to involve and consult patients and the public in service planning and operation, and in the proposals for change. This is a new duty that trusts have to fulfil, as before they involved the public only when there was a planned change to service provision.

All trusts now appoint a manager with responsibility for patient and public involvement. They must draw up an action plan showing how they are involving the patients and public in the working of the trust. This could be through organising focus groups of patients to find out about matters of concern, or inviting patients to be representatives on various committees in the trust.

Patient prospectuses

All PCTs have to produce a patient prospectus entitled *Your Guide to Local Health Services*. These guides are available at GPs' surgeries. In some areas they have been delivered to peoples' homes.

Patient's Charters

In January 2001 the Patient's Charter was replaced by the new NHS charter *Your Guide to the NHS*. This is designed to give patients a clear guide to their rights and responsibilities, as well as to the standards and services they can expect to receive under the NHS Plan. The guide gives information about where to get the most appropriate treatment. It also explains how patients can make a complaint.

Key points include:

* *Responsible use of the NHS:* keeping appointments, returning equipment when it is no longer needed, paying any charges promptly and treating NHS staff with respect.

* *Easier access to information:* users of the guide are encouraged to access the health services that are most appropriate. For example, they could contact NHS Direct or their local pharmacist. They could go to a walk-in centre, or see a nurse. Responsible use of services is encouraged. In the past many people used A&E for minor conditions that could have been dealt with elsewhere, and this meant delays for people with urgent problems.

* *Hospital treatment:* from 2004 patients should expect to wait no more than 17 weeks for an out-patient appointment, and no more than nine months for in-patient care. People with suspected cancer should be seen within two weeks of being referred to a specialist.

* *Cancelled operations:* if an operation is cancelled on the day of surgery the hospital should offer another date within 28 days or pay for an operation at the time and hospital of the patient's choice.

* *A&E waiting times:* no one should wait more than four hours in an A&E department from arrival to admission, transfer or discharge.

* *Right to complain:* any patient complaint must be handled sensitively, effectively and without delay.

Dealing with and responding to complaints

In every NHS Trust there is a designated manager who is responsible for dealing with complaints, and he or she provides a quarterly report on complaints to the trust board. Complaints are studied carefully as they may indicate a failure to provide an adequate service, or a need for staff training.

Complaints in primary care are initially dealt with by the GP practice concerned. However, if this cannot be resolved, the complaint will be referred to the PCT.

Quality assurance and regulation in the social services

A useful website on this topic, www.csci.org.uk, has information on the **Commission for Social Care Inspection (CSCI)**. Regulation and inspection in social services has also been developed in the last few years. The Commission for Social Care Inspection (CSCI) was set up in April 2004 and replaced the work previously undertaken by the Social Services Inspectorate (SSI), the SSI and Audit Commission joint review team, and the social care functions of the National Care Standards Commission (NCSC).

CSCI is responsible for:

* carrying out inspections of all social care organisations (statutory, private and voluntary) against national standards, and publishing reports

* registering services that meet national minimum standards

* carrying out inspections of local social service authorities

* publishing an annual report to parliament on progress in social care and an analysis of where money has been spent

* publishing 'star ratings' for local authorities.

The CSCI sets out regulations, standards and information about specific social care services. These regulations apply to care homes for adults (18–65), care homes for older people, children's homes, domiciliary care, fostering services, nurses' agencies and residential family centres. There are supplementary standards covering services for young people aged 16 and 17.

Care homes for young adults

Support is needed for 16 to 17-year-olds who are moving into adulthood. Homes for these young people should take only 16 to 25-year-olds, and their facilities and services should reflect the needs of this client group.

Education, training and employment are seen as very important and should be considered in the individual care plan, which is then agreed with the young person and reviewed frequently. As many of these young people will be leaving the care of social services, they will need to have a leaving care plan. This outlines the support and assistance a young person will receive in order to enable a successful transition to adulthood. The plan will include arrangements for:

* education, training and employment
* securing safe and secure accommodation
* support necessary for disabled young people
* financial assistance to enable the young person to set up and maintain independent accommodation
* claiming welfare benefits where this is identified as a need
* general and specialised health education, health care, and other specialist services such as counselling
* maintaining existing support networks and creating new networks as defined by the young person.

There are 41 standards attached to care homes accommodating young people. Standards indicate the level of support that should be in place for particular client groups who are in the care of social services – either provided directly by the council or commissioned from the independent sector.

What if?

Standard 14 is related to leisure. Read the extracts from the standards carefully. If you were the care manager of a home for young people, how would you ensure that the teenagers in your care are safe and supported, yet have choice?

Standard 14: Leisure

14.1 Staff ensure that service users have access to, and choose from a range of appropriate leisure activities.

14.7. Birthdays, name days, cultural and religious festivals are celebrated and service users participate in planning these events.

14.8. Activities provide a balance between free and controlled time, are experiential, and provide a mix of time with and without adults.

14.9. Service users under the age of 18 do not have access to, or watch, videos certified as suitable for over-18s, and systems and policies

are in place to safeguard users when computer networking or accessing the Internet.

14.10 Leisure interests and areas in which a service user has talents or abilities are encouraged and financially supported.

Try it out

Look again at Standard 14 for young people.

Can you think of any differences or similarities between young people in care and those who are living at home with their families? Rules may be applied in both cases but usually in family life they are unwritten and they would not be regulated and enforced by a government agency.

Risks are part of life, as we have already seen, and risk-taking, whether it is in a care home, school or family, is part of developing an ability to make decisions. In care work there will be clients who need support in making decisions, and it is the responsibility of the care worker or advocate to enable clients to make a choice about what they do. By developing systems of regulation and inspection, it is hoped that quality care will be maintained in all sectors of health and social care. At the same time, all service users of any age should be encouraged to be as independent as possible and to participate in community life.

Although the CSCI is responsible for inspecting children's social services at the moment, this role will be transferred to **OFSTED (the Office for Standards in Education)** in the future, as children's social services are merging with education departments to form children's trusts, while adult social services are working more closely with primary care and mental health trusts. There have been many changes in the way in which services are regulated and inspected, and with health and social care services working more closely together in the future further changes are likely to occur.

OFSTED was set up in 1993 and was initially responsible for the quality of education in all maintained schools and nursery schools. It has developed its inspection role to cover childminding and out of school care for children up to the age of eight. It carries out four main functions in order to ensure that day care providers and childminders meet the national standards.

1. *Registration:* childminders and day care providers have to be registered by OFSTED. Premises are also inspected.

2. *Inspection:* OFSTED inspects child care providers every three years to judge the quality and standards of the child care provided.

3. *Investigation:* OFSTED investigates any complaints or concerns voiced by parents or members of the public, and follows up issues raised in inspection reports.

4. *Enforcement:* OFSTED can take action if there is a risk to children in the service provided. This may lead to the cancellation of the registration of the childminder or care provider.

For more details on OFSTED, look at the website: www.ofsted.gov.uk.

Summary of Section 7.4

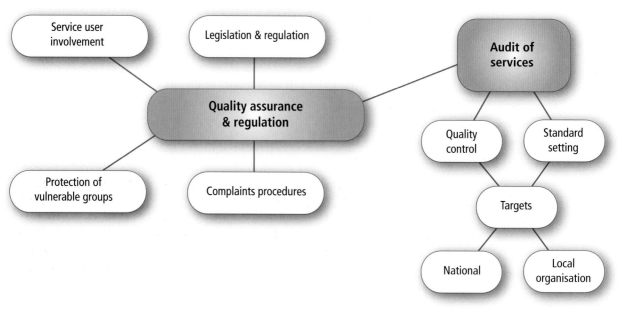

Consider this

At the monthly clinical governance meeting of a PCT, two issues are raised.

There have been a number of complaints about the attitude of a particular GP to patients. This GP has already been the subject of complaints in the past.

The monthly audit of waiting times to see a health care practitioner within 24 hours or a GP within 48 hours shows that the target set by the

Department of Health has not been met in one practice.

1. How should the committee respond to these issues?

2. How could patients' views and patient representation be increased in primary care?

3. Evaluate how far patients' views can influence the organisation of health and social care services.

UNIT 7 ASSESSMENT

How you will be assessed

The external assessment is through a $1\frac{1}{2}$-hour written examination consisting of structured questions based on case studies. The material will include the areas covered in this chapter:

* the structure and provision of services
* meeting individual needs
* the roles of practitioners in health and social care
* quality and regulation in health and social care services.

The examination will test your understanding and ability to apply the knowledge you have gained from studying the unit. You will be expected to analyse the issues and problems presented in the case studies.

The assessment of unit 7 will involve a synoptic test.

> ### Key concept
>
> *Synoptic test:* a form of assessment that explores a student's knowledge gained from studying a range of units. The synoptic test will assess a student's general understanding of core health and social care issues.

Remember to look carefully at the number of marks allocated to each question and try to make the same number of points in your answer. Do not waste time and effort repeating the question, as this will not gain marks. Read through each question completely before attempting to answer it. Candidates often answer a part of a question with an answer that belongs to another part that they have not yet read. You will not be required to give the same answer twice. Unless the question clearly needs a one or two word answer, write your answer in a properly constructed sentence or paragraph. The space allocated to each question is for guidance and you should not write either a great deal less or a great deal more.

Unit test

1. Mrs Brown had a fall in the garden and fractured her hip. She is 80 and lives on her own. She has been in hospital for 10 days and the discharge care manager at the hospital is planning to discharge her. She will have a multi-disciplinary assessment and this will result in a care plan being set up. It is hoped that Mrs Brown will make a full recovery.

    a) What is meant by a multi-disciplinary assessment? (2)

    b) Name two professionals who may be involved in Mrs Brown's assessment. (2)

    c) Mrs Brown's assessment will be based on her needs. Explain the benefits of Mrs Brown having a needs-led assessment. (5)

    d) From the information given in the case study, identify and describe two needs that Mrs Brown in likely to have assessed. (6)

e) Mrs Brown finds it difficult to remember which service provider is dealing with her.

So many people are coming to the ward to see her that she has become confused and anxious about returning home. Her daughter has contacted the local Age Concern so that an advocate can help her.

Outline the role of an advocate and discuss the contribution an advocate can make when organising service provision. (10)

f) Evaluate the importance of supporting Mrs Brown so that she is able to return home. (8)

g) Define the term 'assistive technology'. (2)

h) Give two examples of how assistive technology may help Mrs Brown. (4)

i) Mrs Brown will be able to return home with support from the health and social care public sector. What help may she receive from the voluntary sector? (2)

2. Many health and care workers will be involved in developing a discharge plan and care plan for Mrs Brown. A result of the National Service Framework (NSF) for Older People means that a single assessment process (SAP) has been developed.

a) Define the term 'single assessment process'. (2)

b) The NSF has 8 Standards that include Standard 1, Removing Age Discrimination. How can health and social care workers ensure that discriminatory practices do not occur? (5)

3. After a few weeks at home Mrs Brown complains to her daughter that the nurses do not come when expected and she has not had regular blood checks for her diabetes. She isn't sure how to complain.

a) Who should Mrs Brown complain to in the first instance? (2)

b) PCTs have quality systems in place to ensure that the services they provide are timely, appropriate and meet patients' needs. Identify and explain two ways in which PCTs assess the quality of the services they provide. (6)

c) Discuss the importance of listening to service users and responding to their experiences. (8)

4. Since 1990 there has been an increase in health and social care work performed by the independent sector and a decrease in the amount of work done by the statutory or public sector.

a) Define what the following terms mean and give one example of each:
   * independent sector
   * public sector. (4)

5. The use of the independent sector was part of the government's policy to introduce a mixed economy of care in health and social care.

a) Define the term 'mixed economy'. (2)

b) Describe one advantage and one disadvantage of using a mixed economy approach in health and social care. (6)

6. Discuss how health and social care services are working more closely together, giving examples from at least one client group. (10)

7. Voluntary organisations are now working more closely with health and social care organisations to provide services to a range of client groups.

a) Give an example of a voluntary organisation which works with:
   * older people
   * children. (2)

b) Evaluate the contribution made by the voluntary sector to health and social care services. (10)

References and further reading

Guide to the Social Services in 2004/05 (2000) (London: Waterlow Publishing)

Handy, C. (1993) *Understanding Organisations* (Harmondsworth: Penguin)

HM Government (1997) *The New NHS: Modern Dependable* (London: HMSO)

HM Government (2000) *The NHS Plan* (London: HMSO)

HM Government (2003) Green Paper *Every Child Matters* (London: HMSO)

HM Government (2003) *Fair Access to Care Services* (London: HMSO)

HM Government (2004) White Paper *Every Child Matters: Next Steps* (London: HMSO)

HM Government (2005) Green Paper *Independence, Well-being and Choice* (London: HMSO)

Moonie, N. (2000) *Advanced Health and Social Care* (Oxford: Heinemann)

Moonie, N. (2004) *GCE AS Level in Health and Social Care* (Oxford: Heinemann)

The Princess Royal Trust for Carers (1999) *Too Much to Take On. A report on young carers and bullying* (Derby: The Princess Royal Trust)

Wellards NHS Handbook 2004–2005 (2004) (Wadhurst East, Sussex: JMH Publishing Ltd)

Useful websites

Commission for Social Care Inspection www.csci.org.uk

Community Care Magazine www.communitycare.co.uk

Department of Health www.dh.gov.uk

Department of Health for Scotland www.show.scot.nhs.uk

Department of Health for Wales www.wales.gov.uk

Every Child Mattters www.everychildmatters.gov.uk

Healthcare Commission www.healthcarecommission.org.uk

Home Office www.homeoffice.gov.uk

NHS Direct www.nhsdirect.nhs.uk

NHS website www.nhs.uk

National Institute for Health and Clinical Excellence (NICE) www.nice.org.uk

OFSTED www.ofsted.gov.uk

Promoting health and well-being

This unit covers the following sections:

8.1 Reasons for promoting health and well-being

8.2 Models and approaches to health promotion

8.3 Planning and implementing a health promotion

Introduction

This unit investigates the range of lifestyle choices and societal factors which influence health and well-being. You will investigate the ways in which ill-health can be prevented in care settings and the health-promotion methods that are used by health and social care practitioners. The government has recognised that whilst we now live longer, and the major causes of premature death of the last century are largely under control, the same cannot be said for today's main killers. How we tackle these diseases of the modern day is explored in this unit, including the range of factors that lead to the launch of a health promotion activity and shape its aims, design, target population and subject area. The unit considers the theoretical underpinning of health promotion, exploring the range of models and approaches to health promotion activity. How to plan and implement a health promotion activity brings the unit to a conclusion, explaining how to define your target group, how to set aims and objectives and how to select the appropriate methods and materials.

How you will be assessed

This is an internally assessed unit where you will be expected to carry out your own small-scale health promotion activity which will enable you to learn about the different approaches to health education, and how they are put into practice. As a result you will develop skills in planning, carrying out, and evaluating an activity to promote health and well-being.

8.1 Reasons for promoting health and well-being

Demographic data

One key influence on health promotion is epidemiology or the study of diseases in human populations. It is particularly important in enabling us to understand the spread of infectious diseases and how they can lead to epidemics.

> **Key concept**
>
> *Epidemiology:* this is the study of diseases in human populations. It is particularly important in enabling us to understand the spread of infectious diseases and how they can lead to epidemics. It attempts to understand the factors that influence the number of cases of a disease at any one time, its distribution, and how to control it. This most clearly applies to infectious diseases such as influenza or HIV but is equally applicable to the diseases of the western world such as coronary heart disease and cancer.

Epidemiological data is essential for identifying what health problems are occurring in a population and targeting the relevant health promotion activity to address them. Epidemiological information tends to be of two types:

* information that gives you a picture of the population's health at any one time (incident data)

* information that shows you trends over time (trend data).

Ill-health data, which deals with illness and death, is routinely collected by health organisations and interpreted by a range of organisations, including public health observatories and the Office for National Statistics. For example, the 2005 report by the Statistics Office on cancer in the UK (the 'Cancer Atlas') summarised the trends in past years as follows.

* In the last 50 years of the twentieth century, mortality (deaths) from heart disease, stroke and infectious diseases fell markedly in both males and females. In contrast, mortality from cancer was fairly stable. Consequently, in England and Wales, cancer became the most common cause of death in females in 1969 and in males in 1995.

* The incidence of all cancers combined in England and Wales rose gradually over the 1970s and 1980s by about 20 per cent in males and 30 per cent in females, then levelled off in the 1990s. The trends were similar in Scotland.

This information identifies cancer as a key area for health promotion activity, for example providing a reason for a renewed emphasis on 'stop smoking' activities, the promotion of healthy nutrition and screening programmes like those for breast and cervical cancers. The data was also portrayed graphically to help people visualise the impact of cancer on the nation, as shown in Figures 8.1(a) and (b).

The report also revealed the differences across the country by mapping the incidence of cancer at a point in time. To do this it uses a standardised ratio comparing the rate for lung cancer in each health authority against the average rate for the UK and Ireland. Health authorities with lower than average rates are coloured blue, those with higher than average rates purple.

This demonstrated wide variations. For example, the incidence and mortality rates for cancers strongly related to smoking and alcohol (e.g. those for the larynx, lip, mouth and pharynx, lung – (see Figure 8.2) were generally below average in the South and Midlands of England and higher in a band across the North of England and across the central belt of Scotland. The report pointed out that with such wide

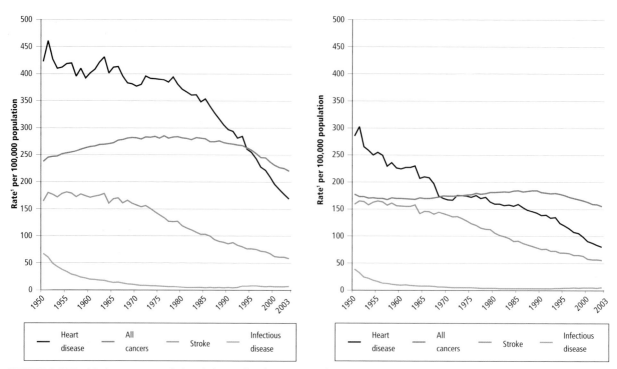

FIGURE 8.1(A) *Major causes of death in males (1950–2003)* (B) *Major causes of death in females (1950–2003)*

Source: Office for National Statistics website

geographical variations, simply reducing the incidence and mortality rates everywhere to those found in the areas with the lowest rates would prevent about 25,600 cases of cancer and 17,500 deaths from cancer each year. The report also points out that around three-quarters of these cases would be related to drinking and smoking.

This information clearly demonstrates that the best population health improvements are achieved by directing resources towards levelling up the health status in the worst areas. In the case of alcohol and tobacco this would mean investing most resources into health promotion aimed at the purple areas on the map.

By contrast, the map for melanoma (skin cancers) reverses the usual cancer patterns (i.e. higher rates in poorer communities). The highest ratios are in the south and south west in particular. This reflects the prevailing weather patterns across the country (i.e. the greatest sun exposure is in the southern counties) and also the relative affluence of these areas, skin cancer being linked to the ability to pay for expensive holidays abroad. However, the picture is not quite as straightforward as a north–south divide; the reduction in cost of package holidays has meant that people in less affluent northern communities now also have access to hot sunny climates.

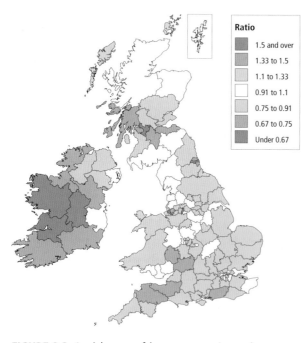

Ratio

- 1.5 and over
- 1.33 to 1.5
- 1.1 to 1.33
- 0.91 to 1.1
- 0.75 to 0.91
- 0.67 to 0.75
- Under 0.67

FIGURE 8.2 *Incidence of lung cancer in males 1991–99*

Figure 8.3 illustrates how activity to promote sun awareness would have to be targeted differently from other forms of cancer prevention, with messages about routine day-to-day exposure (e.g. for building-site workers) being focused on southern areas. Messages about sun safety abroad might be targeted at holidaymakers; welcome packs now frequently include a sun safe guide as part of the health and safety information.

Information about ill-health can be used to prioritise health promotion activity but, as the maps demonstrate, the need for this activity is not evenly spread. Another aspect of health data which needs to be taken into account when planning health promotion activity is that of social class, which has long been used as the method of measuring and monitoring health inequalities.

Since the 2001 census the Office for National Statistics has classified the population into eight layers or social classes, as shown in Table 8.1, specifically picking out the long-term unemployed as a separate group for the first time.

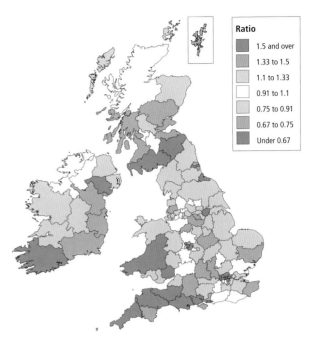

Ratio
▨	1.5 and over
▨	1.33 to 1.5
▨	1.1 to 1.33
□	0.91 to 1.1
▨	0.75 to 0.91
▨	0.67 to 0.75
▨	Under 0.67

FIGURE 8.3 *Incidence of melanoma in females 1991–99*

Source: Office for National Statistics website

1	Higher managerial and professional occupations	
	1.1	Large employers and higher managerial occupations e.g. chief executives of major organisations
	1.2	Higher professional occupations e.g. doctors, lawyers
2	Lower managerial and professional occupations; middle management in bigger organisations; departmental managers, e.g. customer services, physiotherapy, teachers, etc.	
3	Intermediate occupations e.g. clerks and bank workers	
4	Small employers and own account workers e.g. painter and decorator or small manufacturing company owner	
5	Lower supervisory and technical occupations e.g. builders, joiners etc.	
6	Semi-routine occupations e.g. unskilled labouring jobs	
7	Routine occupations e.g. assembly line workers	
8	Never worked and long-term unemployed	

TABLE 8.1 *The Office for National Statistics socio-economic classification*

The long-term unemployed as the lowest social grouping are amongst the most socially disadvantaged, and as a consequence experience significant inequalities in health. They have higher levels of depression, suicide and self-harm, and a significantly increased risk of morbidity and mortality across all causes (see Figure 8.4). For example, men unemployed at the census dates in 1971 and 1981 had mortality rates twice that of the rest of other men of the same age, and those men who were unemployed at one census date had 27 per cent more deaths than would have been anticipated for that group of men.

Morbidity data is information about ill-health as opposed to mortality data, which is information about deaths. Both are useful but morbidity data gives an earlier warning of problems which will later show up as deaths; for example, the rise in deaths due to smoking was preceded by a rise in the numbers of people who were recorded as having lung cancers.

Likewise deaths which are indirectly due to overweight and obesity will be preceded by a rise in the numbers of people with high blood pressure, diabetes and other conditions related to obesity. Both these types of data are routinely collected through health services.

More responsive than either of these two types of data is health-related behaviour information. This might show changes in consumption of fruit and vegetables or physical activity rates. This can be used to monitor the impact of health promotion activities more effectively than either of the other two, since it will respond more rapidly – it is possible to measure changes in people's smoking behaviour within months of a major TV campaign about stopping smoking, but changes in lung cancer rates may take tens of years to appear.

Race also affects life expectancy, particularly because of the differences in culture this may bring. Black and minority ethnic groups have higher risks of mortality from a range of diseases such as diabetes, liver cancer, tuberculosis, stroke and heart disease. Infant mortality and mental illness amongst Afro-Caribbean men have also been highlighted as significant health problems in these communities. However, establishing the cause of these variations has proved difficult. Medical interventions have tended to concentrate on cultural practices, but this does not acknowledge the compounding factors of poverty and low-employment levels in these groups.

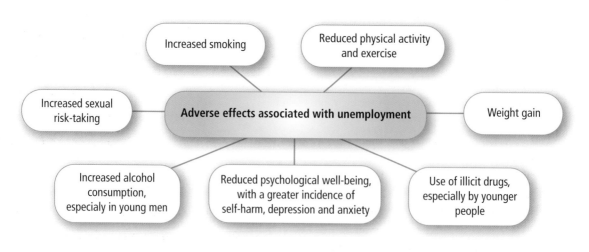

FIGURE 8.4 *Adverse effects of being unemployed*

However we choose to classify the different social strata, most recent research suggests it is the countries with the smallest income *differences*, rather than the richest countries, which have the best health status. Where income differences remain great, as in the UK, health inequalities will persist. For example:

* children in the lowest social class are five times more likely to die from an accident than those in the top social class

* someone in social class 5 is three times more likely to experience a stroke than someone in class 1

* infant mortality rates are highest amongst the lowest social groups

* the difference in life expectancy between a man from one of the most affluent areas in the UK and a man living in Manchester is six years.

Alongside information about social grouping is information about behaviour that affects health, such as smoking, drinking alcohol and taking exercise. This information is not routinely collected other than through major national surveys like the British Crime Survey, Living in Britain, General Household Survey and others. The results of these surveys are routinely presented to PCTs (Primary Care Trusts) to inform their planning for health promotion activity, and are also available on the Office for National Statistics website (www.statistics. gov.uk). Clearly this information is essential to monitor the changes in behaviour, which usually predate the changes in ill-health. For example, the first national fitness survey (Allied Dunbar

National Fitness Survey 1990) provided a wealth of information about the increasingly sedentary lifestyle of the UK population, forecasting an increase in both childhood and adult obesity in years to come. This forecast has duly come to pass, as we shall see in later sections.

National and international targets for health

The European Observatory on Health Systems and Policies describes health targets as follows:

'[Health targets] express a commitment to achieve specified outcomes in a defined time period and enable monitoring of progress towards the achievement of broader goals and objectives. They may be quantitative (e.g. the immunization rate) or qualitative (e.g. the introduction of a national screening programme) and based on outcomes or processors. Ideally they are "SMART" – specific, measurable, accurate, realistic, and time bound. Targets define priorities, create high level commitment, and provide a basis for follow-up and evaluation. Targets can be adopted at international, national or sub-national level.'

Source: European Observatory on Health Systems and Policies website

International targets for health don't fall easily into this model because to set a SMART target would require all countries involved to agree to a single course of action, and this is frequently not possible. Therefore international targets are more usually loosely framed as goals or frameworks which describe broad objectives or common approaches. A good example would be the UN Millennium Declaration, agreed in September 2000. The Declaration, endorsed by 189 countries, set out goals to be reached by 2015. The eight Millennium Development goals are:

* develop a global partnership for development

* ensure environmental sustainability

* combat HIV/AIDS, malaria and other diseases

* improve maternal health

* reduce child mortality

* promote gender equality and empower women

* achieve universal primary education

* eradicate extreme poverty and hunger.

These represent commitments to reduce poverty and hunger, and to tackle ill-health, gender inequality, lack of education, lack of access to clean water and environmental degradation.

A more specific form of international action can be seen in the World Health Organization's Framework Convention on tobacco control adopted by member countries in 2003. These set out broad principles and agreements for action by member states. For example, Article 3 of the guiding principles states:

> 'The objective of this convention and its protocols is to protect present and future generations from the devastating health, social, environmental and economic consequences of tobacco consumption and exposure to tobacco smoke by providing a framework for tobacco control measures to be implemented by the parties at the national, regional and international levels in order to reduce continually and substantially the prevalence of tobacco use and exposure to tobacco smoke.'

Try it out

More detailed information about the Millennium goals and the convention on tobacco control can be found on the Internet.

* What specific targets underpin the broad measures outlined in the Millennium Development goals?

* What actions does the Framework Convention commit signatories such as the UK to undertake?

It is surprising to realise that until quite recently this country had few targets for improving health. It wasn't until the 1992 White Paper *The Health of the Nation* that the country had a first ever health strategy (as opposed to health services). It set for the first time 27 specific targets within five key areas:

* coronary heart disease (CHD) and stroke
* cancers (breast, lung, cervical and skin cancers)
* mental illness
* HIV/AIDS and sexual health
* accidents.

These areas were selected because they were major causes of premature death or avoidable ill-health, as they are today – a fact which provides a consistent thread to the health policy of following administrations. For example, the targets in *Saving Lives – Our Healthier Nation*, the follow-up health strategy to *The Health of the Nation* (released in the first term of the new Labour government in 1999) were:

* *cancer:* to reduce the death rate in under-75s by at least 20 per cent

* *coronary heart disease and stroke:* to reduce the death rate in under-75s by at least 40 per cent

* *accidents:* to reduce the death rate by at least 20 per cent and serious injury by at least 10 per cent

* *mental illness:* to reduce the death rate from suicide and undetermined injury by at least 20 per cent.

This strategy made the first clear commitment to tackle the root causes of ill-health – including air pollution, unemployment, low wages, crime and disorder, and poor housing. This theme was further developed in *The NHS Plan* (2000), a government policy paper which outlined the intention to tackle the health inequalities that divide Britain. This paper set out national targets for tackling health inequalities with the relevant supporting investment, such as:

* a £500 million expansion of 'Sure Start' projects which support families with young children to access health, education and a range of support services

* a new Children's Fund for supporting services for children in the 5–13 age bracket to improve educational achievement, reduce crime and improve attendance at schools, etc.

* a more effective welfare foods programme with increased support for breast feeding

* a 15 per cent cut in teenage conception

* cut the number of smokers by at least 15 million by 2010

* every child in nursery and aged four to six in infant school to be entitled to a free piece of fruit each school day.

Services are provided in group sessions or one to one, depending on the local circumstances and service user's preferences. Most 'stop smoking' advisers are nurses or pharmacists, and all have received training for their role. Services had £138 million available over the three years 2003–06 (£41m/£46m/£51m) with a further £112 million for the two years 2006–08.

The Department of Health funded an evaluation of the NHS 'stop smoking' services programme, which was carried out by a team led by Glasgow University. The main findings were that:

* the services can contribute to a reduction in health inequalities

* long-term quit rates for the services show about 15 per cent of people are still not smoking at 52 weeks, which is comparable with earlier clinical trials

* the services are cost-effective in helping smokers quit.

The evaluation showed that a smoker who tries to quit with the NHS 'stop smoking' service and NRT/Zyban is up to four times as likely to succeed as by will power alone.

The first shift from disease-related targets to health improvement came in February 2001 when the government announced two national health inequalities targets, one relating to infant mortality and the other to life expectancy:

* starting with children under one year, reduce by at least 10 per cent the gap in mortality between manual groups and the population as a whole by 2010

* starting with health authorities, reduce by at least 10 per cent the gap between the quintile (one-fifth or 20 per cent) of areas with the lowest life expectancy at birth and the population as a whole by 2010.

The 2004 public health White Paper, *Choosing Health*

The most recent national document outlining future health strategy is the public health White Paper *Choosing Health: Making Healthy Choices Easier* (November 2004). The detailed action plan *Delivering Choosing Health* (March 2005) set out over 80 pages of actions for delivering better health using milestone targets (delivery of a specific action by a given date).

The White Paper recognised that interest in health was increasing and recommended a new approach to public health that reflected the rapidly changing and increasingly technological society we live in. The document reviewed health and health inequalities and acknowledged the strong role for government in promoting social justice and tackling the wider causes of ill-health and inequality. It also recognised the need to support and empower individuals to make changes in their own lives.

The strategy set out in the document had three underpinning principles.

1. Informed choice: with two important qualifications:

   * protect children

   * do not allow one person's choice to adversely affect another's (e.g. passive smoking).

2. Personalisation: support tailored to the needs of individuals.

3. Working together: real progress depends on effective partnerships across communities.

The strategy's main priorities were to:

* reduce the number of people who smoke

* reduce obesity and improve diet and nutrition

* increase exercise

* encourage and support sensible drinking

* improve sexual health

* improve mental health.

Areas for action

Children and young people

* *Children's personal health plans:* for developing their own health goals with help from their parents or carers, school staff and health professionals.

* *Healthy Start:* a new scheme to provide disadvantaged pregnant women and mothers of young children with vouchers for fresh food and vegetables, milk and infant formula.

* *Support and information for young people:* for example, a new magazine, *FIT*, to get health information across to young men aged 16 to 30.

* *School travel:* by 2010, all schools in England should have active travel plans.

* *Food in schools:* all 4–6-year-olds in LEA-maintained schools in England will be eligible for free fruit or vegetables.

The terms 'activity' and 'exercise' may on the face of it appear to be the same thing, but they are actually subtly different and carry very different meanings for people. Exercise is a term usually applied to sports-related activity whilst activity would include both exercise and the activities of daily living.

> ### Key concept
>
> *Promoting activity not exercise:* 'exercise' is a term usually applied to sports-related activity and in many people's minds is linked to competition and discomfort; it can be a very negative term. However, 'activity' is a less threatening term, being defined as *'any force exerted by skeletal muscle that results in energy expenditure above resting level'.* Activity includes *'the full range of human movement, from competitive sport and exercise to active hobbies, walking and cycling or activities of daily living'.* Current health promotion approaches in this area promote activity because it is less threatening and can be integrated into daily activities. 'Activity' is therefore more attainable for most people than 'exercise'. The 'walking bus' is a good example of this and illustrates a concept called *active transport*, that is transport which requires some energy expenditure, such as walking or cycling.
>
> Source: Department of Health (2004)

Communities for health

Communities for Health is a strategy to promote action on locally chosen priorities for health

FIGURE 8.5 *By 2010, all schools in England should have active travel plans, including the promotion of 'walking buses' to school*

across the local voluntary sector, the NHS, local authorities, business and industry. Its aims are:

* local authorities to work with the national transport charity Sustrans to build over 7,000 miles of new cycle lanes and tracks

* national and local organisations will be invited to develop their role as corporate citizens by making their own pledges on improving health among their workforce or local community

* all government departments and the NHS to be smoke-free (subject to limited exceptions) by 2006.

Health as a way of life

Everyone who wants to will have the opportunity to use a personal health kit to develop their own personal health guide. The suggestion is that in the future, when every house has access to digital TV, information and a personal health promotion portfolio will be available through your TV. Some digital channels already give you access to health information from the government. A new kind of personal health resource will provide NHS health trainers to help people make healthy choices and stick to them.

A health-promoting NHS

All NHS staff will be trained to deliver key health messages effectively as part of their day-to-day work with patients:

* a national screening programme for chlamydia will cover all areas of England

* guidance and training will ensure all health professionals are able to identify alcohol problems early.

Work and health

The NHS will become a model employer promoting the health of its workforce, diversity and equality, and providing family-friendly working conditions. New initiatives will challenge discrimination and improve access to work for people with mental illness.

Concerns expressed by the government

Obesity

Nutrition has recently become a high-profile health issue, as illustrated by its prominence in *Choosing Health*. This is particularly because of startling recent trends in young children where among 3–4-year-olds there has been a 60 per cent increase in the prevalence of being overweight and a 70 per cent increase in rates of obesity. Most adults in England are now overweight and one in five (around 8 million) are obese. (Obesity is defined as a body mass index in excess of 30.) There are currently 30,000 deaths a year linked to obesity, and an estimated cost to the NHS of £500 million a year.

The government's concerns over obesity are best seen in the Health Select Committee's Report on Obesity (2003–04) which summarised the problems as:

'Around two-thirds of the population of England are overweight or obese (see Figure 8.6). Obesity has grown by almost 400 per cent in the last 25 years and on present trends will soon surpass smoking as the greatest cause of premature loss of life. It

---

What if?

Look at the difference between the types of actions in the most recent public health White Papers, **Choosing Health**, and **Our Healthier Nation**. **Choosing Health** is built around programmes of work as opposed to disease reduction targets. If you were Minister for Health:

* What targets would you set that would be meaningful to the public?

* Your maximum term in office is likely to be five years. How would you ensure that you

could demonstrate progress in improving health in this timescale?

* 'It could take ten years to produce improvements in health.' What might be the implications of a change of government before the ten years are up?

* How does this influence campaigning at election times when the health agenda tends to focus on services related to ill-health?

will entail levels of sickness that will put enormous strains on the health service. On some predictions, today's generation of children will be the first for over a century for whom life expectancy falls. Obesity is associated with many health problems including coronary heart disease, diabetes, kidney failure, osteoarthritis, back pain and psychological damage. The strong association between obesity and cancer has only recently come to light. We estimate the economic costs of obesity conservatively at £3.3–3.7 billion per year and of obesity plus overweight at £6.6–7.4 billion.'

Did you know?

Body mass index (BMI)

BMI is a reliable indicator of total body fat, which is related to the risk of disease and death. BMI can be calculated using weight and height with this equation:

$$BMI = \frac{Weight\ in\ kilograms}{(Height\ in\ metres) \times (Height\ in\ metres)}$$

The score is valid for both men and women, but it does have limits. It may overestimate body fat in athletes and others who have a muscular build, and it may underestimate body fat in older persons and others who have lost muscle mass.

	BMI
Underweight	Below 20
Normal	20–24.9
Overweight	25.0–29.9
Obesity	30.0 and above

At its simplest level, obesity is caused when people over-eat in relation to their energy needs. In the early parts of the twentieth century the overwhelming focus of national food policy was on securing enough food, as opposed to improving the diet of the population. This policy had its origins in the Boer War but became firmly established during the global conflicts of the First and Second World Wars. Malnourishment in terms of insufficient fat and protein in the diet was widespread at this time, and remained so throughout the war years until the end of rationing. Current western diet problems are frequently traced back to this point as the origin of the range of choice and widespread availability of food, which we take for granted today. It is this shift to malnourishment in the form of over-consumption that now characterises the major dietary problems of the developed world.

At the same time as people's energy expenditure through exercise has dropped considerably, environmental factors have combined to make it increasingly easy for people to consume more calories than they need. Energy-dense foods (e.g. chocolates, doughnuts, burgers, etc.), which are highly calorific without being correspondingly filling, are becoming increasingly available. People are, generally speaking, aware of what constitutes a healthy diet, but there are multiple barriers to putting this into practice:

* in the absence of practical cookery lessons, children and young people are growing up without the skills to prepare healthy meals

* this can lead to a reliance on convenience foods, which are often high in energy density

* healthy-eating messages are drowned out by the large proportion of advertising given over to highly energy-dense foods

FIGURE 8.6 *Around two-thirds of the population of England are overweight or obese*

Promoting activity

Carrie is the manager of a local physical activity team. The team is funded by the local Primary Care Trust (PCT) and works closely with the local authority; in particular the leisure services department, the park rangers and the community development team.

The goal of the physical activity team is to promote active lifestyles. Their target client group are people who are not active at all and have certain key conditions such as high blood pressure, diabetes, obesity and mild to moderate depression (activity has been shown to be an effective alternative to drug therapy for people with depression).

Her team includes three activity advisers who have sports science backgrounds, with specialist knowledge in the area of activity promotion. The advisers receive referrals from a range of health personnel, including GPs, practice nurses, health visitors, etc. The people are referred based on a strict set of criteria (including one of the specified conditions above), but they must also live in certain postcode areas – i.e. the most deprived wards in the district, those with the poorest health indicators. This ensures that the team are working to address the local health inequalities agenda by prioritising those people with the poorest health and the least disposable income.

People referred to the scheme are encouraged to participate in a wide range of activities (see Figure 8.7): not just gym sessions, but guided walks, gardening, cycling. These constitute 'activity' as opposed to 'exercise', a term that can be a barrier to people becoming more active because they don't see themselves as 'the sporty type'. The local leisure services department works in partnership with Carrie's team, providing discounted rates for clients to use their facilities and free use of community centres where the advisers can deliver group sessions.

* food pricing also makes buying unhealthy food more attractive and economical than healthy alternatives

* food labelling, a key tool to help consumers choose healthy foods, is frequently either confusing or absent.

We are also an increasingly sedentary population, with only just over a third of men and around a quarter of women achieving the Department of Health's target of 30 minutes of physical activity five times a week. Levels of walking and cycling have fallen drastically in recent decades, while the number of cars has doubled in 30 years. Children are also increasingly sedentary both in and out of school. A fifth of boys and girls undertake less than 30 minutes' activity a day. Television viewing has doubled since the 1960s, while physical activity is being squeezed out of daily life by the relentless march of automation. The government response to this situation can be seen in the range of measures listed earlier in the *Choosing Health* White Paper, for example the emphasis on promoting healthy eating and activity in schools.

FIGURE 8.7 *All of these activities can be beneficial to people's health*

Stemming the tide of obesity is seen as the greatest public health challenge facing the country at this time. To see just how complex an issue this is:

1. List as many things as possible which contribute to young people being overweight.

2. Now try and group these into those issues which are about:

   * the individual's responsibility

   * the local community

   * the nation

   * international issues.

3. How did the balance appear between the individual and the wider local, national and international issues?

4. Could you identify any international issues?

5. Now try and suggest changes which could be made to reduce obesity at each of the levels identified.

The result is what would be called a *whole system approach*, one which starts with the individual and works its way out to include national and international actions.

Concerns raised by the media

The role of the media in raising health concerns has been most graphically illustrated through coverage of concerns about the safety of the measles, mumps and rubella (MMR) vaccine. A research paper by Andrew Wakefield (1998) suggesting that MMR vaccination in young children might be linked to autism sparked a controversy. It became the centre of a media storm and went on to include the UK's Department of Health, the World Health Organization, and most broadcast and print media for several days either side of its publication.

Findings from many other researchers provide no support for an MMR-associated form of autism as suggested by Andrew Wakefield. Despite this there has been significant damage to the public confidence in the vaccination, leading to low levels of vaccination and a rise in prevalence of measles, mumps and rubella. (Deaths from measles are common in some European countries, and this is directly related to poor vaccine coverage.) Measles has almost been eliminated in Britain, but high levels of population immunity (greater than 90 per cent) are needed to prevent the recurrence of epidemics.

This collapse in confidence might also be linked to the MMR vaccine becoming a victim of its own success. When disease elimination is close, attention inevitably shifts to the side-effects of the vaccine. Findings from the Health Education Authority (HEA), which had been tracking a random sample of mothers with children aged 0–2 years since 1991, found that 8 per cent of mothers considered that the MMR vaccine presents a greater risk than the diseases it protects against and that 20 per cent consider the vaccine to have a moderate or high risk of side-effects (see Figure 8.8). In October 1994, just before the national immunisation campaign against measles and

FIGURE 8.8 *It is understandable that parents are worried about causing harm to their own children – but who can they trust to give them the right information to help them make the right choice?*

rubella, 55 per cent of mothers considered measles to be a very serious illness; now only 20 per cent do. This mirrors the problems experienced with the whooping cough vaccine, where media coverage about the vaccine throughout the 1970s led to a drop in vaccine coverage from 81 per cent to 31 per cent.

Worryingly, the HEA survey also showed that 67 per cent of people knew that some scientists had linked the MMR vaccine with autism – however, they also thought that the evidence in favour of such a link was evenly balanced, or that the evidence even favoured a link. The long-term media coverage of controversy over the vaccine appears to have led the public to associate MMR and autism, despite the overwhelming evidence to the contrary. The public also thought the take-up of the MMR vaccine had fallen by more than 25 per cent since 1998, when, at the time of the survey, it was down by only 6 per cent.

The fears and concerns of parents are best seen in comments by one researcher, who said, 'They (parents) wanted to trust their doctor and health visitor, but they felt they were being spun a political line.' This indicates the increasing politicisation of health practitioners and the erosion of public trust in their advice. Despite the huge amounts of scientific evidence to back up its MMR policy, the government's medical advisers could not convince the public to simply accept their advice.

As a result, the Department of Health had to overhaul its information about the MMR vaccine, using a wider range of formats to disseminate the information, including the Internet, where parents were increasingly searching for information about the vaccine. The detailed nature of the discussion also meant that parents frequently wanted to see the research evidence, reflecting their scepticism about government information. The Department of Health responded by making available the full texts of relevant research to support the case for vaccination with MMR. This need for information is most clearly evidenced by the establishment of a separate NHS-supported website devoted solely to the dissemination of accurate information about the MMR vaccine (http://www.mmrthefacts.nhs.uk/).

One interesting aspect of this situation is that it showed that parents were becoming increasingly 'consumerist' in their approach to health care and to government policy – in other words, they were more likely to question and reject the advice they received and make up their own minds. This is particularly true of parents in the more affluent social groups.

Try it out

You might want to think about some of these issues in a group.

* Is it the duty of the press to provide balanced reporting?

* If, as in the MMR case, the evidence is overwhelmingly one way, how should the media represent the issue?

* Do you think the public are able to differentiate between the personal standpoint of an individual journalist, for example in an editorial, and a factual assessment?

* The politicians involved at the time of the MMR controversy refused to tell the public whether their children had been vaccinated. Should they have done so to restore confidence in the vaccine?

* Should the NHS have recognised patient choice and provided single-vaccine immunisations for measles, mumps and rubella even though there was strong evidence that this would harm children by reducing immunisation levels?

Concerns expressed by the public

It is unusual for the public to influence national level debate about health promotion; it is more likely the views of local people will influence the path of a small-scale locality project, for example the establishment of a local food co-op. However there is one example where growing public interest in health was given a voice and influenced a range of public policies. This was as part of the nationwide consultation which preceded the production of the government's

Choosing Health White Paper. As part of this exercise people across the country were asked:

* what could really make the difference in enabling people to choose health?

* what should government do?

* what do individuals want to do for themselves?

* what support would they like from the NHS or local government?

* what do they expect of the food and leisure industries?

* what do people want for their children – and what do children and young people want for themselves?

* how can we make choosing health a reality for everyone?

Over 150,000 people responded to the consultations directly or took part in local discussions and surveys. Most people were clear that they wanted to decide for themselves what they should do to make a difference to their own health. Eighty-eight per cent of respondents agreed that individuals are responsible for their own health, acknowledging that health is a very personal issue. People do not want to be told how to live their lives or for government to make decisions for them. The consultation also made plain that many people do want to choose health but that they expect support in making these decisions, particularly the complex ones, and that sometimes they need practical help to stick to them.

This a theme picked up by the government in the opening sections of *Choosing Health*, where it identifies that this interest provides:

'real opportunities to make a practical difference. Health is becoming more and more prominent in news headlines, TV programmes, magazines and everyday conversations. The media is extending the debate through coverage in the press and activities such as the BBC's Fat Nation *and* NHS Day *and ITV's* On the Move *campaign. People's awareness of health issues and their motivation to change means that there is a much greater likelihood of achieving real progress.'*

New scientific evidence

Choosing Health made only brief references to alcohol as a cause for serious health concern, because in 2004 the government released a national alcohol harm reduction strategy. The basis for this wide-ranging health promotion strategy was a precursor report released in 2003 (the strategy unit's interim analysis) which contained one of the most detailed assessments of the impact alcohol was having on society at the time. It stated that although *'the vast majority of people enjoy alcohol without causing harm to themselves or to others – indeed they can also gain some health and social benefits from moderate use,'* for others, *'alcohol misuse is a very real problem'*. The report put an estimate on the cost of alcohol misuse at around £20 billion a year. This figure was arrived at from a combination of impacts, including alcohol-related health disorders and disease, crime and anti-social behaviour, loss of productivity in the workplace, and problems for those who misuse alcohol and their families, including domestic violence. The report identified that the annual costs of alcohol misuse included:

* 1.2 million violent incidents (around half of all violent crimes)

* 360,000 incidents of domestic violence (around a third of the total)

* increased anti-social behaviour and fear of crime – 61 per cent of the population perceive alcohol-related violence as worsening

* expenditure of £95 million on specialist alcohol treatment

* over 30,000 hospital admissions for alcohol-dependence syndrome

* up to 22,000 premature deaths per year

* at peak times, up to 70 per cent of all admissions to accident and emergency departments

* up to 1,000 suicides

* up to 17 million working days lost per year through alcohol-related absence

* between 780,000 and 1.3 million children affected by parental alcohol problems

* increased divorce – marriages where there are alcohol problems are twice as likely to end in divorce.

It also identified that almost one in three adult men and nearly one in five women exceed the recommended guidelines of 21 and 14 units per week respectively, compared to 1988, when one in four men and one in ten women exceeded recommended guidelines. The number of women drinking above recommended guidelines had therefore risen by over fifty per cent in the last 15 years.

The report also identified that people were drinking more regularly, with 38 per cent of men and 25 per cent of women drinking on three or more days per week. This showed a very gradual upward trend which was more perceptible for women. More men drank on five or six days of the week; more women drank on three or four days of the week. In 2001 22 per cent of men and 13 per cent of women drank on more than five days in the preceding week.

Key concept

Safe drinking levels: the Department of Health guidelines for safe drinking state that:

For men: drinking between three and four units a day or less indicates no significant risk to health. Regularly drinking four or more units of alcohol a day indicates an increased risk to health.

For women: drinking between two and three units a day or less indicates no significant risk to health. Regularly drinking over three units a day signifies an increased risk to health.

The strategy unit's interim analysis showed that the group which routinely exceed recommended limits by the greatest amount are people under the age of 25. Never before had a government attempted to describe the impact of alcohol on society in such a way. The proposals to address the problem reflected the wide range of issues associated with alcohol misuse.

Proposals set out in the National Alcohol Harm Reduction Strategy

Better education and communication

The strategy included a series of measures aimed at achieving a long-term change in attitudes to irresponsible drinking and behaviour, including:

* making the 'sensible drinking' message easier to understand and apply

* targeting messages at those most at risk, including binge and chronic drinkers

* providing better information for consumers, both on products and at the point of sale

* providing alcohol education in schools that can change attitudes and behaviour

* providing more support and advice for employers

* reviewing the code of practice for TV advertising to ensure that it does not target young drinkers or glamorise irresponsible behaviour.

Improving health and treatment services

The strategy proposed a number of measures to improve early identification and treatment of alcohol problems. These measures included:

* improved training of staff to increase awareness of likely signs of alcohol misuse

* piloting schemes to find out whether earlier identification and treatment of those with alcohol problems can improve health and lead to longer-term savings

* carrying out a national audit of the demand for and provision of alcohol treatment services, to identify any gaps between demand and provision

* better help for the most vulnerable – such as homeless people, drug addicts, the mentally ill, and young people. They often have multiple problems and need clear pathways for treatment from a variety of sources.

Combating alcohol-related crime and disorder

The strategy proposed a series of measures to address the problems of those town and city centres that are blighted by alcohol misuse at weekends. These include:

* greater use of exclusion orders to ban those causing trouble from pubs and clubs or entire town centres

* greater use of the new fixed-penalty fines for anti-social behaviour

* working with licensees to ensure better enforcement of existing rules on under-age drinking and serving people who are already drunk.

Working with the alcohol industry

The strategy emphasised a need to build on the good practice of some existing initiatives (such as the Manchester Citysafe Scheme) and involve the alcohol industry in new initiatives at both national level (drinks producers) and local level (retailers, pubs and clubs).

At national level, a social responsibility charter for drinks producers will strongly encourage drinks companies to:

* pledge not to manufacture products irresponsibly, for example no products that appeal to under-age drinkers or that encourage people to drink well over recommended limits

* ensure that advertising does not promote or condone irresponsible or excessive drinking

* put the sensible drinking message clearly on bottles alongside information about unit content

* move to packaging products in safer materials – for example, alternatives to glass bottles

* contribute to a fund for new schemes to address alcohol misuse at national and local levels, such as providing information and alternative facilities for young people.

At local level, there will be new 'code of good conduct' schemes for retailers, pubs and clubs, run by a partnership of the industry, police, and licensing panels, and led by the local authority. These will ensure that industry works alongside local communities on issues which really matter, such as under-age drinking and making town centres safer and more welcoming at night.

Health promoters and their role

The promotion of health is multi-layered. It starts with the individual and their health and lifestyle choices, and moves on through local issues and organisations to broader influences at both national and international level. Organisations working at local, national and international level are therefore all involved.

International organisations

These include a range of charities such as Christian Aid, Oxfam and Save the Children, as well as pressure groups such as Greenpeace and key statutory organisations like the United Nations, European Commission, World Health Organization (WHO) and UNICEF.

The World Health Organization (WHO)

The WHO has been instrumental in shaping and influencing health policy across many nations through its *Health for All by the Year 2000* programme. This has been crucial to a move away from medically dominated models of health promotion to a broader-based approach encompassing social and environmental influences. The key feature of this programme was the introduction of the first targets for improving health.

The WHO's constitution defines it as 'a directing and co-ordinating authority on international health work,' its aim being 'the attainment by all peoples of the highest possible level of health'. The following are listed among its responsibilities:

* to assist governments in strengthening health services

* to establish and maintain administrative and technical services such as epidemiological and statistical services

* to provide information, advice, and assistance in the field of health

* to stimulate the eradication of epidemic, endemic, and other diseases

* to promote improved nutrition, housing, sanitation, working conditions, and other aspects of environmental hygiene

* to promote co-operation among scientific and professional groups which contribute to the enhancement of health

* to propose international conventions and agreements on health matters

* to promote and conduct research in the field of health

* to develop international standards for food, biological and pharmaceutical products

* to assist in developing an informed public opinion among all peoples on matters of health.

Source: WHO website

National organisations

The greatest potential for improving the health of the population lies at the national level with government. Simply put (as expressed in the Acheson report, HMSO 1998) the single most effective action at any level to address the level of health inequality is to raise benefit levels.

Government

Government action to make improvements in health takes place across all departments, as was seen in the first health strategy, *The Health of the Nation* (1992). Government routinely reorganises its structures but at the time of writing key government offices included:

* Department of Health

* Department for Education and Skills

* Home Office

* Department of Culture, Media and Sport

* Work and Pensions Department

* Department for Environment, Food and Rural Affairs

* Department of Trade and Industry.

One illustration of the government's role in promoting health can be seen in the work of the Department for Education and Skills, which has been instrumental in leading the development of the National Healthy School Standard and in reducing the levels of unemployment, through initiatives such as the modern apprenticeship and the New Deal.

However, the government is not the only national organisation that contributes to the promotion of health. There are many other national-level organisations that have a part to play in promoting better health, as shown in Table 8.2.

ORGANISATION TYPE	EXAMPLES
Voluntary organisations Produce educational materials such as those on sexual health issues from the FPA or on safety from RoSPA. These organisations become acknowledged as being authoritative on their subject and may be the sole supplier of literature in that field. They also campaign on specific issues, e.g. MIND, which campaigns for improved mental health services.	Family Planning Association (FPA) Royal Society for the Prevention of Accidents (RoSPA) National Childbirth Trust (NCT) National Association of Mental Health (MIND)
Professional organisations Set professional standards and codes of conduct, can strike off professionals who are proved to have breached them and therefore stop them practising. Nurses, for example, cannot be employed without a current registration with the UKCC, which therefore provides a mechanism for managing the quality of the nursing profession.	British Medical Association (BMA) United Kingdom Central Council for Nursing, Midwifery and Health Visitors (UKCC) Institution of Environmental Health Officers (IEHO)

ORGANISATION TYPE	EXAMPLES
Trade unions Advocate and negotiate for their members on issues such as pay and working conditions. They can also co-ordinate activity to campaign for changes, e.g. through strike action or working to rule. For example, the teaching unions have had several periods when they have either withdrawn support for out-of-hours activities or resorted to strike action in response to government activity which affected their working conditions.	Public sector workers (UNISON) Teachers (NUT, AMMA, NASUWT) Miners (NUM)
Commercial and industrial organisations There are roles for large private agencies, e.g. in delivering an efficient and effective rail network which can reduce road traffic and hence pollution levels.	National Rivers Authority (NRA) Network Rail

TABLE 8.2 *Organisations involved in care services*

Local agencies

Whilst national government policy will remain the most effective tool for enabling health to be promoted, it is at the local level that national policy is translated into practice. This relies on a range of local agencies working together effectively on health issues with a common purpose. Examples of local partner agencies and their potential roles are set out below.

Health services

The primary function of the NHS is to treat sick people. Although health promotion activity could and should be a feature of many health service roles, in practice this aspect of health activity has often been seen as secondary to the primary goal of treating the sick. However, *Choosing Health* has a specific target for all NHS staff (both clinical and administrative) to become health promoters. The key local health service is the Primary Care Trust (see Figure 8.9).

The PCT has a key role in local health promotion programmes with several key staff groups who can be partners for local health promotion programmes and projects.

The PCT public health department will usually include both specialist public health practitioners and the health promotion service. The public health team has a key role in assessing the patterns of ill-health locally and identifying what types of health care provision and health promoting activities are required to improve health locally. Public health practitioners provide:

* surveillance and assessment of the population's health and well-being

* promotion and protection of the population's health and well-being

* risk management and evaluation of activity

* collaborative working for health and well-being

* development of health programmes and services and reduction of inequalities

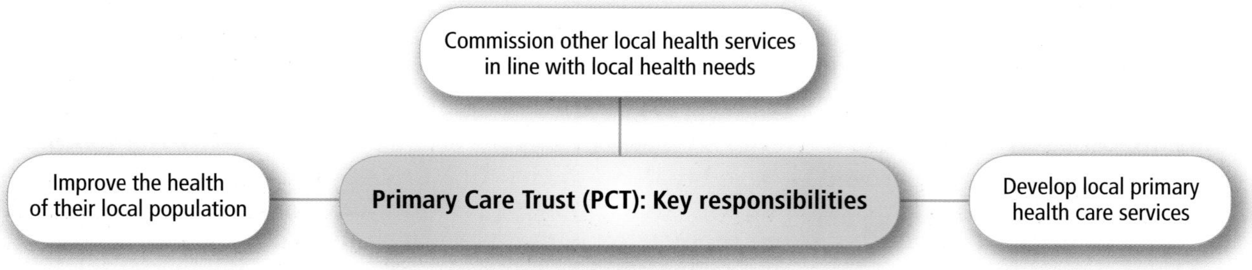

Commission other local health services in line with local health needs

Primary Care Trust (PCT): Key responsibilities

Improve the health of their local population

Develop local primary health care services

FIGURE 8.9 *Key responsibilities of PCTs*

* policy and strategy development and implementation

* working with and for communities

* strategic leadership for health and well-being

* research and development

* ethical principles for health promotion and public health.

Specialist health promotion services

These are usually located within or alongside the public health team. They are a small, specialised service which supports the development of the health promoting role of others and the development of new services and policies which can promote health locally. The role of these services has grown and developed over time, the flexibility to do this being largely due to the fact that the services are not governed by a professional body, enabling teams to grow and develop into new areas of practice in response to local need.

Try it out

Find out where your local health promotion team is based – start with your PCT website.

* What services do they provide?

* What resources can you access which might help you with your project?

SCENARIO

A health promotion specialist's role

Geoff is the local health promotion specialist for schools. He came to this role from a background in teaching, but colleagues in other areas have a wide range of previous roles from youth and community or voluntary sectors. His role is to support local schools in achieving healthy school status as part of the Healthy Schools programme. This is a national initiative which supports local programmes in each local education authority. His role includes:

* *Raising public awareness:* he will raise the profile of key issues through direct campaigning within schools, for example for national days such as No Smoking Day or World Aids Day. He also organises events such as sex education conferences, including liaison with the media.

* *Advice and consultancy:* he offers advice on a school's submission for Healthy School status and on any health-related topics the school is working on.

* *Service development:* as part of the extended schools programme he can encourage the schools to look at developing school-based health services, for example school nurse drop-in sessions.

FIGURE 8.10 *In his work as a health promotion specialist, Geoff often works with young people to find out their views on health-related issues*

- *Policy development:* supporting and advising schools on the development of a wide range of specific policies, including sex education, smoking, substance use, nutrition, etc.

- *Project planning:* the management of specific projects; for example, he is currently working on a project with three local schools to help parents develop effective communication approaches for talking to young people about difficult issues such as sex and drugs.

- *Research:* he is currently undertaking some local research about young people's use of the local sexual health services. He is also involved in some consultation work with young people about local recreational activities they would like to see in the future.

- *Training and education:* Geoff provides in-service training for teachers on a range of health education issues, and will co-facilitate classes to offer models of good practice for health and health-related subjects.

- *Resources:* he will also advise on purchases of new materials, and recommend resources and how best to use them.

Community nursing

Community nurses also contribute to public health practice, working with communities as well as providing care to individuals. The public health contribution of nurses, health visitors and midwives was outlined in *Making it Happen* (Department of Health, 1995). This stressed that nurses, midwives and health visitors were not only 'hands on' professionals delivering care to individuals, but that they also had an important role to play in the development and implementation of local health improvement initiatives.

NURSE	TYPE OF ACTIVITIES
Community nurses	* nursing care (e.g. bandaging and care of wounds in the patient's home)
Community midwives	* monitor and support expectant mothers before and after birth outside the hospital * in some cases carry out home deliveries
Health visitors (or public health nurses)	* monitor child development from first week after birth * carry out regular assessment tests and advise on parenting * respond to a diverse range of local community needs (e.g. establishing mother and toddler groups) * provide a range of training and development groups for parents (e.g. on effective parenting, baby massage, etc.) * support local community activity such as food co-operatives
School nurses	* routine screening of school-age children * support administration of vaccination programme * involved in school-based PSHE programmes (personal and social health education)
Occupational health nurses	* nursing support on site for larger employers * health-promoting activities such as health check-ups and 'stop smoking' advice

TABLE 8.3 *Nursing activities*

General practitioners (GPs)

GPs are independent practitioners – that is, they are in effect small businesses who contract with the local Primary Care Trust to provide a range of services. GPs have a practice population or list, which may be widely dispersed because people who register with a GP build up a relationship with them over many years and may wish to remain with them when they move away from the practice area. GPs form the core of a primary health care team that is the backbone of the local medical services. The WHO defined primary health care in 1978 as:

> 'Essential health care ... made universally accessible to individuals and families in the community… It forms an integral part of both the country's health system, of which it is the central function and main focus, and of the overall social and economic development of the community.'

Primary health care teams are the first point of contact for people who are unwell, and act as the gatekeeper to more specialised or secondary services in hospital settings. The operation of the GP services is governed by the new General Medical Services contract.

Other local key players

It is frequently suggested that the greatest capacity for improving the health of the population lies not with the health services but with the local authority. It provides a range of key services

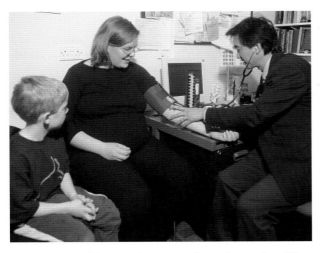

FIGURE 8.11 *GPs are the core of a primary health care team*

which can prevent people becoming ill in the first place. These include provision of affordable housing, availability of leisure facilities to help people become physically active, waste collection, promotion of the arts, and a host of others. Health promotion within a local authority setting most often centres round the environmental health department, which at one time was part of the public health team.

Environmental health department

The environmental health service has a broad public health role covering housing, food safety, water supply, refuse disposal and pollution control. Increasingly the emphasis on the key statutory duties of surveillance and enforcement has left little scope for developing a broader, more comprehensive approach to the improvement of the public's health. Environmental health departments tend to focus their activities around these core statutory functions:

* *Food safety:* the food safety team is responsible for ensuring that all food produced or sold locally is safe. Complaints are investigated and food samples taken for examination. Diseases which could be food- or water-borne are also investigated.

* *Health and safety:* the commercial safety team is responsible for enforcing health and safety legislation in the majority of workplaces, including offices, shops, places of entertainment, consumer and leisure services.

* *Environmental protection:* environmental health also has a role in investigating complaints from the public about a range of environmental nuisances which can affect people's health, including noise, smoke, fumes, odour and dust.

* *Pest control/dog control:* the pest control team treats rodent infestations in domestic and commercial premises throughout the district, as well as other public health pests, such as fleas, cockroaches and wasps. They also undertake an annual programme to control rats in the sewage system. The dog control team enforces the dog fouling laws, provides advice and education on responsible dog ownership and removes stray dogs from the street.

Local education authorities

Local education authorities (LEAs) have responsibility for health education in schools and further education colleges through the work of teachers and lecturers. LEAs may also have advisers with specific responsibility for health education, and other staff who provide advice, support and training in health education for teachers. However, with the introduction in the 1990s of local management of schools (LMS) and LEA resource constraints, many of these posts have disappeared.

There have been considerable developments in the school setting in the last twenty years, including the introduction in 1989 of the National Curriculum, the changing role of school governors and the shift of budget-holding responsibilities from local education authorities to schools themselves (part of LMS). A number of essential functions remain the responsibility of the LEA, including:

* special educational needs

* access and school transport

* school improvement and tackling failure

* educating excluded pupils and providing pupil welfare.

These are functions that cannot be undertaken effectively at the level of the individual school. Their impact on health is twofold. In general, the wider provision of good-quality education is known to improve the chances for future good health, but more specifically, the LEA can ensure that young people with additional needs have those needs met.

Social services

The social services directorate of the local authority provides a wide range of services to help individuals and families with personal and social problems. Service users range from the very young to the very old. Most of the Directorate's work is concentrated on helping the most dependent sections of the community, which include children, the elderly, people with physical or learning disabilities, and people with mental health problems.

On request, social services make a careful assessment of each person's needs, and if the person is eligible for support, they will arrange a suitable package of care. This might include a home help, meals-on-wheels, day care, or – for someone with a disability – special aids and equipment. If support in the community is no longer possible, residential care can be provided. Social services are also responsible for fostering and adoption services, and for the registration of childminders, nurseries, playgroups and residential homes.

Social services have numerous opportunities for promoting better health through their day care and residential services, where health education advice can be offered. There are also opportunities for supporting health-promoting activities among people with special needs, for example in the context of day care services for people with physical or learning disabilities and those with mental health problems.

Police

The police protect the public from crime and violence, take action to prevent misuse of drugs and alcohol, and help to ensure road safety. Many aspects of the police service's work overlap with health promotion. For example, fear of crime particularly affects people's emotional and mental health. It is well documented that people's fear of crime is often disproportionate to the level of crime in their neighbourhood, and in some cases this can damage people's confidence to venture out from home alone. Examples of police initiatives which address the fear of crime include:

* offering crime prevention advice, such as advice relating to home security or to personal safety

* support for Neighbourhood Watch schemes

* action on domestic violence

* tackling hate crime – crimes motivated by prejudice, for example against people of different races or different sexual orientations

* tackling the supply of drugs and supporting drug prevention initiatives

* supporting community safety activities, such as tackling neighbourhood nuisance.

Increasingly the police are active partners in a variety of local initiatives; for example, their work in disrupting local drug markets and arresting dealers. Another aspect of police work is their involvement with community safety, where the issues of crime and disorder can be addressed across organisational boundaries – the police may work with the youth and community services, for example, to address youth-related problems. This might mean co-ordinating the activity of these two services to address neighbourhood nuisance involving young people, or providing training for local police officers in skills for working effectively with young people who are deemed to be causing nuisance. The police have a key partnership role to play in tackling hate crime, which is motivated by intolerance of people of different race, religion, sexuality, etc. Police community liaison officers are at the forefront of much of this work.

Voluntary agencies

The voluntary sector is a diverse range of organisations, each with one or more functions. Most voluntary organisations act as service providers; they provide practical services such as delivering a meal, listening to someone's distressed telephone call, or providing full-time residential care in a hospice for a terminally-ill person. These services fill gaps in the provision made by the statutory authorities. In some instances, voluntary organisations have become the recognised experts in a particular field; St John Ambulance (see Figure 8.12) and the hospice movement are examples.

Voluntary organisations also act as pressure groups, attempting to promote change in large statutory bodies such as the NHS. There are long-standing groups, such as MENCAP (concerned for people with learning disabilities), and ad hoc groups, which campaign for a single short-term aim, for example to save a local hospital from closure. Pressure groups may be extremely effective at mobilising public opinion, which in turn puts pressure on policy-makers to change their plans.

Many voluntary organisations have a role in education and information – they reply to letters, use the media, organise courses, or publish leaflets, newsletters and magazines. There are also telephone

FIGURE 8.12 *St John Ambulance is the UK's leading provider of first-aid training and services*

advice lines which provide information on a wide range of topics and many have Internet sites.

Locally, the Council for Voluntary Services acts as an umbrella organisation for a wide variety of voluntary sector organisations. The organisations they represent will vary from one area to another, but usually there is a high proportion of support groups for people with specific illnesses or disabilities. The Council for Voluntary Services offers one means whereby statutory organisations can communicate with many voluntary sector groups and with carers.

Did you know?

Victim support
The service offered by Victim Support is quite specialised, and has an important, if indirect, effect on the health of clients. Any victim of crime experiences loss and change, from relatively minor losses of property, such as a bicycle, through to the most profound losses associated with serious crimes such as rape or murder. Victim Support lobbies on relevant issues, usually at a national level. Successful lobbying resulted in the establishment of services for victims and other witnesses at all crown courts, funded by government. In addition, where resources permit, Victim Support may from time to time be involved in promotional and awareness campaigns.

Some Victim Support schemes have a specialist service offering helplines and one-to-one support and counselling to victims of sexual crime. Often such victims are adult survivors of childhood sexual abuse who, as a result of this early trauma, have mental and emotional health needs. Survivors of *recent* sexual crime have urgent and specific physical health needs, related to the risks of pregnancy and of sexually transmitted disease.

Volunteers for Victim Support need particular skills and must also know how to make appropriate referrals to other agencies in cases where specialist help is needed.

Try it out

Find out how you can get in touch with your local Victim Support service.

* What services do they offer to victims of crime?

* How do most people access the service?

Defining a health promotion project or programme

There are a range of different influences which affect both the way a health promotion project or programme is designed and the way it is delivered on the ground. The starting point for any health promotion activity should be needs assessment.

Key concept

Needs assessment: this is the starting point for any health promotion activity. Needs assessment means the understanding of local or national patterns of ill-health. This information is routinely available from agencies like the Office for National Statistics, or the Public Health Observatory. It will determine what conditions need to be addressed to bring the greatest health gains, and which people suffer those conditions most. This in turn frames the type of activity and the target audience.

For example, in 1997 new statistics suggested that smoking rates among young adults (16–24) were on the increase – against an overall reduction in smoking across the whole population. As a result, the target audience for mass media campaigns (previously smokers aged between 25 and 40) was changed to address the 16–24 age range. The resulting *Testimonials* campaign ran from 1997 to 1999 and set its target audience as lower socio-economic groups, recognising that smoking rates were highest amongst people in these groups.

Try it out

What information can you find about local smoking rates/smoking-related ill-health?

You can use the Department of Health website, the Public Health Observatory website for your region or your PCT website as a starting point.

Testimonials worked alongside the development of local initiatives such as the development of 'stop smoking' services. Here allocations from the Department for Health are targeted at the areas with the highest indicators for deprivation. The poorest areas of the country receive the greatest amounts of funding for 'stop smoking' services, acknowledging that this is where the levels of smoking will be highest. Local organisations like the PCT and local authority will then be expected to demonstrate how they are targeting their activities into those areas of greatest deprivation, that is targeting wards and neighbourhoods with high levels of deprivation and ill-health, to reduce smoking levels in those areas.

Health and wealth will not be equally distributed in the area where you live.

* Which are the most and least deprived wards/ areas in your district?

* What evidence is there that local services are making efforts to target resources into those areas of greatest need?

You can use lots of sources of information for this; start with the websites for your local PCT and local authority.

Work at the local level will reflect the role each agency plays. For example, it will be the PCT who manages the 'stop smoking' service which will be seeking to support people in the disadvantaged communities to quit smoking. GPs and practice nurses working in practices in these wards might be targeted for training in smoking cessation methods, so they can give basic advice and identify people who want to quit for referral to the 'stop smoking' service.

Find out what action your local PCT is taking to reduce the smoking rates:

* across your area as a whole

* in the most disadvantaged communities specifically.

Is there any evidence of work going on with local schools, the education authority or youth and community services to target young smokers?

The environmental health personnel may seek to promote smoke-free restaurants or pubs to provide areas where people can socialise without risk of breathing second-hand smoke. The specialist health promotion service might work with the health visitors in the target wards to set up community-based projects empowering local people; for example, training local people to offer peer support for their neighbours who want to quit, or to act as lay health advisers (a model similar to that anticipated for the health trainers promised in *Choosing Health*).

Summary of Section 8.1

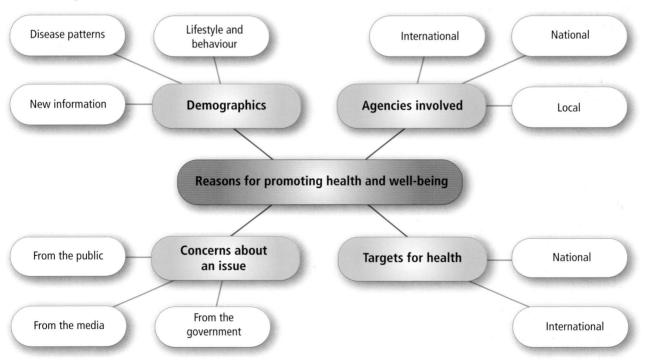

The damage caused by inappropriate use of alcohol has become a major concern for government, the public and a wide range of local agencies.

Using concepts, can you identify?

1. What damage to health can alcohol cause?

2. What information about alcohol drinking patterns will be needed to plan for services effectively which can deal with this likely increase in demand for alcohol support?

Go further – Can you analyse issues using theory?

3. Alcohol-related harm is not just about harm to health. What other types of harm to the local community are related to inappropriate alcohol use?

4. Tackling this range of harms will require a partnership approach. What actions are suggested in the National Alcohol Harm Reduction strategy, and which organisations would be required to make these a success?

5. How can the media contribute both to the problem and the solution?

Go further – Can you evaluate using a range of theories?

6. The underlying causes of both the increase in alcohol use and the shift to binge drinking are wide-ranging. Can you identify causative factors at an individual, local and national level that might have contributed to the changing trends?

8.2 Models and approaches to health promotion

Approaches to health promotion

The term 'health promotion' covers a wide range of different activities, all of which have a part to play in promoting health. None of them is definitively the right way; they are simply different approaches which complement each other. Table 8.4 shows six approaches, but these are by no means the only ones, and, confusingly, people can refer to the same approach using different terminology.

> **Key concept**
>
> *Health promotion:* this covers a wide range of different activities. The balance between them is very much a choice based on personal perspective, influenced by life experience, personal standpoints and values.

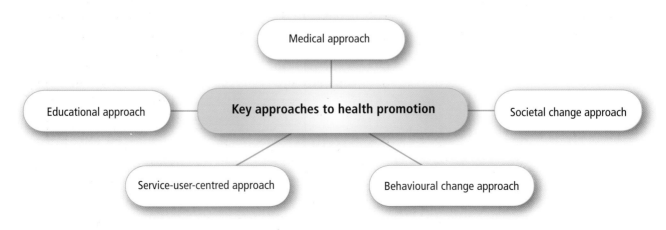

FIGURE 8.13 *Key approaches to health promotion*

MODEL	AIM	HEALTH PROMOTION ACTIVITY	FACTORS INFLUENCING CHOICE OF THIS MODEL
Medical approach (interventionist)	To achieve freedom from medically-defined disease and disability. *(For example, to keep people free from diseases associated with smoking, such as lung and heart diseases.)*	Use medical treatment to prevent or reduce the effects of ill-health. *(For example, encourage people to seek early detection and treatment of smoking-related disorders.)*	Can be dependent upon the availability of an effective screening process and the necessary treatment. Some screening processes remain imprecise and may register false negative or positive values. Screening programmes can be very costly. If the condition is identified it doesn't necessarily mean it can be treated effectively.
Behavioural change approach (behaviourist/ preventive/ persuasive)	To promote individual behaviours in the population which keep people free from disease. *(For example, to change people's smoking behaviour.)*	Encourage adoption of healthier lifestyle by changing attitude and therefore behaviour. *(For example, persuade people not to start smoking, and where they have started, to stop.)*	Evidence suggests this works best with educated middle- and upper-class social groups who respond to these health messages more readily. Lower socio-economic groups respond less well, and as a result 'stop smoking' messages have actually increased smoking-related health inequalities, as they reduce smoking in middle classes but fail to do so in lower socio-economic groups.
Educational approach (educationalist/ informative)	To provide people with the necessary knowledge and skills to enable them to make well-informed decisions. *(For example, to develop people's understanding of the effects of smoking on health and their decision-making skills.)*	Educational activity to disseminate information about health. Development of skills required for healthy living. *(For example, giving information to service users about the effects of smoking. Developing their skills in quitting smoking or resisting enticement to start smoking.)*	As under 'Behaviour change approach' above. Skills development only works with those who have already committed to change; any attempt to engage people who have not decided to change their lifestyle is doomed to failure.

MODEL	AIM	HEALTH PROMOTION ACTIVITY	FACTORS INFLUENCING CHOICE OF THIS MODEL
Service-user-centred approach (empowerment/ client-centred)	To work on health issues on the service user's terms, not your own. *(For example, to ensure that smoking cessation support and advice is available BUT not to offer it unless the client actively seeks it.)*	Allowing the service user to identify health issues, choices and actions which they choose, thereby empowering the service user. *(Here the smoking issue would only arise if the service user selected it. Any further discussion would depend on the service user's willingness to address the topic.)*	Responding to the cues of the patient or client would be good practice in any educational approach. There is evidence that the public expect certain people (GPs, practice nurses, etc.) to question them about their health behaviours so people in key positions can raise the issue without it being challenging.
Societal change approach	To change the physical and social environment to enable healthier lifestyles. *(For example, to make smoking socially unacceptable, to change the way in which society as a whole views the behaviour making it less acceptable to smoke.)*	Working within the political or social system to change the physical/social environment. *(For example, increasing the number of public spaces covered by no-smoking policies, making non-smoking the norm in society, making cigarette sales to children more difficult, banning tobacco advertising and sports sponsorship.)*	This underpins the other approaches, enabling and supporting them. More people are motivated to quit as smoking becomes increasingly unacceptable, with fewer places where they can smoke. Most of this activity is only possible at an organisational, district or national level because it means setting policy either for the organisation or the country.
Fear (Not always included in this list of methodologies – it could be seen as part of the educational approach but it has a very specific approach which might be seen as setting it apart.)	To frighten people into adopting a healthier lifestyle. *(For example, to make the effects of smoking so frightening as to prevent people taking up smoking or to encourage those who do smoke to quit.)*	Educational activity to disseminate Information about the effects of unhealthy lifestyles. *(For example, a campaign using real-life patients talking about their experiences of lung cancer brought on by smoking – see http://www.givingupsmoking.co.uk/ for examples.)*	Although people were reluctant to use this approach at one time, it increasingly has a place in current campaigning approaches – in this case bringing home to young people the message that smoking-related death can happen much earlier than they may think, and emphasising the impact on family etc., through the *Testimonials* adverts. This approach usually requires campaigns only possible at regional or national level.

TABLE 8.4 *Six approaches to health promotion*

Evaluate the following examples of health education approaches to smoking. Try to identify the model of health promotion each is based on.

* A practice nurse discussing an action plan for stopping smoking with a patient.

* A teacher showing a group of children a set of diseased lungs in a jar.

* A youth worker working with a group of young people to develop their decision-making skills.

* A community worker working with a group of single parents on an estate who have expressed a desire to 'stop smoking' to create their own support group.

* A doctor prescribing nicotine replacement therapy for a smoker who has been told they must stop by their consultant.

* A national television campaign to encourage smokers to quit smoking, with a helpline which offers support on how to quit.

* A person working with a quit smoking group for people who have suffered a heart attack.

Ethics

Clearly health education can present serious challenges to the educator. For example, if a health promoter works with a person gradually exploring their health needs and supporting them towards making an informed choice, the result may be that the individual decides not to follow the health promoter's advice and chooses to adopt health-damaging behaviour. This then poses serious ethical issues for the professional. Can they accept and respect that decision and not coerce or persuade the service user to adopt a different choice?

The danger with health education activity is that health promoters become fixed on the goal of improved medical or physical health, to the detriment of other aspects of holistic health. It is all too easy for professionals to adopt a judgemental approach, deciding what is best for the individual to the exclusion of that person's right to self-autonomy. It is important to remember that empowering people is an integral part of effective and ethical health promotion work.

Key concept

Ethical decision making: to act ethically is to act in a principled way. Health promotion is founded on a set of principles which define an ethical approach.

To enable health promoters to stay true to these values and act in an ethical way they can ask themselves the following questions:

* Will the person be able to choose freely for themselves?

* Will I be respecting their decision, whether or not I approve of it?

* Will I be non-discriminatory – respecting all people equally?

* Will I be serving the more basic needs before addressing other wants?

* Will I be doing good and preventing harm?

* Will I be telling the truth?

* Will I be minimising harm in the long term?

* Will I be able to honour promises and agreements I make?

These questions are equally applicable for a midwife in a one-to-one conversation, or planners considering alterations to local roads in a housing estate. For example, the planners might be asking themselves whether they have adequately involved the local people in the decision-making process, and if they have respected local people's input, not valuing it differently from that of other professionals.

Another example might be a midwife discussing smoking with a pregnant woman. Here the midwife has considerable knowledge about the potential damage to the unborn child and the possibility of further health damage if the mother continues to smoke after the birth. However, to be an ethical health promoter she must respect the mother's right to choose whether to continue smoking, and not allow the mother's decision to continue smoking (should that be the case) to change the relationship.

SCENARIO
Ethics

Carolyn is a midwife who has worked her area of the district for the last seven years. She has just finished her first visit (the induction visit) with Alison, a 19-year-old woman who already has a two-year-old called Tom. Carolyn was also Alison's midwife throughout her pregnancy with Tom. Alison is currently smoking 25 cigarettes a day, and on initial enquiries doesn't want to consider quitting. Most of her family smokes, and Alison's mum says she smoked through her pregnancy with Alison and she is OK, isn't she? Alison was smoking a similar amount throughout her pregnancy with Tom, who was born a month premature, weighing only 2 kilograms (4.5 lbs). He has subsequently had problems with asthma and repeated chest infections.

Discuss the following questions:

* Should Carolyn be telling Alison to quit smoking?

* What would the appropriate messages be for her to convey to Alison?

* Is she failing in her role as a midwife if she accepts Alison's wish to continue smoking?

* In this situation, who is better placed to judge what is right for Alison and her family, and how do you justify that decision?

FIGURE 8.14 *Health professionals have to consider ethical issues when discussing health-damaging behaviours such as smoking*

* If Carolyn was very directive, how might this affect her relationship with Alison and what might the implications of any change in the relationship be?

* Should health behaviour be a matter of personal choice, or is it too important to leave to the individual?

Approaches, methods and materials

There are many ways in which you can communicate health promotion messages to your local community.

Interaction

It is hard to quantify the extent to which individual interaction can contribute to health campaigning. However, it is clear that the general public hold certain groups within society in high regard, and respect the information they obtain from people such as doctors, nurses, teachers and environmental health officers. This creates considerable potential for promoting key health messages simply through the day-to-day routine of work. This might mean a doctor suggesting to someone attending a health check that they consider giving up smoking, or a district nurse suggesting that moderate activity is still possible and potentially beneficial for an older service user whilst visiting them at home.

It is quite normal for key health campaigns to engage these health promoters in the communication of a key message. For example, on National No Smoking Day many health practitioners plan specific events to link with the national campaign and offer support to people wishing to quit smoking.

Presentations

Delivering presentations about key messages can be a useful way to reach groups of people with specific information. For example, a health visitor might give information about weaning to a mums and toddlers group, or a physical activity promoter might discuss the benefits of gentle physical exercise with older people at a luncheon club. Presentations are a key tool for many community-based workers. However, presentations:

* cannot disseminate key messages to wider population groups, although they are useful for a small group

* may have a short-term impact, but often lack the necessary follow-up to support people

* require careful planning to engage the audience and hold their attention – the attention span of most adults is about 20 minutes

* may be lacking in a clear purpose and not linked to longer-term priorities and planning

* require effective planning, delivery and evaluation; skills which are not routinely developed in many health promoters

* will not suit all the people in any group session because adults have different learning styles.

Generally, a mix of training and educational approaches is most effective; for example, combining a short presentation with some active group work.

Leaflets

Leaflets are the backbone of health education activity. They serve a wide variety of purposes such as informing people about local services, providing information about specific health conditions, giving advice about specific health promotion issues or encouraging people to consider broader health matters. In many cases leaflets are designed to support specific health campaigns, such as those for immunisation campaigns or for National No Smoking Day. However, it is important to remember that for many people a leaflet will not be an appropriate means of communication. A 2003 national research study for the DfES showed that:

* 5.2 million adults in England lack basic literacy (they had failed to reach the standards of reading and writing currently expected for children at age 11)

* more than one-third of people with poor or very poor health had literacy skills expected for children at age 11, or below

* low levels of literacy and numeracy were found to be associated with socio-economic deprivation

* 53 per cent of all adults surveyed had low levels of practical skills in using information and communication technology (ICT).

Clearly many agencies still do little to take account of people's literacy levels, because another survey of readability of patient

FIGURE 8.15 *Well-designed leaflets catch the reader's attention*

information produced by hospices and palliative care units showed that 64 per cent of leaflets were readable only by an estimated 40 per cent of the population (survey in the *Choosing Health* White Paper).

Therefore, a leaflet on first appearance is a relatively simple tool, but it is important to consider a range of questions when designing or using one.

* Who is the leaflet for? A drugs leaflet appropriate for secondary school children will not be appropriate for primary schools.

* Who produced the leaflet? If it is a commercial company such as a drug company, could they have been selective in their reporting of the information?

* When was it first produced, and is the information still relevant or accurate? For example, information on drug-related harm changes very rapidly.

* Is the language level used appropriate to the target audience? For example, is it too complex, or does it include unexplained abbreviations or technical terms?

* Is it well designed, that is, will it capture the attention of the reader from other leaflets and posters?

* Will it connect specifically with the target audience?

* Are the key messages clearly identified?

* Where is the best place to display it to reach the target audience?

Posters

Posters provide an excellent tool for catching the attention of the target audience and supporting the key broad messages you might then develop in more detail within a leaflet. The factors which draw attention to a poster can be divided into two groups (see Table 8.5).

PHYSICAL CHARACTERISTICS	MOTIVATIONAL CHARACTERISTICS
Size – the whole of the poster as well as parts within it, like key lettering, need to be large enough to attract attention	**Novelty** – unusual features can help attract attention
Intensity – bold headings	**Interest** – it can be a good strategy to make links with items of interest to the target audience
Colour – use of bright colours, such as reds, greens and oranges, and appropriate use of contrast so that dark text appears on a lighter background and vice versa	**Deeper motivations** – e.g. fashion and sex – can also help ensure the target audience looks at your poster
Pictures – using photographs and drawings can help you get your point across as well as making the poster more visually interesting	**Entertainment or humour** – e.g. the use of cartoons to make a serious point

TABLE 8.5 *Well-designed posters catch the audience's attention*

The key point of a poster is that it should be eye-catching and big enough to attract attention. It will need to be in colour, or if in black and white it should use this for impact or dramatic effect. Wording on posters should be minimal and very bold. Posters need to be located carefully in places where the target audience will see them, and routinely changed after a short period because they become almost 'invisible' once people have seen them a few times.

You can find examples of well-designed publicity materials for healthy eating campaigns on the Department of Health website under '5 A Day' (see Figure 8.16). These illustrate two particular points relating to good poster design:

* use of colour to make the material attractive and draw attention to it

* simplicity of the message.

The mass media

Many people would view the use of the media (newspapers, magazines, radio and television) as the most effective means of reaching the population to promote health. People may assume that because the media reaches a large number of people its effect will be correspondingly great. However, there are other considerations to take into account.

The success of a health message conveyed by the mass media will be dependent upon the attitudes and viewpoint of the individual receiving the message. Therefore it is not surprising to find that many research studies have shown that the direct persuasive power of mass media is very limited. Expectations that mass media alone will produce dramatic long-term changes in health behaviour are doomed to disappointment. So what success can realistically be expected when using the mass media in health promotion work? Appropriate aims here might include using the media to:

* *raise awareness of health and health issues:* for example, the link between over-exposure to the sun and the risk of skin cancer

* *deliver a simple message:* for example, that babies should sleep on their backs not their tummies; that there is a national advice line for young people wanting information about sexual health

* *change behaviour, if the behaviour is a simple one-off activity:* for example, phone for a leaflet, which people are already motivated to do and which it is easy to do.

The use of mass media should be viewed as part of an overall strategy which includes face-to-face discussion, personal help, and attention to social and environmental factors which help or hinder change. For example, mass media publicity is just one strand in a long-term programme to combat smoking.

FIGURE 8.16 *Sample materials from the 5 A Day initiative*

Mass media cannot be expected to:

* convey complex information (e.g. about transmission routes of HIV)

* teach skills (e.g. how to deal assertively with pressure to have sex without a condom or take drugs)

* shift people's attitudes or beliefs – if a message challenges a person's basic beliefs, he is more likely to dismiss the message than change his belief (e.g. 'My granddad smoked sixty a day till he died at 80, so saying I should stop smoking is rubbish.')

* change behaviour – unless the change requires a simple action that people are already motivated to do (e.g. the media may encourage those people who are already motivated to be more active to start walking, because this is an easy and accessible form of exercise). However, it will not persuade those who are not motivated to be more active.

Using the local media

Whilst most people are familiar with national and regional media, that is the main national newspapers, local evening papers, national radio and television stations, it is far more likely that you will be dealing with local media. It is unlikely that your news will be sufficiently interesting to grab the attention of the nationals who will be mainly reporting information about national and international events.

The local media can still be a very effective way of reaching people. For example, the local free newspaper will most likely reach every house in your area, but how many people will actually read it? It is worth knowing how to increase your chances of getting the local media to cover your story. Local media, both radio and print, often have a few key permanent staff members who may be with the paper or station for many years, but the reporters are usually juniors working their way up to the regional and national media. This means they may have little experience or understanding about the issues you are trying to get coverage for. The way to overcome this is to provide a press release where you give them the information you want to be

included in the story. In the press release, make sure you give them:

* a title (if it's catchy they may use it directly)

* a brief summary of the main message you are trying to get across (usually 3 points maximum)

* what is happening where and when

* the names of any important people who might be attending

* whether a picture might be possible (either for them to send a photographer or for you to provide one)

* a quote about the news item from someone of interest

* some background facts

* the person to contact for follow-up and their details.

If you write a good press release the paper may largely use it verbatim, or the radio station may read it directly. If they like your story they may wish to interview you. Should that happen, make sure you ask to see the questions they intend

FIGURE 8.17 *Prepare for an interview beforehand*

to ask before the interview. Tell them this will help you prepare the necessary background information and improve the quality of your answers and therefore the interview.

When selecting the media you are trying to gain coverage from, ask yourself, 'Who is their target audience? Does this paper/radio station want to talk to the population I am trying to reach?' It's no use getting massive coverage on Radio Limeswold for a campaign on chlamydia screening aimed at under 25s if the radio station target audience is mainly over 65.

Defining the approach

As we have already seen, the *Testimonials* campaign is one of the longest-running, most comprehensively evaluated health promotion campaigns of recent years. It was a response to new demographic information which re-focused anti-smoking efforts on to young adults (16–25) from the lower social groupings. The strategy for television advertising was to use real-life testimonials. These sought to encourage personal identification with the health risks, and to give a sense of urgency to the idea of giving up. The format used only smokers, not health professionals. The short, 30-second adverts were unscripted. The people chosen had a variety of smoking-related conditions, including cancers, respiratory conditions, amputations and heart disease. The campaign tried to convey the impact of smoking-related diseases on the day-to-day lives of those individuals.

The campaign consciously aimed to use fear as a very effective way of grabbing the attention of the target group (young adults). The use of unscripted personal monologues was also particularly effective. This is not the only effective form of advertising; some highly effective adverts are more humorous. However, using humour can

risk trivialising important information and allow people to distance themselves from the message.

The costs associated with this type of media campaigning make it impossible to support at a local level. The issue of resourcing will greatly influence the type of approach adopted. Clearly from what we have seen so far most major media campaigns can only support simple health education messages. But this means the level of information supplied in these media campaigns is quite superficial. Therefore these campaigns can often do little more than steer people into local services (as in the case of *Testimonials*) where they can access more in-depth support. However, this can be problematic for two reasons:

* The people most likely to respond to these messages are the more affluent and assertive higher social groups – the so-called 'worried well'. This may help reinforce existing inequalities in access to health services.

* In some cases services are unable to cope with the additional demand. When a health district publicised their breast screening service to women in the target age range, the result was a surge in requests for screening which filled the remaining appointments for the year and created a waiting list.

Therefore, local responses may often focus on the other types of approaches, including empowering the service user, and using lower-tech methods such as leaflets and posters. There are many examples of media materials to support the current smoking campaign at: http://www.givingupsmoking.co.uk. Follow the link to the current campaign section where you can view the TV adverts, hear the radio ads and see examples of posters and leaflets which support the campaign.

Summary of Section 8.2

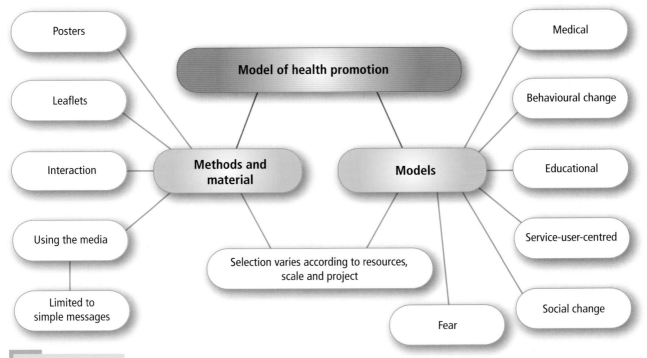

Helen is a teenage pregnancy co-ordinator. Her job is to bring together local agencies to reduce the rate of teenage conceptions in the area where she works. The UK has one of the highest rates of teen conceptions in the developed world and the government has set clear targets for reducing this by 2010, with funding to support it. The initial report from the social exclusion unit identified that teenage pregnancy mirrors other forms of health inequalities, being highest in the most deprived communities. Therefore, work to prevent teenage conceptions is not just founded on promoting safer sex but has many social dimensions. Helen has two main strands to her work:

* preventing pregnancies in the first place

* providing support to existing teen parents to prevent second unplanned pregnancies.

Using concepts, can you identify?

1. Under each model of health promotion suggest a type of activity which would contribute towards reducing teenage pregnancy in Helen's district.

   * medical approach

   * behavioural change approach

   * educational approach

   * service-user-centred approach

   * societal change approach

   * fear.

Go further – Can you analyse issues using theories?

2. If Helen decides to fund a local poster campaign to promote condom use with 16–18-year-olds, where might she want to have posters displayed? What design issues might she need to take account of for the audience? What would be a suitable message for the poster campaign to carry?

3. If she were to consider discussing the campaign with the local press, what would be the advantages and disadvantages of talking to the local newspapers? What messages could she hope to get into their feature articles?

Go further – Can you evaluate using a range of theories?

4. The social exclusion unit report (available from the Teenage Pregnancy Unit site www.dfes. gov.uk/teenagepregnancy) suggests the way to address teenage pregnancy is predominantly through a social change approach. What types of social factors might need to change to deliver the reduction? Which agencies would this require Helen to work with, and what barriers might there be to successfully delivering the required reduction by 2010?

8.3 Planning and implementing a health promotion

To plan effectively requires a clear understanding of what you are trying to achieve. As a health promoter you need to define clear aims and objectives before commencing any form of action. Planning should provide you with the answers to three questions:

* what am I trying to achieve?
* what am I going to do?
* how will I know whether I have succeeded?

What am I trying to achieve?

Identifying your target audience and need

As a health promoter, your first action in undertaking any campaign will be to identify the source of the need you are considering. This will identify who you are targeting.

Identifying your target audience for a campaign starts with the question, 'What is the health need which I should be addressing?' The need for a campaign will usually come from one of four sources:

* **Normative need:** this is defined by an expert or professional according to their own standards. Where something falls short of this standard then a need is identified. An example is the trends in numbers of people who are overweight or obese. A person with a BMI above 30 is classed as obese; this uses a professionally defined measure. Should the numbers of people who exceed this measure rise then this will identify a normative need to address the issue of obesity.

* **Felt needs:** these are needs which people feel, that is things we want. For example, people might want their food to be free of genetically modified (GM) products.

* **Expressed need:** a felt need which is voiced. For example, the felt need to have GM-free food may become a public debate, with pressure groups focusing on the issue.

* **Comparative need:** this arises from comparisons between similar groups of people, where one group is in receipt of health promotion activity and the other is not. Examples here might be one school having a well-thought-out and planned Personal and Social Health Education (PSHE) curriculum but another does not.

The evidence of need for your own project can be established from national, regional and/or local health information. There are many sources for this type of information, including:

* your local Primary Care Trust – the health promotion unit or public health department in particular

* the local authority.

There are also many key websites where you can access data, in some cases for areas as small as individual electoral wards. These include the Public Health Observatory (one for each regional health authority area), the Office for National Statistics, the Department of Health and, in the case of drug and alcohol use, the Home Office. If you were undertaking a project which aimed to address young people's drug use then the most useful sites would be the Home Office and the Public Health Observatory for your region.

Having established the target audience and needs for your health promotion project, you will start to translate the idea of how to meet these needs into aims and objectives.

An aim may have several supplementary objectives within it. Objectives are usually defined as being SMART (see Figure 8.18).

> **Key concept**
>
> *Aim:* a broad overall goal for the whole project – this is often a statement of the underlying intention that will be hard to use to assess the success of a project.

FIGURE 8.18 *SMART objectives*

Objectives which are not SMART cannot be effective aids to planning. They may be aims which require breaking down further into specific objectives. Without this level of detail an objective cannot be measured, and therefore evaluation of the work is undermined.

For example, for a theatre in health education project, one objective might be:

Use a 'theatre in education' approach to engage young people in an accessible, fun but rigorous discussion about the legal, health, personal and social consequences of decisions made in relation to drugs, sex and crime. Plan and deliver this activity within the next school term.

What am I going to do?

Researching the issue

As part of their work a health promoter may need to conduct research. For example, having established the need for a piece of work using national information sources, they may wish to collect local data to build their case for the work. In the case of the theatre in education project referred to above, this might mean carrying out some research to assess patterns of substance use amongst local young people. This information might then be used to specifically tailor the project to meet the local needs, for example by focusing on a specific substance which they find is used most regularly.

When carrying out research, it is important to consider:

1 *purpose and audience:* define the purpose of your research, and identify the target audience

2 *literature review:* review the existing literature – has your research already been carried out somewhere else?

3 *planning:* plan how to conduct the investigation

4 *testing:* test your proposed methodology by carrying out a small-scale pilot study

5 *review:* review the findings of your pilot study, and review your methodology in the light of these findings

6 *research:* carry out the research

7 *analysis:* analyse the data from the research

8 *conclusions:* draw conclusions based on your findings

9 *report*: compile a report of your findings, for the target audience identified in step 1.

Liaison with other agencies

Health promotion is rarely effective when the activity is focused within one organisation. The causes of ill-health are so varied that it requires a wide-ranging response across agencies to influence health for the good. This is reflected in current government thinking; it is now a statutory duty for local statutory agencies like the PCT and local authority to work in partnership ensuring they then plan action together through the local community strategy (an overarching document for a district which describes how agencies will work together to improve that area).

When working with other agencies it is important to know which you need at what stages of the work. You need to include them in your planning, otherwise you may find that they are unable or unwilling to support the work, or can't meet your timescale. For example, you might want to work with local school nurses on a school-based project, or to engage the local community drugs team on a college-based project.

Milestones

These are steps along the way to delivering the outcome or objective. They help you break the objectives down into smaller steps, and so are useful for helping you plan the work effectively.

OBJECTIVE
State your objective here (use a separate sheet for each objective).

KEY TASKS/ACTIVITIES
Briefly describe what service or activity you will be providing, and evaluating, that supports the achievement of this objective.

RESULTS
What do you hope will change as a result of this activity?

MEASURES
How will you measure if the described change is occurring/has occurred?

STANDARD
Define the levels of success for your project.
What will be the best you could hope for? (A great result!)
What will you be happy with? (A satisfactory result)
What will you be unhappy with? (A disappointing result)

TABLE 8.6A *Objective sheet*

For example, the milestones towards an objective which involved recruiting people from local voluntary agencies to participate in a focus group about support for carers might include:

* design publicity materials including leaflets, posters and press adverts
* order sufficient stationery to support mailing the materials
* compile a circulation list for the mail-out
* arrange for materials to be printed
* mail out to relevant people
* visit local community groups to raise awareness about the project.

Milestones can also contribute to the evaluation process for a piece of work. They can be documented as a series of process-related targets which can be easily measured in terms of achievement: 'That milestone was met on time.'

Establishing clear objectives for your own work

If you have been working on your assessment activity you should have done this already as part of your original project proposal. For each objective, draw up an objective sheet like the one in Table 8.6A. The more carefully you describe your objectives and hoped-for outcomes, the easier it is to evaluate the effectiveness of your programme. An example of a project objective worked up in this way is shown in Table 8.6B.

OBJECTIVE

State your objective here (use a separate sheet for each objective).

Use a 'theatre in education' approach to engage young people in an accessible, fun but rigorous discussion about the legal, health, personal and social consequences of decisions made in relation to drugs, sex and crime. Plan and deliver this activity within the next school term.

(One objective from a 'theatre in education' project with Y7–9 students.)

KEY TASKS/ACTIVITIES

Briefly describe what service or activity you will be providing, and evaluating, that supports the achievement of this objective.

Each year group has a session on a different theme, watched by form tutors and other pastoral staff. Y7 Bullying, Y8 Drugs, Y9 Sex and Relationships

Interactive theatre performances by a team of actors with groups of 60–90 students, lasting 90 minutes.

Students will receive preparatory and follow-up work in the school.

Some preparatory and follow-up work will be done with school staff.

RESULTS

What do you hope will change as a result of this activity?

Students will show a greater repertoire of behaviours enabling them to make informed and safe decisions.

Students and staff will feel more confident and informed when discussing the issues raised in the performances.

Staff will feel able and confident to follow up this work.

(Students and staff will feel that the interactive theatre experience can make this learning enjoyable and memorable.)

How will you measure if the described change is occurring/has occurred?

Assess student attitudes before and after the performances.

Assess staff attitudes and confidence before and after the performances.

Observe and evaluate the performances.

(Follow up after six months to review progress.)

Define the levels of success for your project. Start to think about what some of these mean in quantitative terms; for example, does *high level of satisfaction* mean 100 per cent were very satisfied, or 90 per cent, or less?

What will be the best you could hope for? (A great result!)

A highly enjoyable experience with high levels of satisfaction; students have much more confidence in discussion and feedback, staff very pleased, and happy to continue and develop the work; school uses some interactive techniques in its PSHE; we get to do more work with them!

What will you be happy with? (A satisfactory result)

The students and staff enjoy the day; there is evidence of some change in student knowledge and attitudes, and some staff express interest in continuing the work. Some follow-up takes place in school and there is evidence of links to the PSHE curriculum.

What will you be unhappy with? (A disappointing result)

Preparatory work is not done, or done badly; feedback from students and staff is only satisfactory; there is little evidence of increased knowledge or changed attitudes in the students. Staff don't attend the performances and show little interest in following up the work or using or developing the techniques as part of their curriculum.

TABLE 8.6B *Completed objective sheet*

How will I know whether I have succeeded?

Evaluation and outcome measures

Evaluation is something we actively engage in on a daily basis, when we ask ourselves questions such as:

* do I enjoy my job or should I apply for another one?

* will I go to that club again?

or, on a professional footing when we ask:

* how did that session go?

* did I achieve what I set out to do?

* did that patient or service user really understand what I was explaining to her or

was she just being polite when she said she did?

In other words, evaluation is about assessing the value or worth of something, which as these questions show includes an element of subjectivity; our own personal appreciation of it.

In the context of evaluating health promotion activity we are probably considering a more formal approach to evaluation. The evaluation may be more public or open to scrutiny by outsiders. In this type of evaluation there are two key aspects:

* defining what we hope to achieve – aims and objectives

* gathering information to assess whether we have met these.

Evaluation: the question of when to evaluate is closely bound up with the purpose of the evaluation. Is it to be a final *summative* assessment of what has happened? Evaluation of this type, which seeks to establish the worth of work when it has reached its conclusion, is termed an *outcome* evaluation. Or is it an ongoing appraisal of the progress made? Evaluation that involves feedback during the course of a project, when things are still taking shape, is termed *formative* or an evaluation of *process*.

An outcome measure is the end point of the piece of work a health promoter undertakes. This can be a target as challenging as those seen in *Our Healthier Nation*, which refer to reductions in disease but reflect national policy, and therefore require co-ordinated action at national level to deliver them. Conversely, it could be something quite small-scale, such as creating and improving the knowledge and skills of healthy cooking amongst people from a specific geographical community. There will be considerable overlap between outcome measures and objectives here, but it is important not to confuse the two.

Objectives refer to the work required to deliver the outcome. In this example an objective might be to develop a model training programme for delivery with a group of women from the identified community. Outcomes refer to the product of the work. The health promoter will have to identify the desired outcomes in advance of the work to ensure that they design into the process ways of measuring whether the product is delivered. For example, they need to check whether the knowledge and skills of healthy cooking were successfully developed in the community and people then went on to alter their diet and eating behaviours.

It is not always possible to predict the outcome of a piece of work. It can create unintended or unexpected outcomes which are a by-product of the work. In the example above, the by-product might be better community relations due to the sustained programme of group activities during the cooking skills course, or the establishment of local community market gardening initiatives to grow local fresh produce.

So for your assessment activity you need to ask yourself, 'How will I know that this has been a worthwhile activity?' You will need to identify the information required to enable you to prove that your aim has been achieved. You might want to scale down some of your objectives and outcomes when you begin to do this and realise how ambitious you have been.

Evidence for evaluation

Changing behaviour

Activities in the health education arena focus on the need to motivate individuals to change their health-related behaviours, most commonly in areas such as increasing physical activity, quitting smoking, adopting a healthier diet, adopting safe sex messages, etc. As you can imagine it is not easy to monitor the changing behaviour of a group of people over time to assess how successful a health promotion activity has been. This is exactly the problem faced by the smoking cessation services set up with the support of government funding in each health district in 1999–2000. The services must report how many people referred to them set a quit date, how many went on to quit smoking and how many were still not smoking after one month. To assess the effectiveness of the services in this way requires a considerable investment in administration to track the patients, collect the necessary information and collate it for the returns to the Department of Health.

Cost-effectiveness

Whilst much local health promotion activity may be viewed as being relatively cheap in relation to the illness it seeks to prevent, it is also hard to measure the precise outcome of the work. The investment of two or three hours time by a practice nurse to help someone quit smoking is considerably less expensive than the cost of extensive treatment for lung cancer. However, it is impossible to state categorically that the nurse's time led to that individual quitting. Many other factors might have influenced the outcome; that is it isn't an *attributable* outcome.

During recent years, questions about the relation between costs and effectiveness in the field of health promotion have become important. In a world of limited resources costs clearly have to be taken into account. If, for instance, a health education programme is entirely effective in changing the health behaviour of a small group of people but achieves this success through enormous financial and human resource investment, it is important to acknowledge that in the evaluation process. Without this information it is not possible to make comparisons between differing health promotion activities which achieve the same outcome, or health promoting activities and medical interventions.

Disease reduction

As we have already seen, it is virtually impossible to attribute the most important outcome (reduction of a specific disease) specifically to a health promotion intervention. The range of other influences which impact on a person's life make this impossible. After all, if we are not able to state categorically that smoking causes lung cancer (the appropriate statement is that there is a very strong association between the two), how can we say that the time spent with a person counselling them on quitting smoking led to a reduction in lung cancer?

Therefore, targets for disease reduction are usually set at national, regional or district level (as we have seen with the two national health strategies) but are rarely used as health promotion success indicators. Even national health promotion initiatives such as the introduction of smoking cessation services use short-term measures which are more easily attributable to the intervention, for example the number of people setting a quit date, the numbers still not smoking after one month, the numbers still not smoking at three and six months.

It must also be recognised that some disease patterns can take several years to change even if the health promotion intervention succeeds. For example, the 'stop smoking' service can reduce

FIGURE 8.19 *The success of 'stop smoking' services is measured by the number of ex-smokers who don't take up smoking again*

What if?

Imagine you are the project lead for the local 'activity on referral' service which provides support for people who need to be more active (like Carrie's team on page 69). Your team introduces people to gentle exercise such as walking, gardening, or attendance at a leisure club. A variety of local practitioners are able to refer people who wish to become more active to your service for one-to-one and group support.

* What measures could you use to show that the service was having the desired effect on the participants?

* What tests would you have to do to collect this information?

* How often would you need to collect it to monitor changes effectively?

* How practical is all of the above likely to be?

* What benefits other than changes to physical health might participants experience by being involved in the scheme?

the numbers of people smoking but for many people their cancer may already be established but undiagnosed. Therefore it will take time for the impact of reducing smoking levels to take effect. Some health promotion interventions can actually lead to a rise in the incidence of disease, screening campaigns being a particularly good example. Whenever campaigns are undertaken to encourage uptake of screening it is inevitable that the numbers of additional patients seen will lead to an increased number of diagnoses.

Evaluating your own practice

An essential part of being an effective health promoter is to be a reflective practitioner; that is, to review your practice, identify any areas of weakness or improvement, identify what would improve your practice in the future and build that into future work. This is an essential part of adult learning as described by Kolb in the model of experiential learning. This model has four elements: concrete experience, observation and reflection, the formation of abstract concepts and testing in new situations. Kolb represented these in the experiential learning circle (Figure 8.20).

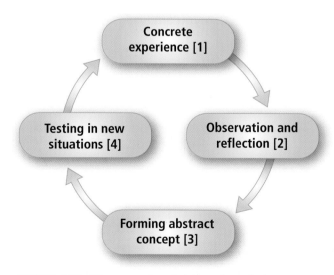

FIGURE 8.20 *The experiential learning circle*

Kolb and Fry (1975) argue that the learning cycle can begin at any one of the four points – and that it should really be approached as a continuous spiral. However, it is suggested that the learning process often begins with concrete experience, where a person *carries out a particular action* – in this case your health promotion activity – and then sees the effect of the action in this situation.

Following this, the second step is observation and reflection. This helps us to *understand these effects in the particular instance* so that if the same action was taken in the same circumstances it would be possible to anticipate what would follow from the action.

In this pattern the third step would be forming abstract concepts; in other words, *understanding the general principle* under which the particular instance falls. An educator who has learnt in this way may well have various rules of thumb or generalisations about what to do in different situations. So you will begin to develop both confidence and competence to deal with managing health promotion activities.

When the general principle is understood, the last step is *testing it out in new situations* within the range of generalisation. Reflective practice is about taking time out to carry out steps 2 and 3 and getting other people's views on how you are performing within a role so you can begin to generalise about your future practice to change and improve it. This could cover any aspect of competence in health promotion, be it acting ethically (e.g. not using inappropriately sponsored materials), managing projects (e.g. keeping to timescales in the milestone plan), or working in partnership (e.g. how well you maintain effective working relationships with your colleagues or other practitioners you are depending upon to get the job done).

Summary of Section 8.3

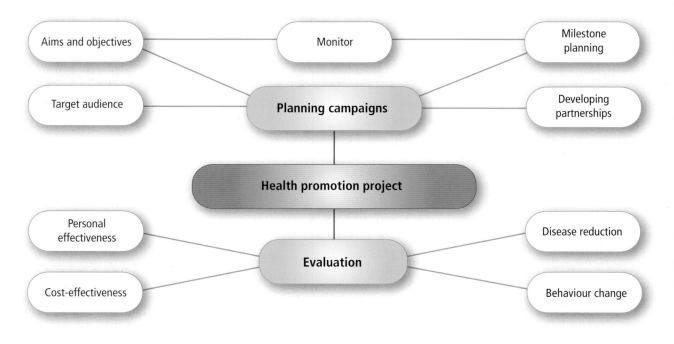

Pat is a school nurse who is working with the local schools health promotion specialist, Geoff, to develop a 'school nurse drop-in' as part of an extended school provision in one of the local high schools. This school is in a deprived area with high teenage pregnancy rates. The drop-in will operate from 3.30 to 5 pm on two afternoons a week and will enable pupils from the school to drop in and discuss any health concerns with her in confidence. This might be a wish to stop smoking, advice about losing weight or dealing with stress, or it could be for a pregnancy test or advice about contraception. It took a great deal of time and effort to persuade the school to support the drop-in; they were particularly concerned about parents' views of the types of advice their children might be getting.

Using concepts, can you identify?

1. What is/are:

   * an aim for the service?

   * three or four key objectives which might fall from this broad aim?

   * any specific ethical issues Pat might need to consider in her planning?

Go further – Can you analyse issues using theory?

2. Who are the 'stakeholders', that is those with an interest in the project?

3. What health information could Pat use to provide evidence of the normative need?

4. How could Pat gather information to describe the expressed need for this service?

Go further – Can you evaluate using a range of theories?

5. What measures could she use to evaluate this project in terms of:

   * personal effectiveness

   * cost-effectiveness

   * behaviour change

   * disease reduction?

UNIT 8 ASSESSMENT

How you will be assessed

Assessment evidence will typically consist of a written report on a small-scale health promotion project that you have carried out. You may work as part of a group, or as an individual, to carry out the health promotion activity, but your report must be an individual piece of work carried out entirely by you. Your health promotion project should take approximately 15 hours to complete.

The topic of your activity may be drawn from any area relevant to health and social care but the target group should be from one of the following client groups:

* people who are ill

* young children

* older people

* people with specific needs.

Your report will demonstrate your knowledge and understanding of the promotion of health and well-being, and show evidence of your ability to conduct a small-scale health promotion project. You can use either existing materials or develop your own materials, to collect evidence for your project. Your report must include evidence of:

* knowledge and understanding of the topic addressed by your project, and a considered and appropriate choice of target group

* the planning of your project, including:

  * aims and objectives

  * the health promotion model(s) and approach(es) chosen

  * the methods used to measure the success of the project.

* implementation of your health promotion project, the use and development of appropriate media and materials, and an analysis of the success of your project

* the evaluation outcomes of your health promotion project.

This unit is assessed through a portfolio of work, with the mark you gain for that assessment being your mark for the unit. As part of the portfolio you will produce a report which describes the planning of, and your participation in, a small-scale campaign to promote good health in a care setting (or your own centre if you prefer).

There may be little time to produce posters and leaflets. Therefore, where possible, use existing campaigning materials, which for the most part can be readily obtained from health-promotion departments, health centres, social services and shops.

To help you understand how your work will be assessed, guidance on what you need to do to achieve the highest marks for each assessment objective (AO) section have been included on pages 107–8.

Key things to bear in mind

Identifying the level of need

You will need to undertake some consultation activity with both service users and service providers about any planned activity which may affect them. If/when you carry out interviews or activities with clients as part of your assessed work, it is essential that you obtain the client's consent and maintain full confidentiality throughout. Some of these people may be workers (such as health visitors, school nurses, community nurses, environmental health officers and GPs), so it will be important to either use opportunities with visiting speakers, or to go out to visit these workers to test out your ideas for the campaign and find out about their roles.

You can find information about government initiatives on most government department websites, for example those for the Department of Health and the Department for Education and Skills. You can find information about the effectiveness of health promotion activity on the HDA website.

Both primary (your own) and secondary (review of other peoples') research would be useful to enable you to develop an understanding of the different factors affecting health and well-being, and the effects of ill-health on service users in various settings.

Defining the approach you will use

In the assessment, you will be expected to provide an explanation of the health-promotion approach you have adopted in the planning and implementation of the campaign. It will be important to have a sound understanding of these approaches before you attempt any detailed planning. You won't be expected to demonstrate an in-depth knowledge of each approach which could be used, but to demonstrate a good understanding of the applied approach.

Most commonly, people use the educational approach which seeks to inform and educate to promote healthy practices, but the preventative approach is also frequently utilised. Increasing in popularity is the use of fear as an approach, particularly when used on television, for example using vivid images of people suffering the consequences of unhealthy lifestyle choices, such as smoking, to instil fear into those who watch. But fear can also be used on a simpler, local level, for example a teacher using a pair of diseased lungs to scare young people about the effects of smoking.

Defining success

It is important to set clear aims and objectives in the plan for the campaign. These will vary with the intended outcomes. For example, improving health and well-being may be the aim of a campaign provided for people who are overweight and inactive and thus at risk of coronary heart disease. Alternatively, a campaign to promote safe sexual practices to young adults may have two aims, firstly to reduce the number of sufferers of sexually-transmitted diseases, and secondly to reduce the number of unplanned pregnancies.

The objectives of the campaign will link directly to the different stages and tasks which need to be completed, to ensure the campaign takes place as efficiently as possible. You also need to consider the intended outcomes of their campaign so that effectiveness can be measured accurately. Try to identify the skills you use, for example practical skills, organisational skills and communication skills.

The evaluation needs to include evidence of reflective practice where you make judgements about your performance and the success of the campaign against the pre-set criteria stated. Higher marks are dependent on demonstrating analytical skills and the ability to make reasoned judgements, together with consideration of both the intended and unintended outcomes; for example pointing out that a campaign which encourages counselling may result in long waiting lists.

You may wish to work in groups to collect materials and when participating in the health-promotion campaign; however, for all other aspects of this unit, you are required to produce your own individual portfolio of evidence.

A worked example

Young people in the age range of your peers are the most likely people to be experimenting with a range of substances, including alcohol, tobacco and various illicit substances. Your project might be based on a need to improve people's awareness of what local services are available for them and to focus specifically on one particular substance which the majority of your student body will be using, that is alcohol. This project might require you to:

* find out information from your local young people's substance misuse services about the services available to you and your peers and how you could access them

* use the Home Office and National Statistics Office websites to access information about young people's drinking patterns; describe the current drinking patterns for your own age range and the trends in drinking patterns over the last ten years

* find out what the current recommended safe drinking levels are

* design a poster to challenge your own student peer group to think about their drinking behaviours and the possible impact these may be having on their health

* design a leaflet to support your poster campaign which provides information about safe drinking levels, helps people calculate their weekly and daily unit intake and provides contact details for local services for anyone who feels they may need to access professional support

* describe the ethical issues this presents for you; for example, how does this work impact on your relationships with your friends when you are out socialising over a drink? Or how would you deal with a friend whom you identify (as a result of undertaking this work) may be drinking too much?

Assessment guidance

AO1 Knowledge and understanding of the topic addressed by your promotion, and a considered and appropriate choice of target group.

Higher marks will be awarded if:

* you demonstrate good skills in obtaining information from at least two sources on the topic of your health promotion

* there is evidence of independent research, and the information is drawn from several relevant sources

* you are able to choose an appropriate target group, and the rationale for your decision is reasoned.

The best marks will be awarded if:

* you demonstrate excellent skills in obtaining information from at least three sources on the topic of your health promotion

* there is evidence of you planning your own methods for obtaining information

* there is evidence the information is drawn from several relevant sources, and from different types of sources

* you are able to choose an appropriate target group, and the rationale for your decision is well reasoned.

AO2 The planning of your promotion including: aims and objectives, the health promotion model(s)/ approach(es) chosen, and the methods used to measure the success of the promotion.

Higher marks will be given where:

* you are able to create a plan for a small-scale health promotion project

* you display a good knowledge of health promotion models and approaches in doing this

* you have at least two stated aims and objectives

* you demonstrate a good understanding of what the aims and objectives mean

* your method for evaluating your project is clear and this shows a good understanding of the evaluative process.

The best marks will be given where:

* you are able to create a plan for a small-scale health promotion project
* you display a high level of knowledge of health promotion models and approaches
* at least three of the aims and objectives are stated, and detailed understanding of them is demonstrated
* a high level of understanding of the evaluative process is shown in your evaluative methodology which is well explained.

AO3 Implementation of your health promotion, the use and development of appropriate media and materials, and an analysis of the success of your health promotion.

Higher marks will be awarded where:

* you are able to carry out your planned promotion
* you show a good understanding of the health promotion models used
* your analysis is based on adequate data, and conclusions are reasoned and based on evidence
* you are able to create the necessary media and materials, and your choice of materials demonstrates clear understanding and knowledge of the health promotion models used
* you can apply methods to measure the success of the project, and demonstrate a good understanding of the process.

The best marks will be awarded where:

* you are able to carry out your planned promotion, showing a detailed understanding of the health promotion models used
* analysis is based on extensive data, and conclusions well reasoned and based on well-founded evidence presented within the report
* you are able to create media and materials, and your choices demonstrate a high level of understanding and knowledge of the health promotion models used
* you can apply methods to measure the success of the project, and demonstrate an excellent understanding of the evaluative process.

AO4 The evaluation outcomes of your health promotion.

Higher marks will be awarded where:

* you demonstrate a good level of evaluative skills
* your report evaluates the health promotion project and indicates the outcomes, with reasoned conclusions
* you are able to discuss and draw conclusions which are based on evidence
* you show a good understanding of at least two of the aims and objectives and evaluative criteria is demonstrated
* you demonstrate some evidence of independent thinking and initiative.

The best marks will be awarded where:

* you demonstrate excellent evaluative skills
* your report evaluates the project and indicates the outcomes, with well-reasoned and detailed conclusions
* you are able to draw valid conclusions from the evidence present, which are clear, well reasoned and detailed
* you demonstrate a high level of independent thinking and initiative.

Unit test

1. What is the difference between health trend data and incident data?

2. What is the difference between morbidity and mortality data and what advantage does health-related behaviour data have over both of these types of data?

3. What are the current safe drinking levels prescribed by the Department of Health and what are the four main strands of the alcohol harm reduction strategy?

4. Using the promotion of physical activity as an example, identify the aim of each model of health promotion and suggest a relevant type of activity for each.

Model	Aim	Health promotion activity
Medical approach		
Behavioural change approach		
Educational approach		
Service-user-centred approach		
Societal change approach		
Fear		

5. When designing a leaflet what are the key questions you would need to consider?

6. A friend of yours has had unprotected sex on several occasions, usually whilst under the influence of alcohol. You are worried that they are regularly putting themselves at risk of catching a sexually transmitted infection (STI) and also are making themselves vulnerable when they are intoxicated. What are the ethical considerations you need to think about if you wish to discuss this with them?

7. If you were to undertake a health promotion project to reduce the unsafe level of alcohol consumption in a particular estate in your locality, you would first need to identify the need for this project. Describe a possible example of:

   * a normative need

   * a comparative need

   * a felt need

   * an expressed need.

8. What does SMART stand for when defining objectives?

9. What is the difference between a summative evaluation measure and a formative evaluation measure? Give an example of each, from your own project if you wish.

10. Give four categories of information you could use to evidence your evaluation. Give an example of each, from your own project if you wish.

References and further reading

D. Acheson, (1998) *Independent Inquiry into Inequalities in Health* (London: HMSO)

American Commission on Chronic Illness (1957) *Chronic Illness in the United States* Vol. 1 (Cambridge, MA: Harvard University Press)

Benzeval, M., Judge, K., Whitehead, M. (1995) *Tackling Inequalities in Health, an Agenda for Action* (London: Kings Fund Publishing)

Dawson, D. (1990) *Women's Cancers, The Treatment Options, Everything you need to Know* (London: Piatkus Publishing)

Department of Health (1992) *Immunisation against Infectious Disease* (London: HMSO)

Department of Health (2000) *The NHS Cancer Plan* (London: HMSO)

Department of Health (2001) *Involving Patients and the Public in Healthcare* (London: HMSO)

Department of Health (2001) *The National Strategy for HIV and Sexual Health* (London: HMSO)

Department of Health (2004) 'At least five a week – evidence on the impact of physical activity and its relationship to health – a report from the Chief Medical Officer'

Downie, R. S., Tannahill, C., Tannahill, A. (1996) *Health Promotion Models and Values* (Oxford: Oxford University Press)

Draper, P. (1991) *Health through Public Policy* (Green Print)

Ewles, L., Simnett, I. (1999) *Promoting Health – A Practical Guide* (London: Bailliere Tindall)

Hall, D. (1996) *Health for all Children* (Oxford: Oxford University Press)

HM Government (1992) *The Health of the Nation* (London: HMSO)

HM Government (1997) *The New NHS: Modern Dependable* (London: HMSO)

HM Government (1997) *Saving Lives: Our Healthier Nation* (London: HMSO)

HM Government (2004) *Choosing Health – Making Healthy Choices Easier* (London: HMSO)

Jones, L., Sidell, M. (1997) *The Challenge of Promoting Health – Exploration and Action* (Milton Keynes: Open University)

Katz, J., Peberdy, A. (eds) (1997) *Promoting Health: Knowledge and Practice* (Buckingham: Macmillan/OU Press)

Kolb, D.A., Fry, R. (1995) 'Toward an applied theory of experiential learning' in *Theories of Group Processes,* Cary Cooper (ed.) (London: John Wiley & Sons)

Montgomery S.M., Morris D. L., Thompson N. P., Subhani J., Pounder R. E., Wakefield A. J. (1998) 'Prevalence of inflammatory bowel disease in British 26 year olds: national longitudinal birth cohort', *British Medical Journal*, Apr., 316:1058–1059

Moonie, N. (2000) *Advanced Health and Social Care* (Oxford: Heinemann)

Naidoo, J., Wills, J. (1996) *Health Promotion: Foundations for Practice* (London: Bailliere Tindall)

Whitehead, M., Townsend, P., Davidson N. (1998) *Inequalities in Health: The Black Report and the Health Divide* (Penguin Social Sciences Series) (Harmondsworth: Penguin Books)

Useful websites

British Heart Foundation
www.bhf.org.uk/
Heart health information, including information about activity and nutrition.

Chartered Institute of Environmental Health Officers
www.cieh.org/
Information about their role and how to train to be one.

Department of Education and Skills
www.mindbodysoul.gov.uk
Provides accurate and up-to-date health information for young people.

Department of Health
www.doh.gov.uk
Search here for links to *Choosing Health*, Public Health White Paper, and health statistics.

Department of Health and Department of Education and Skills
www.wiredforhealth.gov.uk
Provides teachers with access to relevant and appropriate health information.

European Observatory on Health Systems and
Policies
http://euro.who.int/observatory
Supports and promotes evidence-based health
policy-making through comprehensive and
rigorous analysis of the dynamics of health
care systems in Europe.

Home Office
www.homeoffice.gov.uk/drugs/index.html
Information about the National Drugs Strategy
and links to information about current drug
use trends and patterns.

Immunisation
www.immunisation.org.uk/
Information about immunisation programmes.

MMR
www.mmrthefacts.nhs.uk/
Information about the MMR vaccine for
parents, to counter the fall in public confidence
in the vaccine.

National Drugs Agency
www.drugscope.org.uk/
Advice on drugs treatment and prevention
services; includes high-quality information
about patterns of use, information about specific
drugs and advice on how to prevent use.

National Health Service
www.nhs.uk/england/
Connects you to local NHS services in England
and provides national information about the
NHS.
www.nhlbisupport.com/bmi/bmicalc.htm
Calculate your own BMI using the information
on this site.
www.cancerscreening.nhs.uk/
Provides good quality information about
both cervical and breast cancer screening
programmes.
www.givingupsmoking.co.uk
Information about smoking, how to quit and
where to access local services.
www.quick.org.uk
Quality information checklist for young people
to assess the quality of information they find
on the Internet.

National Institute for Health and Clinical Excellence
(NICE) www.publichealth.nice.org.uk/
Information about effective health promotion
interventions.

World Health Organization
www.who.int/en/

Investigating disease

This unit covers the following sections:

Introduction

Unit 9

This unit develops your understanding of health and disease gained from Unit 1, *Human Growth and Development,* and also includes aspects related to Unit 8, *Promoting Health and Well-being*, both at AS level.

You will learn about the disease process, including how diseases are caused, classified, diagnosed, treated and prevented. The information on disease prevention includes how the progress of disease is tracked and the use of data collected by professionals, which is the basis for epidemiology. You will be able to relate certain diseases to appropriate settings such as health, early years, care of older people and individuals with special needs.

How you will be assessed

This unit is internally assessed. You must produce a report of a *comparison* between a communicable and a non-communicable disease, including the following:

* a summary of the biological basis of the disease and the body's response to it
* the causes and distribution of the disease
* facilities for diagnosis and treatment in your locality
* factors that affect the availability and outcome of treatments
* an analysis of support available in your locality
* an evaluation of the strategies to prevent the disease and factors affecting those strategies.

You can choose diseases affecting people at any stage of their lives, but you must agree these with your tutor and produce individual reports. Primary evidence (such as that gained from patients with the disease or professional care workers) and knowledge of facilities within your local area for diagnosis and treatment are crucial to achieving the higher mark bands.

9.1 Health and disease: epidemiology

You have already learned in earlier AS units that defining health is very complex and that early attempts have generally been considered as too narrow and oversimplified. The concept of health leads us into considering the world around us, political and social issues, different cultural norms and different life stages. Every area and aspect of our existence seems to have an implication for the health experience of an individual or group of people.

Health is now viewed as a positive experience of possessing the wherewithal to live life to the full and achieve maximum potential. Two more recent attempts to define health have met with considerable acclaim:

'Health is, therefore, seen as a resource for everyday life, not the objective of living; it is a positive concept emphasising social and personal resources, as well as physical capabilities.'

World Health Organization (1986)

'A person's optimum state of health is equivalent to the state of the set of conditions which fulfil or enable a person to work to fulfil his or her realistic chosen and biological potentials.'

David Seedhouse (1986)

Try it out

Working on your own, or with a small group, take a few minutes to reflect on a non-health issue, event or activity with which you were recently involved. Thinking broadly, analyse the impact, positive or negative, that this activity may have had on your health.

SCENARIO

John

John loves his wife and two young children very much; he likes to indulge them, take them on holidays each summer and maintain a nice home. John's wife does not go out to work and he earns a modest salary as an office worker. John has a new loan for a better car and large amounts on several credit cards. His bank balance reduces at the end of every month to make a larger and larger overdraft. His family is unaware of the looming financial crisis and today John has been asked to make an appointment with his bank manager to discuss his financial situation. This is a non-health issue.

Discuss the potential impact on the health of all members of John's family using your understanding of the concept of health together with the information in the two quotations above.

FIGURE 9.1 *Almost all non-health issues have an impact on health*

You have learned about the terms 'illness', 'ill-health' and 'disease' in the AS units. Illness is a word we use to describe a state of being unwell. It is a subjective or personal health experience when we are aware of something that does not feel right. Ill-health is a longer experience of being unwell and we may or may not know the cause. We tend not to describe ourselves as being in a state of ill-health when the situation is short and temporary – this is termed an illness. Disease tends to be the term which might be used if a doctor or similar professional has made a diagnosis from signs and symptoms shown by the patient and offered treatment, advice or care of some description. A condition of this type can usually be given a name.

Diseases can be classified in several ways. In this unit we will consider the following classification, derived from Unit 1, when we met physical, intellectual, emotional and social aspects of health:

* physical disease, or physical illness

* psychological disease, more usually thought of as mental health disorders

* social disease, or conditions associated with personal lifestyle choices or the environment.

Physical diseases or illnesses are those which affect the functioning of parts of the human body. Examples of physical diseases are:

* coronary heart disease

* bronchitis

* nephritis

* arthritis.

Mental health disorders affect the mind or intellect. They include:

* depression

* anxiety disorder

* bipolar disorder.

Personal lifestyle or environmental disorders are those that arise from social deprivation, relationships or those which have their roots in our personal activities, such as:

* alcoholism

* substance abuse

* sexually-transmitted diseases.

When you examine the examples in this classification, you will find that the classification is not absolute because disorders like depression, bulimia and substance abuse also produce physical effects. Similarly, alcoholism, addictions and arthritis can have psychological effects, and depression and bulimia can be seen as having foundations in modern society.

Another way of classifying diseases is simply into communicable and non-communicable diseases.

Key concept

Communicable disease: this is infectious or contagious disease, which can be transmitted from one living organism to another. Non-communicable diseases cannot be passed between living organisms.

In order to prevent communicable disease, it is necessary to closely investigate all the factors contributing to the infection and its spread.

Key concept

Epidemiology: this was, historically, the study of outbreaks of acute infectious disease or, put simply, the study of epidemics. Today, epidemiology refers to the study of the causes, distribution and determinants (factors) of diseases, communicable and non-communicable, in a defined or set population.

Did you know?

An acute illness is a condition which comes on suddenly and lasts for a relatively short period, whereas a chronic disease is a condition that persists for a long time. Both types of illness may or may not be severe. Generally, acute diseases have signs and symptoms, such as fever and breathlessness, which change rapidly from day to day. The signs and symptoms of chronic diseases change very little, implying a continuous disease process and progressive deterioration.

FIGURE 9.2 *Acute illnesses have dramatic signs and symptoms that change rapidly, whereas chronic conditions change little over a long period and show gradual deterioration*

Epidemiology has been defined as:

'The study of the distribution and determinants of health and disease-related conditions in populations. It is concerned with epidemic (excess of normal expectancy) and endemic (always present) conditions. The basic premise of epidemiology is that disease is not randomly distributed across populations.'

M. Shenker and J. Ladou (eds) (1997)

Did you know?

An epidemic disease is one which suddenly spreads quickly within a community (or defined population) in which it has been comparatively rare. Outbreaks of measles in local areas such as London or the Midlands are often accurately described as epidemics. An endemic disease is one that is constantly present in a community, region or group of people. AIDS is said to be endemic in Africa. A pandemic is a disease affecting a high percentage of the population in a large geographical area, occasionally worldwide. The spread of recent new strains of influenza from Asia to Europe and North America are pandemics.

In simple terms, epidemiology studies both communicable and non-communicable diseases, in groups of people rather than in individuals.

Media reports often compare the prevalence of diseases like heart disease in the West and in countries like China, where such diseases are much rarer. This is comparative epidemiology where determinants in one population (not necessarily in a different country) are compared with those of a different population for a given condition.

Epidemiologists aim to identify the factors that cause disease or the transmission of disease and prevent the spread of both communicable and non-communicable diseases and conditions. They are trained to identify and prevent disease in a particular population. This is different from the role of a clinical doctor who identifies and treats diseases in an individual.

To carry out their studies, epidemiologists need to collect a wide variety of information from the defined population and the environment in which they live. This is known as data collection.

Did you know?

The basic unit values of observation, measurement and presentation are called data. Statistics is the science of handling the collection, measurement, analysis, interpretation and presentation of data.

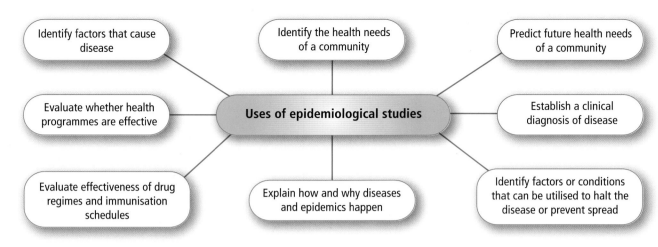

FIGURE 9.3 *The purposes of epidemiological investigations*

A fairly simple epidemiological study might compare the incidence of, say, asthma in an inner city area with that in a rural community.

Members of the populations being investigated are counted and defined in terms of age, gender, race, social class, occupation, marital status, medical histories etc., until a good profile is built up.

The number of new cases in each area each week (or month or year) will be counted – usually with the co-operation of general practitioners in the area. This is known as the *incidence* of the disorder. The counting exercise will be repeated at regular intervals for a set period of time.

The *prevalence* of the disorder is the number of individuals within the population with asthma at any given time. This calculation is also repeated at regular intervals. The data will be analysed and interpreted by statisticians who will present statistical conclusions for the investigative team to consider. The preliminary findings may result in further explorations such as collecting evidence concerning the quantity and nature of pollutants in the two environments.

There are three main types of epidemiological studies.

1. *Descriptive studies*, which describe the distribution of disease by the variations of individual, place and time, to study outbreaks of acute disease and to develop hypotheses about the spread of disease.

2. *Analytical studies*, which identify the relationships between the causes of the disease or associated factors; these are also used to develop hypotheses to test cause and effect.

3. *Experimental studies*, which seek to prove an association between factors and disease outcomes.

You will find more useful information on data collection in Unit 6, *Public health* (pages 265–70).

Try it out

In May 2005, the Health Protection Agency (HPA) warned that epidemics of measles were a real possibility in the London area as take-up of MMR vaccine had fallen from 92 per cent in 1995 to 84 per cent in 2002. The WHO recommends that to prevent outbreaks the immune level of a population should be above 95 per cent. What types of data would have been collected in the lead-up to the HPA's warning?

Summary of Section 9.1

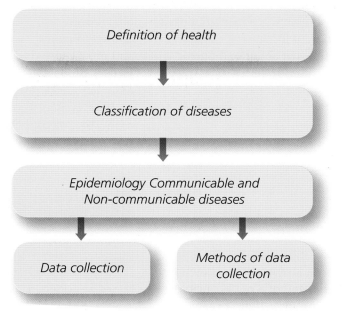

Definition of health

↓

Classification of diseases

↓

Epidemiology Communicable and Non-communicable diseases

↓

Data collection   Methods of data collection

'Sexually-transmitted infections (STIs) are a major public health problem in the 16–24 years age group. Young people are behaviourally, biologically and socially more vulnerable to STI acquisition through a complex set of interactions. Rates of diagnoses of chlamydia, gonorrhoea and genital warts are highest among women aged 16–19 and young men aged 20–24 in England, Wales and Northern Ireland. The burden of chlamydial infection was greatest among women in 2003, with 49,601 diagnoses (of 89,431 in total), of which 73 per cent were those aged under 25. Diagnoses are likely to be an underestimate of the true numbers of chlamydial infection because of high levels of asymptomatic (having no symptoms) infection. In men, rates of gonorrhoea were highest in the 20–24 age grouping in 2003, with significant increases since 1995.'

Source: S. Douglas, *Health Protection Matters*, (Spring 2005)

Using concepts, can you identify?

1. Which group of diseases do chlamydia and gonorrhoea belong to?

2. What data is necessary to produce this report?

Go further – Can you analyse issues using theory?

3. Analyse the implications in this report for the health of young people.

Go further – Can you evaluate using a range of theories?

4. Suggest ways in which this information can be used in health promotion campaigns.

5. How could the campaigns be evaluated?

9.2 Differences between communicable and non-communicable diseases

Communicable diseases

These are caused mainly by micro-organisms transmitted in a variety of ways to humans. Some communicable diseases can be spread by larger organisms such as mites, worms and flukes.

Micro-organisms are too small to be seen by the naked eye and must be viewed with light or electron microscopes, thus giving rise to their collective name.

Micro-organisms which cause disease are also known as pathogens. Not all micro-organisms are pathogenic; humans live in harmony with many micro-organisms and some are even helpful in our physiological functions. For example, bacteria living inside the large intestine produce vitamin K and help in the digestion of food.

In this unit, you will learn about pathogenic micro-organisms, which comprise:

* viruses
* bacteria
* fungi
* protozoa.

Viruses

Viruses are extremely small, one-half to one-hundredth the size of the smallest bacteria, so they were not positively identified until the electron microscope was invented around 1930. They have a simple structure, consisting of a nucleic acid core surrounded by coats of protein subunits arranged in a symmetrical shape.

The nucleic acid may be DNA or RNA depending on the particular type of virus and this is called the viral genome. Viruses are truly parasitic and do not carry out the normal activities to support metabolism. Viruses are known to parasitise all known living organisms and most cause disease. The number of different viruses probably exceeds all other types of living organisms added together.

Viral genomes contain genes capable of replicating or copying the virus, thus making new virus particles. Viruses are only capable of replication when they are inside living cells.

Did you know?

Viruses are from 15 to 300 nanometres in diameter and can only be seen using an electron microscope. One nanometre is one thousand-millionth of a metre!

There are many diseases attributed to viruses. Table 9.1 shows only some of the most well known.

FAMILY OF VIRUSES	COMMUNICABLE DISEASES
Herpes viruses	Chicken pox, shingles, genital herpes, glandular fever
Picornaviruses	Hepatitis A, poliomyelitis
Orthomyxoviruses	Influenza
Paramyxoviruses	Mumps, measles
Coronaviruses	Common cold
Adenoviruses	Respiratory and eye infections
Papovaviruses	Warts
Retroviruses	HIV responsible for AIDS

TABLE 9.1 *Diseases caused by viruses*

Viruses can enter the body via many routes, such as:

* inhaled droplets
* food and drink
* bites

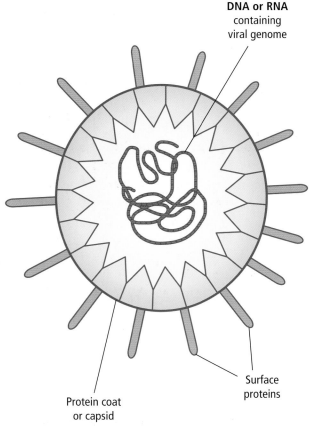

DNA or RNA
containing
viral genome

Protein coat
or capsid

Surface
proteins

FIGURE 9.4 *Structure of a typical virus*

* infected needles
* conjunctiva of the eye
* mucous membrane of the genital tract and mouth.

Having gained entry, many viruses invade the nearest cells and begin to multiply. Some enter the lymphatic vessels, lymph nodes and circulation, from which they can access all parts of the body, even targeting specific organs. Some viruses are even capable of using nerve fibres to travel to their destinations.

After sticking to the body cell, the virus injects itself into the cell interior and loses its protein coats. The released nucleic acid uses the cell's raw materials to make large numbers of copies of itself, and new protein coats. Large numbers of new virus particles are released from the cell, which suffers great disruption and damage and may die.

Cell damage and death may cause serious illness, particularly when the cells form part of

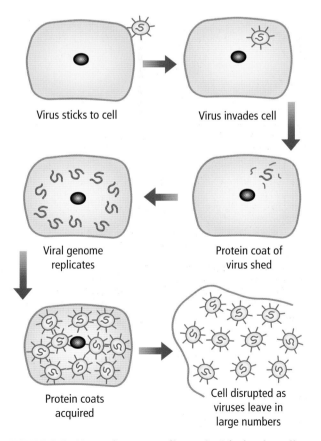

Virus sticks to cell   Virus invades cell

Viral genome replicates   Protein coat of virus shed

Protein coats acquired   Cell disrupted as viruses leave in large numbers

FIGURE 9.5 *How viruses replicate inside body cells*

a vital organ. The body's immune system may respond by pouring out huge numbers of specific antibodies to the invading virus and the resulting antigen-antibody complexes may cause further inflammation or tissue damage.

Some viruses can interact with the chromosomes of body cells and 'switch on' so-called cancer genes (oncogenes), producing body cells which divide repeatedly in an uncontrolled way to form tumours. A form of leukaemia can arise from virus infection.

Another type of virus invades special white blood cells known as T-lymphocytes that have an important role in defending the body against disease. This is what happens in HIV infection, resulting in extremely weakened immune systems providing the opportunity for (opportunistic) infections.

Under normal circumstances, the immune system of an individual will respond after a short period and produce specific antibodies which, in a variety of ways, will neutralise the invasion of viruses. This will normally enable the individual to recover within a few days or weeks. If the virus infection has occurred before, circulating antibodies will pour into the circulation very rapidly and the invasion will be resisted so that subsequent infections are rare. This is why second infections of viral diseases such as measles are rare. Occasionally, the severity and speed of the invasion causes severe damage before the immune system can respond – this can occur with the poliomyelitis and rabies viruses. Other viruses, like the herpes infections (cold sores, shingles), are able to evade the immune system, making recurrence more likely.

Many agents which might disable viruses cannot be used as they would also damage the vulnerable body cells. New anti-viral agents concentrate on preventing the virus from injecting itself into the cells or stopping the viral genome from replicating. Antibiotics are not effective against virus infections and are only prescribed to prevent or treat secondary bacterial infection which might follow a viral infection.

Influenza

This viral infection is often known as 'flu and is commonly mistaken for a feverish common cold.

TYPE OF INFLUENZA VIRUS	CHARACTERISTICS OF VIRUS TYPE	TYPE OF ILLNESS
A	Highly unstable, new strains constantly emerging	Produces classic signs and symptoms
B	Fairly stable, but can produce new strains	Can mimic appendicitis in children, but classic illness in adults
C	Stable, antibodies protect for life	Mild illness like the common cold

TABLE 9.2 *Characteristics of influenza viruses*

Classical signs and symptoms include:

* fever and chills
* headache
* muscular aches and pains
* loss of appetite
* fatigue (extreme tiredness).

Did you know?

A *sign* is something that is observed by the individual, a care worker or others, for example facial pallor or flush. A *symptom* is something complained of by the affected individual, such as a cough or headache.

The classic signs and symptoms are often followed by a cough, sore throat and/or running nose. Fits or convulsions may occur in children, mainly as a result of a high temperature.

Patients often feel weak and depressed after 'flu but generally, the signs and symptoms clear up after 1–2 weeks. Infrequently, a severe form of pneumonia results and this can cause death, even in young healthy adults.

Preventative strategies and treatment

Older people and those with respiratory and circulatory disorders are recommended to have annual 'flu immunisations. These are not totally effective, due partly to the large number of influenza types but also to the emergence of new strains. Many countries and the WHO maintain special laboratories to investigate samples from 'flu epidemics at any time to keep vaccine stocks up to date and in plentiful supply. Vaccines

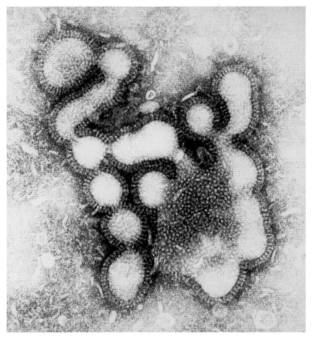

FIGURE 9.6 *Influenza viruses*

contain a mix of different killed influenza viruses. Vaccinations are required annually and are given just before the winter/spring seasons, usually in October or November.

Bed-rest, analgesics (painkillers for muscular aches and to reduce fever) and warm drinks are usually all that is required in the way of treatment, but older people with cardio-respiratory problems may be given an anti-viral drug. Secondary bacterial infection or the risk of it can be controlled with antibiotics.

Bacteria

Some examples of different pathogenic bacteria and the diseases they cause are shown in Table 9.3.

TYPE OF BACTERIA	SHAPE	EXAMPLES OF DISEASES CAUSED
Bacilli	Rod-shaped	Tuberculosis Pertussis (whooping cough) Tetanus Salmonella food poisoning
Cocci	Round	Pneumonia Meningitis Tonsillitis
Spirochaetes	Spiral	Syphilis Yaws Leptospirosis

TABLE 9.3 *Diseases caused by bacteria*

Key concept

Bacteria: these are single-celled micro-organisms that live naturally in water, soil and air. Most are harmless but some are pathogenic. They are generally classified by their shape and have been known about since the seventeenth century.

Bacteria need moist, warm conditions in which to thrive and many survive in the extra-cellular spaces between cells. Aerobic bacteria require

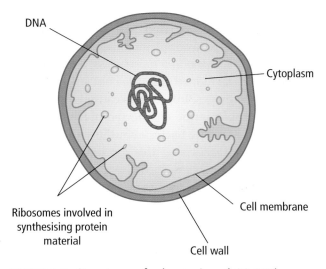

FIGURE 9.7 *Structure of a bacterium (x20,000)*

oxygen for survival so many inhabit the skin and respiratory tract. Others, known as anaerobic bacteria, live deeply in tissues or wounds. Bacteria vary in their ability to move around the body. Those with flagellae (an extended moveable filament like a whip) tend to be highly mobile (motile) while others move only in air or fluid.

Bacteria multiply by simply dividing to form two new bacteria; under ideal conditions of temperature, moisture and 'food' supply, this can take place every twenty minutes. A single bacterium can become a colony of over five hundred in only three hours.

Consider this

You make yourself a packed lunch and forget to wash your hands first. The food is contaminated with about one hundred staphylococci at 7 am. How many bacteria will be on your sandwiches by 12.30 pm when you eat your lunch? Assume your lunch is kept at room temperature in a polythene box to keep it moist.

Some bacteria are capable of becoming encapsulated in a thick membrane so that they can resist unfavourable conditions. These are known as spores. Spores can survive for a considerable length of time in this dormant state, becoming active once again when conditions become favourable. Bacteria causing tetanus, botulism and anthrax are all capable of spore formation.

Like viruses, bacteria can enter the body in a variety of ways:

* inhaled droplets from sneezes or coughs
* contaminated food or water
* cuts and wounds in the skin or through hair follicles
* through the mucous membrane of the genito-urinary tract.

Bacteria cause disease by producing toxins or poisons. Some produce toxins internally into their structure and these are called endotoxins. Disease symptoms take longer to appear as the bacteria have to die before the toxins are released to cause damage. Exotoxins are secreted outside the

FIGURE 9.8 *Red and white blood cells under the electron microscope*

recovered from the disease or an animal, usually a horse, which can manufacture the antibodies without actually suffering from the (artificially-induced) disease.

Good personal and food hygiene (not spreading an infection, washing hands carefully, covering skin infections and not handling food) should prevent the more common ailments. For more serious conditions, such as tetanus, pertussis and diphtheria, active immunisation programmes should be practised.

An active immunisation programme involves injections of killed or very much weakened bacterial agents at various periods of time. These cannot cause active disease, but will still stimulate the formation of antibodies to protect against future infections. More than one injection is usually required to raise the level of antibodies in the bloodstream of the recipient above the threshold for immunity.

bacterial cells and produce symptoms much more rapidly. Food poisoning experts investigating causal bacteria are aware that if the onset of illness is rapid, such as one to three days, the likely cause is an exotoxin-producing bacterium whereas an illness taking longer to appear comes from endotoxins.

After entry into the body, bacteria can be attacked by certain white blood cells capable of surrounding and engulfing the invaders (a process known as phagocytosis). These are the neutrophils, more commonly called phagocytes. Other white blood cells, the lymphocytes, produce antibodies that can attack bacteria direcly. Once again these tend to remain circulating in the bloodstream and can be produced rapidly if infection re-occurs. This means that some bacterial infections, such as scarlet fever and typhoid fever, are unlikely to occur again in the same patient.

Strategies for prevention and treatment

The main method of treating bacterial infections that are not resolved through the immune response is by antibiotic drugs. Many of these drugs can be given by mouth but some are injected. Sometimes antisera are used, particularly when the disease is less well known.

Antisera contain antibodies to the causative agent produced by an individual who has

Tuberculosis (also called TB)

Tuberculosis is an example of a bacterial disease caused by *Mycobacterium tuberculosis,* a disease now rare in developed countries but still common in poorer countries. Infection is caused by inhaling droplets from an infected individual. After inhalation, the bacteria multiply quickly to form a mass; at this stage the immune system may overcome the infection. If so, the mass heals and results in scarring of the lungs.

When the infection is not resolved by the immune system, the bacteria spread via the lymphatics and blood stream to other organs, such as bones, kidneys, intestines and other lymph nodes.

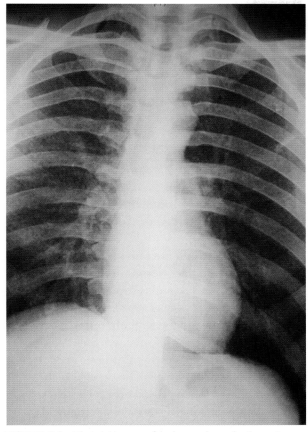

FIGURE 9.9 *Chest X-ray of tuberculous lesions in the lungs – the cloudy mass*

YEAR	NO. OF DEATHS	MORTALITY RATE PER 100,000 POPULATION
1999	383	0.74
2000	373	0.72
2001	375	0.72
2002	386	0.74
2003	393	0.74

TABLE 9.4 *The number of deaths and mortality rate for tuberculosis in England and Wales, 1999–2003*

Adapted from figures produced for the HPA, Dec. 2004

Tuberculosis is a disease associated with malnutrition and poor living conditions. In recent years, it has become more common in the UK as it is an opportunistic infection associated with HIV and AIDS and individuals who are immuno-suppressed, such as transplant patients. Clearly, the disease is more common in people who have contact with a person who already has tuberculosis, those in later adulthood and the population groups in inner-city areas. Around 6,500 cases of tuberculosis are reported each year. In the last 10 years there has been a 25 per cent increase in new cases of the disease. More than 30 per cent of all new cases in England and Wales are immigrant people who have come from the Indian sub-continent.

The main symptoms and signs are coughing, often with blood-stained phlegm or sputum, breathlessness, poor appetite, loss of weight, chest pains, fever and night sweats. The disease can be fatal but in most cases drug therapy restores full health. More serious respiratory complications can occur if untreated.

Diagnosis is usually made from signs and symptoms and a chest X-ray. Bacterial examination and culture of sputum may confirm the diagnosis. A tuberculin test may also be performed. Rarely, a biopsy (small piece) of lung tissue may be sent for pathological examination.

Did you know?

The Heaf test

The Heaf test (a tuberculin test) shows whether an individual has tuberculosis or has been immunised with a BCG injection (see below). A small amount of tuberculin is forced into the surface of the skin in a circle of tiny puncture marks and left for a few days. A positive test is shown by a hard, raised area of tested skin. The test is negative if the skin is almost normal. The test is simple and painless. From September 2005, the Heaf test is replaced by the Mantoux test, used in most other countries. The tuberculin is introduced into the skin by a needle, otherwise the same principles are applied.

Strategy for prevention and treatment

The most important part of controlling TB is identifying and treating those who already have the disease, to shorten their infection and to stop it being passed on to others.

When a case of tuberculosis is diagnosed, the family, close relatives and friends of the individual are traced, tuberculin-tested, X-rayed and examined to ensure that they have not been infected. This is known as contact tracing and is effective at preventing the spread of tuberculosis.

The government chief medical officer published a TB action plan in October 2004 with these aims:

* reduce the risk of new infections
* provide high-quality treatment and care for people with TB
* maintain low levels of drug resistance.

His long-term goal is to reduce and ultimately eliminate TB in this country.

Part of this strategy is to replace the current universal BCG vaccination programme with an improved programme targeting those individuals at greatest risk. The new programme will identify and vaccinate babies and older people who are most likely to catch the disease, especially those living in areas with a high rate of TB or whose parents (or grandparents) were born in a TB high prevalence country.

Modern drugs for TB are very effective. They are given in a combination of three or four different drugs for several months to reduce the formation of drug-resistant strains.

Fungi

Some fungi can cause serious illness and even death in humans while others result in mild disorders. Fungal infections can also give rise to allergic disorders.

Some types of fungi are present on the surface and inside our bodies most of the time, but they are usually in competition with the bacteria in these areas, so rarely get a chance to multiply and cause problems.

Single-celled fungi are known as yeasts and they occur in colonies. A common infection called candidiasis (often known as thrush) is caused by a yeast, *Candida albicans*.

Fungi that invade the skin are often referred to as dermatophytes, and mycoses are diseases caused by fungi. The study of fungi is *mycology*.

Multi-cellular fungi, such as tinea, which causes athlete's foot or ringworm forms thread-like branching structures known as hyphae within the surface layers of the skin. Fungal

FIGURE 9.10 *Candidiasis or thrush is caused by single-celled yeasts – coloured yellow*

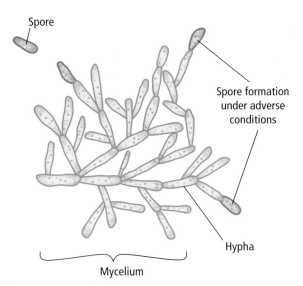

Spore

Spore formation under adverse conditions

Hypha

Mycelium

FIGURE 9.11 *Fungus mycelium and spore formation*

hyphae grow into a colony known as a mycelium and, like bacteria, these have cell walls.

Fungi are unable to make their own food. Most are parasites gaining their nourishment from surroundings by secreting external enzymes to liquefy the tissues before absorption through the hyphal walls. This type of fungus is capable of forming reproductive bodies called spores. Spores can resist unfavourable conditions and start to grow again when conditions improve, to form more hyphae.

Athlete's foot or *Tinea pedis*

Athlete's foot is a communicable disease caused by a dermatophyte, *tinea pedis*. It is more common in teenagers and males, but anybody can get it. The feet provide a warm, moist environment, ideal for fungal growth. People who go barefoot rarely catch this infection, demonstrating that the wearing of shoes is an important factor in maintaining ideal conditions for the dermatophyte. Shower rooms used by many people are frequently the sources of original infections, as the fungus thrives in the warm, damp conditions. However, it can also spread from bedding and clothing.

An itchy, scaly rash appears between the toes, or on the soles or sides of the feet; this is followed by inflammation and blisters. When the blisters burst, the raw skin underneath is exposed and inflamed causing pain and swelling. This stage can last up to ten days, but the infection may persist for months or years.

Toenails are usually infected as well and these are harder to treat; the nail becomes crumbly and hard to cut. Other parts of the body can become infected through scratching the infected area and touching elsewhere such as the groin (jock itch).

Strategies for prevention and treatment

The infection may go away if the area is washed frequently, dried carefully and dusted with talcum powder or foot dusting powder. There are also many good 'over the counter' preparations.

> **Did you know?**
>
> Good foot hygiene prevents athlete's foot.
>
> * wash and dry the feet well every day, particularly between the toes
> * use talcum powder to reduce perspiration
> * avoid close footwear like boots in warm weather
> * use cotton socks to keep feet dry.

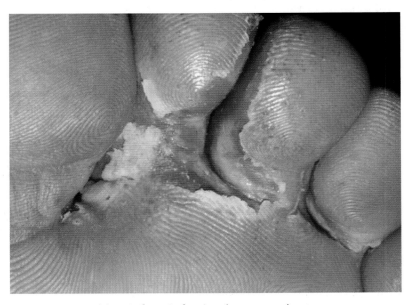

FIGURE 9.12 *Athlete's foot infection between the toes*

DISEASE	CAUSATIVE ORGANISM	TYPE OF ILLNESS
Amoebiasis	Entamoeba histolytica	Diarrhoea often with fever
Trichomoniasis	Trichomonas vaginalis	Sexually-transmitted disease
Malaria	Plasmodium	Serious disease affecting organs and high fever
Sleeping sickness	Trypanosoma	Serious disease affecting organs and high fever

TABLE 9.5 *Protozoan parasites*

Anyone infected with athlete's foot should not walk around barefoot in order to protect others. Special socks are available for wet areas.

Protozoa

Several protozoa are parasites of humans, including those shown in Table 9.5.

Malaria

Malaria is a disease found mainly in Africa, where it causes nearly one million deaths each year. It is also found in Asia, the Middle East, central and southern America, but only 10 per cent of malaria deaths worldwide occur in these countries.

You might not think that many cases of malaria would occur in the UK, as it mainly occurs in hot countries. However, with business people and tourists travelling further and further afield as cheaper airline packages become available, there are now about 2,000 cases of malaria in Britain every year.

> **Did you know?**
>
> An uninfected individual becomes infected by a bite from an infected mosquito and an uninfected mosquito becomes infected by biting an individual with malaria. The mosquito must be a female of the type *Anopheles*.

The malaria-causing protozoon plasmodium, of which there are four species causing disease in humans, spends part of its life cycle in the mosquito and part in human beings.

> **What if?**
>
> If you were suddenly offered the opportunity for a safari holiday in Kenya next week, would you take the risk of getting malaria, a serious, potentially life-threatening disease? You have not got the time to take the full course of anti-malarial drugs and there is no available immunisation.

> **Try it out**
>
> Anti-malarial drugs do not offer 100 per cent protection against contracting malaria. Find out about other precautions that are recommended in a malaria-prone country.

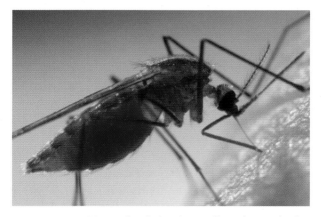

FIGURE 9.13 *Mosquito injecting saliva through the skin surface*

The symptoms of malaria appear within a week or two after being bitten by an infected mosquito; this is often after the individual on holiday has returned to the UK. Many people initially believe that they have influenza.

The mosquito injects saliva into the bite and the parasite uses this as a route to gain entry, first travelling to the liver to multiply and then invading red blood cells.

Did you know?

A vector is an organism that carries pathogens from one host to another. The mosquito is acting as a vector in the transmission of malaria.

Fever, shivering and chills are the first symptoms to appear and coincide with the bursting of infected red blood cells to release more plasmodium organisms into the circulation. One of the four species of plasmodium affects more red blood cells than the others and produces a more severe effect.

The released protozoa invade more red blood cells, multiply again and the cycle is repeated. Infected individuals begin to have a pattern of shivering and fever followed by a high temperature and then heavy sweating.

The destruction of so many red blood cells leads to anaemia and often jaundice.

Did you know?

Jaundice occurs when a high level of bilirubin occurs in the blood. Normally, when old red blood cells are broken down, bilirubin, formed as a by-product of haemoglobin degeneration, is released into bile produced by the liver. This is the pigment that colours faeces brown and so it is eliminated from the body. In malaria, there are so many red blood cells being ruptured that the liver cannot cope and the excess bilirubin gives rise to yellowing of the skin and the whites of the eyes, called jaundice.

In malaria, the feverish (febrile) attacks and the anaemia, together with severe headache, vomiting and malaise (feeling of being unwell) leaves individuals weak and exhausted.

Infected red cells tend to stick together and may block capillaries of vital organs, such as the kidneys and the brain, with serious consequences. Kidney failure, coma and fits are common complications of malaria.

Some red cells become infected with different forms of plasmodium that then infect mosquitoes when the individual is bitten.

Try it out

Create an annotated diagram to illustrate the cycle of infection in both the mosquito and humans.

Strategy for prevention and treatment

Anti-malarial drugs such as chloroquine and primaquine are used in treatment. Severe cases might require blood transfusion.

Anti-malarial drugs are used to decrease the likelihood of getting malaria and regimes are constantly being updated. Additional precautions are recommended – you have researched these on page 128.

Did you know?

Experts in climate change have warned of the possibility of malaria becoming endemic in the UK and Europe in the future.

Immunisation against malaria is the subject of research in many countries but as yet there are problems with the length of immunity and other aspects. The World Health Organization has undertaken a massive attempt to control this disease, but resistance to anti-malarial drugs and insecticides by mosquitoes have prevented improvement. It continues to be a serious problem in a large part of the world.

Try it out

In the unit assessment, you need to compare and contrast a communicable disease with a non-communicable disease. As a practice exercise, compare and contrast influenza and malaria.

Non-communicable diseases

This group of diseases cannot be transmitted from one human being to another in the various ways described for communicable diseases, that is by inhalation, sexual contact, etc. There are no causative micro-organisms that can be identified, although in many non-communicable diseases a cause can be attributed to effects such as a faulty gene, excessive wear and tear, or lack of (or excess of) a particular substance in the diet.

Just as it was possible to categorise communicable diseases into viral, bacterial, etc., so it is possible to subdivide non-communicable diseases, depending on either the type of illness produced or the cause of the condition. In this unit, non-communicable diseases are subdivided into:

* degenerative diseases
* deficiency diseases
* lifestyle/environmental diseases
* inherited diseases.

Degenerative diseases

You will have learned about degenerative changes that take place during the ageing process in Unit 1, *Human growth and development,* but these are natural changes and not disorders. In degenerative disorders, the changes tend to occur earlier than natural changes and are often more rapid and selective in their distribution.

In many of these disorders, the specialised cells making up the tissues are destroyed and replaced by connective or fibrous (scar) tissue.

Some degenerative disorders are given in Table 9.6.

> **Key concept**
>
> *Degenerative disease:* this is a collective term for a number of conditions that demonstrate a decline in the structure and function of organs or parts of the body, when the conditions do not arise as a result of inflammation, infection, malignancy (cancer), altered immunity or damage from external sources.

Some of the conditions shown in Table 9.6 are now recognised as genetically inherited and others (known as familial disorders) are thought to 'run in families'.

Arthritis

> **Key concept**
>
> *Arthritis:* this means inflammation of joints, causing pain and stiffness on movement. There are many different types of arthritis, the main type as a degenerative disease is osteoarthritis.

Osteoarthritis

This is a very common disease that many people over 60 years of age suffer from; the disease can also occur earlier in life, especially when there has been excessive wear and tear on joints.

Women are three times more likely to be affected than men and there is no cure for the condition.

Osteoarthritis is more likely to occur when certain precipitating factors exist, such as:

* joints have been injured
* an individual is obese (extra weight carried)
* other disease processes affect the joint, e.g. gout

DEGENERATIVE DISORDER	PART OF BODY AFFECTED	BRIEF SUMMARY OF CONDITION
Osteoarthritis	Joints	Joint cartilage wears away and bone distorts
Muscular dystrophy	Skeletal muscles	Profound muscle weakness
Retinitis pigmentosa	Eyes	Early blindness
Alzheimer's disease	Brain	Early dementia
Parkinson's disease	Brain	Abnormal movements and stiffness

TABLE 9.6 *Some degenerative conditions*

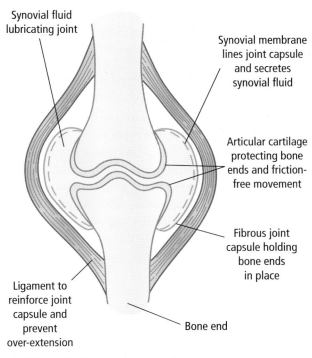

Synovial fluid lubricating joint

Synovial membrane lines joint capsule and secretes synovial fluid

Articular cartilage protecting bone ends and friction-free movement

Fibrous joint capsule holding bone ends in place

Ligament to reinforce joint capsule and prevent over-extension

Bone end

FIGURE 9.14 *The structure of a joint*

* excessive sports or dance activities have been carried out (e.g. professional footballers, tennis players, ballet dancers)

* a congenital deformity or incorrect alignment of bones exists.

All these predisposing factors result in increased wear and tear, or stem from a long-standing condition.

Articular (joint) cartilage lines bone surfaces within the joint cavity and forms a smooth, slippery surface which protects the underlying bone and allows virtually friction-free movement.

Cartilage, which is not as hard as bone, does not have a direct blood supply as this would interfere with its function; instead it is nourished by nutrients from the underlying bone. This means that cartilage has reduced powers of healing, unlike most tissues of the body with good blood supplies. Cartilage cells (chondrocytes) are imprisoned in spaces between their glassy secretions and are therefore poorly nourished. As a consequence of these factors, repair of cartilage tissue does not take place. For example, veteran boxers can often be distinguished due to 'cauliflower' ears from repeated injuries to their ear cartilages.

In osteoarthritis, the worn cartilage can be missing in certain joint areas and can become rough and flaky in other places. Some bits of cartilage may actually break off and lie freely within the joint cavity. These are termed 'loose bodies'; they can cause the joint to lock temporarily and can be quite troublesome.

In affected joints, certain bone cells become active and cause overgrowth and distortion of bone at the margins – these are called osteophytes. The whole joint may look swollen, enlarged and deformed.

Due partly to the osteophytes and partly to the pain, the stiffened joint is not used as much, resulting in the surrounding muscles becoming weaker. The patient complains of pain, swelling, stiffness of the joint and being unable to carry out normal daily activities.

Doctors will diagnose the condition from the signs and symptoms and from X-rays of the affected joints.

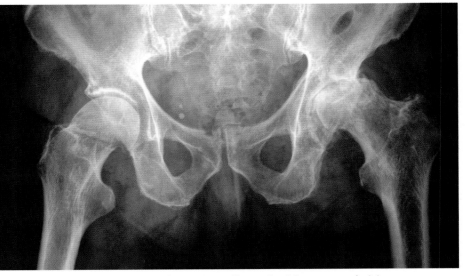

FIGURE 9.15 *X-ray to show a hip joint affected with osteoarthritis*

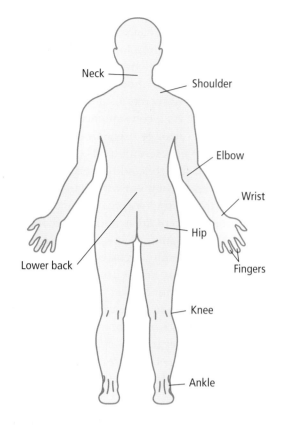

FIGURE 9.16 *Main joints affected by osteoarthritis*

The main joints affected by osteoarthritis are the weight-bearing hips, knees and spine, but shoulders, elbows, wrists, ankles and fingers can also cause trouble.

Strategy for prevention and treatment

One of the most important ways to both prevent and treat osteoarthritis is to maintain an ideal weight for height, especially into middle and later adulthood, to avoid carrying excess weight on the skeleton and joints.

Losing weight can benefit obese sufferers by providing considerable relief from symptoms. Analgesics or painkillers and physiotherapy exercises will also help. Swimming is an ideal way to maintain muscle strength while not bearing weight on the joints. Steroid injections may help some people, but ultimately the patient might have to undergo a joint replacement with an artificial joint (arthroplasty) or have the joint, if practicable, immobilised (arthrodesis).

Deficiency diseases

Dietary deficiencies are fairly rare in developed countries and conditions related to diet are more likely to involve over-consumption.

Individuals who practise very restricted diets, have problems absorbing nutrients from food, or are alcoholics are the main groups of patients presenting with dietary deficiencies in the UK.

Deficiency diseases, once diagnosed, are relatively easy to treat as the deficiency can be addressed relatively simply in western countries.

> **Key concept**
>
> *Deficiency diseases:* this group of conditions arises when one or more components necessary for a healthy life is lacking from the body. The term is mostly used in conjunction with dietary deficiencies, particularly in poor countries.

Two serious conditions found in children of poor countries are *kwashiorkor* and *marasmus*. Both afflict children under three years old, who have been weaned from the breast on to a diet lacking in the proteins and calories needed for growth and health. Untreated children may die. Children who receive treatment may have stunted growth and mental impairment.

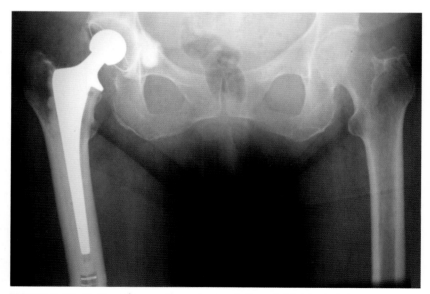

FIGURE 9.17 *X-ray of an arthroplasty at the right hip joint*

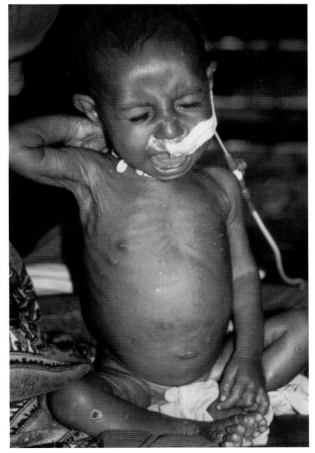

FIGURE 9.18 *Infant with protein deficiency disease*

Anaemia

Possibly the most common deficiency disease in the UK is *iron-deficiency anaemia*.

Anaemia occurs when the requirements for iron and loss of iron from persistent bleeding or menstruation is greater than that gained from the diet. Although menstruation stops temporarily during pregnancy, the demands for the growing baby tend to push most women into a degree of anaemia, requiring iron supplements.

Most of the iron from old red blood cells is recycled and stored in the liver, but there is always a small loss, from shed skin, and from intestinal lining cells. Any disease process causing bleeding, such as peptic ulcers, haemorrhoids, tumours of various kinds and heavy menstrual losses, may lead to anaemia.

Inadequate iron intake may arise in older people who live alone, individuals on slimming diets, children with food fads and pregnant women. Plant iron is less well-absorbed than iron from animal meat but generally vegans and vegetarians manage to maintain iron balance; this may be due to a high intake of vitamin C which facilitates iron absorption.

Individuals who are iron-deficient have pale mucous membranes (such as inside the mouth), facial and nail bed pallor, and complain of breathlessness on exertion, fatigue, headaches and sometimes chest pain.

These signs and symptoms may be in addition to those of any underlying causative disease process.

Try it out

Some other vitamin deficiency diseases are called night blindness, beriberi, rickets and pellagra. Find out:

* which dietary components are lacking

* the main symptoms produced

* whether particular life stages are affected as with kwashiorkor and marasmus.

Collect your data and compile a table for presenting your research.

Scurvy

Scurvy is a deficiency disease caused by a lack of vitamin C or ascorbic acid. This is important in the formation of connective tissues which are the 'binding and fastening' tissues of the body. Inadequate supplies of ascorbic acid lead to weak connective tissue formation, frail blood vessels and poor healing.

Individuals with scurvy have bleeding gums and loose teeth, evidence of haemorrhaging in the skin (and elsewhere, but these are less visible), leading to the appearance of bruising. Bleeds into bones and muscles cause severe pain and children may have stunted growth. There are often other associated vitamin deficiencies.

Scurvy can be fatal if untreated, but the incidence is rare in developed countries as fresh fruit and vegetables usually form part of the diet. Liver, kidney and milk also contain ascorbic acid, but in lower amounts than fruit and vegetables.

Treatment of scurvy is by large doses of vitamin C. Prevention is by maintaining an adequate intake of fresh fuit (particularly citrus fruit, strawberries and blackcurrants) and vegetables.

Diseases associated with lifestyle or the environment

The actions and habits of individuals may predispose them to health hazards, as may the environment in which they carry out their daily activities.

Many conditions fall into this category, such as alcohol dependency, drug dependency, lung cancer and heart disease as a consequence of smoking, skin cancers due to solar exposure and even dental caries.

You have already learned about some of these conditions in Unit 1, *Human growth and development,* and may wish to revise these and perhaps carry out further research.

To extend your knowledge further, this section of this unit will examine solar exposure and dental caries.

Skin cancer due to solar exposure

Skin cancer is one of the most common malignant conditions. There are three types, all of which seem to be related in some way to solar exposure over a long time.

Basal cell carcinoma

The bottom layer of the skin epidermis is an actively growing layer that pushes new cells towards the surface to replace (in time) the dead cell layers that are shed from the outer surface of the skin. Exposure to ultra-violet radiation may cause some of these cells to react abnormally. This layer also contains special cells called melanocytes which produce a black/brown pigment called melanin. Fair-skinned individuals have few melanocytes whereas dark-skinned people have a large number. Melanin absorbs UV radiation and protects deeper layers of the skin, so damage from UV radiation is less likely to occur.

When basal cells are out of control and start to divide more rapidly a flat, slow-growing 'spot' appears on the face or neck. As this grows larger the edges become 'heaped' up or rolled and the centre begins to ulcerate. The most common areas are above a line drawn from the mouth to the ear. This type of facial tumour is often called a 'rodent ulcer' because if untreated, it erodes the tissues underneath and can become very deep. Usually, an individual will seek medical help before the carcinoma becomes too large, mainly because it is located on the face. When diagnosed early, recovery is good.

Strategy for prevention and treatment

Fair-skinned people should not expose their skin to sunshine for long periods. Hats and other protective clothing should be worn and a high-factor sunscreen preparation or even total sun-block should be used as regularly as necessary depending on the climatic conditions. Sunshine around mid-day should be avoided whenever possible by staying indoors or in the shade. In hot countries, fair-skinned people should be particularly careful. In the UK, there are an estimated 30,000 cases annually and with higher temperatures due to global warming and the fashionable appearance of looking tanned, these figures are rising. Fair-skinned people should resort to fake tan and sun protection. Treatment can be by radiotherapy, surgical removal or cryosurgery (freezing with liquid nitrogen).

Malignant melanoma

In the bottom layer of the epidermis of the skin, there are special cells producing a black/brown

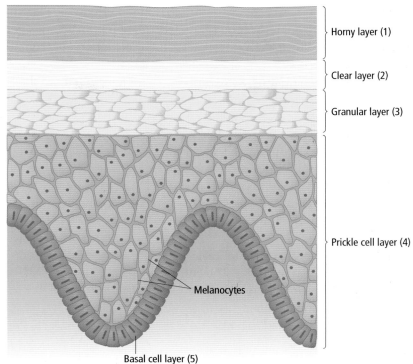

Horny layer (1)

Clear layer (2)

Granular layer (3)

Prickle cell layer (4)

Melanocytes

FIGURE 9.19 *Section through the skin*

Basal cell layer (5)

pigment that protects against solar radiaton. These cells, called melanocytes, may also divide in an uncontrolled fashion to produce a melanoma.

Melanomas can appear on any part of the body and unlike basal cell carcinoma, can spread to other parts of the body and can prove fatal. Melanomas start commonly from a mole although they can start from normal skin. Moles are rather like pigmented birthmarks. The mole gets larger and lumpier, and may change colour and bleed.

Strategies for prevention and treatment
Early diagnosis is very important to prevent spread. Many people now have suspect moles surgically removed to prevent melanomas developing. Any mole that starts to get larger should be referred for medical opinion quickly. Surgical removal of the mole is carried out and radiotherapy and anti-cancer therapy used as appropriate. The condition, once again, is more prevalent in fair-skinned people over 60 years of age.

Squamous cell carcinoma
This cancer is also related to solar exposure for many years and associated with pale skins and people over 60 years. The tumour occurs in people who have worked with certain chemicals such as oils, coal tar and paraffins, and those who have been exposed to the sun. Hands, ears and lips are common sites. The cancer starts as a firm painless lump, often resembling a wart or ulcer that slowly gets bigger. This cancer can spread to other parts of the body and can be fatal.

Strategies for prevention and treatment
Any suspicious lesion on the skin surface should be referred to a doctor. A skin biopsy is carried out and if diagnosed, surgical removal of the tumour is follwed by radiotherapy and anti-cancer drugs as appropriate.

Try it out

* Discuss your own behaviour in the sun with a small group of peers. Would you change your behaviour in the light of the information you have gained?

* Design a questionnaire to survey the sun behaviour of a group of other peers. Analyse and present your findings.

* Design a leaflet to provide health-related information to young people on the dangers of exposure to the sun.

Dental caries

Dental caries is the professional term for tooth decay caused by the sticky substance on teeth known as plaque.

Plaque is a mixture of food debris, saliva, mucus and the bacteria that normally inhabit the mouth. When plaque is not removed regularly by brushing and flossing, the bacteria, nourished by sugary deposits from food, produce an acid as a by-product. The acid gradually erodes the hard enamel covering the teeth. When the enamel is holed, the destruction will continue deeper into the dentine layer and the pulp cavity if the tooth is not treated.

Pain or toothache is a feature of dental caries that has advanced deeper into the tooth. The entry of bacteria into the body through here may be a more serious problem for some patients, such as those who are immune-suppressed as a result of organ transplantation.

Strategy for prevention and treatment

Good dental hygiene and regular check-ups by the dentist will enable small cavities to be treated early. Tooth removal or extraction may be necessary in some instances. Using fluoride toothpaste or adding fluoride to drinking water hardens the enamel of teeth making it more resistant to decay. The latter course of action can meet with resistance from certain groups who object to mass treatment by interference to water supplies and the removal of individual choice.

NHS dental practices are declining rapidly as more and more dentists change to private practice (where full fees are charged for the work). Some dentists have been encouraged to come to Britain and work in the NHS dental service, but there are still dentally-deprived areas. Many people cannot afford private dentistry, resulting in large geographical areas having no 'free' dental services for several years. This means that many children and adults will suffer from advanced dental caries in the future.

Modern diets containing increased quantities of sugars and refined carbohydrates will also produce greater levels of dental caries. Although drinks like cola have long been known to be linked to caries, there has recently been a report showing that drinks perceived as 'healthy' also contain unacceptably large quantities of sugar.

Source: *Public Health News*, July 2005

Inherited diseases

Key concept

Inherited diseases: this is a group of diseases passed from one person to another by the genes they inherit from their parents or forebears.

Did you know?

Human beings have 23 pairs of chromosomes in the nuclei of their body cells. One of each pair has come from the father and the other from the mother. A characteristic, such as hair colour, is located in the same place on one pair of chromosomes. Each chromosome carries one half of a gene, known as an allele. The alleles may be both the same, say for black hair or blonde hair, or may be different (one allele for black hair and one for blonde hair). In this example, the hair colour from mixed alleles will be black because black is the dominant allele and the blonde allele is recessive. A recessive allele will not show itself in the individual when a dominant allele is present. This means that an individual with blonde hair must have two recessive alleles whereas black hair may result from two dominant alleles or one of each.

Alleles responsible for inherited diseases may be either dominant or recessive.

Two 'normal' parents may have a child affected by an inherited condition because they have both donated a recessive allele responsible for that condition. They may be totally unaware that they carry an affected allele.

Recessive alleles are usually denoted by a lower case letter and dominant alleles by an upper case letter.

For more information on inheritance and the many conditions which fall into the category of inherited diseases, see Unit 1, *Factors affecting human growth and development*.

In this unit, you will learn about cystic fibrosis and haemophilia. The former is a recessive autosomal disorder whereas the latter is a sex-linked recessive condition.

Cystic fibrosis (CF)

This disorder is also known as mucoviscidosis as it is characterised by the production of very thick (viscid) mucus (muco-) that is unable to flow easily and lubricate the intestines, nose, mouth, throat, bronchi and bronchioles. CF remains a serious disorder causing chronic lung infections and an impaired ability to absorb fats and other nutrients from food. People with CF are affected from birth, and previously most sufferers died in childhood. With modern antibiotic treatment, physiotherapy and replacement pancreatic enzymes, most patients with CF now reach adult life.

Some individuals carrying two recessive alleles develop early symptoms but others may not show anything for a long time.

Typically, there are recurrent infections, particularly of the upper respiratory tract and of the chest, and these can cause lung damage. Motions are often putty-coloured, greasy and 'smelly'. This is due to the sparsity of pancreatic enzymes. Sweat glands often do not function well and sweat is extra salty; this may give rise to heatstroke in hot weather.

Infertility can occur in both sexes and the condition may be diagnosed in adult life as a result of investigations by infertility clinics.

Children may be classed as 'failing to thrive' and growth may be impaired. The condition affects about one in 2,000 births, but seems to be more prevalent in the white caucasion population.

Strategy for prevention and treatment

Genetic research studies have found that the allele for cystic fibrosis exists on chromosome 7, and it is now possible for both parents to have tests for cystic fibrosis and to receive genetic counselling. Parents may choose to have the pregnancy terminated if a foetus is found by CVS or amniocentesis to have the condition. Not every couple has pregnancy tests like these; there has to be an element of known risk, such as a family history of the condition.

SCENARIO

A case of cystic fibrosis

Barry and Jean have a young son, Darren, who is two years old. Darren has been hospitalised three times for chest infections in his short life and has recently been diagnosed with CF. His parents have been extremely anxious about him many times and Jean has given up her part-time job to take care of him. She has learned to give Darren physiotherapy exercises twice every day and other special measures.

Barry and Jean would love to have another baby next year but fear that they could not cope with having another child affected with CF. The consultant has explained that there are tests that can be carried out during pregnancy to detect CF (chorionic villus sampling and amniocentesis). Barry and Jean wish to know the extent of the risk of having a baby with CF.

Obviously, Barry and Jean both carry a recessive allele for CF as Darren has CF.

Work out the chances of a second baby in this family also having CF.

Heart/lung or lung transplants can be given to individuals with cystic fibrosis who have suffered serious lung damage.

Physiotherapy to drain the viscid mucus and pancreatin supplements, together with a nourishing diet enhanced by vitamin supplements, enable individuals with CF to reach adulthood.

Try it out

Use the Internet to investigate the types of support given to adults and children with CF.

Haemophilia

This is a sex-linked recessive inherited disorder that results in blood failing to clot properly due to the lack of a specific factor known as Factor VIII. Technically, both sexes can inherit the condition but in practice it is almost exclusive to males. The haemophilia recessive allele is carried on an X chromosome. The normal allele for blood clotting is dominant.

Did you know?

An individual who has an affected recessive allele for a disorder such as haemophilia, but does not themselves suffer from the condition (because a normal dominant allele is present on the other chromosome of the pair), is often called a 'carrier'.

Haemophilia is commonly called the bleeding disorder. Most individuals suffer from spontaneous or accidental bleeds from minor

Try it out

Using your knowledge of genetics, find out why individuals suffering from haemophilia are nearly all males and a female haemophiliac is extremely rare. Demonstrate your knowledge by creating appropriate patterns of inheritance with explanatory annotations.

injuries. Bleeds are often into muscles and joints, causing severe pain and frequently deformities of joints. Bleeds also occur elsewhere in the body and necessitate frequent hospitalisations. Problems start to arise when children start to be mobile, and in the past, many children with haemophilia did not reach adulthood.

Strategy for prevention and treatment

Modern treatment has enabled haemophiliac children to survive into adulthood, but quality of life is variable. Factor VIII is now available in synthetic form and from pooled donor blood. Regular infusions can be given to prevent bleeding episodes or after injury to stop bleeding. Many haemophiliacs are able to administer Factor VIII for themselves.

Haemophiliacs must be careful to choose activities that provide exercise without the risk of major injury, such as swimming.

Try it out

Investigate sources of support for adults and children with haemophilia using the Internet and other sources of reference.

SCENARIO

A case of haemophilia

Sally has a brother with haemophilia and has learned at first-hand how the condition affected his quality of life.

During Sally's first pregnancy she learned that she was a carrier of haemophilia, and Sally and her husband have been carefully counselled during each of her three pregnancies. She had a termination of a male foetus after two years of marriage and now has three daughters. Her last baby was born three months ago and several neighbours and friends have commented on

'another girl' and how they must have 'hoped for a boy this time'. Try to imagine how Sally and her husband feel receiving comments such as these. They do not explain as most people would not understand the pattern of inheritance or have heard about haemophilia.

* Discuss suitable responses for well-minded but ignorant friends.

* Find out about the risks of one of Sally's daughters being a 'carrier' of the haemophiliac allele.

Genetic counselling is available for families with a history of haemophilia, although identifying the sex of a foetus is important here due to the rarity of female haemophilia.

In the past, individuals with haemophilia were given transfused blood from donors and many developed viral hepatitis, HIV and AIDS from infected blood. Some sexual partners were infected too.

> **Try it out**
>
> In the unit assessment, you will compare a communicable disease with a non-communicable disease. As a practice exercise, compare and contrast these two inherited conditions, CF and haemophilia.

Differences between communicable and non-communicable diseases

You have learned about many communicable diseases and non-communicable diseases in this section and now need to identify the differences between them.

Causes of diseases

Communicable diseases are caused by micro-organisms such as *viruses, bacteria, fungi* and *protozoa.* Non-communicable diseases are not caused by micro-organisms.

Non-communicable diseases may be caused by unexplained or explained tissue deterioration, deficiency of a substance necessary for health, inherited genes, lifestyle choices or environmental effects.

Communicable diseases are not caused by these factors, although the same factors may influence the outcome and spread of a communicable disease. For example, tuberculosis is more prevalent in poor living conditions and influenza spreads rapidly in overcrowded situations.

Spread of diseases

Communicable diseases spread from one organism to another – usually from human to human, but sometimes using a vector.

Non-communicable diseases do not spread from one organism to another. They are not infectious.

Communicable diseases must have a 'portal of entry' or a gateway into the body such as through inhalation, ingested food or drink, through punctures of the skin, sexual contact or direct contact. Most non-communicable diseases begin internally although external stimuli may be an important factor, as with smoking and lung cancer.

Life stages of affected individuals

Communicable diseases generally can affect people at any life stage. Many infections result in immunity of various lengths. This does not mean the individual is never invaded by the micro-organisms again, but rather that the 'full-blown' disease never develops because the body defences rapidly overcome the infection. Some infections have, therefore, a greater impact at specific life stages such as infancy and childhood, for example measles and diphtheria.

Non-communicable diseases are often linked with specific life stages. For example, Alzheimer's disease and osteoarthritis are linked with later adulthood and CF and haemophilia with infancy and childhood.

Treatment of patients

Communicable diseases are most often treated by anti-microbial drugs whereas non-communicable diseases are not. The latter are mainly treated palliatively, that is to bring about the easing of symptoms but not a cure. Sometimes replacement organs or other parts of the body may also be necessary, for example joint replacement for osteoarthritis. This is not usually the case in communicable diseases.

Immunity plays a large part in preventing communicable disease, but so far immune responses are seldom available for non-communicable diseases.

Communicable diseases tend to clear up with treatment whereas non-communicable diseases tend to get gradually worse.

Support for diseases

Temporary support for communicable diseases may be necessary but non-communicable diseases tend to require long-term support from family, friends, relatives, NHS personnel and possibly social services.

Self-help groups and charitable support agencies are plentiful for non-communicable diseases but are far less common for communicable diseases.

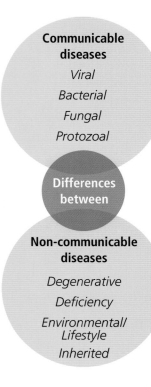

Communicable diseases

Viral

Bacterial

Fungal

Protozoal

Differences between

Non-communicable diseases

Degenerative

Deficiency

Environmental/ Lifestyle

Inherited

Try it out

In small groups, make lists of all the voluntary agencies that you can think of, either locally or nationally. Sort them into lists of those giving support for communicable and non-communicable diseases.

Try to categorise the non-communicable diseases supported by these agencies into degenerative, deficiency, lifestyle/environment and inherited conditions.

Consider this

Mary has two children; James, aged 4, and Kylie who is 6 years old. James has haemophilia and had a severe nose bleed last week and Kylie is ill with viral gastro-enteritis, which seems to be going round her primary school.

Compare and contrast these two conditions in terms of:

1. the biological basis of the disease
2. the body's response to the disease
3. the causes of the conditions
4. the distribution of the conditions in Mary's locality.

9.3 Diagnosis, treatment and support of disease

Key concept

Clinical diagnosis: this occurs when an individual, usually a doctor or another health care worker, is able to establish the nature of the disease mainly by giving the condition a name, such as meningitis.

Differential diagnosis: a few conditions may appear similar and the doctor cannot provide a clinical diagnosis as he/she is unable to distinguish one from the other. This consists of a more generic label or name, for example chest infection or kidney infection.

Clinical diagnoses can often be determined from the signs and symptoms that the patient displays.

With some diseases, particularly those resulting from infections, there may be similar signs and symptoms such as fever, headache, rapid pulse and breathing rates. In this case, the diagnosis may be of the differential type. Swabs of secretions and blood and urine samples may be sent for laboratory examination and culture. Laboratory technicians grow the micro-organisms from swabs or samples of fluid in a special medium so that there are enough organisms for analysis and identification. There are many other more specialised investigative techniques that can be used if diagnosis is proving difficult.

Rarely, a specific diagnosis may never be reached and the patient gradually recovers, probably due to an immune response.

Diagnosis and treatment by the individual

Many common conditions can be diagnosed and treated by the affected individual without the need for appointments with the family doctor or hospital visits. There are more and more 'over-the-counter' preparations for treating common ailments.

Service users may also use NHS Direct or the Internet to assist them with a diagnosis and treatment.

Diagnosis and treatment by a local health practice

When an individual feels that he or she is unable to deal with a health problem, an appointment is made with the GP or practice nurse in the local health centre. Most service users expect to get a diagnosis and medication as a consequence of this visit. Appointments can be subject to one or two days' delay when the matter is not deemed to be urgent, and sometimes the patient begins to improve and does not attend. This is an expensive waste of time and resources for the practice, so it is important to cancel the appointment as soon as possible so that another patient can be attended to.

Especially in the winter months, many patients attend with viral infections of the upper respiratory tract, such as colds and influenza. Unless the patient has a pre-existing medical condition, such as heart or lung disease, there is little that a doctor can do other than suggest keeping warm, plenty of rest and fluids, and staying home to limit the infection of others.

Many people do not understand this and feel 'cheated' when they do not receive medication. There are a large number of cold and 'flu remedies on the market that people can use, and although they appear expensive they are cheaper than obtaining prescriptions.

Obviously, many people attend the health centre for more worrying 'new' symptoms and might need the first stage of laboratory investigations together with a full examination and history-taking. Some patients will be successfully treated at the health centre while others will need referral to a hospital for a more in-depth investigation, specialist help and/or treatment. Other patients in the practice will attend for regular checks on the progress of long-term conditions such as angina, hypertension, arthritis, heart or renal failure. Such patients might be seen by the practice nurse who will refer the patient to the doctor as necessary.

Most health centres offer more specialist clinics for family planning, maternity, hypertension, immunisations, etc.

Large numbers of patients registered to a general practice may not visit the centre in years, but feel safe knowing that the help is there when needed. Others suffer extreme anxiety in the presence of health care workers and put off visiting the practice with the most urgent of symptoms. It is always surprising what some individuals will suffer in the terms of signs and symptoms before consulting a doctor, while others are constantly making appointments for trivial health problems. When the nature of the illness is very sensitive, such as infertility, incontinence, impotence, fear of pregnancy or sexually-transmitted disease, a patient will often make an appointment to discuss a totally different health problem, and just as they are about to leave approach the real difficulty with a, 'By the way, while I am here...'. Doctors frequently refer to this as 'the hand on the doorknob' complaint.

Each individual receiving prescriptions over a long period must periodically undergo a review of their medication. This is often carried out by the practice nurse.

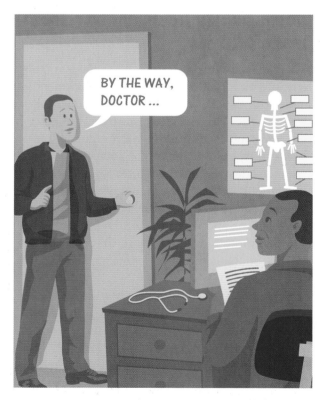

FIGURE 9.20 *The 'hand on the doorknob' complaint*

Pharmacy Stamp

CKM

NHS No:

Name
Address
of service user

Please don't stamp over age box
Number of days' treatment
N.B. Ensure dose is stated

Endorsements

HOSPITAL PRESCRIBER

HP

FP10NC0403

Prescriber's name and initials in block capitals

Signature of Prescriber

Date

13/09/05

For dispenser
No. of Prescns. on form

HP

Name
Address
of Health Care Unit

L7 8XP

RQ6

NHS PATIENTS – please read the notes overleaf

44521422918

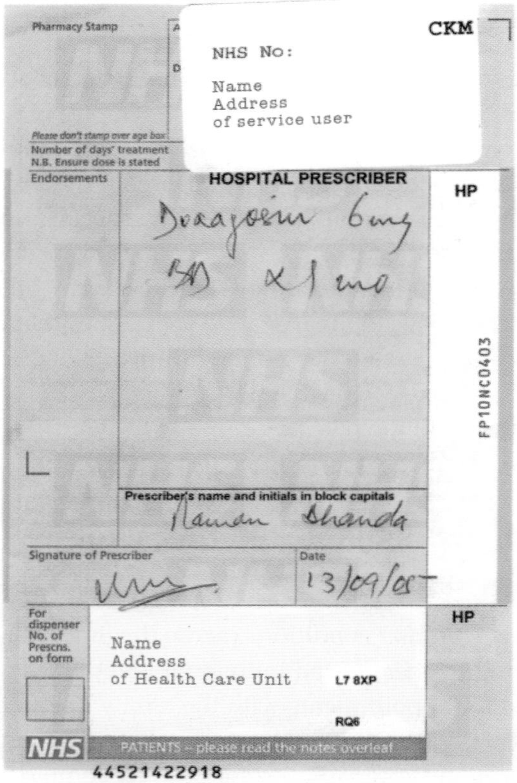

FIGURE 9.21 *A standard prescription form*

Diagnosis and treatment by a local hospital

A GP may refer a patient to a hospital for a variety of reasons. Some of these are:

* for more detailed investigations such as X-rays, scans, ultrasound scans, electrocardiograms, special laboratory investigations

* to book a bed for childbirth and support the practice with pregnancy monitoring

* for surgical procedures

* for closer monitoring and care

* for psychiatric, medical and surgical emergencies

* when a patient is ill and has nobody at home to act as carer

* if a patient has a serious infection, such as pneumonia, tuberculosis or malaria, requiring specialist care and treatment

* when a patient has a serious non-communicable disease that needs specialist care, such as heart and renal failure, cancers and some inherited diseases

* when a GP is unable to provide a precise clinical diagnosis.

Patients can use the hospital without GP referral when an accident or emergency arises and where there is an 'out of hours' GP service actually based in the hospital through an appointment system.

The hospital always works closely with the GP who provides the initial details of the need for referral. The hospital, via the consultant of the department, keeps the GP informed of the type of care being given and drug regimes.

This is important because after discharge, the GP will continue to provide the medication even though the service user may still be visiting the hospital as an out-patient. Both the GP and the hospital personnel will regularly review medication and care received.

A health district with a population of 250–500,000 people will have a district general hospital providing medical, surgical, obstetric and gynaecological, psychiatric and paediatric services.

Diagnosis and treatment at a specialist national centre

You may live near a specialist hospital or have read about the work of national centres.

Not surprisingly, many national specialist centres are located around the capital or close to renowned universities where research is conducted. However, there are other centres, often located in large cities, which have become highly specialised. Some are listed in Table 9.7 below.

Table 9.7 is not a definitive list, and you may be able to add several more specialist centres. For instance, there are important and famous children's hospitals in Sheffield and Birmingham.

Try it out

Using the Internet investigate the work of national centres for special conditions.

All hospitals produce annual reports and you can get further information from these – most are on the Internet.

Not everybody with cancer will be able to visit a national oncology centre, and not everybody with an eye disease will go to Moorfields Hospital. However, these are leading diagnosis, care and treatment centres in their areas of excellence. They also produce research papers to keep treatment at other hospitals up to date. Consultants visit the specialist centres and may even work there for a time. Conferences are also held to share experiences and knowledge.

Facilities to support individuals with diseases

As well as key medical personnel in general practice and hospitals, there are many other agencies that provide support to individuals, and particularly those people with non-communicable diseases who need long-term support. Support may be of the self-help type where information is shared between individuals to assist daily living or to provide information. Some agencies aim to improve the quality of life by the provision of social activities, including fund-raising events and outings.

NAME OF SPECIALIST CENTRE	LOCATION	SPECIALISM
Stoke Mandeville Hospital	Near Aylesbury, Bucks	Spinal injuries
Papworth Hospital	Cambridge	Cardiothoracic surgery
Gt Ormond Street Hospital	London	Paediatrics
Moorfields Hospital	London	Eye complaints
Royal Marsden Hospital	London area	Cancers (Oncology)
Royal Brompton Hospital	London area	Cardiothoracic diseases and surgery
Nuffield Orthopaedic Hospital	Oxford	Orthopaedics
Clatterbridge Hospital	Wirral, NW England	Cancers (Oncology)
Walton Hospital	Liverpool	Neurology and neurosurgery
Royal Liverpool and Broadgreen University Hospital	Liverpool	Cardiothoracic diseases and surgery
Christies Hospital	Manchester	Cancers (Oncology)

TABLE 9.7 *Some specialist hospitals*

Useful assistance with daily living tasks may be provided by groups such as social services or 'meals on wheels'.

Support from charities and support groups

There are too many charities and support groups to provide a full list but here are a few to get you thinking of others:

* MIND supports mental health patients

* Cystic Fibrosis Trust

* Age Concern supports older people, especially those in poverty and illness

* Terence Higgins Trust is for people with HIV and AIDS.

Support groups attached to local hospitals or health promotion units may be related to strokes, cancers and heart attacks.

Try it out

Working in small groups, write on sticky notes all the names of charities and support groups for people with diseases in your local area. Attach these to a large piece of paper and try to find examples of the ways in which they offer support to people. Search the Internet to add to your knowledge.

As a group, select two agencies from your list and invite speakers to provide first-hand information. Decide on an activity to support those two groups, perhaps helping on a flag day, or at an open day.

A friend or family member may have received support from a group and be willing to be interviewed or give a short talk on the type of support given.

Support from clinics

Many patients receive ongoing support from clinics specialising in one particular condition. There are diabetic clinics, various transplant clinics, hypertension, cervical smear and family planning clinics, to mention only a few. Each medical clinic will monitor particular aspects of a person's health, often by regular checks on blood chemistry (glucose, creatinine, urea, etc.). Regular physical checks (blood pressure, cells visible in smears, films from mammography units, and the status of contraceptive devices) can also be used to provide support.

Service users who might be on continuous medication, such as anticoagulants or immuno-suppressive drugs, will need levels of these drugs in the blood monitored at frequent intervals to maximise their potential, and to prevent over-medication or serious side-effects. Such checks are carried out in clinics and out-patient departments. The number of visits to the latter can be minimised by short frequent clinic visits often managed by specialist nurses.

Try it out

Interview someone you know who regularly attends a clinic, to investigate the activities carried out there.

Support from domestic care

As well as family, relatives, neighbours and friends there are also people employed by other agencies, who will support people with illnesses in their own homes. The principal agency is social services, but there may also be assistance from the NHS, charities and voluntary groups. Some local businesses will also provide home visits, such as chiropody and hairdressing services. Many supermarkets will now provide home delivery services of groceries and household items for a charge, although access to the Internet is usually required.

What if?

You live alone in a first-floor apartment and have broken a leg. Apart from this, you are in good health. How will you manage your daily activities? Find out what equipment you might need and the agencies that might supply such equipment.

In order to assist service users or provide information within your assessment, you will need to establish the needs of patients and obtain accurate information about the availability of services in your locality. Rural areas are not likely to have as many local services as urban areas. Deprived inner city areas with high crime rates will probably have poorer facilities than suburban areas as voluntary providers are reluctant to serve there, so each locality will be different.

Try it out

Invite a speaker from your local social services to provide an overview of home services in your area.

Service users may not be aware of any specific needs in their daily lives and good listening skills may be necessary to identify physical, social, intellectual or emotional needs. After identification of needs, most service users will not be aware of available services. It is wise to take time for a service user to get used to the idea of assistance and not to make snap judgements. If a service user is involved with a care plan, his or her needs may already be known and handled by professional carers, such as social services.

The service user must be able to move at their own pace with regard to support and must be in agreement with any suggestions. However, if a service user does not have a care plan, some suggestions may be offered when the time is judged suitable. Information regarding support must be offered in small doses to avoid confusion.

Did you know?

The Citizens Advice Bureau (CAB) is a valuable resource for information. You might ask your teacher if a speaker from your local CAB could be invited to tell your group about agencies likely to provide support for people with illnesses in their own homes.

You should have heard of some of the following services:

* mobile libraries
* mobile shops
* Internet banking
* home helps (social services, other providers)
* services provided by faith organisations
* Council for Voluntary Services
* Meals on Wheels
* bereavement support organisations
* toy libraries
* Age Concern.

Try it out

Construct a group database of services which support people in their own homes, using a computerised database or a card system. Provide the name, address, telephone number and email address, with a short description of the types of support available.

SCENARIO

Meg

Meg is a 79-year-old widow with severe osteoarthritis in her hips and knees. She depended on her late husband for transport, shopping and household chores as her mobility is severely impaired. Her beloved husband died suddenly from a heart attack three months ago. She is a neighbour of yours and you have hardly seen her since the funeral. When you pay her a visit, you are shocked at her decline; Meg has lost weight, her house and personal hygiene have seriously deteriorated and she seems very depressed. Meg is an independent person and will not use social services as she feels that these services are for other people, not her, and she will be letting her husband down by going to them for help.

How would you approach the situation in order to help Meg?

Factors which may affect the availability of support, investigations and treatment regimes

In theory, everyone in the UK has the right to the diagnosis, treatment and support of an illness. In practice this does not always work out in the best way possible for the service user. There may be a mistaken or unclear diagnosis, delayed investigations due to lack of available equipment, lack of specialised staff, lack of hospital beds, or treatment that cannot be supplied because of cost.

Self-diagnosis and treatment

When individuals diagnose an illness for themselves, such as a headache, a pain or sore throat, they may be masking more serious illness by treating the condition with over-the-counter medicines. Unless they contact local health services, investigations will not be carried out and support will not be offered.

In some circumstances, this may have serious consequences and a correct diagnosis will be made too late for correct treatment and support.

On the other hand, the self-diagnosis and treatment of minor ailments will release more time for doctors, laboratory technicians and support personnel to devote to people suffering from more serious complaints.

Cost of medicines and other consumables

Some service users are exempt from paying prescription charges (pensioners, unemployed people), but others have to pay a designated sum for each item on their prescriptions. There are certain schemes whereby people on long-term medication can pay less, but for some people prescription charges can be a considerable burden on their income. Consumable items such as dressings, micropore tape and incontinence pads also attract prescription charges when prescribed by the doctors in a general practice.

There are many people on low incomes who avoid visits to a general practice for as long as possible because of the relatively high cost of prescription items. As a result, people may suffer unnecessarily from conditions that could be treated or supported.

On the reverse side of a prescription, there is a list of tick boxes for persons who are exempted from charges to complete. Many service users believe that all medications and consumables are cheaper by prescription than from a pharmacy – this is not always so. You can find out the real cost of prescription items from the guide called *MIMS*, which is produced for pharmacists, or the *BNF (British National Formulary)* guide, which is produced for doctors.

Try it out

Investigate the categories of people who are exempt from paying prescription charges.

Using *MIMS* or *BNF*, find out the real costs of the following:

* aspirin
* penicillin
* cyclosporine (immunosuppressant)
* sodium bicarbonate capsules
* ferrous sulphate tablets (iron tablets).

Compare the cost of each of these medicines with the current prescription charge.

The media often report on the shortage of specialist equipment in hospitals and provide profiles of sick people who cannot get the correct treatment as a result. One of the most often reported situations is that of patients with renal failure who cannot have dialysis using a kidney machine because of the lack of equipment or specialist staff.

Kidney machines cost several thousand pounds whereas scanners, MRI (magnetic resonance imaging) and cyclotrons (particle accelerators used in cancer treatment) cost hundreds of thousands of pounds.

Early in 2005, a new type of scanner became theoretically available, but is so expensive that very few areas of health care will be able to afford any. The new scanner is able to peel through layers of the body to look at organs, muscles and the skeleton.

In 2005, the media reported that in most areas waiting lists for traditional scans was nearly a year.

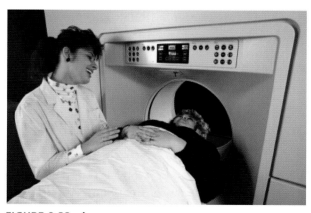

FIGURE 9.22 *A scanner*

Availability of specialist staff

If you see, hear or read media reports, you will know that service users frequently do not get the treatment they need due to a lack of specialist staff.

Theatre staff in specialist areas of health care, for example paediatrics, are often in short supply.

There are no specialists in eating disorders affecting young people; most are cared for by general psychiatric staff. The NHS is short of doctors, yet we hear that currently many doctors cannot find work, particularly those who are in the first years of a career. The need is there, the personnel are trained, but the NHS cannot afford to employ any more doctors. Consultants are specialists in particular areas, taking many years to train and qualify, but in 2005 numbers of consultants were cut.

There is such a chronic shortage of nurses in the NHS that nurses are being encouraged to come from overseas to staff our hospitals. If we could retain trained nurses within the NHS, this would not be necessary. It costs thousands of pounds to train one nurse, who may then leave due to the stress of working in a situation with staff and equipment shortages.

The need for specialised equipment

You have already learned about some specialist equipment such as kidney machines, but some sorts of equipment for imaging and cancer treatment are so expensive that they can only be made available in specialist centres.

MRI scanners are hailed as the biggest breakthrough in diagnostic techniques since X-ray machines. They produce finely detailed and three-dimensional images of body structures without producing harmful radiation. Diagnostic X-ray machines are not penetrating enough to treat active cancers so higher voltage machines (from

10,000 to 30 million volts) are necessary. The lower voltage machines (10,000 volts) are similar to X-ray machines, but the higher voltage machines are of special design and require specialist operators.

When a service user lives near a specialist centre, such as Clatterbridge, Royal Marsden or Christies in Manchester, treatment can be as prompt as waiting lists allow and as frequent as necessary. However, if a service user lives in, say, rural mid-Wales, travelling is both exhausting and expensive and may not be as prompt or frequent as desirable. Some service users may become in-patients during a course of cancer treatment,

but this further complicates the allocation and availability of hospital beds. Some people have called this a 'postcode lottery', meaning that the health care received by patients can depend on their home location.

Try it out

Using the Internet and any other sources of reference available to you, such as media reports and people you know, compare and contrast treatment for a particular condition, such as cancer of the colon, in two different areas of the country.

Summary of Section 9.3

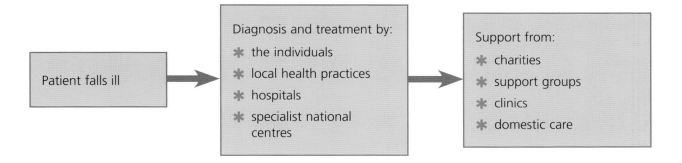

Consider this

Angus, a retired farmer living in rural Scotland, seven miles from his nearest neighbour, has severe osteoarthritis in his knees. His mobility is impaired and he needs two sticks to manage the uneven ground around his home. George is a retired farmer in Shropshire suffering from the same chronic complaint in his knees. George has recently moved into sheltered accommodation. He lives near to a specialist centre for orthopaedics.

Using concepts, can you identify?

1. What are the signs and symptoms that would have led to the diagnosis?

2. What are the clinical or laboratory investigations that might have been carried out?

Go further – Can you analyse issues using theory?

3. What systems of support and treatment should exist to support a service user with osteoarthritis?

Go further – Can you evaluate using a range of theories?

4. Compare and contrast the treatment and support that might be available to each man.

9.4 Strategies for prevention of disease

At every level, government, regional, local and personal, there is a pressing need to prevent people from becoming unwell. People who are ill for long periods of time have a poorer quality of life, may suffer pain and discomfort, and be unable to fulfil their potential. People with illnesses need to be supported economically, physically, socially and mentally by the state. This costs a great deal of money which has to be found from taxes. There must be a balance between the needs of those requiring support and those paying for it through taxation. Currently, despite the large amounts of extra money being ploughed into the NHS and social services, at least 25 per cent of health trusts are in deficit and this figure is likely to increase. For the benefit of the individual and the economy of the country, there must be national, regional, local and personal efforts to prevent disease.

National strategies to prevent disease

You have already learned about some national strategies in Unit 1, *Human growth and development* and Unit 6, *Public health*. It would be beneficial to return to these units, your class notes and your unit assessments for revision before beginning this section of this unit.

National strategies to prevent disease are processes employed over the whole country to reduce disease and thus improve the health of the population.

The government commissions reports on health care and prevention of disease from independent authoritative bodies every few years. Some of these influential reports are:

✳ *Inequalities in Health* (Black Report, 1988)

✳ *Independent Inquiry into Inequalities in Health* (Acheson Report, 1998).

Reports like these stimulate white papers from the government which set out national strategies and policies for future years, such as:

✳ *Saving lives: Our Healthier Nation* (1997)

✳ *Choosing Health – Making Healthier Choices Easier* (2004).

In addition to reports like those mentioned, the government is advised by the government Chief Medical Officer (who provides an annual report), the Department of Health, the World Health Organization, the European Commission, the Health Protection Agency, parliamentary committees, political quangos, various institutes and university research documents.

Consider this

Are there too many advisory reports?

Do important health issues get 'lost'?

Do the general public get confused with conflicting health reports?

Is there a need for one independent reporting body to be responsible for advising the government on health matters?

How far should political influence be allowed to affect issues of health care and disease prevention?

Do the media play a useful role in translating and summarising the findings of governmental reports into material suitable for public understanding?

Are the general public aware of national strategies?

Debate these issues.

Try it out

The National School Fruits scheme has been well publicised, as has the 'Five-a-Day' recommendation. Carry out a survey of people, across a wide range of life stages, to determine the level of public knowledge of these schemes.

Another group might survey awareness of the controversy which led to changes being made in funding and provision of school dinners.

Compare the results of the two groups to see whether 'celebrity publicity' makes a difference in the dissemination of information to the public.

Local strategies to help prevent disease

Health trusts, health promotion units, social services, education and public health observatories (PHOs) will in various combinations identify specific health problems in communities and mount campaigns to address these. Such campaigns might be part of national strategies addressed locally, or particular problems for the local community. A community with a large Asian population, for example, may find that levels of immunisation in young children are lower than national levels, so the community is at higher risk of epidemics. In this case, a health promotion campaign targeted at Asian mothers – information (talks, leaflets, posters, etc.) – could be provided through various centres in suitable languages, and the results collated through health centres and mother and baby clinics.

There are racks of useful information leaflets in general practices, dentists, libraries, health centres and even supermarkets.

Well-women and well-men clinics are ways to provide information in a friendly, informal setting to encourage self-examination of breasts and testicles, and to become informed about contraception, cervical smears, blood pressure checks and many other health issues. Centres like these may be located in health promotion units or health centres.

Fitness centres provide applicants with health checks related to exercising and may pick up on individuals with high blood pressure, high BMIs, erratic pulse rates and high blood cholesterol levels.

Pharmacies will often offer blood pressure and blood cholesterol monitoring.

In broad terms, over half the adult population in the UK is overweight or obese, and many children are also in this category. Obesity is said to be an epidemic in this country and experts have said that many children will die before their parents. Obesity is associated with cardiovascular disease, Type II diabetes and orthopaedic problems.

The causes of this problem are believed to be a lack of physical exercise and diets loaded with fat and sugar. See also Unit 1, *Human growth and development*, page 24.

Personal lifestyle choices in the prevention of disease

Every individual is unique with hopes, desires and wishes for fulfilment; everyone in a free society also has the choice of how to live their life. You can choose what to eat and drink, how clean you keep yourself and your environment, how much physical activity to take and whether or not to abuse substances or indulge in behaviour that might involve risks to your health.

Individuals also have moral responsibilities to keep themselves and others around them as safe as possible. These rights and responsibilities can often be in conflict, especially if peer pressure, fashion and social trends exert powerful influences over people.

Hygiene

Personal hygiene is important in the prevention of disease because it involves regularly removing bacteria from the skin surface, hair, nails and teeth. You have learned that bacteria double their numbers by reproduction every 20 minutes. When bacteria are allowed to build up, then any break in the skin surface can lead to infection, mainly by staphylococci bacteria which reside on everyone's skin. Clean hair and nails are important for the same reasons.

Severe infections can reach the blood circulation causing septicaemia, which is life-threatening.

Dental caries is formed from the waste acidic products from bacteria in the mouth. By constantly removing the accumulated bacteria the risk is significantly reduced.

Body odour is unpleasant and is also caused by accumulated bacteria using secretions such as sweat for their metabolism.

Recently, friends and relatives have been urged to bathe or shower before visiting people in hospital in order to reduce the number of MRSA infections. Visitors are thought to be a significant route for bacterial contamination.

Diet

You have studied the relationship between diet and health in:

* Unit 1, *Human growth and development* pages 24–5

* Unit 4, *Social aspects and lifestyle choices* pages 169–70, 176

* Unit 6, *Public health* pages 284, 292.

A balanced diet with the correct quantities of protein, carbohydrate and fat, and plenty of fresh fruits and vegetables to supply vitamins, minerals and fibre, will help you keep to the right weight for height, provided physical activity is also adequate. Water is an important component of the diet, but only a small number of people drink the recommended quantities of fluid per day.

Did you know?

Water is the medium for all the chemical reactions taking place in the body and too much or too little water can kill cells.

The recommendation is to drink 8 glasses of water each day.

An unbalanced diet can lead to malnutrition, Type II diabetes, cardiovascular disease, skeletal and joint problems, renal, endocrine and neurological disorders, to name but a few. Eating disorders such as anorexia nervosa disturb the menstrual cycle and fertility. Many of these conditions can lead to disabilities and death.

Exercise

A few decades ago, people generally were more physically active as there were far fewer cars. It was normal for children and adults to walk or cycle to school and work. Public transport, mainly buses, may have been available between walks. There were fewer labour-saving devices like washing machines and dishwashers, so household chores were more physically demanding.

In modern society, fewer people walk or cycle and most household chores are performed by machines with little more activity involved. Most families travel even short distances by car, and children rarely play in streets or parks as these are deemed too dangerous.

For most people then, exercise is a positive choice taken for health benefits and many choose not to do so. For people who are overweight, this in itself tends to limit exercise due to the difficulties encountered. The benefits of exercise are multiple (see Figure 9.23).

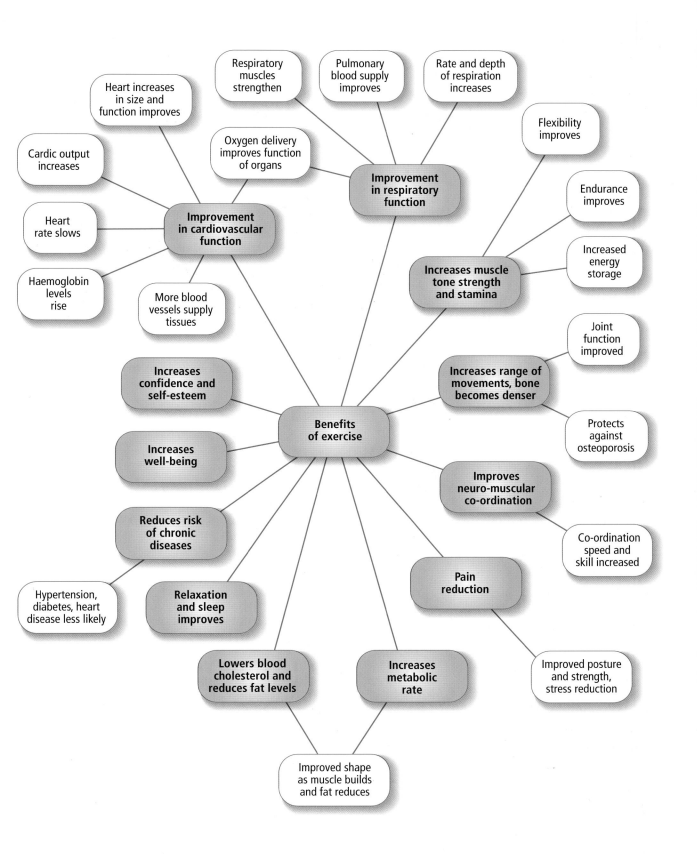

FIGURE 9.23 *The benefits of exercise*

Health risks

Substance abuse is widespread today. Although the numbers of people smoking are decreasing, there is a worrying trend that younger and younger children are taking up the habit. The trend is similar for alcohol consumption and illegal drug abuse. Revise the risks associated with these addictions in Unit 1, *Human growth and development* pages 28–30.

Experts have also warned about the risks of drinking at home, as quantities poured are larger, there are no risks attached to travelling and alcohol is easily available from supermarkets with the family shopping. Individuals may not realise that they are exceeding the recommended number of units per week, often by three or four times.

Many people consume wine far more readily at home, believing that it is relatively safe. However, the recommended number of units of alcohol dates from a time when wine glasses were much smaller than those used today. In addition, wine today tends to contain a higher level of alcohol than previously, so drinking half-a-bottle or more of wine each night as a means of relaxing from work puts an individual well above the recommended levels and at risk of developing liver and other organ disease.

Risk behaviours increase under the influence of alcohol and drugs. Increases in the number of rapes, muggings and other violent attacks have been attributed in part to abuse of alcohol and drugs. Unprotected sex, with its risk of sexually-transmitted disease and unplanned pregnancy, can also be related to alcohol and drug abuse. So-called 'binge drinking' and 'yob culture' is fuelled by substance abuse and there are reports of related accidents and deaths almost daily in the media. Many people seem to believe you cannot 'have a good time' unless under the influence of alcohol or other substances. This is causing the government, police, local councils and residents much concern, and the planned relaxing of licensing laws to allow 24-hour drinking does

FIGURE 9.24 *Relaxing after work*

Try it out

Survey newspaper reports for one week for examples of risk behaviours attributed to substance abuse.

Find out what proportion of young people in school or college understand the risks to health from substance abuse and still drink or take drugs.

What if?

You have met a group of friends to celebrate a friend's eighteenth birthday in a club. Later in the evening and already rather merry, your friends start betting one another to drink more and more alcohol. Most of your friends are not used to large quantities of alcohol because of the cost, but this time the parents have provided a 'free bar' and people are keen to make the most of it. A lot of pressure is put on you to join in. You are told that it's only for a laugh and that you are spoiling the party by refusing.

How can you cope in a situation like this?

How will you respond?

Is it easier to give in and drink?

Discuss your options.

nothing to allay those fears. In 2005, over 90 per cent of retailers of alcohol applied for extended licenses.

Peer pressure is thought to be a powerful influence in the encouragement of substance abuse and risk behaviours.

Factors that interfere with the prevention and control of disease

The prevention and control of disease in the twenty-first century with immunisation, antibiotics and sophisticated treatment sounds fairly complete but, as well as 'new' diseases appearing, there are man-made and micro-organism changes that mean it is a constant battle for doctors and scientists to keep abreast of disease.

Public perception of risk

People are influenced by news reports in the media. Pictures on our television screens are particularly powerful – for example, there was an extraordinary public response to the tsunami disaster in South East Asia on Boxing Day in 2004. Only a few months afterwards, relief agencies were warning of the impending famine disaster in remote Niger. However, it was not until television crews arrived in Niger that the public and governments started to respond with aid. It was too late for some adults and children, but the response saved many lives. Everyone agreed that the emergency could have been avoided if notice of the impending disaster had been taken months earlier.

Reports from a particular source in the 1990s, linking the MMR vaccination with autism and bowel disease dealt a savage blow to immune levels for those diseases in the population. The research in the report was found to be questionable, but there are still the same fears among parents of young children today. Thus, despite the Department of Health and the World Health Organization repeatedly reassuring the general public of the safety of MMR vaccination, the public perceive that the risk is still present.

Certain newspapers in 2004 castigated the government for not stockpiling vaccines against so-called bird flu which was sweeping through birds in Asia. At that time, there was no evidence of transmission between birds and humans, but the media sensationalised what was perceived as a threat to British citizens. At the time of writing, there is still concern over bird 'flu spreading to birds in Europe, mainly via migrating birds. Certain newspapers are once more highlighting that people in key positions in government, London officials and doctors have vaccines stockpiled for their use. The public are becoming concerned that there are no stockpiles for ordinary people because of this publicity. However, we know that the influenza virus changes frequently by mutation. If the bird-to-human transmission occurs, producing widespread epidemics, there is likely to be a mutation which would render the original vaccine inactive. We can be assured that the UK government and the global influenza centres are monitoring the situation very closely.

Other groups and charities can also sensationalise, mainly through the medium of television. Fund-raising advertisements provide figures and images that shock the viewing public without putting the figures in perspective. They also insinuate that making donations of a few pounds every month will enable the abuse, disability or disease to cease without providing any explanation of how this could be achieved. Organisations like these have to compete for public donations and it gets harder every year so, the greater the emotional appeal, the more likely they will achieve success. However, it must be said that charities and voluntary organisations do carry out valuable work and depend on the generosity of the public.

People also have a lowered perception of the risk of serious disease even when well informed. There is a denial or perception that 'it wouldn't happen to me', particularly when symptoms appear suddenly and there is no family history of the condition. Despite statistics to the contrary, many motor cyclists and car drivers who travel fast do not perceive that they are in any danger. One insurance company has said that seven out of ten drivers are uninsured. If true, this means that many people incurring disabilities or death resulting from accidents have no financial support.

Contraception is now easily available to most people in this country to protect against unplanned pregnancies, but some people still do not take responsibility for their own sexual behaviour. Young people might find themselves with parental responsibilities and financial commitments at a very young age. Condoms provide the only method of protection against sexually-transmitted diseases. Too many young women, to their cost, believe that the contraceptive pill is the only protection necessary.

Patient–doctor concordance

Concordance means agreement, in this case an agreement between patient and doctor about the patient's health care.

Previously, the patient, although autonomous, sought the doctor's help for a health problem and was then seen as a passive recipient of the doctor's instructions, which may or may not be followed. Much more emphasis is now placed on patient–doctor interaction and the need for agreement between the participants.

This is largely due to the need for consent to protect the patient's rights and a secondary need to conserve resources. There is little point in the consultancy taking up precious resources, including time, if the patient then proceeds to ignore the results of the consultancy and fails to improve in health.

Patients do not undergo training or education to become patients, so they may be unaware of the advantages that concordance brings to the patient–doctor relationship. Most people would probably say that they want a doctor who is:

* effective in diagnosis and treatment
* trustworthy
* kindly, considerate and sympathetic
* knowledgeable and up to date
* a good communicator and easy to talk to
* always available
* not time-constrained
* concerned for patients
* not financially-constrained
* confidential
* not patronising.

This list is not in any order and you may be able to add some points of your own. Certainly, not many patients would insert 'concordance' or 'someone I can agree with' into that list. However, it is likely that patients will find it easier to reach

Try it out

Carry out a mini-survey of people in different life stages, to determine the five qualities they most desire in their GP.

Add any other qualities you think should be on the list, but do not make it too long.

Ask people (either the same group or a different group) to rank the qualities in order of importance.

Another group might survey qualities not desired in a GP and ask for these to be ranked.

Groups could compare and contrast the results.

SCENARIO

Concordance

A patient weighs 22 stone and consults his or her GP because of severe pain and stiffness of the knee joints. The doctor diagnoses osteoarthritis of the knee joints and explains that the treatment consists of prescribed painkillers until the patient loses 8–10 stone in weight.

The patient is offended by these remarks, buys painkillers from the local pharmacy when necessary and does not visit the doctor again.

Identify and explain:

* why the doctor focused on the patient's weight
* the consequences of not achieving concordance at this consultancy, for both doctor and patient
* how concordance could have been achieved
* the benefits of achieving concordance, for both parties.

concordance with their doctor if he or she has all these qualities.

Patient compliance

'Patient compliance' is when patients take action following a request or instruction by therapists, nurses, doctors or pharmacists.

One of the most common examples of non-compliance occurs when patients do not complete courses of antibiotics. Both the GP and pharmacist emphasise the need to complete the whole course of antibiotics for an infection. Frequently, as soon as the service user feels better, returning to school or work, the antibiotics are forgotten or taken haphazardly. Apart from the possibility of the infection recurring, this type of behaviour encourages the formation of resistant strains of the micro-organism.

Try it out

In small groups, think of times when you have not been patient-compliant. Were there any consequences?

In the scenario on page 156, there was no concordance and also no patient compliance, a complete waste of resources. It would seem pointless to consult a doctor and not heed advice or instructions, but hundreds of thousands of pounds are probably wasted every year through non-compliance. An extreme example would be someone who received a liver transplant after a life of alcohol dependence and who then returned to heavy drinking after the operation. Most would view this as a waste of resources, but would probably never consider the cost of non-compliance of millions of other individuals for smaller sums.

It is the responsibility of everyone to look after their own health and comply with advice and treatment.

Antibiotic resistance

Scientists and medical researchers constantly battle to combat micro-organisms that have developed resistance to common antibiotics. Combinations of drugs against, for example, tuberculosis have to be used because of this problem. Antibiotics are only effective against bacterial infections and are ineffective against viruses.

Most people know about MRSA (methicillin-resistant staphylococcus aureus) and the disabilities and deaths which have resulted from hospital infections. Staphylococcus aureus is a common pathogen normally resident on skin and up noses. The rise in the resistance has been attributed to dirty hospital wards and poor hygiene practices, but there may be other contributory factors. MRSA infections have been around for several years, but the rate has been increasing annually.

Some antibiotics are kept in reserve to tackle MRSA and other resistant infections and doctors are encouraged not to use these unless absolutely necessary. The government is committed to eliminating MRSA infections within the next few years. New hygiene practices have been introduced, including vigilant approaches for nurses and doctors in cleansing the hands with special alcohol-gel rub between patients. Matrons have been appointed to oversee hospital cleanliness.

In 2005 there were reports of another serious infection linked to dirty hospitals, widespread use of antibiotics and poor hygiene. This was due to *Clostridium difficile*, which is more common than MRSA and responsible for a thousand deaths and 45,000 cases annually. A more prudent use of antibiotics and attention to hygiene would control this infection.

Resistance also occurs in other countries, particularly where antibiotics have been available as over-the-counter preparations. Although this has not been the case in the UK, antibiotics may have been too easily obtainable in general practice for treating minor infections. The public is partly responsible because patients insisted on antibiotic prescriptions for low-degree infections rather than allowing natural, aquired immunity to build up.

Funding available

The shortfall of funds for many health authorities may be compounded from 2005, as general practices become eligible for extra finance under a new points system for quality of care and services provided. The extra money will come from health authority budgets, not central government.

The government has stated that health authorities have already received a massive increase in funding and they must manage their resources better.

As treatment regimes and equipment become increasingly expensive, the funding available for fighting disease becomes crucial to the availability of health care.

Try it out

Find out how your local general practice matches up to others in the area by using the Internet. You could also invite a practice manager to help you understand funding allocations.

Did you know?

Health authorities produce annual reports for public perusal. Contact your health authority for a copy and investigate funding allocations and performance against prevention of disease.

Summary of Section 9.4

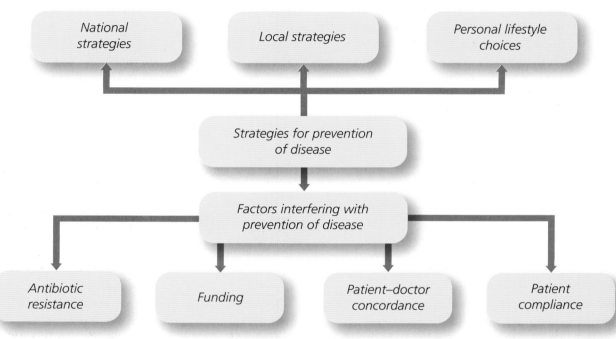

Consider this

A large company, specialising in oral health products, surveys the state of primary school children's teeth every year.

For the last three years, the same health authority, a former coal-mining area, has been at the bottom of the list for poor quality oral health in these age groups.

Using concepts, can you identify?

1. What factors might have contributed to these results?

2. What data might be collected?

Go further – Can you analyse using theory?

The health authority has over the last two years encouraged several new dental practices to move into the area.

3. Suggest why this has not significantly improved oral health in the area.

4. Suggest other local strategies that might be used to improve oral health in primary school children.

Go further – Can you evaluate using a range of theories?

5. Evaluate how far personal lifestyle choice influences children's oral health.

UNIT 9 ASSESSMENT

How you will be assessed

The assessment of this unit will consist of a report *comparing* two diseases. One disease must be a communicable disease and one a non-communicable disease. You will need to think carefully about the diseases on which you choose to base your report and agree these with your tutor.

You may choose one disease the same as your peers providing that the second disease is different. The report produced must be an individual piece of work.

Your work must include evidence of:

* a brief summary of the biological basis of both diseases and the body's responses to them
* information about the causes and distributions of both diseases
* analyses of the support available and the facilities for diagnoses and treatment in your locality
* factors affecting the availability and outcomes of the treatments
* evaluations of the strategies for prevention of the diseases and factors affecting them.

ASSESSMENT OBJECTIVE	DETAILS
AO1 Biological basis of diseases	You must describe the biological basis of the disease and how the body responds to the disease.
AO2 Causes and distribution of diseases	You must explain the factors affecting the causes and distribution of the diseases and demonstrate the ability to compare and contrast the communicable and non-communicable disease
AO3 Support, diagnosis and treatment	You must analyse the facilities for diagnosis, treatment and support including factors affecting the availability and outcomes of treatment.
AO4 Strategies for prevention of diseases	You must evaluate strategies for prevention of the diseases and factors affecting them.

Assessment guidance

Your choice of communicable and non-communicable diseases can be crucial to achieving higher mark bands as you are required to analyse the availability of support and facilities for diagnosis and treatment in your locality and compare these with national provision. In addition, you need to be able to examine distribution of disease and strategies for prevention, identifying issues impacting on the prevention. Having a family member or friend to interview can prove advantageous in identifying local issues, such as facilities for support and treatment, providing consent has been obtained and confidentiality maintained. You could compare a communicable disease that you have had with a non-communicable disease suffered by someone that you know, or vice versa.

It can be useful to make rough notes identifying points of comparison for any pair of diseases you are considering. Choosing diseases which impact on the same life stage can be helpful in providing a standard for comparing and contrasting, but choosing different life stages can provide more points to make. You are recommended to read through the whole of this guidance before commencing.

AO1 Biological basis of diseases

You will need to explain the biological nature of the two diseases. For example, measles is contracted through viral infection (measles virus) and cystic fibrosis is inherited through two recessive alleles. This should be followed by the body's response to the diseases, for example high temperature and rash, or thick viscid secretions and glandular abnormalities. You should then be able to explain how the different signs and symptoms are produced and shown, linking these to the way the diagnosis is made and any clinical or laboratory investigations used to clinch the diagnosis. Remember that comparisons need to be made throughout the work and you can do this in the text by using link words such as, 'but' and 'whereas'. You may prefer to write the information you have gathered in your own words and then compile a table of comparable points at the end of each section. An example is given below.

CHARACTERISTIC FOR COMPARISON	NAME OF COMMUNICABLE DISEASE, E.G. MEASLES	NAME OF NON-COMMUNICABLE DISEASE, E.G. CYSTIC FIBROSIS
Biological basis of disease	Infection by measles viruses	Not caused by a virus
	Not inherited	Inheritance of two recessive alleles for cystic fibrosis

Notice how two points have been made; when making comparisons it is important to be comparing the same characteristic. For example, you would not say, 'Mary has blonde hair but Sandra has blue eyes'. It is not a true comparison. You would need to say, 'Mary has blonde hair but Sandra has not' and, 'Sandra has blue eyes whereas Mary has brown eyes'; so two points of difference are recorded.

AO2 Causes and distribution of diseases

In this section, you will need to explain factors affecting the cause and distribution. Using the same example, being in contact with someone in the infectious stage of measles, not being immunised or not having an adequate immune threshold would be factors affecting the cause.

To compare distributions, you might need to visit websites such as the Department of Health, National Statistics, netdoctor, specific organisations or similar. Do not forget to make your comparisons. Use specialist vocabulary as appropriate, but remember to use your own words and acknowledge sources that you use.

AO3 Support, diagnosis and treatment

You will describe how the diseases are diagnosed and treated and how provision differs. Note that the example used, measles, does not offer much scope as viral diseases such as measles are mainly self-limiting and no treatment is offered other than antibiotic cover to prevent secondary infection. However, if you choose a viral disease it can offer good comparisons with a disease such as cystic fibrosis because of the contrast in treatment and support. You will need to compare the support available locally and nationally and provide justifiable reasons for differences between the two diseases, as well as making links to work-related problems and issues, such as requiring special facilities or needing to rest more often. Demonstrate how you have gathered information from a variety of sources by referencing.

AO4 Strategies for prevention of diseases

You must explain the strategies for prevention of the diseases and then evaluate these, describing strengths and weaknesses, to draw conclusions. You should include reasons why prevention strategies are not always completely successful and suggestions for how these issues impact on available prevention, support and treatment. Candidates working at the higher mark bands must demonstrate independent thinking and initiative.

Unit test

1. Match the following diseases to the main types of micro-organisms that cause them.

   1. Thrush   A. viruses
   2. MRSA   B. protozoa
   3. Malaria   C. fungi
   4. Influenza   D. bacteria

2. Circle the communicable diseases in the list below, leaving the non-communicable diseases.

   Osteoarthritis

   Dental caries

   Rubella (german measles)

   Athlete's foot

   Coronary heart disease

   Cystic fibrosis

   Scurvy

   Chicken pox

   Measles

   Lung cancer

3. Explain the difference between clinical diagnosis and differential diagnosis.

4. Identify the missing word in each statement from the list below.

   a) Malaria is transmitted from one person to another through _____.

   b) Common colds spread rapidly in a classroom due to _____.

   c) Diarrhoea and vomiting can be caused through flies contaminating _____.

   d) _____can become contaminated by sewage during land upheaval, causing cholera.

   e) Verrucas are transmitted by _____ with viruses.

   f) HIV is mainly transmitted by _____.

   direct contact; sexual contact; food; droplet inhalation; drinking water; a vector.

5. Distinguish between a symptom and a sign and give three examples of each.

6. Explain the differences between the following pairs:

   a) gene and allele

   b) dominant and recessive

   c) autosomal and sex-linked conditions.

7. Using examples to illustrate your answer, explain patient–doctor concordance and patient compliance.

8. State four examples of facilities for diagnosis, including one that might be found in a specialised centre.

9. Describe two national and two local strategies to reduce the incidence of lung cancer from smoking.

10. Non-communicable diseases can be divided into:

    1. degenerative

    2. deficiency

    3. inherited

    4. lifestyle or environmental.

    Match the correct group to the following conditions:

    A. Haemophilia

    B. Cirrhosis of the liver

    C. Alzheimer's disease

    D. Rickets.

References and further reading

Acheson, D. (1998) *Independent Inquiry into Inequalities in Health* (London: HMSO)

Dorling, D., et al. (1999) *The Widening Gap: Health Inequalities and Policy in Britain* (The Policy Press)

Douglas, S. (Spring 2005) 'HIV and STIs: a disproportionate burden' *Health Protection Matters*

Ewles, L., Simnett, I. (2003) *Promoting Health – A Practical Guide* (London: Balliere Tindall)

Health Protection Matters, quarterly publication by the Health Protection Agency

HM Government (1997) *Saving Lives: Our Healthier Nation* (London: HMSO)

HM Government (2004) *Choosing Health: Making Healthier Choices Easier* (London: HMSO)

Moonie, N. et al. (2000) *Advanced Health and Social Care* (Oxford: Heinemann)

Public Health News, monthly publication (London: Chadwick House Publishing)

Seedhouse, D. (1986) *Health: The Foundations for Achievement* (New Jersey USA: Wiley)

Shenker, M., Ladou, J. (ed.) (1997) *Occupational and Environmental Medicine* (Connecticut USA: Appleton Lange)

World Health Organization (1986) 'A discussion document on the concept and principles of health promotion'

Any medical or biological text covering diseases.

Useful websites

BBC www.bbc.co.uk

Department of Health www.doh.gov.uk

Government statistics www.statistics.gov.uk

Health Education Authority www.hea.org.uk

Health Protection Agency www.hpa.org.uk

Our Healthier Nation www.ohn.org.uk

Using and understanding research

This unit covers the following sections:

10.1 The aims and use of research in health and social care

10.2 Research methods

10.3 Carrying out a research project

Unit 10 Introduction

This unit will give you an appreciation of the key purposes of research, and in particular how it is used in practice in the fields of health and social care.

A range of research styles and methods are described, and there is practical advice on the design and administration of different types of data collection tools. The analysis and interpretation of data is explained in some depth. Finally, guidance on how to conduct a research report is set out, from the planning stage through to implementation and evaluation.

How you will be assessed

This unit is internally assessed. You must produce a research proposal and final written report.

10.1 The aims and use of research in health and social care

The role of research in health and social care

The importance of research to the development of health and social care practice should not be underestimated. Worldwide, hundreds of journals are devoted to reporting the findings of numerous research projects relating to new developments in medicine, health care or the impact of new initiatives in social care. There are numerous Internet websites devoted to new research, and the many books that are published annually on related topics rely heavily on research findings to give authenticity and weight to their authors' arguments. News bulletins (on TV or radio) report the outcomes of significant pieces of research, and every day most of the more reputable newspapers are likely to contain reference to newly published results from investigations into a range of topics.

What is research?

The term 'research' denotes a systematic enquiry that is designed to add to existing knowledge and/or to solve a particular problem (Bell 1993:2).

Over time, specific approaches and methods for carrying out such enquiries have developed, some of which are linked to particular disciplines.

Laboratory experiments, for example, are often used when developing new drugs. Clinical procedures in a controlled environment may assess, for example, the impact of damage to the human brain following a stroke. Outside the laboratory environment, questionnaires may be used to find out how people respond to the provision of a new service, or the observation of behaviours might be employed to give an insight into the impact of a certain environment on the ways that people interact.

Researchers will choose and adapt from a range of approaches and methods in order to seek answers to the questions or hypotheses that they wish to test. The important thing about all research is that whatever method is used, the findings are reported systematically and scientifically, in as clear and honest a fashion as possible.

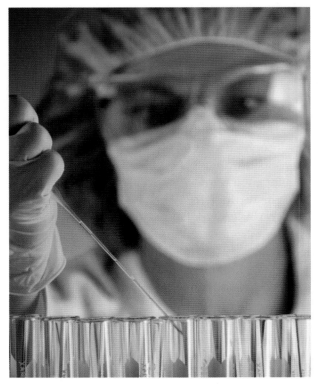

FIGURE 10.1 *Researcher in a laboratory*

Who does research?

Anyone can do research. A brief trawl through the Yellow Pages to find names and addresses of all the dentists in a given location is, in a sense, a piece of research. In this unit, however, rather more elaborate projects are studied.

Some of the main bodies undertaking research in health are:

* universities

* hospitals

* national bodies such as the Medical Research Council

* the Research Council for Complementary Medicine

* the Prince of Wales's Foundation for Integrated Health

* private organisations such as large pharmaceutical companies.

In social care, there are a number of bodies in the UK that sponsor or promote research. The Joseph Rowntree Foundation, for example, sponsors research that will impact on the development of social policy (see page 171), as does the Institute for Public Policy Research (IPPR). These are only two of a number of bodies and organisations that promote social care related research.

In the UK, the government initiates a great deal of research, sometimes in-house (i.e. within specific government departments) and sometimes commissioned from outside organisations or independent researchers. Each government department, such as the Department of Health, has its own website, and details of ongoing and published research can be accessed easily.

The Office for National Statistics (ONS) is the government department that deals with information from the national census, the most recent of which was in 2001. The website for this department (www.statistics.gov.uk) may be searched for easily accessible data on the population of England and Wales, with links to census data for Scotland and Northern Ireland.

The study of population characteristics is known as *demography*. Demographic data often provides an essential background to research studies of many kinds.

As well as national government, local authorities also often have their own research units or departments. Demographic data is vital to the effectiveness of government, whether local or national.

For example, consider a local council which has received Sure Start funding for a new day centre for single parents with young babies. The council's research unit processes data from the 2001 census to locate the areas of greatest potential need within the authority's boundaries. The census data reveals that there is a significant concentration of lone-parent households with dependent children in two Output Areas (these are the small local divisions within which census data is counted). These Output Areas lie adjacent to each other. The council decides to look for suitable premises in either of these two small areas.

Using research

Investigating new care-related situations

In June 2005, the organisation Carers UK published the results of a survey that investigated the concerns of carers – people who have the responsibility for caring for others on an unpaid basis (access this survey via www.carersuk.org). Over 2,900 carers responded to the survey by completing a questionnaire. The results indicated that 65 per cent of those who took part felt that their career prospects had been adversely affected as a result of their caring responsibilities, whilst 74 per cent of respondents often took annual leave in order to care for someone else. This survey was commissioned in response to the concerns of carers, and represents a systematic effort to provide statistical backing for their demands.

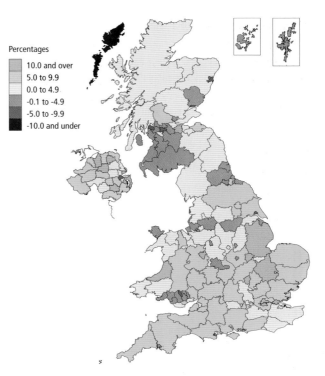

Percentages

	10.0 and over
	5.0 to 9.9
	0.0 to 4.9
	-0.1 to -4.9
	-5.0 to -9.9
	-10.0 and under

FIGURE 10.2 *Population change in the UK, 1993–2003*

Source: *Social Trends* (2005)

Carers UK will use the information to call for greater flexibility on the part of employers who may have carers on their staff.

A smaller study, this time of 124 young people with substance-related mental health and family problems, reports the relative effectiveness of an intervention known as ecologically-based family therapy (EBFT) (Slesnik and Prestopnik, 2005). All the young people in the study had run away from home. They were randomly assigned to one of two interventions, EBFT or the usual service available via a shelter. Researchers reviewed the situation at the start of the study, just after the end of the intervention, and then at 6 and 12 months afterwards. They found those who had received EBFT reported greater reductions in substance misuse than the young people in the control group.

These examples show that the investigation of care-related situations often involves the collection of qualitative data of some kind.

> **Key concept**
>
> *Qualitative data:* purely qualitative data cannot be expressed simply in numbers. It is often concerned with people's values, attitudes and/or opinions.

Testing and reviewing existing knowledge, treatments and practices

Research into medical treatments and knowledge is continuous and exhaustive. Worldwide, scientists in research laboratories seek to establish the mechanisms underlying certain diseases or medical conditions, or to test the reliability or effectiveness of specific drugs or treatment methods. Such studies often involve the collection of quantitative data. This is data that can be expressed in terms of numbers, percentages and so on.

> **Key concept**
>
> *Quantitative data:* this is expressed in numerical form. It can be presented in tables, bar charts, pie charts or graphs.

Currently, the 'gold standard' for the testing of medical knowledge and treatments is the *randomised clinical controlled trial* (RCCT). A randomised trial is based on a randomly selected sample of subjects who receive a particular drug or treatment. Another set of subjects, or 'control' group, receive either the standard treatment or no treatment at all, and the outcomes for the two groups are compared. When a large number of such trials have taken place, researchers can then take a look at all the results by means of a *systematic review*.

> **Key concept**
>
> *Randomised clinical controlled trial (RCCT):* a research method involving more than one sample group. One sample receives the treatment being investigated and the other doesn't, and the results are compared.
>
> *Systematic review:* a thorough and systematic comparison of RCCTs to produce convincing evidence for the effectiveness (or otherwise) of a particular drug or treatment.

Sometimes, the results of research are inconclusive or even controversial. The current debate on the safety of the combined MMR (measles, mumps and rubella) vaccine is an interesting example of this. In the late 1990s, Dr Andrew Wakefield published a study in *The Lancet* suggesting a possible link between the MMR vaccine and the condition known as autism, together with associated gut and bowel abnormalities (Wakefield 1998). When this research received media coverage, many parents stopped having their children vaccinated with the combined drug. This alarmed health officials, who feared that uncontrolled outbreaks of diseases like measles might result. Over the years since 1998, a great deal of attention has been paid by researchers (and the press) to the question of whether or not the MMR vaccine can have serious and undesirable consequences. The Department of Health has since concluded that the MMR vaccine is 'safe and extremely effective'. Despite this, there are still researchers who dispute the Department of Health conclusions, and the debate continues within the scientific community. The government's position on this, together with lists of research articles, can be accessed via the Department of Health website. A conflicting view can be explored via the What Doctors Don't Tell You website.

Explaining the relationship between factors affecting health and well-being

In the last ten years or so significant amounts of research have demonstrated the complex relationship between health and a number of other factors including:

* diet
* lifestyle
* environmental circumstances
* psychological factors.

SCENARIO

Stress and the common cold

Cohen and colleagues studied 420 volunteers (men and women) who agreed to be given the common cold virus via nasal drops. All the volunteers were housed in a residential unit in Salisbury, at the British Medical Research Council's Common Cold Unit.

Before the test, the stress levels of each person were measured using standard psychological methods. In particular they noted significant life events during the preceding year, emotional state at the time of the experiment and each person's perception of how well they could cope with the ups and downs of life.

Cohen found that the people with the highest stress measures were more likely to:

* become infected by the virus
* develop colds.

Sources: Cohen 1991; Cohen 1993

The outcomes of research such as this led eventually to the emergence of a new discipline known as *psychoneuroimmunology* (PNI) (Martin 1997). PNI studies have demonstrated the complex relationship between the mind and the body, and in particular how a person's state of mind can have an effect upon his or her health, both positively and adversely.

Key concept

Psychoneuroimmunology: a scientific discipline that explores the relationships between the mind and various systems within the body, in particular the immune and hormonal systems.

Similarly, some research studies have demonstrated very effectively the relationship that can exist between the environment and the health of individuals. Such studies often involve the use of the technique of *epidemiology*. This method uses mapping to explore the potential causes of disease.

Key concept

Epidemiology: the study of the geographical incidence of disease in order to demonstrate potential causes (and cures).

There is a famous early example of an epidemiological study from the mid-nineteenth century, which led to a deeper understanding of the cause of cholera, a devastating disease which was responsible for many deaths at that time, particularly between 1831 and 1866 (see scenario, page 170).

Evaluating service interventions and policies

When money and time has been invested in the provision of new services, it is vital to conduct evaluative studies to assess the impact and effectiveness of such new initiatives.

Such studies might use a mixture of both qualitative and quantitative methods. Consider the example of the new Sure Start project described on pages 166–7. After receiving funding and developing this new service, both the local council and the government department that supplied the funding would seek evidence of its effectiveness. Quantitative data would be needed to show, for example:

* how many people were using the centre
* how far they were travelling to get there
* the most popular times
* the most popular activities.

Qualitative data would also be needed, and it would be a good idea to ask the centre users:

* what they thought of the new service
* whether things could be done better or differently
* what other activities/facilities could be in place.

Dr John Snow and the Broad Street Pump

Until the late 1850s, it was commonly believed that cholera was an air-borne disease. Matter, such as rotting corpses or food and the contents of sewers and cesspits, was considered to exude bad air or 'miasma'. People breathed in this miasma, and as a result became ill with any number of diseases, including cholera.

Dr John Snow, a London anaesthetist, observed incidents of cholera in the neighbourhood of Soho in London during the outbreak of August–September 1854. He noticed that they were clustered around a water-pump in Broad Street. He followed up his observations with a properly documented study, including inspection of the water from the pump. He took a list of those who had died of cholera from the General Register Office, and then made further enquiries about each of these people.

He found that nearly all the deaths were of people living very close to this particular water-pump. Furthermore, five people who lived closer to another water-pump were found to always send for water from Broad Street. Nine people using a local coffee-shop, which used the Broad Street water, also died from cholera. A number of other Broad Street residents, who worked for a local brewery, always drank the free beer provided by their employer. None of these people were infected with the disease.

Snow persuaded the Board of Guardians of St James's parish to remove the handle of the Broad Street pump to prevent its further use.

Dr Snow supported his hypothesis with maps and tables documenting the incidence of the disease. He considered possible alternative explanations for seeming anomalies (such as the apparent immunity of the brewery workers). In 1857 he published a paper in the *British Medical Journal* demonstrating that

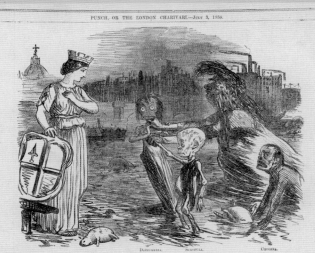

FIGURE 10.3 *The 'Great Stink' of London*

customers of the Southwark water company had a cholera death-rate that was six times higher than customers of the Lambeth water company (Halliday 2001). Snow suggested that this was because in Southwark, customers received water drawn from a particularly polluted section of the Thames. Initially, support for Snow's hypothesis was limited; but after the 'Great Stink' of 1858, when MPs were unable to enter the House of Commons because of the smell from the Thames, the notion that polluted water was the cause of diseases like cholera was taken more seriously. Shortly after this, the engineer Bazalgette was commissioned to construct a new sewage system for London, and this took much of the effluent away from the city.

Snow's epidemiological studies provided evidence which gave new insights into the spread of cholera, leading ultimately to improved sanitary conditions in the city of London. His studies provided a clear demonstration of the relationship of disease and environment, in this case between cholera and polluted water.

Sources: Snow (1855); Halliday (2001)

FIGURE 10.4 *Evaluative studies of new initiatives in care are essential to inform further developments, and to secure funding for institutions such as Hartrigg Oaks*

The evidence could justify further development of the project, either by application for more funding, or by the local council making financial provision within its own budget to continue the service.

A real-life study of this kind can be investigated on the Joseph Rowntree Foundation website. The Joseph Rowntree Housing Trust has developed the UK's first Continuing Care Retirement Community, Hartrigg Oaks, which represents a new concept in residential provision for older people. The scheme is experimental not only in its provision of a community environment in which residents are expected to be active participants in the running of the facility, but also in its promotion of imaginative financial arrangements to fund the development. Hartrigg Oaks opened in 1998, and the Joseph Rowntree Foundation then commissioned the University of York to evaluate its effectiveness.

Research into practice: how research findings affect the work of health and social care practitioners

Policy making and service planning

We have seen how a local authority used census data to find the best location for a new Sure Start centre for single parents with young babies (pages 166–7). We have also seen how Dr Snow's research into the causes of cholera eventually influenced the politicians of the day, resulting in a new drainage system for London that dramatically improved public health.

Demographic and epidemiological data is used constantly by politicians and service planners to make informed decisions about new service developments.

An excellent example of the use of such data is provided by the annual report of the government Chief Medical Officer (CMO), which can be accessed easily via the Department of Health website. This report presents the recommendations of the CMO on a number of issues, based on research which is explained and fully referenced. In 2003, topics covered included the impact of smoking on skin ageing, the economic case for creating smoke-free workplaces and public places, and the importance of early diagnosis of HIV.

The CMO's recommendations often find their way into law, as is the case with the ban on smoking in public places. In other instances, the findings set out in the annual report are indicated as the basis for further research or action. Another article in the 2003 annual report spotlights some local health problems and trends in England, revealing some rather specific local issues (see Table 10.1).

Try it out

Go back to the facts and figures you produced for the exercise on page 167. What are the issues in your local area?

See what else you can find out by getting hold of information from your local authority.

What research is the authority using to support its plans for service development?

North East	Dental health of 5-year-olds (non-fluoridated areas)
London	Health of Black and ethnic minority communities
East Midlands	Notifications of tuberculosis
West Midlands	Obesity in women aged 16–64 years
North West	Deaths by drowning
East of England	Increase in poly drug use
South West	Health of people over 65 and relationship to crime
Yorkshire and Humber	Fuel poverty
South East	Difficulties in accessing NHS dental treatment

TABLE 10.1 *Government Chief Medical Officer's report 2003, areas of concern: England*

Try it out

Find out how public health information is collated and used in an area of the UK other than where you live. For example, if you live in England, you might choose to find out about public health data in Scotland; if you live in Wales, you might study public health data for Northern Ireland.

The development and testing of medical and other treatment interventions

Worldwide, there is considerable research into medical and other treatment interventions. Hospitals, university departments, charitable organisations (such as Cancer Research UK) and private companies invest significant resources into testing existing procedures and pharmaceutical products, and into the search for new and more effective interventions.

The Research Council for Complementary Medicine has published *An Introduction to Research* (1999) which sets out the range of types of study that can be conducted into health interventions (see Table 10.2).

Key concept

Case reports: these are used to describe a particular case in detail, particularly if that case is very rare, or perhaps if a practitioner has observed a new phenomenon.

Surveys: these are also descriptive, but their scope is broader than just an individual patient. Studies of dental health in children, such as those referred to in the Chief Medical Officer's annual report, include survey data.

Cohort studies: these are used to study the impact of a treatment amongst a group of patients. A new drug, such as Beta Interferon (now used in the treatment of some people with multiple sclerosis), would be administered to a defined group (a cohort), and its impact carefully monitored.

TYPES OF RESEARCH STUDY	
PURPOSE	**METHOD**
To describe something	Case reports Surveys Cohort studies
To explain something	Qualitative research (e.g. interviews, surveys)
To test a hypothesis	Quantitative research (e.g. clinical trials)
To make generalisations	Multi-centre trials Systematic reviews of trials

TABLE 10.2 *Research into medical treatments*

Source: From *An Introduction to Research* (1999) published by Research Council for Complementary Medicine. Reproduced with permission

The validity of the findings of a cohort study is limited by the absence of a control group. There is also the possibility that changes in patient health may be due to factors that the study does not pick up.

In contrast a *clinical trial*, particularly when the subject group is randomised, is a more rigorous method of determining the effectiveness of a specific intervention. A clinical trial of the drug Beta Interferon would involve giving the drug to one group of patients and comparing their progress with a second group who do not receive the drug. The second group may receive no treatment, receive an existing 'standard' treatment, or they may be given a placebo. A *placebo* is something that looks like a medical intervention (e.g. an injection or a capsule), but in fact does not contain any active treatment.

Clinical trials are randomised, in that patients are first selected according to a number of criteria (e.g. medical condition, age, gender), and are then randomly allocated to either the treatment or the control group. These trials are deemed to be even more effective if the researchers do not know which patients are receiving the real treatment, and which are receiving the placebo. In such cases, the researchers are said to be 'blinded'.

It is unlikely that one clinical trial will be conclusive. Researchers attempt to replicate and refine the findings of other trials on the same subject. This, in turn, enables *systematic reviews* of the research into the same topic to be made. Such a review will attempt to assemble the evidence for a particular intervention for a range of settings and patient groups. This kind of research activity is called *meta-analysis*, and it can sometimes reveal a common 'global' outcome from specific research.

In the UK, an online research facility, known as the Cochrane Collaboration, established in 1993, systematically collects and makes available existing reviews of research about the effects of health care interventions. This organisation also promotes clinical trials and other studies of such interventions. The Cochrane Library is a collection of evidence-based medicine databases. Although full access is by subscription, some of the Cochrane's services are free, including details of the findings of systematic reviews.

In practice, researchers may make use of several methods of data collection. A clinical trial, for example, may be preceded by more qualitative data collection from patients to ensure all the parameters have been taken into consideration. It might also be supplemented by qualitative data

SCENARIO

Too cramped for comfort

Two large teaching hospitals have combined their resources to research the incidence of a specific type of disease in women of a certain age group. The sample to be studied has been randomly selected, and the initial data collection (the completion of questionnaires and the taking of blood samples) commences at two designated centres. The women are to have a second set of tests after 12 weeks.

However, it is noticeable that at one of the centres, women are failing to turn up for the second appointment. At the other centre, patients are turning up as requested.

Telephone follow-up of several of the non-attenders from the first centre, reveals a high level of discomfort with the environment in which the research was being carried out. A number of basement rooms had been set aside, but these were airless and extremely cramped. There was not much privacy for the taking of blood samples, and there were no facilities for people with disabilities.

As a result of this brief qualitative review, the research organisers manage to find alternative premises for their study.

✳ How could researchers have prevented this situation from arising?

✳ If resources are a problem, what might researchers do to ensure their subjects are willing to co-operate in the study?

This example demonstrates the advisability of supplementing quantitative research with qualitative information.

from people taking part in the study, to make sure that patients are not being adversely affected by, for example, environmental issues.

Systematic reviews are extremely important in the production of guidance for practitioners. The National Institute for Health and Clinical Excellence (NICE) provides national guidance (in England and Wales) on the promotion of health and the prevention and treatment of ill-health. NICE uses a range of methods, both qualitative and quantitative, to produce technology appraisals, clinical guidelines and advice on interventional procedures. NICE's guidelines are based on reviews of clinical and economic evidence. NICE also invites interested parties, such as manufacturers, patients, carers and health professionals, to give evidence on the use and effectiveness of specific interventions and treatments. The resulting guidelines are then publicly available, to both professionals and patients.

Try it out

Choose a medical condition that interests you. Make an Internet search to find out what organisations currently sponsor or conduct research into that particular condition.

What kinds of research are being done (qualitative, quantitative, clinical trials, etc.)?

Assessing user satisfaction with health and social care services

Those who plan and deliver services, including Primary Care Trusts (PCTs), local authorities, voluntary and charitable organisations, and even private service suppliers, will routinely evaluate the impact of the services they deliver.

In the case of the hypothetical Sure Start centre described above (pages 166–7), the local authority made a user-satisfaction survey of those using the centre, as well as monitoring the centre's use by means of quantitative data.

Similarly, the satisfaction of residents of the Hartrigg Oaks Community initiative was very closely evaluated by a specially commissioned study by the University of York (page 171). The first report, published in 2003, provides

qualitative data in the form of tables and bar charts, giving basic statistical information (numbers of residents, age profiles, short-term use of the facility, etc.), and also information about satisfaction levels. Some of the latter is expressed quantitatively (e.g. a bar chart showing satisfaction levels), whilst qualitative data is given in the form of direct quotations of residents' observations and comments. Researchers used two postal surveys, face-to-face interviews and discussion groups with both staff and residents to gather the evaluative data. The full report can be accessed via the Joseph Rowntree Trust website.

Summary of Section 10.1

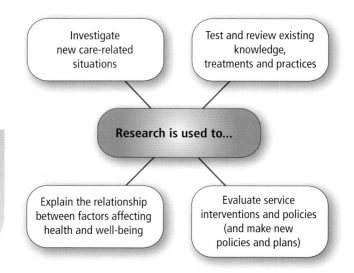

Consider this

An investigation into how growing older can sometimes have an impact on a person's mental health has shown how physical, social and biological factors can be interrelated.

1. What would you say was the main aim of this piece of work (using the categories highlighted in the summary above)?

2. How might this work be of practical use?

3. Which of the following professionals might be interested to learn more about these findings: GP, health visitor, social worker, care worker, home care worker, social services manager, health service planning manager. Describe briefly how each professional might put information from the investigation into use.

10.2 Research methods

The aims of research

Research may be carried out to achieve one or more of several aims:

* to describe something
* to explain something
* to test a hypothesis
* to make generalisations.

Researchers may use more than one method of data collection and analysis within a given study, but if the aims of that study are not clear and explicit right at the beginning, then the research runs the risk of drifting, and the tools of analysis chosen may not be appropriate to the task.

Research methods in social care

The types of study used in the field of medical treatments and interventions were set out in Table 10.2 (page 172). Research methods in the field of social care are very similar, with the addition of a number of other techniques (see Table 10.3). It would be misleading to suggest that the fields of health and social care research are two separate disciplines; there are many overlaps between the two.

Case studies

The *case study* technique is common in social care research, and can involve just one person, or a group of people such as a social care team. Data might be collected by several methods, including observation and interviews with the subjects concerned.

STYLE	PURPOSE	TYPICAL METHODS	TYPICAL EXAMPLES
Case study	To identify the key processes and features of a specific situation.	Observation Interviews Questionnaires	Study describing the introduction of a new home care service.
Survey	To establish facts and to answer the questions What? Where? When? How?	Questionnaires (either self-completed, or completed by the researcher) Analysis of existing data (e.g. medical records, census)	The UK census Survey to find out what kinds of service are preferred by people with disabilities.
Experiment	To establish a causal relationship.	Comparison of experimental group with control group.	Cohen's study of the impact of stress on the immune system (page 169). Study of the impact of EBFT (page 187) on young people.
Ethnographic study	To make an in-depth study of an aspect of a culture or group of people.	Observation	Study of relationships between staff and service users in a day unit for people with learning disabilities.
Action research	To analyse and evaluate an ongoing situation.	Questionnaires Diaries Interviews Case studies	Evaluation of the strengths and weaknesses of a new way of recording users' needs.

TABLE 10.3 *Styles of research in social care*

Suppose that a research organisation such as the King's Fund wants to find out more about the local use of joint community care teams (teams where staff from local authority social services departments and health authority units combine within the same management structure to provide a more joined-up service). The research organisation might commission a piece of research involving a number of case studies of such teams. The researchers would identify several teams, and then design research to assess the impact of the new working arrangements, including:

* daily working practices

* user satisfaction

* cost-effectiveness.

Methods used might involve observing the team at work on a daily basis, interviews with staff (both singly and as a group), interviews with people who use the service and questionnaires, either for interviews, or sent by post for self-completion.

Surveys

Surveys are also extremely common research tools. The UK census is a classic example of a survey, in which questionnaires are completed and quantitative data is systematically collated and analysed. The census poses specific questions to all UK residents, enabling researchers to analyse the population according to certain parameters (see pages 166–7). Surveys are a useful tool when, for example, a local authority wishes to assess levels of satisfaction amongst users of a specific service.

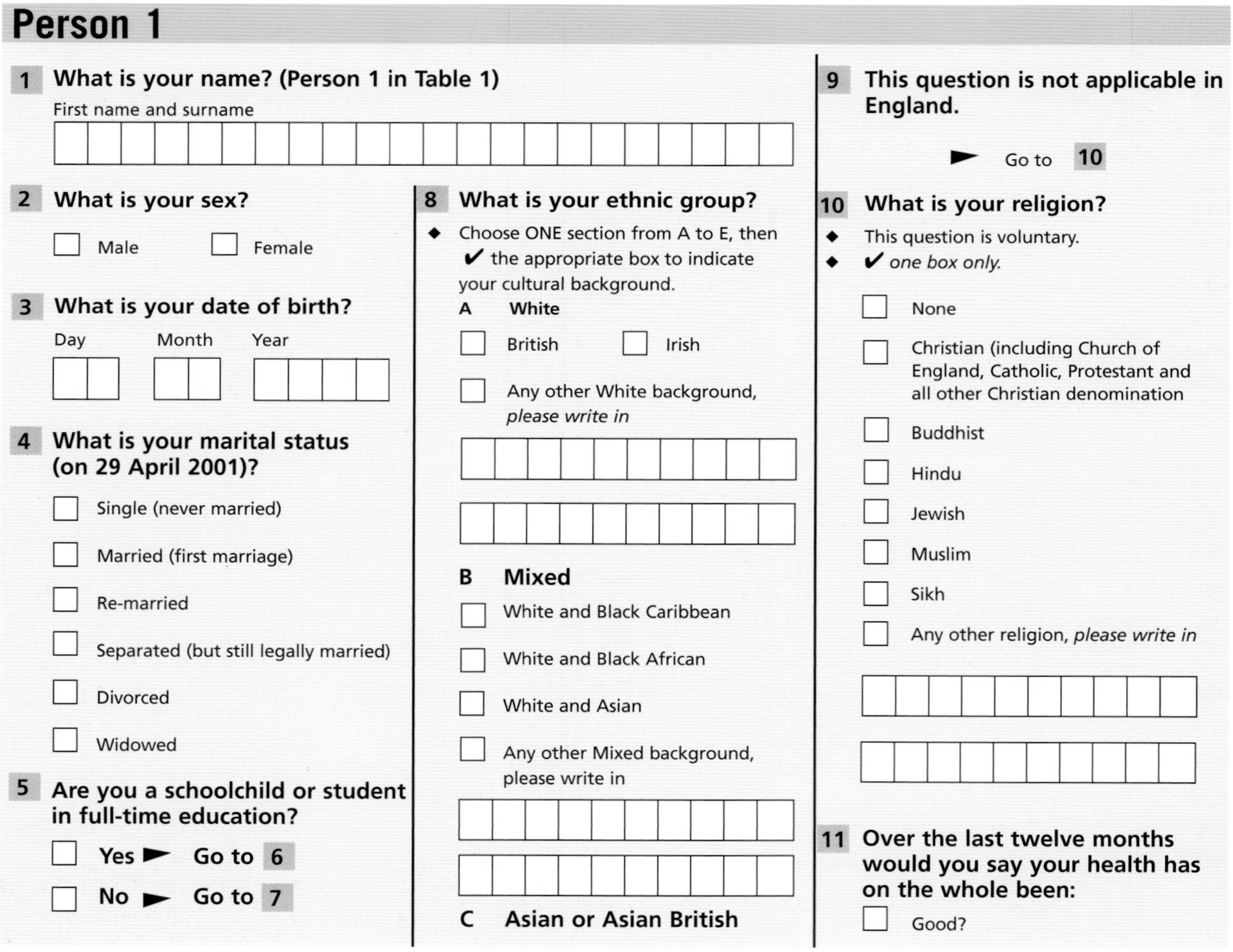

Person 1

1 What is your name? (Person 1 in Table 1)
First name and surname

2 What is your sex?

☐ Male   ☐ Female

3 What is your date of birth?

Day   Month   Year

4 What is your marital status (on 29 April 2001)?

☐ Single (never married)

☐ Married (first marriage)

☐ Re-married

☐ Separated (but still legally married)

☐ Divorced

☐ Widowed

5 Are you a schoolchild or student in full-time education?

☐ Yes ► Go to **6**

☐ No ► Go to **7**

8 What is your ethnic group?

◆ Choose ONE section from A to E, then
   ✔ the appropriate box to indicate
   your cultural background.

A White

☐ British   ☐ Irish

☐ Any other White background, *please write in*

B Mixed

☐ White and Black Caribbean

☐ White and Black African

☐ White and Asian

☐ Any other Mixed background, *please write in*

C Asian or Asian British

9 This question is not applicable in England.

► Go to **10**

10 What is your religion?

◆ This question is voluntary.
◆ ✔ one box only.

☐ None

☐ Christian (including Church of England, Catholic, Protestant and all other Christian denomination

☐ Buddhist

☐ Hindu

☐ Jewish

☐ Muslim

☐ Sikh

☐ Any other religion, *please write in*

11 Over the last twelve months would you say your health has on the whole been:

☐ Good?

FIGURE 10.5 *The UK census collects data from all households in the UK*

Experimental method

The *experimental method* involves the comparison of two groups, to identify the potential impact of a specific factor (or variable). For example, one group of people with a specific medical condition may be given a new drug. A second group with the same condition will not be given the treatment. Over time, the health of each group will be monitored, including quantitative data from tests on blood, urine, body tissue, etc., or on measures of mobility. All such tests must be relevant to the specific medical condition. Researchers may also seek qualitative data about the subjects' state of mind or sense of well-being. If the group receiving the drug shows significant improvement using these measures, then there is a possibility that the drug is having an effect.

One important aspect of the experimental style is that it can be replicated by other researchers. The experiment is at the heart of the randomised clinical controlled trial (RCCT) (page 168) and surveys of such work are usually made to allow scientists to compare and contrast the findings. Agreement between a number of RCCTs is often held to be convincing evidence for the safety or efficacy of a new treatment. Cohen's studies of the impact of stress on the immune system (page 169) used the experimental style of research.

Ethnographic research

The *ethnographic* style of research is similar to a case study; it focuses on aspects of behaviour in a certain situation. However, it is usually much broader, and often involves the researcher becoming involved in the situation that he or she is observing. An example might be that of a researcher who wants to discover how a day unit for people with learning disabilities works, including dynamic processes and key relationships. In this case, the researcher might spend weeks or even months observing life in the unit, so that service users and staff accept his or her presence. Such a detailed process is extremely time-consuming, and is not likely to be suitable for a small-scale study.

Action research

Action research focuses on a particular task or problem. The project is conducted by a group of people (often a group of colleagues) who regularly review and monitor aspects of an issue, to make decisions about how it should be tackled. An example might be that of a group of health staff, who want to make improvements to the way that patients are assessed and then admitted to a treatment programme. Staff might keep diaries of what is going on, interview patients and also analyse service use data. As time goes by, they will introduce changes to the system, and then monitor the impact of those changes. As this style involves the collaboration of a group of people over time, and in the context of an ongoing work situation, it is unlikely to be relevant to a small-scale project. However, the findings of action research projects may provide useful secondary information.

Key concepts in research

When conducting research, a key distinction is made between primary data and secondary data.

Primary data

Primary data is the information collected by a researcher during the course of a study. Such information might include:

* information from questionnaires
* notes made during the observation of a person or group of people
* notes/transcripts/recordings made during an interview
* experimental data.

The collection and analysis of primary data will be discussed in the sections on collecting and analysing information. With respect to the project undertaken for this unit, primary data will be the information you collect directly in relation to the topic you are investigating.

> **Key concept**
>
> *Primary data:* the actual data collected by a researcher during the course of a study.

SCENARIO

What difference has it made?

Nas is studying the impact of a series of reminiscence sessions in a residential unit for older people.

His primary data includes:

* notes made when observing one of the sessions

* the views of people attending the sessions (collected by questionnaire)

* the views of both the unit manager and other staff (collected by interview).

1. What other methods of data collection might Nas consider?

2. What ethical principles should Nas observe when collecting this data?

FIGURE 10.6 *Nas used several data collection techniques*

Secondary data

Secondary data is that collected by people other than the researcher (see Figure 10.7). Someone doing research will collect data from other sources to put his or her investigation into context, to make comparisons or to draw analogies. Sometimes, a researcher will make particular reference to other studies that appear to lend support to the findings of his or her piece of work.

Key concept

Secondary data: the data collected by people other than the researcher of a given project, and found in other published or Internet sources.

Sources of secondary data

* official statistics (e.g. census data)

* books on the relevant topic

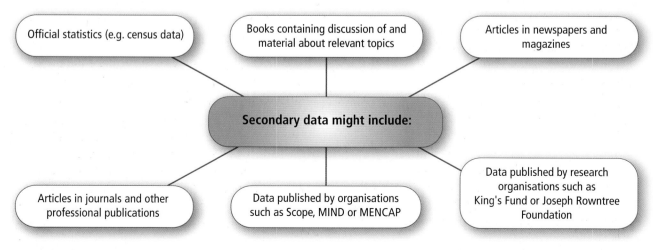

Official statistics (e.g. census data)

Books containing discussion of and material about relevant topics

Articles in newspapers and magazines

Secondary data might include:

Articles in journals and other professional publications

Data published by organisations such as Scope, MIND or MENCAP

Data published by research organisations such as King's Fund or Joseph Rowntree Foundation

FIGURE 10.7 *Sources of secondary data*

* articles in newspapers and magazines
* articles in journals and professional publications
* data published by organisations such as Scope, MIND or MENCAP
* data published by research organisations such as King's Fund.

A piece of primary research, such as the evaluative study of Hartrigg Oaks commissioned by the Joseph Rowntree Foundation becomes secondary research when it is cited by someone else in another study.

Quantitative data

Quantitative data is that which can be expressed numerically (i.e. it can be quantified). It is difficult (but not impossible) to express purely qualitative data numerically. A number of examples of quantitative data have already been cited. Such data is useful to a researcher because it allows conclusions or inferences to be drawn from the information collected. The interpretation of data will be discussed more fully below (page 195).

The production of quantitative data is an important element of scientific enquiry. For example, it would be unscientific to say that 'most of' the patients in a piece of research responded well to a certain treatment. This means little in scientific terms. It is more meaningful to quantify this and to state that, for example, 80 per cent

SCENARIO
Research in context

For her research project, Natalie is going to describe a new initiative in communicating with people who have learning disabilities. She is studying group sessions in one of the day units of her local authority, where staff are using special techniques to help people with learning disabilities to express themselves. She is also going to investigate how effective these new techniques are.

She needs to find out about similar projects elsewhere, to provide background information and points of comparison. To find this secondary data she starts with the Valuing People website. Here, she finds some of the information she needs, together with links to the websites of other helpful organisations, and references to other published secondary sources.

1. What other sources of secondary data might Natalie use?
2. How can she use this information to help with her project?

Natalie uses the secondary data she collects to put her research into context. She discovers that there are other places where new ways of empowering people with learning disabilities are being tried. These include advocacy, self-advocacy, mentoring and facilitation. One of these projects has actually been evaluated, so she decides to adapt one of the questionnaires for use in her own project. She cites this other research in her own report, giving a full acknowledgement.

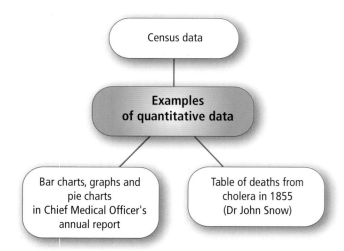

FIGURE 10.8 *Examples of quantitative data*

quantitative data about the incidence of a particular disease, failure to collect qualitative information about the feelings of the women taking part in the study resulted in a high drop-out rate, so the results were not as comprehensive as they might have been.

of patients in a clinical trial of 3,000 people responded well to the same treatment. Note, too, that in a well-conducted research study, both the results of the treatment and the total number of people in the sample are quantified.

Qualitative data

Qualitative data is concerned with abstract concepts such as values, attitudes and opinions and cannot always be expressed numerically. Such data is expressed by the subjects of a study in their own words, and is often concerned with how people feel, how they view particular issues or events, what they would like to do or what kinds of service they would like to receive.

In social research projects, researchers will often leave a space somewhere on the questionnaire for people to add their own comments. Indeed, qualitative information can be very useful in the design stage of a piece of research. It is good practice to obtain the views of people who are likely to be involved. Such opinions can alert researchers to key issues, and to help them avoid making serious errors of judgement with respect to the design and implementation of the research. This is true for both evaluative and experimental types of research.

In the scenario on page 173 the example was given of poor design with respect to a clinical study of a particular disease. Although the ultimate focus of this study was to produce

SCENARIO

A question of quality

A private research company has been asked to evaluate the impact of a new community centre on an estate where there are a number of high-rise blocks.

At a very early stage in planning the project the researcher, Jon, attends several local group meetings (e.g. the pre-school playgroup, the residents' association) and meets with a number of other people, such as the local community police officer, to explain the research and to ask people what they think. He tape-records what people tell him, and then uses the information to plan his research.

1. **What basic principles should Jon observe before and during this initial fact-finding exercise?**
2. **How might he prepare for each of these meetings?**

In this example, Jon has started his enquiries with an open mind. He doesn't ask people to fill in questionnaires at this point, but he does have some questions of his own. By asking open questions such as 'What do you think about the new community centre?', or simple specific questions such as 'Who do you think I need to talk to?', he starts to build up a general picture of the current situation. From this initial enquiry, he can start to focus in on key people and issues to investigate in a more structured way.

Qualitative data can be useful to supplement quantitative material. The Hartrigg Oaks research uses the actual comments of residents to augment and explain the more numerical information expressed in tables and bar charts.

Planning your research

When planning your own research project, it is a good idea to consider how you will use both qualitative and quantitative data.

Structured and unstructured data

The terms *structured* and *unstructured* are used with respect to methods of data collection. Broadly speaking, data which is collected in a structured way can be quantified, whereas unstructured data cannot.

Jon, in the scenario above, began collecting qualitative data about his research in a fairly unstructured way. He didn't take along questionnaires to standardise the responses of the people he consulted, and made no attempt to quantify what he was told. He was content to record the responses, to listen and to accept information in whatever format people wished to express themselves. In contrast, as he moved into the next phase of the project, he began to devise ways of standardising responses. There are several ways to standardise responses to questions, including ticking boxes or circling numbers. This is what is meant by the term structured data collection (see Figure 10.9), and if used appropriately it can provide a way of quantifying qualitative responses.

The first two questions on the questionnaire in Figure 10.9 collect structured data. This can be analysed numerically. Once all the questionnaires have been completed, the researcher can add up the number of answers to each question, and then express the results in terms of numbers or percentages. For example, the results might show that 40 per cent of respondents considered the community centre offered a good service, 40 per cent felt the service was just average, and 20 per cent thought it was poor.

In contrast, Question 3 makes no attempt to structure what people want to say and, in theory, any responses are possible here. Of course, it is always possible that the researcher can classify these 'free-ranging' responses into broad areas. He might be able to say, from such an analysis, that about 30 per cent of respondents indicated they would like to see different opening hours to the ones currently operating, or that 23 per

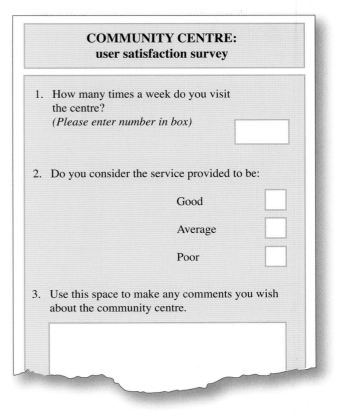

COMMUNITY CENTRE: user satisfaction survey

1. How many times a week do you visit the centre?
   (Please enter number in box)

2. Do you consider the service provided to be:

   Good

   Average

   Poor

3. Use this space to make any comments you wish about the community centre.

FIGURE 10.9 *A simple questionnaire*

cent found the centre difficult to access because they had particular mobility problems. However, because of the unstructured nature of the way this information is collected, any conclusions drawn will have to be cautious, and may need further investigation.

Try it out

Design a very short questionnaire for people to complete by themselves. The task is either to find out what medication or what services respondents receive. The subjects are a group of people aged over 75 years.

Selecting a group of subjects

Identifying who to include as the subjects of your research depends on your objectives and the topic chosen.

Subject: as well as meaning a 'topic' (such as maths or English), the term subject(s) is used in research methodology to indicate the person or people who are being studied in a particular piece of research.

Population: as well as meaning the people who live in a particular country or area, this term is used in research methodology to indicate the total number of people who are being studied. Sometimes, the population of a study is composed of households rather than individuals.

Case studies and defined populations

In a small-scale study such as the one you will undertake for this unit, the choice of population may be straightforward. In the demographic study described on page 166 (location of a new Sure Start day centre) the researchers needed to find out about all single parents in the borough. Census data enabled them to establish the geographical location of this particular population. In the study of Hartrigg Oaks, the population of the two postal surveys included all residents of the community.

Sampling

Sometimes it is not possible to include all relevant subjects within the scope of a piece of research. It would be very difficult, for example, to measure the physiological changes resulting from smoking by studying every smoker in the UK. This would involve testing possibly hundreds of thousands of individuals, and the logistical problems would be immense. For larger-scale studies such as this, a procedure known as *sampling* is necessary in order to reduce the population to a manageable size.

Sampling: the selection of a representative cross-section of the population being studied.

Opportunity sampling

Even when a population is well-defined, the researcher may have to be content with whoever

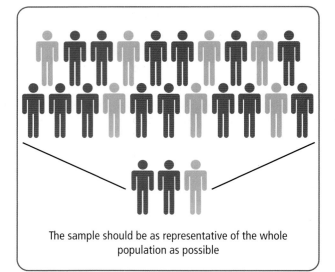

The sample should be as representative of the whole population as possible

FIGURE 10.10 *The sampling technique*

is available to form the subject group. Not everyone may be willing or able to take part in a survey, for example. Similarly, members of a group that is being observed may not all be present at the time the observation is made. This is very likely to be the case in a small-scale study where time and human resources are limited.

Random sampling

Researchers may use a number of different sampling methods to arrive at the population of a study. One such method is known as random sampling. Before random sampling can be done, a sampling frame has to be drawn up. This is basically a comprehensive list of potential subjects.

If, for example, researchers want to monitor the effectiveness of a new diagnostic technique designed to pick up early signs of cancer in older women, the total population may be defined as all women living in a certain area aged 50 plus. One way to make a random sample would be to ask all GP surgeries in that area to print out lists of all their female patients of that age. This list would then be the sampling frame. The next stage would be to select names from that list, perhaps every tenth name, in order to give a smaller scale list of subjects for study. A better way to ensure a truly random sample would be to generate a random list of numbers by computer, and then to ask GPs to produce those names corresponding to those numbered places on the sampling frame list.

Stratified random sampling

Sometimes, researchers will want to use a different sampling technique, especially if it is important to make sure that key sub-groups within a population are properly represented.

Suppose that the objective is to establish satisfaction levels amongst people using a new community outreach scheme. An initial survey of everyone using the scheme might be done easily by using a very simple questionnaire, but there might be too many users to do in-depth interviews with everyone. The sampling frame would be the list of all people known to use the service. However, if the list showed that there were far more women than men using the scheme (e.g. 70 per cent of users being women), then researchers would need to make sure that the sample chosen for the in-depth interviews represented this 70:30 gender split. This means that if 100 people were selected for interview, 70 should be women and only 30 should be men. This technique is known as proportionate stratified sampling.

There is yet another kind of stratified random sampling known as disproportionate stratified sampling. Suppose that a very small number of people using the outreach scheme are from a particular ethnic community. Perhaps only five people are from this cultural group, and they represent less than 1 per cent of the total population of the study. If proportionate stratified sampling were to be used, only one out of the 100 people selected for interview would be from this group. However, if cultural issues were felt to be important, then researchers might want to make sure that the views of all five people in this cultural group should be determined. There might be important reasons why people from this group were not using the outreach facility, and interviewing all five people might provide important information for service planners.

In this case, the researchers have deliberately structured the way in which subjects are selected in order to make sure that small but significant groups within the study population are properly represented. The data from such small groups can also be analysed and presented separately, to highlight any differences between them and the rest of the study population.

Quota sampling

Yet another sampling technique is known as quota sampling. This is often used by market researchers, who might be instructed to stop a specified number of, for example, men of a certain age in the street, and then to ask them questions, perhaps about a particular product or service. If, for example, a council wanted to assess reactions to a new one-stop shop facility in a shopping centre, then the quota sampling method might involve interviewers stopping 100 men and 100 women as they left the premises, in order to get their views on the service.

> ### Did you know?
>
> Many councils and health authorities now have 'one-stop shops', often situated in easily accessible places such as shopping centres. Here, local people can get information and advice about what's on offer, including health, social care, leisure, environmental health and many more services and facilities.

It will not be necessary for you to demonstrate use of these more sophisticated sampling techniques in the small-scale study for this unit. However, knowledge of how populations are sampled may help you to evaluate some of the secondary research collected at the start of your study.

Triangulation

Sometimes, particularly in larger studies, researchers will cross-check their findings by collecting data from a number of different sources and informants. A case study of group behaviours in a mental health day centre, for example, may be compared with data from a different centre elsewhere. Such a comparison will allow a more balanced account to be made of observed behaviours. This process is known as triangulation.

You may be able to use triangulation in your own project, if you are able to obtain data relevant to your project from another source.

Methods of data collection

Questionnaires

It may be that some of the data needed for your research is best collected by means of a questionnaire. You will have to decide whether the questionnaires will be self-completed (by the people taking part in your study), or whether they will be completed by yourself in conversation with each subject in an interview-type situation. Interviews will be considered more fully below (pages 188–91).

> ### Key concept
> *Respondent:* a person who takes part in a survey, and who 'responds' to the questions (either by self-completion of a questionnaire, or during an interview).

The information in this section applies mainly to self-completion questionnaires. Advice on conducting interviews is given later.

FIGURE 10.11 *'I'll never get this in an envelope, even if I do complete it.'*

When questionnaires are self-completed, clear instructions must be given, and the form must be user-friendly and easy to complete. Short, simple forms are more likely to be completed fully than long, complicated ones.

The distinction between structured and unstructured data was discussed above, and a mini-questionnaire was shown giving examples of questions designed to collect both types of data. To remind you, structured data is that which can be expressed numerically, whilst unstructured data is less easy to quantify.

Questions to collect unstructured data

Unstructured data is usually collected by means of the verbal or open question. Open questions cannot be answered simply by 'yes' or 'no', so a respondent has to find his or her own words to give an answer. Open questions usually begin with the words 'what', 'why' and 'how'.

> ### Key concept
> *Open question:* one which cannot be answered by 'yes' or 'no', and requires a response to be made in someone's own words.

Open questions are useful in questionnaires for collecting qualitative data, such as respondents' views or opinions, or where researchers are interested in exploring all angles of an issue, including some that they had maybe not thought of. Some examples are:

* What are your views about the meals on wheels service in your locality?

* What differences have you observed as a result of taking this drug?

* Why did you choose to use this service?

* How are you feeling as a result of having acupuncture?

Open questions are often used on questionnaires to gain qualitative information that is additional to the quantitative data collected in the structured part of the form. Sometimes, such data can be analysed and expressed numerically, especially if the researcher can detect a trend in the responses. However, you need to be very experienced in order to do this well, particularly if there are a lot of questionnaires to analyse.

Questions to collect structured data

There are a number of different options when seeking to collect structured data by questionnaire, six of which are set out in Table 10.4 (following Bell 1993: 76–7).

The straightforward closed question can also be used. A closed question can be answered 'yes' or 'no', and can be useful in determining which categories a respondent falls into. For example:

✱ Do you use medication to control your condition?

✱ Does your child need physiotherapy?

✱ Do you need help in getting in and out of bed?

The closed question can also be used in conjunction with a technique known as routing. If a respondent answers in a certain way to a closed question, then he or she can be redirected on to a different part of the form. For example:

> 3. Do you use medication to control your condition?

> If 'no', please go straight to question 7.

(Questions 4, 5 and 6 would then deal with aspects of taking medication. The person who answered 'no' at this point would not need to answer these particular questions.)

The *list* (Table 10.4) is useful when you want to establish which of several options applies to

TYPE	EXAMPLE
List	Which of the following services do you use? (Please tick all that apply to you) Home care Meals service Residential care Other (please specify)
Category	Which of the following age groups do you belong to? (Please tick one category only) 19 years or under 20–25 years 26–30 years 31 years or over
Ranking	Place the following leisure activities in order of their importance to you by giving a number to each (1 = least important, 5 = most important): swimming movement and music art classes drama group craft activities
Quantity	How many times have you visited your GP in the last six months? (Please enter the number of times in the box)
Scale	The service given at my local GP surgery is: Excellent Good Average Fair Poor 1 2 3 4 5 (Please circle the number that most closely corresponds to your opinion)
Grid	See Table 10.5 for an example of a grid to collect data.

TABLE 10.4 *Question types: structured data collection*

each of your subjects. A respondent can tick as many items in the list as are applicable. You may also want to pre-code items in the list for ease of analysis. This can be done by splitting questions down into the categories that will later be used for analysis (e.g. the age of subjects can be subdivided into meaningful bands, such as birth–5 years, over 65 years etc). A number can be allocated to each of these; analysis can then proceed by totalling the instances of each number (e.g. twenty instances of number 16, etc). With the category type of question, a respondent will tick only one of a number of boxes, and again you may wish to pre-code each item for future analysis. As with lists, it is often useful to add the category 'other' to allow for options that you may not have anticipated.

The ranking type of question is normally used to establish the relative importance that a respondent attached to specific characteristics, qualities or even services. You might use this method to find out which activities potential users of leisure services might value and use.

The scale has a similar use, and can be used to ask respondents to attach values to specific characteristics or services. In the example above (Table 10.4), people have been asked to rate the service provided at the local GP surgery. Here, respondents have been allowed a choice of five scores, allowing them to select a mid-point score if they feel ambivalent about an issue. Some researchers would offer only a four-point scale (e.g. excellent, good, fair, poor), as it is claimed that a five-point scale allows people to sit on the fence, and leads to meaningless scores of 'average'. However, others criticise the four-point scale on the grounds that it can polarise scores artificially;

people may be genuinely ambivalent about certain issues, and should have the opportunity to express this. Forcing them to choose between 'better' and 'worse' ends of a scale may not necessarily lead to meaningful scores.

The grid (see Table 10.5) can be used to express more than one parameter at the same time, and collates the data into more than one category. Using the grid below, for example, the researcher could produce tables to show the total number of people using each service, and the number using each supplier. Preferences towards particular types of supplier would show up, for example if the people in the sample preferred the Age Concern day facilities to those provided by the council.

Using one or more of these types of structured questions will provide you with data than can be analysed numerically, even if it concerns people's views and opinions. In practice, researchers often use a number of different types of question on the same questionnaire, although they keep it simple by grouping question types together. Structured questions can be supplemented by unstructured data collection on the same form.

Questionnaire design and layout

It is important to give careful consideration to the design of a questionnaire, which should be neither too complex, nor too long.

Points to consider include:

* type the questionnaire
* consider the font size and design; will any of your respondents have visual problems?
* use plenty of white space; this aids clarity
* make instructions clear

Please indicate by ticking the appropriate boxes which services you receive and who provides them.

	Council	Age Concern	NHS	Private company	Don't use this service
Day facilities					
Meals service					
Chiropody					
Community nurse					

TABLE 10.5 *Structured data collection using a grid*

* explain abbreviations, acronyms and jargon

* if using tick-boxes, align to the right-hand side of the sheet

* leave complex questions to the end.

Consider this

A bit too vague

Andrea is studying transport use by people who attend a day facility for people with physical and sensory disabilities. She wants to find out about the frequency of use of the council's buses.

Her first attempt is:

How much do you use the council's bus service?

(Please tick) Very often
　　　　　　　Sometimes
　　　　　　　Not very often.

1. What problems might be anticipated if this wording is used?

2. How might the questions be improved?

Piloting the questionnaire

Even in a small-scale study, it can be useful to have a 'dry run', to test out the questionnaire before moving on to the collection of 'real' data. Asking other people to complete the prototype form may throw up some unforeseen ambiguities or problems.

A pilot exercise involving three centre users reveals that Andrea's questions are too vague and won't give her very reliable data. Each of the three choices is open to personal interpretation. 'Very often' to one person might mean every week, whilst to another it might mean every day.

On reflection, she therefore opts for a quantity-type question, which limits respondents to specific choices which can be quantified.

Andrea's revised question

How many times a week do you use the council's bus service?

☐

(Please enter a number in the box. If you do not use this service, please enter a zero.)

There are a number of other potential problems with respect to the wording of questions, some of which are shown in Table 10.6 (see Bell 1993: 79–81).

QUESTION TYPE	EXAMPLE	NOTES
1. Leading question	In your opinion, why is the council's decision a good thing?	Expects respondent to agree that this decision is indeed a good thing.
2. Presuming question	Why should CAMS be available on the NHS?	Like (1), makes assumption that respondent agrees with the proposition (i.e. that complementary therapies should be available on the NHS).
3. Double questions	Do you use physiotherapy and the day hospital service?	If a respondent uses only one of these, it is not clear how s/he should respond.
4. Hypothetical questions	If you satisfied the eligibility criteria, which services would you choose?	Unlikely to give anything worth measuring.
5. Sensitive questions/ insensitive wording	Are you too disabled to access this building?	This question labels the respondent; it would be better to ask: 'Do you have problems accessing this building?'

TABLE 10.6 *Questions to avoid*

Interviews

Interviews can be structured, unstructured or semi-structured in the way they are designed and carried out. Whichever method you use, it is important to value and respect your interview subjects.

Valuing the person

If you choose to collect data by interviewing your subjects (either face-to-face or by telephone) then there are a number of additional considerations to keep in mind. The people you are interviewing are not simply sources of data for your project, but are unique individuals, each of whom has a right to be treated with respect. You will need to have the right attitude if an interview is to be a success.

Ethics and interviews

The subject of ethics in research will be considered in some depth below (pages 204–5). However, this is a good point to note that the British Psychological Society (BPS) has produced a code of ethical principles for conducting research with people, in order to guide psychologists. The BPS code is actually intended for use by chartered psychologists, but it represents good practice, and does provide a point of reference for the ethics of interview (and other) research. The code's key principles for research with people are:

* obtaining consent
* avoiding deception
* providing debriefing
* enabling withdrawal from investigation
* maintaining confidentiality and the anonymity of participants
* protecting participants from harm.

You will be asking a number of people to help you by answering some very personal questions, and/or to give you personal (and maybe difficult) details about themselves. Because you are asking for their help, it is vital that you get their consent to taking part in your research project. You must therefore explain the nature of your project, and how you will use any information that you get. It can sometimes be a good idea to allow participants to talk about their part in the project afterwards – this is known as debriefing. For example, evaluation of a project might include the opportunity for subjects to tell you what they thought about how it was conducted. Taking an ethical approach applies equally to the collection of data by self-completed questionnaires.

You must guarantee that you will not use the person's real name or any details (such as addresses, details of relatives or photographs) that could identify who they are. In other words, you must provide a guarantee of anonymity.

Your questions and checklists should be prepared well in advance, and (as discussed above) preferably piloted before the 'real' interviews take place. You must check out with your tutor, or another professional who knows your subjects, how you intend to conduct your interviews. Be sure that your questions will not threaten your subjects or cause offence. The single most important consideration when interviewing people is to respect and value their personal identity.

Interviewing people with learning disabilities

If your research requires you to interview people with learning disabilities, you will need to take expert advice about the best way of structuring both the interview itself and also the way that you collect data. There are now a number of specialised ways of empowering people with learning disabilities to express themselves, including using an advocate, self-advocacy and facilitated sessions to make it easy for people to choose between options or to express their views. Information about empowering people with learning disabilities is available on the Valuing People website.

FIGURE 10.12 *Facilitated sessions are often used to empower people with learning disabilities to express themselves*

Conducting an interview

Thorough planning is essential to conducting successful interviews. There are a number of practical considerations to bear in mind, and these are set out in Table 10.7.

Interviews can be structured, semi-structured or unstructured or a combination of two or all of these techniques.

Structured/semi-structured interviews

In the structured interview, the researcher uses a schedule which might be very similar to the self-completion questionnaire. The interviewer will read out each question, completing or ticking the boxes, and circling the relevant responses as required. If the respondent doesn't understand something, the interviewer can explain as required.

Time	Choose times that are mutually convenient for both interviewees and yourself. Make sure that your interview sessions don't clash with something else that people would normally be doing.
Pacing	Don't take on too many interviews at one time. Conducting even one interview can be very tiring, depending on its length and content.
Venue	Choose a venue that is convenient for everybody who is going to be involved. It should be suitable for holding private, quiet conversations. The room needs to be comfortable, neither too hot nor too cold, and well-ventilated.
Furniture	Furniture should be comfortable, but not so as to cause drowsiness. Consider whether you will need a table to lean on (to take notes) or whether you will have your papers on a clip-board.
Accessibility	This is another factor to consider with respect to the venue. If you or your respondents have mobility problems, for example, you will have to make sure that everyone has easy access to the building/room you have chosen.
Additional help	Consider whether you will need a signer (for any deaf people) or an interpreter. You may have your own sensory or language needs. In either case, you'll need to check out whether the venue is adequate to accommodate yourself, your subject and any helper who is present. Similarly, people with learning disabilities may require the presence of an advocate or carer.
Recording unstructured data	Consider whether you will: – use a tape recorder – take notes – bring a second person to take notes. The interviewee must be quite comfortable with whatever method of recording you choose.

TABLE 10.7 *Preparing to conduct an interview session*

There are a number of advantages to using a structured interview, as far as the quality of data is concerned:

* all or most of the questions are likely to be answered (respondents may leave unanswered questions in a self-completed questionnaire)

* the risk of misunderstanding questions is minimised

* the risk of collusion between respondents is avoided

* the interviewer can dictate the pace of the interview

* additional responses/reactions may be observed by the interviewer

* problems of reading, writing and comprehension can be overcome

* quantitative data will be produced in a standardised way

* sensory and physical problems can be overcome.

When conducting a structured interview, the researcher aims to ask the questions in the same way for each respondent. This is to make sure that data collected is standardised, and to minimise bias (for more on bias, see below, pages 202–3).

The interviewer may also have a list of prompts or probes to help respondents provide further detail in specific areas, for example:

> Question 6
> Do you consider that you receive enough practical support?
>
> Yes   Go to Question 7
>
> No   Why is this?
>   Would you like to get your existing service more frequently?
>   What else would you like to receive?

Here, the technique of routing is also used. If the respondent answers 'Yes' to Question 6, then the interviewer moves straight on to Question 7. If the answer is 'no', then the interviewer moves to

a series of prompts to elicit further data from the respondent.

This use of a combination of question types is also known as semi-structured interviewing. This method involves starting from a list of prepared questions, but then allowing the respondent to answer these in his or her own words. The technique can also be used to allow interview subjects to introduce their own themes within a given topic (see Table 10.8).

TOPIC	OPEN QUESTIONS/PROMPTS
Social circumstances	Tell me about yourself. What's it like where you live?
Health	Tell me about your current state of health. What's your state of health like at the moment?
Service use	Why do you come to this drop-in centre? Tell me about the things you do here.

TABLE 10.8 *Collecting semi-structured data*

Unstructured interviewing

Unstructured data collection occurs when interviewees are allowed to talk about anything they want to, without any further prompting on the part of the interviewer. Although the interviewer will probably initiate the topic, after that there will be little attempt to control what the subject wants to disclose. This method is also known as in-depth interviewing, as it often allows a respondent to say what he or she really thinks about something. An example of the opening of an unstructured interview follows.

> Topic
> Sleep clinic at GP Surgery
>
> Opening prompt
> 'Now that you've been attending the sleep clinic for a few months, we'd like to know what you think about it.'

The interviewer wants the subject (in this case a new mother) to talk about her personal experiences of attending the sleep clinic with her baby. Using a totally unstructured approach, the conversation may go anywhere that the respondent wishes. However, the interviewer may need to clarify certain points. The subject may even begin to talk about some personal problems which are nothing to do with the sleep clinic as such. The interviewer will have to be prepared for this, and to offer other support as necessary.

In practice, and in the context of specific research, it is likely that the researcher will want to retain ultimate control of the interview, whether it is structured, semi-structured or unstructured.

Observation

Another method of data collection is that of observation. Observation is often used when making case studies (e.g. observing aspects of service use in a mental health drop-in centre) or ethnographic studies (e.g. watching the interaction of a group of young children and adults). It can also be used in conjunction with the experimental method. An example of this might be when two groups are observed separately, one of which is subject to certain conditions but the other is not. The objective in this case is to see if there are noticeable behavioural differences between the two groups.

Observation can be by a participant (i.e. someone who takes part in the activities with the subjects of the study) or by non-participant observers (see Table 10.9).

An excellent example of a participant-observation is that made by Croft (1999). She wanted to study the ways in which men at a residential establishment (Esplanade) expressed their individual identities through speech and story. She spent a considerable time in the house with them, sometimes helping them with tasks like laundry (although this was discouraged by the centre staff). Gradually, she learned how each of the residents liked to be listened to, and became accepted by them. As a result, she elicited a number of conversations and stories which she later recorded and used as the basis of her study.

However, one of the problems with the

METHOD	TECHNIQUES USED
Participant	– researcher works/lives alongside the subjects of the study – data collection is often unstructured – researcher records significant behaviour, situations and events.
Non-participant	– researcher watches events whilst remaining as unobtrusive as possible – may use grids or charts to record what goes on (e.g. interaction between individuals in a group) – the process may be video-recorded or tape-recorded.

For more on this, see Bell 1993:109–21

TABLE 10.9 *Observational research methods*

SCENARIO
The observer's paradox

Kit wants to find out about the importance of art sessions in a day unit for people with learning disabilities. She plans to attend a session so she can see what they do, and she decides she will also take part by doing some painting herself.

On her first visit, the instructor introduces her to the group, and they are so interested in Kit that they crowd around her, asking lots of questions. The session takes longer to get going than normal, and even then people sometimes stop what they are doing to go and talk to or watch Kit. One young woman becomes very jealous of the attention the others are paying to Kit, and there is a brief disagreement between her and another group member.

Kit's presence in the group has thus affected their normal behaviours and, to some extent, their relationships.

1. What can be done to minimise the impact of this effect (known as the observer's paradox)?
2. How does this need to be built into your research plan?
3. How might the presence of an observer affect the validity of data?

participant method of observation is that subjects will often modify their behaviour, simply because of the presence of a stranger (the researcher). See scenario on page 191.

In contrast, the observers in the scenario below deliberately remain apart from their subjects. They are thus non-participant observers.

In this example, the researchers are particularly keen to note how the children react with each other. The presence of an adult would interfere with this process.

When using the observational method, it is extremely important to decide exactly what is being measured or recorded. Bell notes that the focus of observation is usually one or more of the following (1993:111):

* content (what happens)

* process (the way in which something happens)

* interaction (how participants respond or react to each other)

* the way in which participants contribute to what is going on

* specific aspects of behaviour (violence, concentration span, etc.).

(See Figure 10.14 for specimen observation sheet.)

When conducting interviews or observations, it is essential to work with supervision. In practice, this means having a professional worker such as a care worker or manager present while you are working with a service user. This protects your interests, as well as those of your subject. Such a professional person might also advise you on questionnaire design, and how best to conduct an interview or an observation. Always take such advice when it is given, and observe any house rules or regulations when conducting your research.

There are some very sophisticated classification systems for describing behaviour which are too complex for inclusion here. These are discussed and documented in Bell (1993:112–14). The successful observation of behaviour requires a high level of skill and specialist knowledge. Unless you are very confident and experienced in this kind of work, avoid aiming to produce a very detailed analysis of interactions and behaviours.

SCENARIO
Keeping a distance

Researchers want to observe the response of young children watching TV programmes, in particular to establish whether boys and girls react differently.

The children watch TV in a room which has a one-way observation glass panel fitted in one wall. Observers note how long the children concentrate when watching different kinds of programme, and how they interact.

They record their observations on specially pre-prepared forms. They also video-record the children's behaviour for further analysis.

1. **How should children be protected during the course of a research project?**
2. **Are there any specific ethical considerations where children are concerned?**
3. **How much should be explained to the children beforehand?**

FIGURE 10.13 *Researchers can use one-way observation glass panels to observe how children interact when no adults are present*

SPECIMEN: OBSERVATION SHEET

Observing social interaction in service users in a day unit for people with a learning disability.

Group ....

Number in group ....

Date ....

Time from: .... To ....

Aim:

Activity during observation

Are there any 'friendship groups' evident within the group as a whole?

Are there any individuals who appear not to get involved with the activity?

Are there any obvious group leaders?

Are there any individuals who seek more attention from the session tutor than the others?

Do people share equipment with each other?

Do people help each other?

Are there any individuals who appear to be actively avoiding interaction with the others?

Candidate's Signature ....

Supervisor's Signature ....

Notes:

FIGURE 10.14 *Specimen observation sheet*

Experiments

Experiments involve the setting up of specific situations in order to test the validity of particular theories or hypotheses. Experiments are often concerned with establishing causal relationships, for example that music therapy helps control post-operative pain. In principle, the researcher is in control of all the variables and parameters within an experiment, which should provide quantitative data for analysis. A good experiment is capable of *replication*; it can be repeated using exactly the same conditions so several sets of results can be compared. If results are similar over a number of experiments, firm conclusions may be made from the data.

Some experiments are relatively straightforward to design and control, such as the testing of pharmaceutical products. A sampling frame will be set up according to pre-defined criteria (e.g. age, medical condition) and a population selected at random from this sampling frame. This group will receive the new drug. A second or control group (which satisfies the same criteria as the first group) will either receive no treatment, a placebo, or the existing standard treatment, as in the scenario below. This method is very common in clinical trials (see pages 168–9). Experiments can also be used to compare and contrast the impact of different kinds of treatment on people with the same medical condition.

SCENARIO

Early intervention in multiple sclerosis: a longitudinal study

Researchers want to test out the hypothesis that early intervention with people who have multiple sclerosis (MS) has a greater impact on the progression of this disease than treatment which is given at a later stage.

MS is a condition in which the immune system goes into overdrive, and the body's T-cells start to attack the myelin sheath that surrounds the spinal cord.

The scientists have recruited 180 patients known to be in the early stages of MS, two-thirds of whom will receive a new drug, Campath-1H. The remaining third of the sample will receive Beta Interferon, which is currently quite commonly used to treat this disease.

Subjects in both groups will be monitored regularly for five years, and the final results will not be available for seven years.

Source: Coles and Cox (2002)

1. **In an experimental study, how can researchers avoid influencing results?**
2. **Why is it important to do longitudinal research to test a new pharmaceutical product?**

The kind of project described above is known as a *longitudinal study*, because it lasts for a significant period of time. This particular study contrasts two groups, one receiving a new treatment, and the other a conventional, existing treatment. Researchers can avoid prejudicing the outcome of an experiment by not telling subjects which group they belong to. This eliminates any possible psychological bias. This is considered to be even more effective when researchers themselves do not know which group subjects have been allocated to. This is known as a double-blind trial, and is often used when the control group receives a 'placebo' rather than another pharmaceutical product.

Key concept

Longitudinal study: a research study that lasts for a significant period of time, allowing the impact of a number of variables to be taken into account.

Experiments to measure or predict human behaviour are harder to set up and control. Nevertheless, researchers, especially psychologists, do use the experimental method to investigate aspects of human behaviour. They often combine the setting up of an experimental situation with aspects of the observational method of data collection.

This research described in the scenario below raises a number of ethical questions. It also indicates that sometimes an experiment can run out of the control of researchers. The 'prison' situation became so realistic that when asked if they would forfeit the money earned from participating in the study by taking an early 'parole', 'prisoners' who agreed were even prepared to wait for the decision of a 'parole board' as to whether or not their request was accepted. They seemed to have forgotten that they could, in theory, walk away from the experiment at any time.

Some other data collection methods

There are a number of other data collection techniques that are worth bearing in mind. These include diaries, logs and a technique known as critical incident analysis.

SCENARIO

Prisoners and guards

In the early 1970s, researchers wanted to show that sadistic and cruel behaviour by prison guards resulted from the nature of the conditions, rather than from an innate disposition to cruelty. They set up a 'mock prison', and selected 24 subjects from a group of 75 men who responded to a newspaper advertisement, asking for volunteers to take part in a study of 'prison life'. Each of the 24 subjects was randomly allocated to the role of either 'guard' or 'prisoner'. One 'guard' dropped out before the start of the experiment, and two 'prisoners' were put on stand-by.

Both groups wore uniforms, and the 'guards' also wore reflective sunglasses to prevent eye-contact with 'prisoners'. To make it more realistic, the 'prisoners' were 'arrested' in their own homes, taken to the experimental prison and subjected to a humiliating admission procedure.

As the experiment progressed, both 'guards' and 'prisoners' displayed increasingly negative attitudes and behaviours. Guards became aggressive and insulting, whilst prisoners became passive and compliant, some of them exhibiting a range of behaviours including depression and anxiety. Some displayed rage and anger.

The experiment was terminated early after six days, as behaviours were becoming destructive.

Source: Haney, Banks and Zimbardo (1973)

Researchers want to assess the usefulness of a new piece of equipment designed for use when assisting people with disabilities to move between the bed and a chair.

They ask care assistants in a residential unit to try out the equipment when appropriate, keeping diaries of what they do. In particular, they want care assistants to note any difficulties, and also to record any specific incidents – good or bad – relating to the new device.

They also ask the people who have been assisted to move in this way to keep similar diaries.

After a six-week period, researchers study the diaries and accounts of these specific instances (which are also referred to as 'critical' incidents). They also interview the care assistants and residents to obtain further qualitative data. The number of occasions on which difficulties were experienced (and the types of difficulty encountered) can be expressed quantitatively.

1. **Can you see any potential difficulties with the diary technique of data collection?**
2. **How objective might such data be?**
3. **Does this matter?**

You might want to combine the use of questionnaires with one or more of these techniques, depending on what it is you are seeking to research.

Interpreting and presenting data

How good is your data?

In research methodology, there are two concepts that relate to the quality of the data collected, and consequently to the significance of the conclusions reached. These are *reliability* and *validity*.

Reliability relates to the extent to which a set of results can be reproduced by repeating a piece of research. When researchers do systematic reviews of randomised clinical controlled trials (page 168), for example, they are looking to see (among other things) how far test results have been repeated under similar conditions. If the same results are found time and again, then the findings may be said to be reliable.

The reliability of survey data can be assessed by asking how far similar answers would have been given to interviewers on different occasions.

For a small-scale research study, it should not be necessary to apply scientific tests of reliability. However, it will be important to demonstrate an awareness of the ways in which the reliability of data may be affected by the circumstances under which they were collected, and to build this into any conclusions or inferences made at the end of the project.

The second key concept relevant to drawing conclusions from data is *validity*. Data is valid if it accurately measures what it is supposed to measure. This means that the questions devised and the methods of data collection must be designed to collect exactly what is needed to tackle the question which is the subject of the study. For example, it is of little use to ask extensively about the use of leisure time, if the real focus of a piece of research is personal mobility.

In a small-scale study, it isn't usually necessary to spend a great deal of time on the measurement of validity. However, it is important to make sure that you focus on your objectives, and design data collection tools to do the task in hand.

What does the data show?

Bell advises that in working through data, you should be 'constantly looking for similarities and differences, for groupings, patterns and items of particular significance' (1993:127).

It is advisable to query the data in as many ways as possible. Are there, for example:

✳ differences between men and women in the sample?

✳ are there differences between people of different ages?

✳ is there anything particularly significant about one group of people (e.g. those who have been using a service for a long time, or who have a particular disability)?

The different categories that can be distinguished within data sets are referred to as variables.

A variable might be social class (e.g. in census data), use of a particular drug (in medical research) or a type of mental health problem (e.g. in a piece of social research). The concern of researchers is often to establish whether one particular variable has a causal relationship to another. For example, they might be seeking to establish whether or not people of a certain social class or group tend to have fewer qualifications than people from a different group. Researchers may also be looking for variables that suggest further lines of enquiry. For example, people of a certain ethnic background might be under-represented in a group of service users. Researchers would want to find out why by designing further studies.

In some cases, researchers may say that the data allows them to establish a *correlation* between data sets, or between certain variables. If a pattern is distinguished, for example a high proportion of people who smoke also experience early ageing of the skin, researchers can say there is a correlation to be made between these two variables. In some cases, the data may be strong enough for a *causal inference* to be made. In the government Chief Medical Officer's annual report from 2003, a causal inference has been made between smoking and facial ageing, based on a relatively high number of separate studies. It is important to remember, however, that correlation of two variables does not necessarily imply causality. Data has to be substantiated from a number of studies, and the potential impact of other variables has to be taken into account before a causal inference can be made.

In small-scale studies, conclusions will often be expressed tentatively in terms of simple correlation or suggestion, particularly since the sample size is small.

Other key concepts in the expression of findings are *relatability* and *generalisation*.

Presenting quantitative data

It is essential to express data as clearly as possible so that readers can, firstly, understand the points being made and, secondly, form their own opinions as to how the data might be interpreted.

Suppose 50 people aged over 50 have taken part in a survey about transport use. Among other things, they have been asked if they use a travel pass. A simple way of expressing this is as a table on which both numerical values and percentages may be easily shown at the same time.

A good table will always show the total number of people in the sample, and should be self-explanatory. Tables must always add up correctly. In this case, the total in the 'Number' column must add up to 50, and in the 'Percentage' column must add up to 100.

It is not advisable to give percentages alone in a table, particularly in small-scale studies. A small sample size does not necessarily give conclusive results, and percentages by themselves can give a misleading impression that data is more conclusive than it really is. A figure of 80 per cent is impressive, until it is revealed that this represents 8 out of only 10 respondents.

The data in Table 10.10 could also be expressed visually as a bar chart (see Figure 10.15).

In Figure 10.15, the bars represent the percentage values of each group (i.e. travel pass users, non-travel-pass users). It would be equally informative to give each bar the numerical value of each group. Visual presentation in this way can be quite striking, particularly if there is a significant point to be made about a particular variable.

Similarly, a pie chart is a good way of expressing data visually (see Figure 10.16).

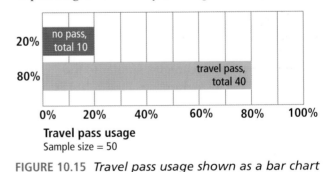

Travel pass usage
Sample size = 50

FIGURE 10.15 *Travel pass usage shown as a bar chart*

	NUMBER	PERCENTAGE
Travel pass user	40	80%
Non-travel-pass user	10	20%
Total	50	100%

TABLE 10.10 *Travel pass usage (sample size = 50)*

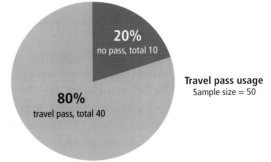

FIGURE 10.16 *Travel pass usage shown as a pie chart*

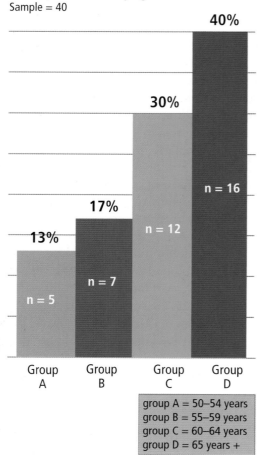

Travel pass users – by age
Sample = 40

40%

30%

n = 16

17%

n = 12

13%

n = 7

n = 5

| Group A | Group B | Group C | Group D |

group A = 50–54 years
group B = 55–59 years
group C = 60–64 years
group D = 65 years +

FIGURE 10.17 *Travel pass users by age shown as a histogram*

AGE (YEARS)	NUMBER	% (UNROUNDED)	% (ROUNDED)
50–54	5	12.5	13
55–59	7	17.5	17
60–64	12	30	30
65+	16	40	40
Total	40	100	100

TABLE 10.11 *Travel pass users by age (Total = 40)*

Another visual technique, similar to the bar chart, is the histogram (see Figure 10.17). In the histogram, the bars touch each other, to indicate that the variable is continuous. Suppose, for example, the ages of people using travel passes are to be expressed visually. Age has been recorded (on the data collection form) into four categories: 50–54 years, 55–59 years, 60–64 years and over 65 years. These are now coded as Groups A–D.

Using the histogram for this example emphasises the gradual increase in travel pass usage with age. The key retirement ages of 60 (for women) and 65 (for men) are retained as potential milestones with respect to travel pass usage. Although retirement ages are changing, there are still a considerable number of individuals for whom these ages have significance.

In doing the arithmetic for these figures, the researcher has had to make a couple of decisions with respect to the percentages, as shown in Table 10.11.

Arithmetically, 5 is 12.5 per cent of 40, whilst 7 is 17.5 per cent. Fractions are usually not considered acceptable when expressing data of this kind (in contrast to some complex scientific experimental data, where differences lower than whole numbers may be of significance). Therefore, the percentages involving less than whole numbers have to be *rounded* upwards or downwards. One convention is to round downwards any fraction that is less than 0.5, and to round upwards figures of 0.5 and above. In this case, rounding up the two age categories in question would give new whole figures of 13 and 18, which would in turn give a percentage total of 101 per cent. This is not good practice, and a decision has to be made which will produce a final total of 100 per cent. In this case, the 50–54 year age group has been rounded up (to 13 per cent) and that for the 55–59 year group has been rounded down (to 17 per cent). Because this is a slightly larger number to start with, rounding down will have a little less impact. However, on sample sizes this small, any conclusions drawn from percentages will have to be treated carefully.

Graphs are also useful for expressing continuous variables, and can be used to compare trends in more than one set of figures at the same time.

The graph in Figure 10.18 compares the mean ages of travel pass users and non-travel-pass users in each of the four age groups, A–D. From this it can be seen easily that in this population, the non-

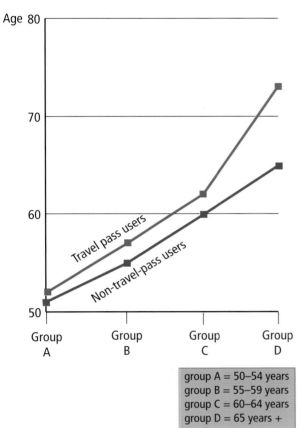

Travel pass usage
By mean age

FIGURE 10.18 *Travel pass users by mean age*

group A = 50–54 years
group B = 55–59 years
group C = 60–64 years
group D = 65 years +

users of travel passes tend to be younger than the users.

The concept of the *mean* is a very useful one for interpreting data. This, along with a number of other mathematical and statistical concepts, will now be considered in the next section.

Conclusions from quantitative data

This is not a textbook on statistics (see References for useful further reading), but if meaningful inferences are to be made from quantitative data, a few basic mathematical concepts can be helpful. These are the mean, the median, and the mode. The statistical concept of probability is also useful, but you are not required to be able to calculate probability for the purposes of passing this unit.

Mean, median and mode

Mean, median and mode are three kinds of measures of a set of data. The mean has already been used in Figure 10.18, and is very similar to the 'average' in simple arithmetic. All score values are added, and then divided by the total number of scores. Table 10.12 shows how this was done for the 'non-travel-pass users' in Figure 10.18.

GROUP A 50–54 n = 5	GROUP B 55–59 n = 3	GROUP C 60–64 n = 1	GROUP D 65 YEARS+ n = 1
50 50 50 50 53	55 55 55	60	65
253	165	60	65
Divided by 5 = 51	Divided by 3 = 55	Divided by 1 = 60	Divided by 1 = 65

TABLE 10.12 *Non-travel-pass users calculation of mean ages*

Sometimes, two different groups may give the same arithmetical mean, even if the actual values in each group are very different. In such cases, another way of finding an average is needed. The *median*, or middle value, can be useful here. Table 10.13 shows how to deduce the median scores for the ages of travel pass users in this example.

Where the number of scores is odd (e.g. Groups A and B), then the middle value is the median (53 and 57 for these groups). If there is an even number of scores, then the median is the average of the two middle scores (Group C = 63, Group D = 73). In this case, median and mean are very similar for all four age groups.

The *mode* is the most frequently occurring score in any group, but this is not used very often in small-scale studies. In the case of the analysis by age, it is not likely to be very useful, but it might be helpful in answering another question. Suppose respondents were asked how many times a week they used their passes. Figure 10.19 shows the answers to this question by people aged 60–64 years.

GROUP A 50–54 n = 5	GROUP B 55–59 n = 7	GROUP C 60–64 n = 12	GROUP D 65 YEARS+ n = 16
50	55	60	65
50	56	60	65
53 Median	57	60	65
54	57 Median	61	65
54	59	62	67
	59	63 Med = 63	71
	59	63	71
		63	73 Med = 73
		63	73
		64	73
		64	73
		64	75
		64	75
			75
			81
			81
			85
Mean = 261 divided by 5 = 52	Mean = 402 divided by 7 = 57	Mean = 748 divided by 12 = 62	Mean = 1160 divided by 16 = 73

Med = Median

TABLE 10.13 *Travel pass users by age calculating median and mean scores per age group (n = 40)*

Responses to question:

How many journeys per week do you make using your travel pass?

2

2

4

4

4

4

4

4

4

4

10

20

20

Modal score = 4

Arithmetical Mean = 7

FIGURE 10.19 *Travel pass users aged 60–64 years (numbers of journeys per week calculation of modal score N = 12)*

Using the mean score in Figure 10.19 would indicate that most people in this age group used their travel pass to make an average of seven journeys per week. In fact, the high usage by just three users has pushed up the mean score. If the mode is taken, it can be seen that most users in this category make just four journeys a week (seven respondents) or less (two respondents). In this instance, the mode gives a more meaningful picture of travel pass use.

How significant are the results?

There are statistical methods for testing out whether figures in the data have *statistical significance*, or whether they might be expected and show nothing unusual.

The charts and figures so far have used travel data for a hypothetical group of 50 people analysed according to age. Suppose that another

Key concept

Statistical significance: when figures satisfy certain statistical tests, they are said to have statistical significance.

variable is studied, this time that of having a long-term disabling condition.

Table 10.14 shows that below the age of 60 (the former retirement age for women), with a few exceptions, those who use a travel pass also have a disabling condition. This is a striking correlation and looks to have significance.

Harris (1986:121) explains the concept of significance using the illustration of tennis balls and a large black plastic bag. Suppose 20 tennis balls are put into the bag, 10 of which have been marked 'Travel pass' and the other 10 marked

	DISABLING CONDITION	NO DISABLING CONDITION	TOTAL
Travel pass	10	2	12
No travel pass	1	7	8
Total	11	9	20

TABLE 10.14 *People aged 50–59 years: travel pass usage by disabling condition*

'No travel pass'. They are shaken up, and then drawn out, the first ten being allocated to the category 'disabling condition' and the second set of ten to the 'no disabling condition' category. How likely is it that scores similar to Table 10.14 would result? In other words, do the figures in Table 10.14 have statistical significance (i.e. that travel pass users under the age of 60 are more likely to have a disabling condition), or are the figures nothing out of the ordinary?

There are mathematical ways of testing what can be inferred from the data. One of these is the chi-square test, which looks for an association between two variables. Chi-square measures the *probability* of any given set of data occurring. A data set with a probability of 1 is inevitable; that with a probability of 0 is impossible. The lower the probability, the more significant the data. The understanding and application of the chi-square test is not a requirement of this unit, but a number of items listed in the references section will provide further reading on this. Unless you feel exceptionally confident it is probably not advisable to attempt complex statistical techniques as part of your study. However, an awareness of these techniques and how they are applied may help in the evaluation of any secondary research used.

Strengths and weaknesses of research styles and methodologies

Research styles

When choosing a research style or methodology, it's important to consider which approach or approaches will best suit the aims of the project. Several styles of research have been highlighted in this section. Table 10.15 (page 202) sets out the advantages and disadvantages associated with four of these.

In the case of a small-scale project, case study and survey are likely to be the most easily managed research styles, although in certain circumstances it might be possible to design a project containing an experimental element. Ethnography and action research are complex approaches and can be costly both in terms of time and human resources. Such styles are probably not advisable for A-level project work.

Research methods

The basic methods of data collection – questionnaire, interview and observation – each have associated advantages and disadvantages.

Self-completion questionnaires
Some advantages to consider:

* relatively cheap
* can include a large number of participants
* some respondents may prefer this to being interviewed
* no danger that interviewer can influence the answers.

Some disadvantages to consider:

* questions may be misunderstood
* respondents may collude in answering the questions
* some questionnaires may not be returned (especially if being sent by post)
* some questions may be left unanswered
* some responses may be hard to understand
* questions may be wrongly completed (e.g. two boxes ticked instead of one).

Using questionnaires in interviews
Some advantages to consider:

* all questions will be answered
* all questionnaires will be completed
* interviewer can ask extra questions (via probes)

STYLE	ADVANTAGES	DISADVANTAGES
Case study (Methods: observation, interview)	– allows intense focus on one particular situation – findings can be related to other, similar situations	– findings cannot be generalised – results may be limited – it may be hard to correlate with other studies – 'observer's paradox' may influence behaviour of subjects
Survey (Methods: questionnaire, interview)	– allows detailed description and comparison – allows facts to be established – can be cheap and quick – can gather both qualitative and quantitative data	– harder to establish causal relationships – questions may have different meanings for different people – hard to make sure that sample population is representative
Experiment (Method: comparison of groups under controlled conditions)	– useful when measuring clearly identified single causes – researcher can control circumstances – quantitative data usually collected – others can repeat the experiment	– hard to measure changes in human behaviour – artificial nature of situation may distort behaviour
Ethnography (Method: observation)	– findings can be relatable to other situations	– time-consuming – group may not be representative, so findings cannot be generalised – 'observer's paradox' may influence behaviour of subjects
Action research (Methods: questionnaires, diaries, interviews, case studies, use of quantitative data)	– practical in its application; tackles real problems and issues in the place where they occur	– time-consuming – requires commitment from a number of people – findings not necessarily applicable to other situations (although may be of interest to others)

TABLE 10.15 *Research styles: advantages and disadvantages (with acknowledgements to Bell, 1993)*

* data will be uniform if researcher uses same format each time
* interviewer may also collect extra (unstructured) data.

Some disadvantages to consider:

* requires more researcher time (and therefore usually involves a smaller sample)
* respondents may be hard to contact/ convenient times hard to arrange
* respondent may give answers s/he thinks the researcher wants (bias)
* respondent may take a dislike to the interviewer (bias)
* questionnaire format may restrict responses.

> **Key concept**
>
> *Bias:* the distortion of the results of a piece of research, due to the undue influence of a specific factor.

Unstructured interviews

Some advantages to consider:

* much qualitative data will be collected
* respondents can say exactly what they think and feel
* interviewer can probe/follow through on any topic of interest
* useful at the planning stages of a research project.

FIGURE 10.22 *The semi-structured interview combines the advantages of both the structured and unstructured approaches*

Some disadvantages to consider:

* very time-consuming, so sample may need to be smaller
* interviewer needs very good communication skills
* potential for bias, because of personality of interviewer
* applicability of results may be limited
* very hard to produce quantitative data
* findings may be limited to sample group.

In practice, particularly if time and resources are limited, the semi-structured interview probably combines the advantages of the structured and the unstructured approaches (see above, pages 201–2). The interviewer starts from some structured questions, but the potential for collecting unstructured data is built into the interview format.

Direct observation

Some advantages to consider:

* observer can watch subjects in their own environment
* observer may see behaviours that subjects are not aware of
* useful for non-literate subjects (e.g. young children)

* both interpersonal interactions and group behaviours can be observed
* may be recorded to view again.

Some disadvantages to consider:

* some ethical problems – especially if the observation is secret
* observer may misinterpret behaviour
* some behaviours may be missed if note-taking is recording method
* what happens may not be relevant to the aim of the research
* behaviours may be affected if the observer is visible to the group.

Participant observation

Some advantages to consider:

* observer gains in-depth and accurate knowledge of group behaviours
* valid data is produced
* can give access to hard-to-reach or closed groups (e.g. homeless people).

Some disadvantages to consider:

* presence of observer will inevitably affect behaviours to some extent ('observer's paradox')
* ethical problems if observer does not disclose true identity
* time-consuming
* advanced social skills needed
* observer may lose sense of objectivity
* non-acceptance by group may limit value of data.

It takes courage, time and dedication to become a participant-observer, and there are also ethical issues involved if the researcher's true identity is withheld. Recording and publishing details of people's behaviour without their permission is arguably bad practice. However, it should be possible to gain permission before engaging in an observation exercise. Spending time with a group to allow them to become accustomed to your presence before data collection starts is not only courteous to the subjects, but also increases the chances of natural behaviours being observed. The issue of ethics is discussed more fully in the next section.

Ethics in research

The British Psychological Society code of ethical principles (page 188) sets out some guidelines for conducting research with people. These principles include obtaining consent, avoiding deception, providing for debriefing, enabling withdrawal, maintaining confidentiality and anonymity, and protecting participants from harm.

The following scenario describes a controversial controlled observational study conducted in the 1960s by Professor Stanley Milgram of Yale University (Milgram, 1963). The study has become famous for the ethical issues it raises as much as for the subject matter itself.

How far will they go?

In Milgram's study, the subjects were ordered to administer electric shocks to 'victims' who were in fact in collusion with the researchers. The ostensible purpose of the study was to test the impact of 'punishment' on memory and learning. In actual fact, the true aim was to see how far people were prepared to obey authority, even if it involved doing something against their better judgement or moral principles.

Subjects had volunteered to take part in the study, which had been advertised (in the press) as a study about memory and learning. They were paid to take part. The subjects were led to believe that both they and the 'victims' were all volunteers, and that they had been randomly allocated to their respective roles. Considerable care was taken when setting up the study to convince the volunteers that this was the case. Forty males, aged 20 to 50 years, took part in the study.

The subjects were ordered (by an authority figure) to administer 'electric shocks' on command to the victims who had been instructed to react according to the 'voltage' delivered. In reality, no electric shocks were given, but the subjects had initially been given small electric shocks to convince them that the situation was real.

Milgram discovered that 65 per cent of the subjects were prepared to keep giving shocks of up to 450 volts (at which point, the victims might have died had the experiment been real). Despite the agonised cries of the victims, on being told 'the experiment requires you to continue', or 'you have no choice, you must go on', it was not until shock levels reached 300 volts that volunteers began to refuse to continue. Twenty-six of the volunteers continued to give shocks up to the maximum 450 volts.

Whilst the volunteers were pressurised to continue, many showed signs of extreme nervousness and discomfort, and one suffered a convulsive fit as a result of the stress.

All of the volunteers were debriefed afterwards, and told that they had not harmed anyone. A year later, they were sent questionnaires to check for any longer-term emotional damage. A more detailed description of Milgram's study can be found in Gross 2003 (pages 103–23).

What do you think?

Does the deception involved in Milgram's experiment breach ethical principles, or could it be acceptable?

1. How is the behaviour of the volunteers in this study similar to that of the subjects in the 'prisoners and guards' study described above (page 194).

2. How important is it for people taking part in any study to be fully informed about what is going on?

3. How might such information affect people's behaviour during the course of the study?

4. Is deception ever justified as part of a research project?

Milgram's findings about people's willingness to conform to authority are quite shocking. However, his work is probably now more famous for the ethical issues it raises. The application of ethical principles in research is now expected, and research such as this and the prisoners and guards study has, in part, been instrumental in the development of such principles.

Summary of Section 10.2

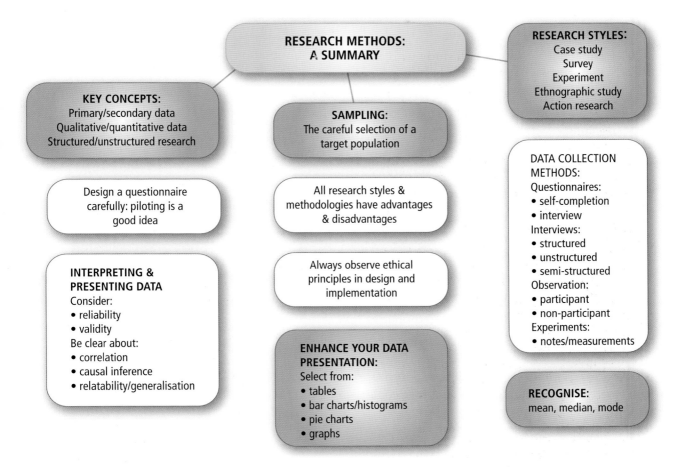

RESEARCH METHODS: A SUMMARY

RESEARCH STYLES:
Case study
Survey
Experiment
Ethnographic study
Action research

KEY CONCEPTS:
Primary/secondary data
Qualitative/quantitative data
Structured/unstructured research

SAMPLING:
The careful selection of a target population

Design a questionnaire carefully: piloting is a good idea

All research styles & methodologies have advantages & disadvantages

DATA COLLECTION METHODS:
Questionnaires:
• self-completion
• interview
Interviews:
• structured
• unstructured
• semi-structured
Observation:
• participant
• non-participant
Experiments:
• notes/measurements

INTERPRETING & PRESENTING DATA
Consider:
• reliability
• validity
Be clear about:
• correlation
• causal inference
• relatability/generalisation

Always observe ethical principles in design and implementation

ENHANCE YOUR DATA PRESENTATION:
Select from:
• tables
• bar charts/histograms
• pie charts
• graphs

RECOGNISE:
mean, median, mode

Consider this

Imagine that you wish to test out the hypothesis that the way people are dealt with by staff affects their perception of the quality of service they receive.

You decide to do some research at a local GP surgery, to find out whether the way in which reception staff receive and welcome patients has a bearing on satisfaction levels with the service as a whole (including the treatment they receive from the doctor).

1. How might this research be designed?

2. What sampling method(s) might you use?

3. How would you collect data on satisfaction levels?

4. What ethical issues might be involved?

10.3 Carrying out a research project

In this section there are a number of checklists designed to assist with the process of carrying out a research project.

Planning the project

It is essential to begin a research study with a clearly defined task with explicit objectives.
Research might involve:

* testing a hypothesis (e.g. that smoking can cause lung cancer)

* investigating a research question (e.g. where is the best place to locate a new GP surgery).

In health and social care, topics might relate to:

* care-related situations and problems

* testing or review of existing knowledge, treatments and practices

* explaining relationships between factors affecting health and well-being

* evaluating service interventions and policies.

Some of the scenarios in this unit describe projects which might be suitable for a small-scale study. Andrea, for example, is studying transport use by service users attending a day unit for people with physical and sensory disabilities (page 187), whilst Natalie is looking at the impact of a new technique for helping people with learning disabilities to express themselves (page 179). In both cases, the target population is easily defined, and the studies are manageable because of the relatively low number of people involved.

CHECKLIST 1 PLANNING A RESEARCH PROJECT

Action	Notes
1. Select a topic.	
2. Define the hypothesis or question to be investigated.	Are the objectives clear? Is the project manageable in the time and with the resources available?
3. Do some background reading into the topic (secondary research).	Has a similar topic been studied elsewhere? If so, is the methodology helpful?
4. Produce a research proposal.	See below.
5. Identify the sample population	Will some kind of sampling method be needed, or will this be an opportunity sample?
6. Decide on the data collection method	Is this to be by survey, interview, observation, etc., or a combination of several methods? If you have time, consider some limited unstructured data collection first to give you some ideas.
7. Design the data collection tools, e.g. questionnaires, interviews, observation checklists.	See advice on constructing data collection tools (pages 184–93)
8. Pilot the data collection tools and adjust as necessary.	Unstructured interviewing might also be useful at this stage, if not before.

Following the steps set out in Checklist 1 will help to ensure that the project is adequately planned. Doing some background reading can be useful for gathering ideas on the potential aims of the study, and also on methodology. Asking advice at this early stage will enable you to assess how feasible the proposal is. It's no good working up a plan to study a group of under-fives, for example, if you do not have access to a group of young children with adequate supervision. Piloting any data collection tools you devise may eliminate any errors or misleading questions, and will help you to assess how much time the main data collection exercise is likely to take.

Once you have done the preliminary work, you can then produce a research proposal.

A good research proposal will include:

* aims

* rationale for the study

* methodology to be used

* details of any piloting or preliminary activity

* specimen data collection tools

* time-scale for the project.

Aims must be very clear. Examples might be:

* to establish levels of satisfaction amongst users of a specific service

* to test the hypothesis that girls have better social skills than boys in a group of 7-year-olds

* to describe the characteristics of a local population using census data.

The rationale for a study sets out the reasons for choosing this particular topic and methodology, and may refer to secondary research. The importance of piloting and initial testing of feasibility has already been discussed. Production of a time-scale is vital, as it is a way of working out whether or not the proposal is feasible in the time available.

Conducting the research project

Checklist 2 highlights key stages in conducting a research project.

CHECKLIST 2 CONDUCTING A RESEARCH PROJECT

Task	Notes
1. Give advanced notification of the study.	Notify everyone concerned, giving full information about the nature of the study and what is involved. A good research proposal might be used at this stage to give information to key individuals.
2. Ask permission where appropriate.	Permission will be needed from the subject population if personal information is sought. Managers and/or staff in health or social services facilities should also give their assent.
3. Give assurances of confidentiality and anonymity.	Consider yourself bound by the BPS code of ethics as much as any professional researcher.
4. Keep appointments, be punctual and courteous.	
5. Collect data using the tools as designed.	Make sure that a supervisor is present, particularly if working with children or people in a social services or health care facility.
6. Record data carefully on to questionnaires, observation sheets etc. Use video or tape-recording as appropriate.	Anonymise your notes and questionnaires. Store all data securely.
7. Analyse quantitative data, selecting appropriate techniques.	Consider whether mean, median or mode are significant. Compare and contrast relationship of different variables.
8. Analyse qualitative data systematically.	Do any themes emerge? Does it throw light on the quantitative data collected?

It is essential to follow ethical principles and to observe the basic rules of courtesy towards everyone you approach. You are, in fact, dependent on the good will and interest of everyone concerned, and it is vital to keep all parties informed of what is going on. Be sure to ask permission to go ahead, both from the subject population (where personal data will be collected) and from managers and/or staff (if the study is to take place in a health or social care facility). Make sure that you will be adequately supervised during the course of the project.

Data must be recorded as accurately as possible and stored securely. Anonymity and confidentiality must be preserved at all times. This means that names should be deleted from any case notes or records that you are allowed to see, and that you should not record information in a way that is traceable to specific individuals. You should not disclose personal information to anyone else, except to people who have a right and/or need to know it. Usually, personal information can only be disclosed to others if you are given permission to do so by the subject of that information. Data in a survey is always reported anonymously, that is it should not be possible to identify specific individuals in the report. If a study concerns individuals, a researcher will usually give new names to these people, or simply refer to them as X and Y.

As the data is analysed and manipulated, ask questions constantly about the significance of what has been collected. For example, does there seem to be a relationship between certain variables? Perhaps everybody above a certain age dislikes a particular food, or the women in the sample are opting out of a certain activity. Are there any themes emerging? Perhaps, in open questioning, a significant number of people mention the fact that they feel better after having their hair done. Are there any comparisons between the findings of your study, and any secondary research that has been consulted? Perhaps another researcher, in a different location but with a similar population, has produced similar findings. This adds weight to your conclusions.

Writing the report

As part of the analytical process, it will be necessary to manipulate quantitative data into a visual form (e.g. tables, graphs, etc.) to show the significance of the data collected. For the final report, choose only the graphics that demonstrate the key findings of the study. If the findings are inconclusive, this is itself worth reporting.

CHECKLIST 3 PROFESSIONAL RESEARCH REPORTS KEY ELEMENTS	
1. Abstract	* summary of study, with key findings.
2. Introduction	* aims * rationale * relevant secondary research/background information.
3. Methodology	* research methods * tools * sampling method * sample size * process followed.
4. Presentation of data	* key tables * bar charts * diagrams, etc.
5. Findings	* significant trends * relationship between variables.
6. Conclusion	* possible causal inferences * relatability to other populations * highlight inconclusive data.
7. Evaluation	Critical reflection on the study: * strengths * weaknesses * how things might be done differently next time.
8. Possible future research	* lines of enquiry suggested by findings.
9. Appendices	* specimen data collection tools * data from other sources (if relevant).

A professional research report always begins with an abstract, which is a short summary of the project, together with its key findings. The introduction sets out the aims and rationale of the study, and may also include any interesting secondary research used to inform the project. The methodology section explains how the study was conducted, including how the population sample was chosen, sample size, length of study, and the data collection methods and tools used.

Actual specimens of data collection tools can be put into an appendix. The presentation and analysis sections of the report should be as succinct as possible. Quantitative data should always be expressed visually (e.g. tables, bar charts, etc.) as well as in words.

The conclusion should make the findings and inferences clear. Often, a researcher will describe how the findings might relate to similar situations, or if inferences may be made from this study to a wider population. There will usually be limited scope for this in a small-scale study.

It is helpful to evaluate the study after it is finished. Try to distinguish what went well from things that could have been done better. You may decide, for example, that the questionnaire used was actually misleading in parts, and that this would be redesigned should the study be repeated. It is always good to reflect on practice, as in every other aspect of professional work.

Finally, it might be possible to see how the study could be followed up. Suppose, for example, in a small study of a reminiscence session, eight out of ten people were found to have trouble getting to the venue. This is an important finding, and would be worth following up with another piece of research.

Summary of Section 10.3

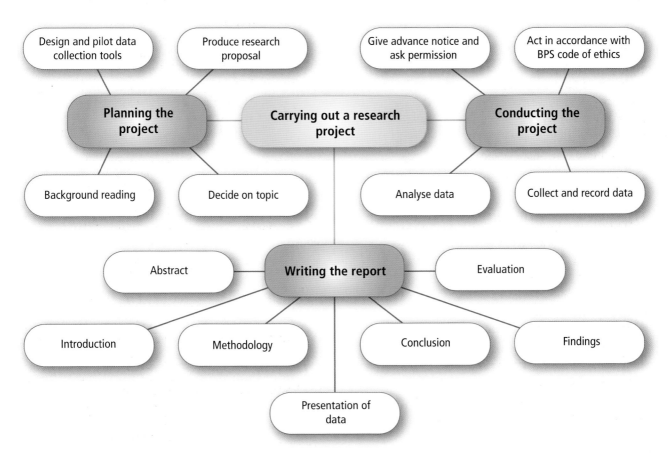

Shashi is about to make a study of a small group of six young children in an early years centre. Staff have introduced some new musical activities (involving percussion instruments and whistles), and Shashi is going to observe the children's reactions to these.

She is especially keen to test the hypothesis that music may help shy children to participate more in a group. She will be watching one child in particular, Stacey, who is currently very withdrawn, and who does not appear to have made any special friendships amongst the other children.

1. What decisions will Shashi have to make about how she collects her data?

2. What data collection tools and techniques might she use?

3. Which visual modes of presentation might be especially helpful in presenting the data?

4. How important will it be for Shashi to be supervised, and who should do this?

UNIT 10 ASSESSMENT

How you will be assessed

To be successful in this unit you will need to plan and research on a topic of relevance to health and social care, with particular relevance to one of the following service user groups:

* people who are ill
* young children
* older people
* people with specific needs.

You must produce a research proposal, together with a final written report. These documents must demonstrate:

* knowledge and understanding of research methodology
* the use of relevant data collection tools and techniques
* the ability to analyse research data
* the ability to evaluate the project and the methodology used.

Assessment guidance

AO1 Identification of the topic and production of the research proposal

You may wish to use Checklist 1 (page 206) to help with this part of the assignment.

The purpose and aims of your study should be absolutely clear, together with a description of how you plan to go about the project.

Good marks will be obtained for:

* a clear statement of purpose and aims

* an explanation of the rationale for the study

* clear reasons for the choice of methodologies and data collection tools

* clarity about how and why the target population has been chosen

* setting a realistic timescale

* use of key concepts, including:
    qualitative data
    quantitative data
    primary and secondary research
    sampling
    population
    research styles (e.g. case study, survey, etc.).

Higher marks will be obtained for demonstrating all of the above, plus:

* awareness of the issues associated with the chosen methodology (or methodologies), including the advantages and disadvantages

* good reasons for the choice of research style and data collection tools

* an awareness of the context in which the study is being conducted

* good use of secondary research as part of the rationale and background to the study (including awareness of sampling techniques and methodologies used in secondary research cited)

* excellent planning skills, including keeping everyone informed, seeking consent, observing ethical principles, etc.

AO2 Production of data collection tools and implementing the project

Checklist 2 (page 207) may be useful when planning the data collection process.
Good marks will be obtained for:

* systematic and thorough planning prior to data collection

* awareness of the strengths and limitations of the data collection tools and methods chosen

* obtaining sufficient appropriate data for analysis

* sensitive application of the data collection tools, paying due regard to the needs of each individual involved in the study

* observation of the principles of anonymity and confidentiality in recording and storing data

* application of key concepts (as appropriate):
    structured data
    unstructured data
    structured, semi-structured, unstructured interview
    non-participant observation
    participant observation.

Higher marks will be obtained for all of the above, plus:

* demonstration of independent thinking in the design and use of data collection tools

* flexibility when designing and administering data collection tools (this may include piloting the data collection tools and responding appropriately to feedback)

* a positive response to any problems or issues that arise during the course of the study

* demonstration of the appropriateness of the data collection tools to the research situation

* sensitive use of questioning, prompts and probes (as appropriate) if using interview method

* good interpersonal skills if using participant-observer method

* maintaining objectivity throughout the data collection process.

AO3 Analysis of data

Checklists 2 and 3 (pages 207–8) may be helpful when analysing your data.
Good marks will be obtained for:

* analysis that makes clear and coherent links between the data and the original purpose and aims of the study

* making valid and justifiable conclusions from the data

* good use of key concepts, such as:
  variable
  relatability
  generalisation
  aggregation
  correlation.

* clear presentation of data in appropriate visual form (e.g. tables, bar charts, graphs etc.)

* a well-structured research report.

Higher marks will be obtained for all of the above, plus:

* demonstration of awareness of the potential for bias in data

* a thorough exploration of all the data collected to establish its significance

* awareness of the limitations of small-scale studies

* use (or awareness) of key concepts, such as:
  reliability
  validity
  bias
  observer's paradox (if appropriate)
  causal inference
  statistical significance
  mean, median, mode.

* awareness of the ways in which data can be manipulated statistically (e.g. concept of probability)

* conclusions that contextualise the outcome of the study, and may make reference to secondary research.

AO4 Evaluation of research study

The discussion of the advantages and disadvantages of different research methods and data collection tools (pages 201–3) may be helpful in completing this part of the research report.
Good marks will be obtained by:

* explaining the strengths and weakness of the study

* evaluating how far the purposes and aims of the study were met

* suggesting how improvements might be made were the study to be repeated
* awareness of how research contributes to developments in health and social care
* awareness of possible implications of key concepts, including:
    bias
    reliability and validity
    observer's paradox (if appropriate).

Higher marks will be obtained by all of the above, plus:

* a high level of analytical thinking
* critical self-awareness at every stage, including planning, choice of methods/tools, implementation and analysis
* awareness of having made choices, and the reasons for those choices
* critical awareness of the context for and purposes of research in the health and social care fields.

Unit test

1. Name four key purposes of research.

2. How is research used in the fields of health and social care?

3. Explain the differences between:

    a) primary and secondary data

    b) qualitative and quantitative data.

4. Why is secondary research so useful?

5. Name four principles of the British Psychological Society's code of ethics.

6. How is structured data different from unstructured data?

7. When might an unstructured interview be used?

8. Why is it important to give numbers as well as percentages on a table of data?

9. In what ways might bias creep into data collected during an interview situation? Is it possible for a structured interview to result in biased data?

10. Why does correlation not necessarily imply causality?

References and further reading

Bell, J. (1993) *Doing Your Research Project* 2nd edn. (Buckingham: Open University Press)

Cohen, S. et al (1991) 'Psychological stress and susceptibility to the common cold', *New England Journal of Medicine*, 325, 606

Cohen, S., Tyrrell, D.A. and Smith, A.P. (1993) 'Negative life events, perceived stress, negative affect and susceptibility to the common cold', *Journal of Personality and Social Psychology*, 64 (1), 131–40

Coles, A. and Cox, A. (2002), 'Does early treatment of multiple sclerosis prevent the progression of disability later on?', *Way Ahead*, 6(1): 4–5

Croft, S.E. (1999), 'Creating locales through storytelling: an ethnography of a group home for men with mental retardation', *Western Journal of Communication*, 63 (3): 329–45

Department of Health (2004), *On the State of the Public Health*: Annual Report of the Chief Medical Officer 2003, accessed via Department of Health website

Gross, R. (2003) *Key Studies in Psychology* 4th edn. (Abingdon: Hodder and Stoughton)

Halliday, S. (2001) 'Death and miasma in Victorian London: an obstinate belief', *British Medical Journal*, 323: 1469–71

Haney, C., Banks, C. and Zimbardo, P. (1973), 'A study of prisoners and guards in a simulated prison', *Naval Research Reviews*, 30 (9): 4–17

Harris, P. (1986) *Designing and Reporting Experiments* (Buckingham: Open University Press)

Martin. P. (1997) *The Sickening Mind* (London: Harper Collins)

Milgram, S. (1963), 'Behavioural study of obedience', *Journal of Abnormal and Social Psychology*, 67: 371–8

Slesnik, N. and Prestopnik, J.L. (2005) 'Ecologically based family therapy outcome with substance abusing adolescents', *Journal of Adolescence*, 28 (2), April, 277–98

Snow, J. (1855) *On the Mode of Communication of Cholera* (London: John Churchill), accessed via www.ph.ucla.edu/epi/snow/showbook_a2.html

Wakefield, A. J. et al (1998), 'Ileal-lymphoid-nodular hyperplasia, non-specific colitis and pervasive developmental disorder in children', *The Lancet*, 351: 637–41

Useful websites

Carers UK www.carersuk.org

Census data (local) www.neighbourhood.statistics.gov.uk

Cochrane Collaboration www.cochrane.org

Department of Health www.dh.gov.uk

Institute for Public Policy and Research (IPPR) www.ippr.org.uk

Joseph Rowntree Foundation www.jrf.org.uk

Medical Research Council www.mrc.ac.uk

National Centre for Social Research www.natcen.ac.uk

NHS Gateway www.nhs.uk

National Institute for Health and Clinical Excellence (NICE) www.nice.org.uk

National Statistics Online www.statistics.gov.uk (Census data – national)

Prince of Wales' Foundation for Integrated Health www.fimed.org.uk

Research Council for Complementary Medicine www.rccm.org.uk

Sociological Research Online www.socresonline.org.uk

Stationery Office www.parliament.the-stationery-office.co.uk (access to government publications)

Valuing People www.valuingpeople.gov.uk

What Doctors Don't Tell You (WDDTY) www.wddty.co.uk

Social issues and welfare needs

Unit 11

This unit covers the following sections:

11.1 Origins of social and welfare issues

11.2 Demographic change and social and welfare issues

11.3 Social issues in context

11.4 Government responses to social issues and welfare needs

This unit covers a variety of social issues and welfare needs which exist in the UK. Some of these issues have existed for many years and others are more recent concerns. Social issues and welfare needs are relevant to workers in health and social care as they impact on service users in a range of health and social care settings. Section 11.1 covers the origins of social issues in the UK and how these are linked to social change and to an unequal society. The second section identifies demographic changes which have impacted on the provision of health and social care. In Section 11.3, social issues in the contemporary UK are examined. Finally the role of government in responding to social issues and welfare needs is explored.

How you will be assessed

This unit is assessed internally. You must produce a written report on a social issue or welfare need of interest to you. To prepare for this it may be useful to keep a folder to store information about your chosen issue, which could come from press items, the Internet and any handouts you are given on your course.

11.1 Origins of social and welfare issues

This section examines the origins of social issues through the social changes that have occurred in the UK in the past 100 years, with particular reference to social changes as they affect age, gender, ethnicity and social class.

Many factors influence social change (see Figure 11.1). To understand how contemporary social and welfare services have developed, we need to look at these factors and how they have influenced these changes. They may include:

* industrialisation
* cultural change
* political change
* economic change.

Key concept

Social change: the process whereby societies or aspects of a society move from one state to another. An example of social change affecting a whole society could be the change from an agricultural society to an industrial society. An example of social change affecting only part of society could be the changing state of the family and marriage, where many births now take place outside marriage in the UK.

FIGURE 11.1 *The range of factors that can influence social change*

Industrialisation

Industrialisation is the process by which a society moves from a predominantly agricultural base to one where the economy is dominated by manufacturing and the factory system. Industrialisation began in Britain in the 1740s, and the process continued until the late nineteenth century. As part of the process, transport systems to move goods and workers also developed. Industrialisation resulted in a large-scale movement of the population from the villages and countryside to towns and cities, a process known as urbanisation. Industrialisation and urbanisation have also meant that the numbers of people working in agriculture in the UK have declined in the last 100 years and more people are living in towns. This may change in the future; ease of Internet access may enable more people to work from home, in which case it will not be necessary for so many people to live in towns and cities.

Urbanisation has also had an impact on family life. With the movement to towns and cities for work, families were split up. Geographical mobility is still increasing all the time and with the development of global capitalism and international companies, many people are further split from their extended families.

In the nineteenth century, industrialisation and *urbanisation* created public health problems in major cities such as London, Manchester, Liverpool and Birmingham. In 1801 London had a population of 800,000. By 1851 the population had increased by a further million. The population of Britain as a whole doubled during that period. The increase in population took place without an increase in resources such as housing, sanitation, drainage, refuse clearance and water supplies, and so health, social and welfare issues were bound to arise. Many of these problems are still an issue in the contemporary UK (e.g. housing, overcrowding, refuse disposal).

Cultural change

Cultures develop to give people a guide as to how they should behave. In different cultures people behave differently because they learn their culture from their parents and society. A particular culture usually develops to help people cope with their situation. Cultures are always changing, but the main cultures are passed on from one generation to another by parents and others who influence people when they are young – including their peer groups and the media.

Key concept

Culture: the collection of values, norms, customs and behaviours that make one group of people distinct from others. A person's culture will influence the development of their self-concept.

Try it out

Make a list of all the factors that have influenced you – what you wear, how you spend your leisure time, how you spend your money. Compare your list with a friend who is in the same age group. Do you think the factors on your list would be different if you were:

* a member of the opposite sex?
* 40 years old?
* from a different ethnic group?
* from a different social class group?

In the past, the church was a strong influence on how people in the UK thought and behaved, but the influence of religion has declined since the middle of the twentieth century.

Secularisation

This is the process by which religious thinking, practices and institutions lose their significance. Evidence of secularisation is usually presented in terms of a decline in church attendance and religious observance, and the declining power of Christianity and Christian religious practice in everyday life. However, many people still believe in a deity of some kind and there has been an increase in the influence of other religions, such as Islam. With the decline of the influence of the church, especially on matters related to marriage and the family, secularisation could be seen as one factor influencing certain social changes. An example might be the increase in one-parent families. However, any social change is usually the result of a range of different factors, and cannot be directly attributed to one particular factor such as secularisation.

Political change

Social change does not take place in a vacuum, and we have already seen that a range of factors influence the changes in a society. Political change can also have a pronounced effect on society. Political change can be seen either as a response to social change, or as bringing about social change.

SCENARIO

Means testing and universal provision

Following the First World War (1914–18) there was a severe economic depression in the UK. The government brought in an extension of unemployment insurance and a retirement pensions system was set up. The government also introduced 'means testing' for these and other benefits.

Key concept

Means testing: a way of identifying those who are most in need, based on an appraisal of household income. Supporters of means testing argue that this approach allows benefits to be targeted towards those who are in most need.

Following the Second World War (1939–45), the Labour Party won the election in 1945 and formed a government. In 1948 the NHS was set up and various ministries were established as part of the welfare state. Many benefits were organised on the basis of universal provision.

The type of social policy that is developed by a political party is affected by the party's ideas about:

* the role and function of the state

* the model of social welfare provision that is seen as appropriate

* the criteria that are used to identify those who are in need.

Models of welfare

There are three main models of welfare that have been applied to welfare policy since 1945 in the UK:

* *the universal model of welfare:* in this model the state provides welfare services to all by right. The state is responsible for all its citizens

* *the residual model of welfare:* in this model the state should provide welfare if the family, individual or private sector is unable to do so

* *the institutional model of welfare:* in this model welfare provision is an important aspect of policy, but it is provided by a combination of private, voluntary and statutory sectors which will provide services on the basis of cost-effectiveness.

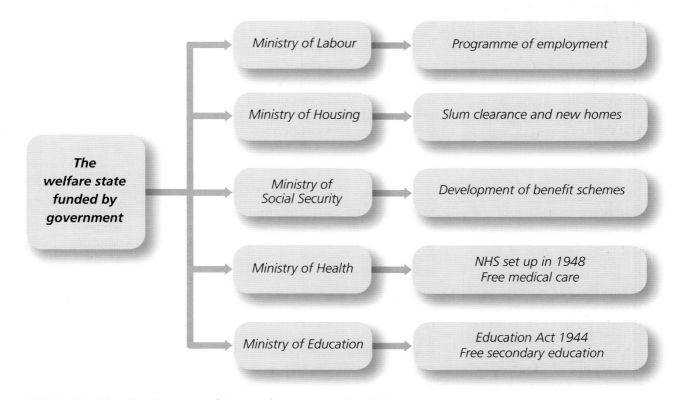

FIGURE 11.2 *The development of the welfare state in the 1940s*

	NEW RIGHT ANTI-COLLECTIVE MARKET MODELS	COLLECTIVIST OLD LABOUR	'THIRD WAY' NEW LABOUR	FEMINIST CRITIQUE	ANTI-RACIST CRITIQUE
Core values	Family values Market and economy Law and order Residual welfare	Equality State provision and control of services Universal welfare model	Family Equal opportunities Consultation Mixed economy	Equality and redistribution of power between men and women needed	Equality and redistribution of power between White and ethnic minority groups needed
Role of the state	State intervention must be limited	State intervenes to ensure stability and quality	State works with other agencies, private and voluntary sector	Male-dominated, acts in interest of men	Acts in interest of White majority Discriminatory
Provision of welfare services	A range of providers will deliver effective services	State should provide services	Mixed economy approach using a range of providers	Needs to reflect women's needs and be anti-discriminatory	Welfare services reflect racism
Means testing	Efficient way to target those most in need	Stigmatising Bureaucratic Inefficient	Used to provide services for those most in need	May adversely affect women	Stigmatising and degrading
Universal provision of services by the state	Inefficient Increases demand and dependence	Committed to universal provision of services	Residual model used – targets those most in need	Reflects traditional view of women as wives and mothers dependent on men	Services do not reflect needs of minority groups
Voluntary organisations	One of the providers of services	Main role to act as pressure group but may provide some services	An important provider of services	Useful resource to help women Needs to be led by women	Needs to be led by minority groups Can reach marginalised groups
Private sector	Encourages choice and competition for services	Leads to division between rich and poor Choice for wealthy	Works in partnership with state	Increases inequality because of women's oppressed position	Increases inequality in society

	NEW RIGHT ANTI-COLLECTIVE MARKET MODELS	COLLECTIVIST OLD LABOUR	'THIRD WAY' NEW LABOUR	FEMINIST CRITIQUE	ANTI-RACIST CRITIQUE
Self-help	People should be independent and organise their own care	Provides help for self-help groups but state is major provider	Personal responsibility encouraged	Women need to support each other	Collective approach helps ethnic minorities

TABLE 11.1 *The key ideologies related to social policy and welfare provision*

Government welfare policy in the UK

1945–1970s

The main approach during this time reflected the view that the state should control and provide welfare provision through the **universal model of welfare**.

1979–1997

When the Conservatives came to power in 1979, one of their key aims was to reduce state spending on health and welfare. Conservative governments followed the **residual model of welfare** and promoted a mixed economy of welfare provision using statutory, private and voluntary agencies.

1997 onwards

A Labour government took office in 1997, and developed the approach sometimes called the 'Third Way'. State intervention has increased in some instances, for example with setting NHS targets, but it has been reduced in other instances through the expanding use of private and voluntary sector agencies. This approach is linked to the **institutional model of care**.

Alan Milburn (a former Labour Health Secretary) addressed voluntary organisations in London in 2004 and told the groups present that charities and the voluntary sector should be given a 'central role in delivering health services'. He stated the view that the voluntary sector can often work closely with marginalised groups and may be more sensitive to the needs of individuals and communities. In 2005 it was proposed that voluntary groups should take over the running of the 'Social Fund' from the Department for Work and Pensions. It is evident that the voluntary sector will take on more responsibility for delivering welfare services from the statutory sector in the future.

> **Key concept**
>
> *Social Fund:* a source of money set up by the state that can be used for a range of payments. Payments such as the winter fuel payment come out of this fund, and there are other payments that communities or individuals can apply for. These include community care grants that can help people move from residential care or prison into the community. Interest-free loans are also available to people on income support.

Criticisms of the organisation of welfare provision

The feminist critique

Feminists suggest that welfare policies tend to reflect the patriarchal attitudes in society. The caring role of women, as mothers and as carers for the disabled or older family members, meant that women were not financially supported by the state. Instead they have been used as unpaid workers. Recently there has been additional legislation and support for carers, but many carers feel the payments do not reflect the true cost of caring.

The anti-racist critique

This perspective identifies the welfare state as part of institutionalised racism in society, denying Black and minority ethnic groups access to all aspects of welfare provision, including health care, benefits, housing and access to employment.

The welfare state is seen as a mechanism used to control immigrants and refugees, and the police are seen as racist and failing to protect people from minority ethnic groups.

Economic change

In the nineteenth century Karl Marx (1818–83) described the UK as a capitalist society. That is, the way goods and services are produced is controlled by individuals so that they can accumulate wealth and profit for themselves. Capital from the sale of these goods and services is used to develop the system further, employing more people and selling more goods. In a capitalist society people do not work to produce what they need. They work for others to produce things so that they may then buy what they need with their wages. Marx criticised capitalism as it depended on a free-market economy, which led to booms and slumps which destabilise society. This lack of stability has most impact on society's most vulnerable members.

> **Key concept**
>
> *Capitalist society:* one in which private ownership of the means of production is the dominant way of providing goods and services.

Private enterprise

In the NHS we have seen the development of private enterprise through the Private Funding Initiative (PFI), whereby private investors provide funds to build new hospitals. These investors expect a return for their investment, just as you would if you put your savings into a building society. Since 1979, state funding of key industries such as utilities (gas, water and electricity supplies), transport and other essential services has been withdrawn and nationalised industries have been sold to the private sector. These privatised industries are funded through the stock exchange by shareholders, who seek a profit in return for their investment. There is a conflict between the interests of investors (who want a return on their money) and consumers (who want a reliable and economic service).

Supply and demand

UK society has developed into a free-market economy. This means that if there is an imbalance between the supply of goods and services and the demand for these good and services, a crisis situation can arise where certain groups may be disadvantaged.

> **Key concept**
>
> *Free-market economy:* one where the market is self-regulating and there is limited interference from the government.

For example, in the 1970s there was a rise in the price of oil which led to a petrol shortage and this affected industries which depended on transporting their goods. It also affected car owners who had to pay more for their petrol. The cost of goods increased, inflation increased, people had to pay more for goods and services, and the real value of the money they had to spend went down.

Similarly, in 2004 there was a shortage of houses for people who work in essential jobs such as teaching, the fire and police service, and nursing. This housing shortage has been fuelled by the increase in house prices in the 1990s, which meant that many people could not afford to get a mortgage as their pay levels had not increased in line with the price rises. In turn, there is pressure on rented accommodation and many younger people continue to live with their parents, because they cannot afford to rent accommodation or get a mortgage. Sometimes groups of friends have clubbed together to buy a house, when previously they might have expected to buy houses individually.

Employment and unemployment

Another economic factor that influences social change is the job market. If there is a high level of unemployment, wages can be kept low and people may decide they are better off on benefits than in a low-paid job. The government has to respond to economic factors and develop policies to ensure that people return to work and reduce the cost of benefits. Recently we have seen examples of government initiatives intended to address this, such as 'back to work' schemes. If people are in work, they pay income tax and other taxes which the government uses to spend on services such as health and social care. If there is high unemployment the government has to fund benefits out of a reduced amount of taxation. Furthermore, people on benefits cannot afford to spend much money on goods and services, which means less money goes back into the economy. In this situation, the economy is likely to remain depressed and unemployment is likely to remain high. From these examples, it is apparent that economic factors are very important in influencing social change and social policy.

Other influences on social change and social policy

The mass media

The mass media is the term used to cover all forms of mass communication such as newspapers, magazines, television and radio. The mass media developed in the nineteenth century with the development of mass circulation newspapers, and continued in the twentieth century with radio and television. Other forms of mass media, such as the Internet and mobile phone technology, are still developing.

The mass media can have a great effect on how people live their lives, with easy access to global and national news, celebrity information, etc. There is some debate about whether the mass media reflects or influences society. It clearly has an influence on government policy. For example, media campaigns on 'yobbish behaviour', 'asylum seekers' and 'dirty hospitals' have led to a reaction by the government and to changes in policy.

International influences

The European Union came into being in 1957 under the Treaty of Rome. Six nations joined together to form the European Economic Community (EEC). These were Belgium, France, the Netherlands, Italy, West Germany and Luxembourg. This grouping was later called the European Community, or EC, and is now known as the European Union (EU). In 1973 the UK, Ireland and Denmark joined, followed by Greece in 1981 and Spain and Portugal in 1986. Sweden, Austria and Finland joined in 1995. In 2004 the EEC further increased its membership to include Poland, Lithuania, Latvia, Estonia, the Czech Republic, Slovakia, Slovenia, Hungary, Cyprus and Malta.

In 1992, economic integration came a step closer when the Maastricht Treaty was signed by the 12 member states, including the UK. The purpose of this Treaty was to unite Europe still further through the following five main objectives:

* a closer European Union with closer co-operation between governments
* a common foreign and security policy among all member states
* the same laws would apply to home affairs and justice policy
* a single European currency – the euro
* European citizenship – all nationals of the EU would share the same rights and would have free right of travel across the community.

The European Parliament was given additional powers governing the treatment of children and working conditions.

Social policy and the European Union

Under the terms of the European Union, people from the member states have free access to the UK (as well as to all the other states of the union). Social policy in the UK covers the provision of health and welfare services to the population, including access to education, housing and employment, as well as health and social care. Living conditions and social policy in some of the new member states can be less favourable than those in the UK, so people from these states may decide to come to the UK for economic reasons. An influx of people from the new member states could cause difficulties for UK social policy in terms of pressure on:

* housing
* the health service
* the job market (if new arrivals accept lower wages, this may depress wage levels for other workers in the UK).

Under EU rulings, companies are allowed to employ workers from anywhere in Europe. This may mean that some businesses will move to areas of the EU where wages are lower, potentially reducing employment prospects in the UK. However, many people see the further development of closer links between the UK and Europe as beneficial, particularly in the context of the development of the Social Charter.

The Social Charter programme

The EU Social Charter of Fundamental Social Rights was signed by 11 member states in 1989, but Margaret Thatcher, the British prime minister at the time, opposed it. In 1997, the Labour prime minister Tony Blair signed up to the Charter. The Charter covers the following rights:

* free movement within the EU
* a weekly limit on working hours
* sex equality
* minimum health and social security provision
* minimum pension rights
* protection for disabled workers.

It is expected that welfare and social protection will develop along similar lines across the European Union.

We are now seeing some of the effects of European legislation on working practices in the UK. In 2004 the European Working Time Directive restricted the number of hours worked by doctors in the NHS. Although this has been welcomed by some, it has caused problems in arranging sufficient cover for busy acute hospitals.

Human Rights

The Human Rights Act of 1998 in the UK is a further example of the influence of the European Union. The Act reflects the European Convention on Human Rights, and this will influence many aspects of welfare provision in the UK. Cases related to informed consent and fair access to treatment for people with mental health problems or learning disabilities may now be referred to the European Court.

An unequal society

Studies of inequality are traditionally concerned with analysing the unequal distribution of wealth in a society, and this issue will be covered in greater depth in section 11.3. In this section we will look at inequality related to age, gender, ethnicity and social class. Inequality can lead to the social exclusion of certain groups.

> ## Key concept
>
> *Social exclusion:* 'this is more than income poverty. Social exclusion happens when people or places suffer from a series of problems such as unemployment, discrimination, poor skills, low incomes, poor housing, high crime, ill-health and family breakdown. Social exclusion can happen as a result of problems that face one person in their life. But it can also start from birth. Being born into poverty or to parents with low skills still has a major influence on future life chances.'
>
> Source: Social Exclusion Unit

Social exclusion affects particular groups in our society; here we will discuss how this happens and the resulting welfare issues.

The Social Exclusion Unit (SEU) was set up by the prime minister in 1997 to understand the causes of social exclusion and to help improve action to reduce it. The government's approach to reducing social exclusion and poverty has four main aims.

* Decent family incomes – with employment for those who can work and support for those unable to work.

* High-quality public services for everyone.

* Preventing social exclusion by addressing risk factors.

* Reintegrating those who become excluded from mainstream society.

Marginalisation is another term that can be used instead of social exclusion.

This is the process by which certain groups or individuals are pushed to the margins of society and excluded from full participation in mainstream society. Socially excluded groups are also marginalised. These groups can be excluded on the basis of age, gender, ethnicity and social class.

Inequality in relation to age

The SEU Report published in 2005 (*Multiple Exclusion and Quality of Life amongst Excluded Older People in Disadvantaged Neighbourhoods*) highlights the experience of older people whose lives have been affected by multiple forms of exclusion.

The report focused on the social exclusion experienced by older people and also looked at how factors of age, gender, ethnicity and health status may affect the older person (Figure 11.3).

The report included 32 in-depth interviews and 10 case studies. The sample was drawn from people aged over 60 living in deprived neighbourhoods in Liverpool, Manchester and the London Borough of Newham. The interviews took place between 2001 and 2002 and covered issues such as older people's sense of well-being, experience of daily life, perceptions of the local neighbourhood, the management of household finances and social relationships. The study concluded that the origins of social exclusion in later life are complex. Figure 11.4 shows some of the reasons for social exclusion in later life.

The most common form of social exclusion in the study was exclusion from social relations – 26 out of the 32 participants experienced this.

Excluded from basic services

Excluded from neighbourhood

Excluded from civic participation

Excluded from material resources

Excluded from social participation

FIGURE 11.3 *Effects of social exclusion for older people*

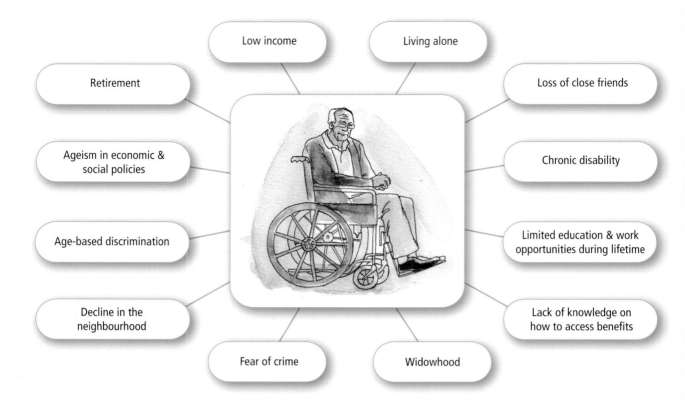

FIGURE 11.4 *The reasons for social exclusion in later life*

CASE NO.	NAME	KEY CHARACTERISTICS	FORMS OF SOCIAL EXCLUSION	QUALITY OF LIFE
3	Joan Richards	85 years, White, widow, lives alone, in good health	Material resources, civic participation, basic services	Good
5	Pauline Fields	81 years, White, widow, lives alone, in very good health	Material resources, neighbourhood	Very good
8	Joseph Lee	85 years, White, widower, lives alone, health neither good nor poor	Material resources, social relations, neighbourhood	Good
11	Peter Brown	68 years, White, single, lives alone, in very good health	Social relations, civic participation	Poor
16	Donald Lloyd	74 years, White, single, lives alone, in poor health	Social relations, neighbourhood	Good
20	Flora Peters	60 years, Indian, widow, lives with son, in poor health	Material resources, social relations, civic participation	Very poor
21	Elizabeth Farmer	69 years, White, widow, lives alone, in poor health	Material resources, social relations, civic participation	Poor

CASE NO.	NAME	KEY CHARACTERISTICS	FORMS OF SOCIAL EXCLUSION	QUALITY OF LIFE
22	Mary Johnson	71 years, White, widow, lives with son, in good health	Material resources, social relations	Poor
25	Edna Walker	74 years, Black Caribbean, widow, lives with son, in good health	Social relations, basic services	Good
31	Waris Abdi Duale	66 years, Somali, widow, lives alone, health neither good nor poor	Material resources, social relations	Good

TABLE 11.2 *Summary of case studies*

Source: HMSO

Try it out

Look at Table 11.2 and describe the patterns you see. How do the experiences of these people differ, and how far are they the same? Can you think of possible reasons for these forms of social exclusion?

Becoming and staying excluded

In the SEU research study, social exclusion seemed to reflect the combinations of age-related factors and disadvantages experienced during working life. Limited education and work opportunities in earlier life affected income, social relationships, and also the kind of housing and neighbourhood lived in. The research study shows that social exclusion is a complex issue in later life. Widowhood, living alone, and loss of close family members, friends and neighbours had an impact. Chronic health problems, leaving work, the experience and fear of crime also affected levels of social exclusion. Recommendations from this research suggest that intervention in adulthood could have an impact on social exclusion in later life.

The purpose of community development and regeneration programmes is to bring together vulnerable groups such as families with young children, different minority ethnic groups and long-term residents. Several of these projects have been developed in deprived neighbourhoods.

SCENARIO
Greenacres

Greenacres has been identified as a community that reflects the problems described in the SEU research. It is a large estate built in the 1930s. There are high levels of:

* unemployment
* truancy
* single-parent families
* teenage pregnancies
* drug-related crime
* deaths from cancer and respiratory disease.

The voluntary services, with representatives from the local Primary Care Trust (PCT) and the council, held a series of meetings to ask people living in Greenacres what they wanted to see happen on the estate. These were the issues raised by the residents:

* they wanted the strategy to be led by the community, not dictated by professionals
* they wanted adequate funding to be given directly to residents and community and voluntary groups
* they wanted the funding to be long term, 5 or 10 years, rather than short-term funding for one year
* they wanted excluded groups to participate – refugees, unemployed, older people
* they wanted people to be helped into work
* they wanted IT skills training.

As a result of the consultation with the community, the following services have been put into place:

* IT skills training at the local community centre
* close working with the police to reduce anti-social behaviour
* a community warden has been introduced
* house-letting procedures have been reviewed and improved
* arts and sports programmes have been implemented for all age groups in the area
* a local community project has been set up based on a co-operative where community members buy fresh fruit and vegetables at a reduced price
* a drop-in service has been set up at the local community centre to advise residents on benefits
* a local community nurse holds a surgery three times a week to advise on aspects of child care, health and contraception
* a local chiropody service has been set up
* refugees and asylum seekers have access to English classes.

The main lesson to be learned from Greenacres is the importance of involving the community in developing services that are relevant to their needs, so that factors affecting social exclusion are addressed throughout life. The case studies in the SEU research showed that social exclusion is often the result of a lifetime spent in deprivation.

Stereotyping of older people

A stereotype is a fixed and often simplistic generalisation about a particular group. These stereotypes are often negative and unflattering, but they may be based on a grain of truth. Stereotypes may lead to prejudice and discrimination if they are widely held, especially by people in power.

It is often difficult to change a stereotype. This is particularly true of the stereotypes of older people, who are seen as deaf, stupid, slow and unable to take on new ideas. In spite of campaigns by organisations that support older people, such as Age Concern, attitudes towards older people are still mainly negative.

What if?

If you visit a hospital or care home, observe how the staff behave towards older patients.

1. Do they show them respect?
2. Do they call them by their preferred name?
3. Do they use terms like 'dear', 'gran' or 'love'?
4. Do they shout at them?
5. Do they speak to an older person's relative or carer rather than to them directly?

Many of these issues have also been the subject of complaint by various disabled groups who also experience discrimination and stereotyping. Stereotyping, whereby all older people are treated in the same way, adversely affects an older person's sense of self-worth.

Labelling is linked to stereotyping. If you apply a negative label to someone, they may adopt certain behaviour as a result (this is known as a self-fulfilling prophecy). If older people are treated as though they have nothing useful to contribute to society, they will withdraw further and may become isolated.

Discrimination

Discrimination is about treating a person or group unfairly because of a negative attitude towards them based on a social factor such as age, ethnicity, social class or gender. Although there has been legislation against discrimination on the grounds of ethnicity and gender, age discrimination is still to be outlawed by legislation (although this is currently due to take place in 2006). As we have already seen in Unit 7, the government has developed health and social care policies related to older people in order to improve their experiences in later life. The First Standard of the National Service Framework (NSF) for Older People is to remove age discrimination in all aspects of the health and social care services. Services and treatment should be available on the basis of need – not decided on the basis of age.

Older people can experience discrimination in a variety of ways, including social stigma, since in our society being older may mean having a lower status.

Older people and employment

Although the age at which the state pension can be claimed is currently 60 for women and 65 for men, it will soon be equalised for both men and women at 65. However, many people face difficulty getting a job once they are over 40, especially if they have been made redundant or if they are returning to work after caring for children. Having a job gives a person status and if you are retired or unemployed, your status and income level are reduced. Age is only one factor; gender and ethnicity can also affect one's chances of employment.

Financial services

Older people often have difficulties accessing insurance, getting loans or mortgages, and arranging credit. They tend to have to pay higher premiums for car insurance (if they are lucky enough to have a car) and holiday or health insurance.

Inequality in relation to gender

Just as age can lead to discrimination and unfair treatment in society, so can gender. Women tend to be seen as responsible for the care of family members who are vulnerable, and this is seen as an extension of their maternal and parenting role. Feminists explain the discrimination experienced by women as related to a society in which traditional stereotypes of women have focused on their maternal and family responsibilities, and these stereotypes are seen to operate in the interests of a male-dominated society in which wealth and ownership of property is dominated by men. Factors, including the influence of the feminist movement in the 1960s and 1970s, led to legislation related to gender issues in the workplace being passed to improve the situation of women:

* the **Equal Pay Act (1970)** stated that men and women doing the same work should be paid the same rate

* the **Sex Discrimination Act (1975)** made it unlawful to treat anyone less favourably on the grounds of sex.

Men as well as women can experience discrimination based on gender, especially if they are seeking employment in what is seen as a traditionally female occupation. Examples have included male midwives and nursery nurses qualifying and being unable to find a post.

The Sex Discrimination Act also set up the **Equal Opportunities Commission (EOC)** in 1976, whose role it was to investigate incidents of discrimination and offer support to women experiencing discrimination. It now investigates complaints related to the unfair treatment of both men and women. Discrimination is seen as being *direct* or *indirect*.

Key concept

Direct sex discrimination: treating someone less favourably on the basis of their sex.

Indirect sex discrimination: setting conditions of employment that indirectly discriminate against one sex (e.g. imposing conditions that are not directly related to the job but which would ensure that applicants of one sex are unlikely to be appointed).

Gender and poverty

Women are more likely than men to be in poverty for the following reasons:

* interrupted employment record due to caring responsibilities
* lack of occupational pension opportunities
* lower incomes compared to men.

We will look at this in more detail in section 11.3.

Gender and employment

Women are less likely to be in full-time employment than men, and more likely to be in lower-paid posts. They are also more likely to be in part-time work because of family commitments. The stereotypes of women as being mothers and carers can affect their promotion prospects, and men are more likely to be in higher-paid management positions even in traditionally female employment areas such as nursing and teaching.

However, recent trends towards men working part-time and becoming responsible for child care can lead to policy changes, such as paternity leave, that can benefit both men and women.

Gender and housing

Single, separated, or divorced women often have limited access to housing. Access to a mortgage may also be difficult. Lone parents may be placed in accommodation by local councils and these tend to be of poor quality.

Gender and benefits

Until recently, the welfare system in the UK was based on the assumption that women would marry and their husbands would support them and be the main breadwinner in the family. Pensions and a wide range of state benefits are still based on this assumption.

Although family patterns are changing and more women are entering the workforce, women still experience discrimination and disadvantage. Social factors such as age, ethnicity and disability increase this disadvantage still further. Some men have also felt discriminated against by the benefits system. One example is the widowed parents allowance which was formerly only paid to women. Men now also receive this benefit.

Inequality in relation to ethnicity

We have already discussed stereotyping and prejudice against older people and against women. Stereotyping of ethnic minorities involves holding negative views about a particular ethnic group. These stereotypes can be based on a shared religion, culture, dress and language but tend to focus on negative aspects. Racial prejudice is based on people being liked or disliked simply because they belong to a particular ethnic group.

Negative attitudes towards ethnic minorities are often inflamed by the media. Stories about asylum seekers and illegal immigrants have increased prejudice and fear among some white people. In the 2005 general election several campaigns were fought by the BNP (British Nationalist Party) on the basis of fear and prejudice against ethnic minority groups. These stories and campaigns are an important factor in causing people from ethnic minorities to become marginalised and socially excluded.

As with all generalisations, we need to be careful not to assume that all ethnic minorities experience the same levels of inequality in society. Many people from Indian groups have high educational qualifications and have highly paid jobs in the professions, but people from Pakistani and Bangladeshi groups are more likely to experience inequality.

Legislation related to racial discrimination

The **1976 Race Relations Act** made it illegal to discriminate either directly or indirectly in the provision of goods and services. Discrimination was also illegal in employment or housing. It also became illegal to incite racial hatred. However, as we have seen with discrimination against women, it is difficult to identify and prove indirect discrimination, and conditions for certain jobs may exclude people who do not have English as their first language. In these cases, the employer would have to show that the qualifications asked for were essential for the job being undertaken.

The **Commission for Racial Equality (CRE)** was set up and a network of racial equality councils (RECs) was developed. There should be a council in your area.

Try it out

Contact your local REC and find out about its work.

Ethnic minorities and employment

Members of ethnic minorities are more likely to be in less skilled occupations and to be in lower grades of employment than their qualifications would suggest. The recent report *Ethnic Minorities in the Labour Market*, based on 2002 figures and published in 2003 by the Strategy Unit, found the following:

* people from ethnic minorities have lower levels of economic activity than White people, and also higher levels of unemployment

* there are age variations – people aged 16–24 have some of the lowest levels of economic activity, especially among Pakistani and Bangladeshi groups

* people from ethnic minority groups have lower levels of occupational attainment and progression than White people, particularly among Pakistani and Bangladeshi men

* ethnic minority households are more likely to have lower incomes – half of Pakistani and Bangladeshi working households have incomes that are 50 per cent below the national average income

* even when a range of factors, such as age, gender and qualifications, are held constant, ethnic minority groups still have the worst position in the labour market.

The report concludes that much of the inequality in employment is due to racism.

Ethnic minorities are more likely to experience unemployment. In 2002 the UK unemployment rate for White people was 4 per cent, while that for ethnic minorities was 8 per cent. Unemployment levels among different ethnic groups also differed. They were highest among Black African and Bangladeshi groups, at 11 per cent, with 10 per cent for Black Caribbean, 8 per cent for Pakistani groups and 5 per cent for Asian groups.

Unemployment for White women was 3 per cent in 2002, but for ethnic minorities the figures differed across groups. Nine per cent of Black African women, 8 per cent of Black Caribbean women, 7 per cent of Pakistani women and 6 per cent of Indian women were unemployed.

The report *Ethnic Minorities in the Labour Market* (2003) shows that, with the exception of Indian and Chinese men (who have relatively low levels of unemployment), very high unemployment figures among ethnic minorities have persisted over a long time. In 1992 the unemployment rates for Bangladeshi, Pakistani, and Black Caribbean men were 15–20 per cent higher than those of White men. By 2000, the difference had decreased but there was still a gap of between 10 per cent and 15 per cent between the two groups. Similar differences still exist for women.

Ethnicity and older people

We have already seen that gender is a factor affecting social exclusion in older age. Ethnicity is also a factor. Pensioners from ethnic minorities are more likely to be living on less than 40 per cent of the national average income and are less likely to speak fluent English, which in itself can lead to disadvantage and social exclusion.

Ethnic minorities and health and social services

Compared with White children, a relatively high proportion of children from Afro-Caribbean backgrounds are taken into care. Families from this ethnic group are more likely to be referred because of breakdown in family relationships and financial hardship.

Mothers from this ethnic group are more likely to be referred for mental health problems. Men from Afro-Caribbean backgrounds are more likely to be sectioned (forcibly detained in hospital) and diagnosed as having severe mental illness. Black and Asian groups are more likely to be treated using drugs for mental health problems rather than be offered psychotherapy or counselling. These differences in treatment could be seen as further evidence of racial discrimination.

Social class is also a factor in accessing and receiving health and social care services, so if you are Black and working class you are more likely to experience discriminatory treatment.

Ethnic minorities and state benefits

Because of the impact of low wages and intermittent employment, people from ethnic minorities are less likely to receive benefits based on National Insurance contributions. Therefore many people from ethnic minorities may receive 'safety net' benefits that are of lower monetary value.

Ethnic minorities and housing

In the last 30 years demand for housing in the UK has increased due to population growth and the trend towards smaller households. Housing tenure varies according to ethnic group.

Key concept

Housing tenure: this describes whether accommodation is owned or rented.

ENGLAND					PERCENTAGES
	OWNED OUTRIGHT	OWNED WITH MORTGAGE	RENTED FROM SOCIAL SECTOR	RENTED PRIVATELY	ALL TENURES (= 100%) (MILLIONS)
White					
British	30	42	19	9	18.0
Irish	25	35	27	13	0.3
Other white	26	31	17	26	0.8
Mixed	11	39	32	18	0.2
Asian					
Indian	27	53	8	12	0.3
Pakistani	24	48	13	16	0.2
Bangladeshi	9	26	55	10	0.1
Black					
Black Caribbean	13	37	42	8	0.2
Black African	2	21	47	29	0.2
Chinese	14	39	12	34	0.1
Other ethnic groups	17	29	31	23	0.2
All households	29	42	19	10	20.4

TABLE 11.3 *Housing tenure by ethnic group*   Source: Survey of English Housing, Office of the Deputy Prime Minister

Look at Table 11.3 and describe what you see. People of Indian origin are more likely than some other groups to own their own home, but those from Bangladeshi groups are more likely to live in rented social housing. Black African and Black Caribbean people are also more likely to rent from the social sector. According to recent research (*Housing and Black and Minority Ethnic Communities* (2005), Office of the Deputy Prime Minister), people of Pakistani and Bangladeshi origins are likely to have the lowest income of any of the main ethnic groups. This means that they are more likely to:

✳ live in overcrowded and poor housing conditions

✳ be dissatisfied with their home and want to move.

People of Black origin are also relatively disadvantaged compared with White and Indian households. Members of Black and minority ethnic households make up 22 per cent of households accepted by local councils as homeless. These groups are also more likely to see racist harassment as a serious problem, especially if White women are with Black men and have mixed race children. People from Black and ethnic minority groups often choose to live in areas with other similar ethnic groups in order to have social support.

Inequality and social class

In 1921 the Registrar General set up a classification of society into five social class groups. However, as the twentieth century progressed, this classification began to be seen as problematic. Society was changing rapidly, and as jobs changed the status attached to certain jobs also altered. In 1971 class III was divided into two groups – manual and non-manual. Social classes IV and V were related to unskilled manual occupations.

Households were classified according to the job of the head of household, and with changes in women entering the workforce this also became problematic. The old system worked for men of working age but didn't reflect the position of older people and women. In 2001 the Office for National Statistics introduced eight new categories for the 2001 census, including a category for self-employed people and one for people who

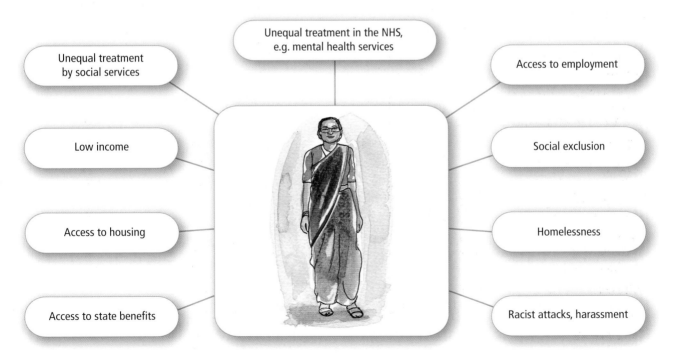

FIGURE 11.5 *Inequality experienced by ethnic minority groups*

Social class categorisation used by the Registrar General

I. Professional occupations

II. Managerial and technical occupations

III. Skilled occupations

(N) non-manual   (M) manual

IV. Partly skilled occupations

V. Unskilled occupations

FIGURE 11.6 *The five categories of social class classification*

THE NATIONAL STATISTICS SOCIO-ECONOMIC CLASSIFICATION – ANALYTIC CLASSES

1	Higher managerial and professional occupations Large employers and higher managerial occupations, e.g. chief executives of major organisations Higher professional occupations, e.g. doctors, lawyers
2	Lower managerial and professional occupations Middle management in bigger organisations, departmental managers, e.g. physiotherapists, teachers, police
3	Intermediate occupations, e.g. clerks, bank workers
4	Small employers and own account workers, e.g. painters, decorators, small manufacturing company owners, taxi drivers
5	Lower supervisory, craft and technical occupations, e.g. plumbers, builders, joiners, train drivers
6	Semi-routine occupations, e.g. shop assistants, hairdressers, labourers
7	Routine occupations, e.g. cleaners, refuse collectors, assembly workers
8	Never worked or long-term unemployed

FIGURE 11.7 *Social class categorisation after 2001*

have never worked and those who are long-term unemployed. This new system of classifying social class is now the current one, and the previous five-category classification has been replaced. However, many of the tables we will be looking at in this section use data from before 2001; these tables still use the previous classification system.

Social class and health

Inequalities between social class groups are still prevalent, especially related to health. Infant mortality rates have fallen in the last 20 years, but there is still a difference between the middle class and the working class.

Social factors such as gender, class and ethnicity all have an impact on health, just as we have seen they also have an impact on poverty.

Socio-economic factors are seen as a key influence in determining a person's health. If we look at mortality and morbidity rates we can see marked differences between the higher and lower social classes (see section 11.2, page 237).

Life expectancy and social class

A man in social class I is likely to live about seven years longer than a man in social class V.

Child mortality

A child born into social class V is twice as likely to die before the age of 15 as a child born into social class I.

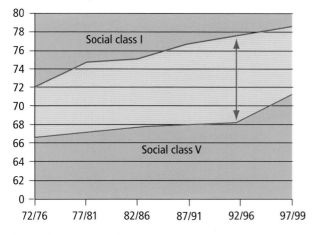

Life expectancy at birth for men in social classes I and V, England and Wales, 1972–99

FIGURE 11.8 *The differences in life expectancy between males of different social class groups*

Source: Health Statist\ics Quarterly; Office for National Statistics (ONS)

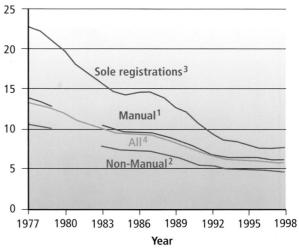

Health inequalities in infant mortality
(by social class and for sole registrations)

Rate per 1,000 live births

Year

1 **Manual = Social classes IIIM, IV and V**
2 **Non-Manual = Social classes I, II and IIIN**
3 **Sole registrations = Births registered outside marriage by mother only**
4 All = Includes all social classes, sole registrations and other registrations

Three-year rolling average plotted against middle year

Data for social class for 1981 is not available because of industrial action by registrars in that year

FIGURE 11.9 *Differences in infant mortality rates based on social class*

Source: Department of Health Statistics Division analysis of data from the Office for National Statistics (ONS)

Causes of death

There are key differences between the causes of death in men and women in social classes IV and V compared with those in social class I.

Long-standing illness

There are twice as many reports of long-standing illness among men and women in social class V compared to those in social class I (see 2001 census). Income and wealth differences still remain between social class I and social class V, and these reflect a range of unequal life chances for the two groups.

Educational opportunities and social class

In spite of the 1944 Education Act and the development of comprehensive schools, there is still a difference in educational achievement between people from different social classes. Although government policy encourages universities to take students from working-class backgrounds, financial problems mean that many working-class students go into work rather than continue their education. Educational achievement assists with employment and higher incomes, so the gap between the social class groups continues.

Housing and social class

There is a difference between the standard of housing experienced by social class I and social class V. With the shortage of social housing and affordable housing many working-class people are unable to rent or buy a property. Homelessness also affects working-class people. Local councils have a statutory duty to ensure that housing is available for applicants who are homeless through no fault of their own. Lone mothers tend to form the highest proportion of homeless people and are among the most likely to seek accommodation from the council. Thirty-five per cent of all homeless households in 2002–03 were single mothers with dependent children.

Summary of Section 11.1

In this section we have seen how social factors such as gender, age, ethnicity and social class interrelate to explain the marginalisation of certain groups in society.

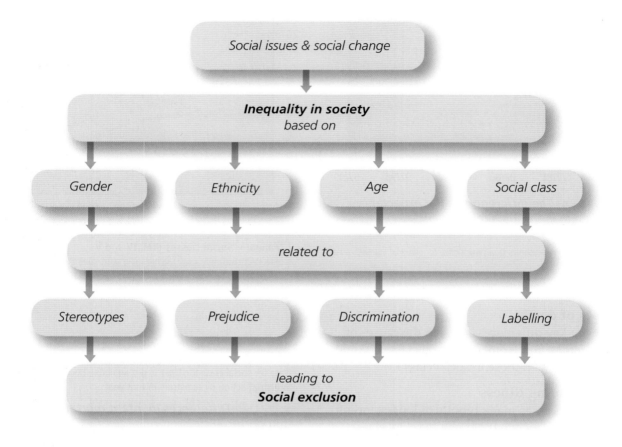

Social issues & social change

Inequality in society
based on

| Gender | Ethnicity | Age | Social class |

related to

| Stereotypes | Prejudice | Discrimination | Labelling |

leading to
Social exclusion

Consider this

Anna is a 55-year-old woman who wants to return to work now her children have left home. She only wants to work part-time because her mother (who lives nearby) has Alzheimer's disease and Anna is her main carer. Anna's husband died two years ago, and although Anna has a widow's pension she is finding it difficult to manage financially. Anna has been for several interviews but she has been unsuccessful in getting a job. She wants to work in an office but she admits her computer skills need updating.

Using concepts, can you identify?

1. What factors in Anna's story may make her more likely to experience unequal treatment?

2. How could the government help to reduce the inequality that Anna may experience?

Go further – Can you analyse the issues using theory?

3. Discuss each model of welfare outlined in this section and indicate how far this approach could assist Anna.

Go further – Can you evaluate using a range of theories?

4. Evaluate the three models of welfare.

5. How might you evaluate the success of government policies related to reducing inequality?

11.2 Demographic change and social and welfare issues

A major factor affecting social issues and welfare needs is the impact of demographic changes. In this section you will develop an understanding of how demographic factors have influenced the nature of social and welfare issues in UK society – for example, the development of a multi-cultural society and an ageing population. You will also develop knowledge of how statistical data can be used to help us understand social issues and welfare needs in the planning of services, the targeting of services, redeployment of resources, assessing service provision and developing future policy objectives. This section overlaps with section 11.4.

Key concept

Demography: the study of populations, with particular reference to their size and structure and how and why these change over time. Demographers study birth, death and marriage rates, patterns of migration and other important factors which affect population growth or decline, such as climate, food supply and the availability of employment.

Morbidity rates: information related to the nature and extent of illness in a population. Morbidity rates can be measured using hospital admission rates, the incidence of disease, such as TB, and self-reported illness rates.

Mortality rates: the number of deaths per 1,000 of the population per year. These rates are often broken down to show differences by age, gender and social class.

Birth rate: the number of live births per 1,000 of the population per year.

Infant mortality rate: the number of deaths of infants under one year old per 1,000 live births.

Population changes

Population changes are among the key factors affecting social policy and the provision of welfare services. The speed of population changes depends on the net natural change – the difference between the numbers of births and deaths, and the net effect of people migrating to and from the country. Most of the population growth in the UK during the twentieth century can be attributed to these changes. However, in recent years net inward migration has become an increasingly important determinant of population growth in the UK, and this is expected to continue in the future.

Births[1,2] and deaths[1]
United Kingdom

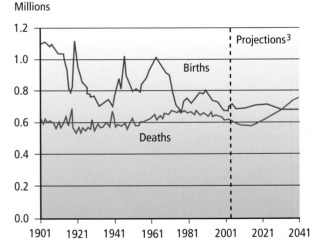

1 Data for 1901 to 1921 excludes Ireland which was constitutionally a part of the United Kingdom during this period.
2 Data from 1981 excludes the non-residents of Northern Ireland.
3 2003-based projections for 2004 to 2041.

FIGURE 11.10 *Birth and death rates from 1901 to 2041 (predicted figures)*

Source: Office for National Statistics; Government Actuary's Department; General Register Office for Scotland; Northern Ireland Statistics and Research Agency

Look at Figure 11.10 and identify the changes you see. What is the gap between births and deaths in the UK at the present time and what are the implications for this pattern?

When birth rates and death rates remain the same, the population is said to be stable. However, if the death rate remains the same and the birth rate increases, as during the 'baby boom' years after World War II and again in the 1960s, this could mean an increase in population overall and also an increase in the proportion of children and young people as opposed to older people. This will have implications for the planning and organisation of health and care services for children and mothers. More maternity services, primary schools and other health and welfare services will be needed for this increase. So you can see that changes in the composition of the population are very significant when planning services to meet health and welfare needs.

Infant deaths

Death rates also include infant mortality rates – deaths in children under one year old per 1,000 live births.

Look at Figure 11.11 and identify the changes in infant mortality that you can see. In your group, discuss factors that may have reduced infant mortality.

Infant mortality rates are an indicator of the standard of living in a country. A fall in infant mortality is due to improved health services, including antenatal and post-natal care, as well as the development of immunisation programmes, improved standards of nutrition, housing and public health. If you look at some of the global statistics you will see that there are many countries in the developing world that still have a high level of infant mortality.

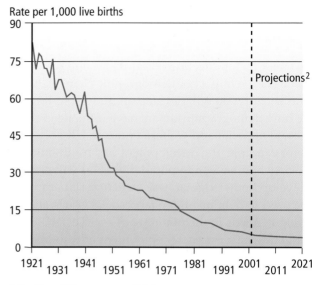

Infant mortality[1]
United Kingdom

Rate per 1,000 live births

1 Deaths within one year of birth.
2 2002-based projections for 2003 onwards.

FIGURE 11.11 *How infant mortality rates have fallen since 1921 with projections for the twenty-first century)*

Source: Office for National Statistics; Government Actuary's Department; General Register Office for Scotland; Northern Ireland Statistics and Research Agency

Morbidity rates

Morbidity rates are the nature and extent of disease or illness in a population. Certain diseases have declined in the last 100 years because of better standards of living and immunisation programmes to protect people from disease. Morbidity rates tend to differ between different groups in the population.

Morbidity rates related to gender

Women

The most common cancer in women is breast cancer and this accounts for 30 per cent of all new cancers in women. Large bowel and lung cancer are the next most common cancers. Using the 2001 incidence figures (Figure 11.12) we can see the pattern of cancer in women.

Apart from cancer, the most common causes of serious illness in women are coronary heart disease, stroke and other circulatory conditions.

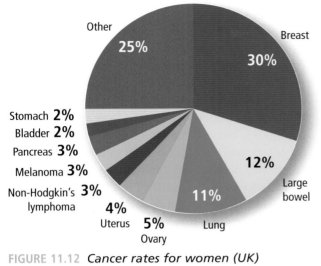

FIGURE 11.12 *Cancer rates for women (UK)*

Source: ONS

Men

The most common cancer in men is prostate cancer. This is responsible for a fifth of all new cases of cancer in men. The incidence of lung cancer is continuing to fall as a result of the decrease in smoking in recent years. Using the 2001 incidence figures we can see the pattern of cancer in men (see Figure 11.13).

Apart from cancer, the most common forms of serious illness among men are coronary heart disease, stroke and other circulatory conditions.

Morbidity rates related to ethnicity

Some genetically determined conditions affect various groups whose origins are African, Afro-Caribbean, Middle Eastern or from the Indian subcontinent. They include blood disorders such as sickle cell anaemia and thalassaemia, as well as diseases that are also present in the population as a whole. Data from a Department of Health survey (*Ethnicity and Health* 1993) showed that there were significantly higher morbidity rates from certain illnesses among ethnic minority groups than among the population as a whole. These included:

* *coronary heart disease:* the death rate among people under 65 from the Indian subcontinent from coronary heart disease is 50 per cent higher than the average for England and Wales

* *stroke and hypertension:* the death rate from stroke and hypertension in people under 65 who were born in the Caribbean is nearly twice as great as the average for England and Wales

* *diabetes:* the incidence of diabetes is four to five times greater in Asians than in non-Asians.

As a result of these findings, the 1999 White Paper *Saving Lives: Our Healthier Nation* gave priority to ethnic minorities. In areas where there was a high proportion of ethnic minorities, health improvement programmes were set up particularly to address these issues. In some areas of the UK, health action zones were established. These aimed to raise awareness of health issues affecting particular ethnic groups; for example, encouraging awareness of diabetes among Asian women. Health action zones also stressed the importance of antenatal care for Bangladeshi and other Asian women, since infant mortality rates were higher among these groups. Women from these groups often experienced difficulty in accessing mainstream antenatal services due to language problems and cultural issues.

The morbidity rates among ethnic groups compared to the White population are carefully noted and health professionals have received training on these issues. Higher morbidity rates among ethnic groups are not necessarily related to genetically determined conditions. For example, pulmonary tuberculosis is higher among ethnic minority groups, but this could be due to factors of poverty and poor housing.

Schizophrenia rates are high for Afro-Caribbeans and also raised for Asians.

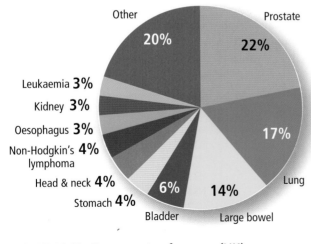
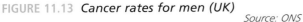

FIGURE 11.13 *Cancer rates for men (UK)*

Source: ONS

Morbidity rates related to social class

As we have already seen, social class is a key factor in determining many life outcomes. According to statistics showing chronic sickness rates by sex and age in 2003 in Great Britain, routine and manual groups are more likely than groups from a higher social class to suffer chronic conditions in every category. These categories include musculoskeletal problems, heart and circulatory problems, respiratory conditions, and digestive problems. Many of these conditions could be related to heavy manual work, but social factors related to housing and lifestyle are also relevant. Manual workers are still more likely to smoke than managerial and professional groups, so health professionals need to focus health programmes, such as smoking cessation support, on these groups. Both male and female manual workers have higher morbidity rates than managerial and professional groups.

Morbidity rates related to age

As we age we are more likely to experience health problems related to heart conditions, arthritis and respiratory problems. Type 2 diabetes is more likely to occur in older people, although it has been noted in younger people who are obese. Cancer rates increase with age; 64 per cent of new cases occur in people over 65. In young children the most common cause of cancer is leukaemia, and this represents one-third of all childhood cancers. In young men aged 20–39, testicular cancer is the most common cancer. In the 2003 statistics showing the incidence of chronic sickness, people over 75 were more likely to suffer from arthritis and rheumatism, hypertension and other heart complaints.

Morbidity data

Research is undertaken each year when GP practices are asked to compile figures on the common conditions presented by patients within each practice. In a Primary Care Trust (PCT) in South London in 2000, figures reflected the national patterns of cancer, lung and heart conditions, but asthma seems to be increasing, especially among older people in this area. Morbidity data is useful in helping PCTs plan services to meet the needs of their populations. For example, as a result of their findings this PCT will allocate more funding to support asthma services. Both national and local data is used to plan health care provision.

Migration and emigration

The UK figures on migration are split into two categories:

* *emigration:* the movement of people from the UK to other countries

* *immigration:* the movement of people from other countries to the UK.

> **Key concept**
>
> *Migration:* the movement of people from one area to another. Internal migration is the movement of people from one area to another in the same country. External migration is the movement of people from one country to another country.

The pattern of people entering and leaving the UK has changed during the twentieth century. Since 1983 there has been a net migration into the UK. In Table 11.4 you can see that more people

| | 1993–1997 | | | 1998–2002 | | |
	INFLOW	OUTFLOW	BALANCE	INFLOW	OUTFLOW	BALANCE
Work-related	59.2	85.3	-26.1	103.4	92.8	10.6
Accompany/join partner	72.3	64.0	8.2	77.2	51.1	26.0
Formal study	61.8	13.0	48.8	91.2	13.7	77.5
Other	93.2	70.6	22.6	164.6	99.3	65.3
No reason stated	20.6	23.8	-3.2	27.7	49.2	-21.5
All reasons	307.1	256.7	50.4	464.0	306.0	158.0

TABLE 11.4 *Migration rates in 1993–1998 and 1998–2002 ('000s)*

Source: Office for National Statistics

are entering the country than leaving it. In 2003 an estimated 151,000 more people arrived to live in the UK for at least one year than left to live elsewhere. Net international immigration into the UK from other countries is projected to remain at a high level over the next 25 years. Nationals of the European Economic Area (the European Union plus Iceland, Liechtenstein, and Norway) have the right to live in the UK provided they are working or able to support themselves financially. Nearly all other overseas nationals wishing to live permanently in the UK have to be accepted by the Home Office for settlement (grants of settlement). Between 2002 and 2003 the number of grants of settlement increased by 26,000 to 144,000 (see Figure 11.14).

In 2003, 28 per cent of grants of settlement were granted to Asian nationals and a further 31 per cent to African nationals. In Table 11.4, the main reason given for immigration was 'other', and this includes asylum seekers.

Refugees and asylum seekers

Britain has had a long tradition of supporting refugees, from the Huguenots in the seventeenth century to European Jews in the twentieth century. In recent years there has been an increase in refugees from the former Yugoslavia and Turkey. A high percentage of refugees have come from Asia and Africa, some seeking asylum, others are married to spouses already in the UK. The increased level of immigration has meant that health and welfare services have had to be reviewed to take account of the particular needs of these groups. Advocates and interpreters play an important part in enabling people to access services. PCTs have organised specific services to meet the needs of patients whose culture require a different approach. For example, in one Sure Start centre there is a drop in clinic for Somali women which is staffed by a health visitor and an interpreter. This covers a range of health issues related to child care and family life. Voluntary organisations have developed to support certain groups, such as refugees, and these often work in partnership with the local health and social services. At the same time, immigrant groups can offer skills in a range of work settings, including health and social care.

Changes in life expectancy

Life expectancy is one indication of the standard of living in a country and the increase in life expectancy is linked to improvements in housing, health care and nutrition. Life expectancy in the UK is rising by about two years every ten years, but there is still a significant difference between

Grants of settlement: by region of origin
United Kingdom

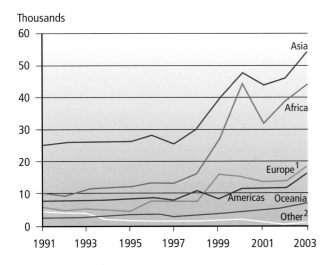

1 European Economic Area (EEA) nationals may apply for settlement, but are not obliged to do so. The figures do not represent the total number of Europeans eligible to stay indefinitely in the UK. Data on EEA nationals granted settlement have not been recorded since 1998.

2 Includes British Overseas citizens, those whose nationality was unknown and, up to 1993, acceptances where the nationality was not separately identified; from 1994 these nationalities have been included in the relevant geographical area.

FIGURE 11.14 *The number of people accepted through grants of settlement*

Source: Home Office

social classes. Some poorer countries in the world still have low life-expectancy rates. For example, at the present time the life-expectancy rates for males in Nigeria and Sierra Leone are 54 and 48 respectively.

Economic effects of changes in life expectancy

If there are fewer economically active adults working and paying taxes, and a larger economically dependent population of older people, economic and social policy will need to reflect these changes to enable the government to raise sufficient funds to support older people.

The government has developed proposals that include:

* raising the retirement age to 65 for everybody

* encouraging people to work as long as they wish
* encouraging the use of private pension schemes, so that only the most needy will depend on state pensions
* means testing for state pensions, so that people who already receive an occupational pension may not receive a state pension as well
* means testing of all benefits for older people.

Impact on housing

With an ageing population, more supported housing will be needed for older people. Local councils are already developing care programmes that enable people to live at home independently for longer (see Unit 7, pages 12–13). If living in their original home no longer seems possible, older people would be encouraged to move to smaller units where they would continue to live independently.

Impact on health services

If there is an increase in the UK population of over-75s in the twenty-first century, there will be increased demand for health services for older people. This includes intermediate care services for people being discharged from hospital who cannot manage independently at home. Conditions that affect older people, such as diabetes, heart disease, arthritis, osteoarthritis and eye problems, will increase as the older population increases, and demand will increase for services for these conditions as well as for chiropody and other community services. The drugs budget will also increase. Additional health staff will be needed to provide services, but recruitment may be a problem

UNITED KINGDOM								YEARS
	1961	1971	1981	1986	1991	1996	2001	2003
Males								
Life expectancy	67.8	69.1	70.8	71.9	73.2	74.2	75.7	76.2
Healthy life expectancy	–	–	64.4	65.3	66.1	66.6	67.0	–
Females								
Life expectancy	73.6	75.3	76.8	77.7	78.7	79.4	80.4	80.5
Healthy life expectancy	–	–	66.7	67.4	68.5	68.7	68.8	–

TABLE 11.5 *Life expectancy rates by birth and sex between 1961 and 2003 in the UK*

Source: Government Actuary's Department; Office for National Statistics

if there are fewer younger people in the population as a whole. However, workers migrating to the UK may help fill the gap.

Education and employment

If the birth rate continues to fall and the under-25 population declines, fewer people in this age group will enter training and further education. Fewer school leavers will be entering employment. Employers may need to recruit older people into jobs previously done by young people. There may be an increase of people in their late-50s and 60s working full-time or part-time to make up the shortfall.

Summary of Section 11.2

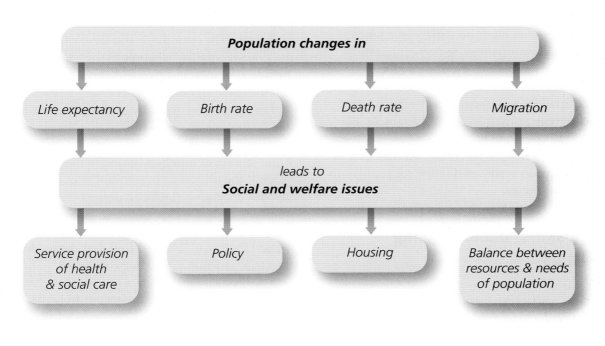

The public health team attached to a PCT is preparing its annual report. This involves collecting a variety of health statistics and analysing them so that an action plan can be drawn up. They notice the statistics show the following:

✷ the numbers of people over 65 have increased in the last ten years

✷ deaths from lung cancer and coronary heart disease have reduced slightly but are still the main cause of death among men in the 45–55 age range

✷ the birth rate is continuing to decline

✷ the proportion of ethnic minorities in the area has increased from 10 to 15 per cent in the last five years.

Using concepts, can you identify?

1. What factors could have influenced these changes?

2. Would you expect similar patterns to be repeated elsewhere in the UK? If not, why not?

Go further – Can you analyse the issues using theory?

3. Use concepts covered in this section to explain changes in population patterns.

Go further – Can you evaluate using a range of theories?

4. Using concepts covered in this section, evaluate the impact of demographic changes in the UK.

11.3 Social issues in context

This section critically examines social issues and welfare needs of concern in contemporary UK. These include a range of interrelated issues. We have already seen that poverty is linked to unemployment, which in turn can lead to mental illness. You need to understand how these factors work together to affect the life experience of certain individuals and groups in UK society, as well as having an effect on society as a whole.

Government responses to current issues are constantly evolving, and include the development of legislation and policy, as well as setting up units and departments whose role it is to deal with current issues. For example, the Social Exclusion Unit has been researching the problems experienced by certain groups, and this body makes recommendation for changes in government policy.

Study skills: understanding statistics

In this section we will be looking at a range of data from various sources, including government statistics. When we look at data it is important to be aware of how the statistics are presented and some of the terms used in the tables. When you look at a table for the first time you need to ask yourself certain questions:

1. Where was the data derived from?

2. When was the data collected?

3. If the data comes from a government department or a political party, what do we need to be aware of? Is there a political bias?

4. What are figures in the table – are they in percentages (per cent) or thousands ('000s)?

5. Are there any terms used that you aren't clear about? If so, you may need to refer to a dictionary or glossary, but you will find that there are often definitions given at the foot of the table.

Mean, median and mode

In many statistics that relate to averages, the terms *mean*, *median* or *modal* may appear. The *mean* average is worked out by adding up all the values and dividing by the total number of values in the set (e.g. the mean of the values 5, 7, 6, 7, 5, 5 is 5.8; in other words, 35 divided by 6). However, the mean average is not always a good representation of the data. For example, if you were calculating the average salaries of people in the UK you would include very high incomes and very low incomes and the resulting mean could be very misleading.

For this reason, in many of the tables we will be looking at, you will find that the *median* average is used. The median average is the middle value of a set of numbers arranged in ascending order. If the set has an even number of values then the median is the mean of the two middle numbers. So in the case of the set 5, 7, 6, 7, 5, 5, we would rearrange the numbers from lowest to highest (5, 5, 5, 6, 7, 7) and find that the median is the mean of 5 and 6; in other words, 5.5.

The modal average refers to the value that appears most frequently. In this example the modal average would be 5. This type of average is not usually used in official statistics.

In some statistics it may not matter too much whether the median or the mean is used – for example, in looking at the height of policemen in London at the time when there was a minimum height requirement there would be a limited range. In this unit you will find that most averages are the median average.

In this section we will consider the following factors that have an impact on current social issues and welfare needs:

* income and wealth distribution
* economic activity and employment
* poverty
* the ageing society
* mental illness and suicide
* disability and dysfunction.

Income and wealth distribution

Income is an important factor affecting people's health and well-being. If people have a reasonable level of income they can spend money on goods and services that improve their standard of living.

Key concept

Income: money from wages, benefits, interest payments on savings and rent from property.

Wealth: the ownership of assets such as property and valuables. A person's wealth can change for a variety of reasons – for example, if a person's wealth is determined by the value of their house and house prices fall, their wealth will also decline.

National Income – Gross Domestic Product

Key concept

Gross Domestic Product (GDP): this measures the economic activity of the UK. It is the total value of goods produced and services provided in the UK in one year. If the GDP is improving in real terms, the economy is expanding and there is more money available for the government to distribute to services such as the NHS and to individuals through benefits.

Household income

An individual's income is subject to income tax, local tax and contributions towards pensions and National Insurance. The amount of money remaining is called disposable income – the amount people have to spend or save. Disposable income is seen as one way to measure a person's 'economic well-being'.

The more disposable income people have, the more money they have to spend on leisure, food and transport. Between 2002 and 2003 the disposable income of all households in the UK grew by 1.8 per cent, and the GDP grew by 2 per cent. GDP needs to keep ahead of household disposable income levels in order for the government to maintain a reasonable standard of living for all the population through spending on health and welfare provision.

From Table 11.6, it is clear that wages and salaries form the largest percentage of household income. This shows the importance of employment in determining income levels. In households where there is at least one person in full-time work, wages and salaries range between 85 per cent and 96 per cent of total income. If people are working they do not need to claim benefits, thus reducing government spending. In families where people are retired, most of their income is from benefits, as we can see in Figure 11.15.

	WAGES & SALARIES	SELF-EMPLOYMENT	INVESTMENT INCOME	TAX CREDITS	RETIREMENT PENSIONS	PRIVATE PENSIONS	DISABILITY BENEFITS	OTHER BENEFITS	OTHER INCOME	ALL INCOME
Self-employed	20	71	2	1	1	3	–	2	2	100
Single or couple, all in full-time work	96	–	1	–	–	1	–	1	1	100
Couple, one in full-time work, one in part-time work	91	2	2	–	–	2	–	2	1	100
Couple, one in full-time work, one not working	85	–	2	1	1	4	2	3	2	100
One or more in part-time work	41	11	4	5	6	16	2	7	8	100
Head or spouse aged 60 or over	–	–	6	–	42	34	7	9	2	100
Head or spouse unemployed	–	–	3	2	–	6	5	73	11	100
Head or spouse sick or disabled	2	–	2	–	–	8	32	52	4	100
Other	3	–	4	1	–	12	1	45	35	100
All benefit units	65	9	2	1	6	7	2	6	3	100

TABLE 11.6 *Composition of household income*

Source: Family Resources Survey, Department for Work and Pensions

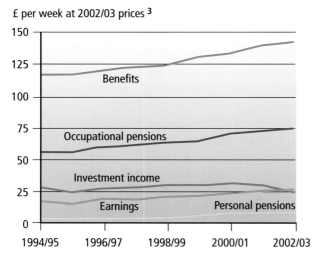

Pensioners'[1] gross income: by source [2]
Great Britain

£ per week at 2002/03 prices [3]

FIGURE 11.15 *Pensioners' gross income by source*
Source: Pensioners' Income Series, Department for Work and Pensions

1 Pensioner units are either pensioner couples where the man is over 65, or single pensioners over state pension age (65 for men, 60 for women).
2 Excludes 'other income'.
3 Adjusted to 2002/03 prices using the retail prices index less local taxes.

Figure 11.15 also shows that pre-tax income levels for pensioners increased between 1994 and 2003.

Statistics show that household disposable income has increased since 1997, but we cannot assume that there is an equal sharing of resources between household members. Section 11.1 showed that women tend to earn less than men, and that pensions for men tend to be higher than those for women. Men's net incomes exceed those of women throughout the life cycle.

Low income

In 2002–03 low income groups tended to be the following:

* one-parent families
* single pensioners
* families with children in workless households
* unemployed people
* large families
* families where the head of the household is from an ethnic minority, particularly Pakistani or Bangladeshi.

Low income is an important measurement of poverty, but material deprivation also measures people's living standards. The Department for Work and Pensions' *Families and Children Study* analysed 34 deprivation items causing four dimensions of material deprivation – food and meals, clothing and shoes, consumer durables, and leisure activities. Lone-parent families are most likely to experience material deprivation.

Wealth

Wealth means the ownership of assets that can be sold (see Figure 11.16).

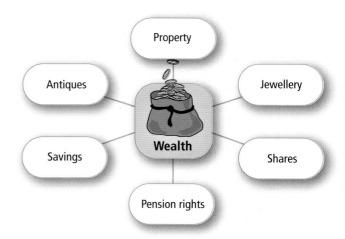

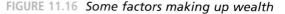

FIGURE 11.16 *Some factors making up wealth*

During the twentieth century the distribution of wealth has become more equal. In 1911 it was estimated that the wealthiest 1 per cent of the population owned 70 per cent of the wealth in the UK. By 1945 this had fallen to 42 per cent. In the 1970s and 1980s, the share of the wealthiest 1 per cent of the population fell from around 22 per cent to 17–18 per cent in 1985. However, since the 1980s, the distribution of wealth seems to have become more unequal, with the wealthiest 1 per cent of the population owning 23 per cent of the wealth in the UK. In an equal society all groups would have an equal share.

Did you know?

Look at Table 11.7: in recent years the wealthiest 50 per cent own 94 per cent of the wealth – this means that the remaining 50 per cent of the population only own 6 per cent of the wealth.

Problems in measuring wealth

It is difficult to measure wealth. As we have already discussed, wealth may be assessed at a different monetary level depending on the price of property, price of shares, etc. Statistics on the distribution of wealth are based on inheritance and capital transfer taxes which have been sent to the Inland Revenue as part of people's tax returns. Tax returns are seen to be an unreliable source of data as they may not reflect the true picture. This is one reason why it is difficult to be sure how much wealth exists at any one time and who owns it.

Economic activity and employment

People are considered to be economically active or 'in the workforce' if they are aged 16 and over and are either in work or actively seeking work. In the last ten years employment rates have continued to be high in the UK. However, the percentage of men in the UK who are economically active has declined from 89 per cent in 1984 to 84 per cent in 2004 (Labour Force Survey). The percentage of women who are economically active has increased from 67 per cent in 1984 to 73 per cent in 2004. These changes are due to a range of factors, including the decline of the manufacturing industry, changes in technology, changes in the skills required of the workforce and the changing role of women.

The economic activity rate (percentage of people in the workforce) is linked to the economic cycle. As the UK experiences economic growth, the number of jobs increases and unemployment

UNITED KINGDOM					PERCENTAGES
	1991	1996	2000	2001	2002
Marketable wealth					
Percentage of wealth owned by:					
Most wealthy 1%	17	20	23	22	23
Most wealthy 5%	35	40	44	42	43
Most wealthy 10%	47	52	56	54	56
Most wealthy 25%	71	74	75	72	74
Most wealthy 50%	92	93	95	94	94
Total marketable wealth (£ billion)	1,711	2,092	3,131	3,477	3,464
Marketable wealth less value of dwellings					
Percentage of wealth owned by:					
Most wealthy 1%	29	26	33	34	35
Most wealthy 5%	51	49	59	58	62
Most wealthy 10%	64	63	73	72	75
Most wealthy 25%	80	81	89	88	88
Most wealthy 50%	93	94	98	98	98

TABLE 11.7 *The distribution of wealth*

Source: Inland Revenue

falls. As the economy slows and goes into recession, unemployment tends to increase. The recession in the 1990s had a greater impact on unemployment among men than among women, as traditional manufacturing industries were most affected. The number of people deemed to be unemployed in 2004 was 1.4 million, but these figures are problematic, as the 'economically active' figures include those who are actively looking for work but are unemployed.

Unemployment

Reasons for unemployment (or economic inactivity) vary by age and gender. Long-term sickness or disability is the main reason for economic inactivity, particularly among 35–49-year-olds. In 2004 there were 7.8 million economically inactive people of working age in the UK and 60 per cent of these were women.

Long-term sickness and disability was the most common reason given for economic inactivity by working-age men in 2004. For women the most common reason was looking after a family or home. Forty-two per cent of lone-parent households were workless in 2004 and as we know most lone-parents are women.

Try it out

Look at Table 11.8 and describe the pattern you see.

Can you think of any additional information that would be helpful in analysing the figures?

We have already seen that people from ethnic minority groups are more likely to be in low-income households. If ethnicity were included in the table, it might give us additional understanding of factors affecting unemployment.

Regional variations in employment rates

Unemployment rates vary across the UK; unemployment is low in southern and central England, but some inner-city areas, such as Newham in London and parts of Manchester, the North East, East Anglia and Cornwall, have high unemployment rates. Northern Ireland and Scotland also have high unemployment. Unemployment can be linked to the decline of traditional manufacturing industries in some areas. The collapse of the Rover car company in 2005 will have a great impact on unemployment in the Birmingham area and also on companies

UNITED KINGDOM					PERCENTAGES
	16–24	25–34	35–49	50–59/64	ALL AGED 16–59/64
Males					
Long-term sick or disabled	5	38	60	53	37
Looking after family or home	1	12	17	4	6
Student	84	25	4	–	30
Retired	0	0	–	31	13
Other	10	26	18	12	14
All males	100	100	100	100	100
Females					
Long-term sick or disabled	4	10	24	42	21
Looking after family or home	22	72	59	27	45
Student	64	8	4	1	19
Retired	0	0	–	15	4
Other	10	10	11	16	12
All females	100	100	100	100	100

TABLE 11.8 *Reasons given for economic inactivity*

Source: Labour Force Survey, Office for National Statistics

supplying Rover. The globalisation of industry has also increased unemployment in the UK as traditional industries such as steel manufacture have moved to countries such as China.

Unemployment and educational achievement

One of the key factors affecting unemployment is educational achievement. In 2004, 45 per cent of men with no qualifications were unemployed, for women the rate was 44 per cent.

Poverty

There have been many discussions about how to define and measure poverty. In the nineteenth century poverty was defined as not having enough resources to live on. There was a minimum income level reckoned as sufficient to support an individual, and everyone whose resources were below this line was considered to be in poverty. This was called 'absolute poverty'.

During the twentieth century there were several studies into poverty and how to measure it. Townsend in his *Poverty Study* (1979) defined the term 'relative poverty', according to which those in poverty were unable to participate in society because of lack of adequate resources. It was recognised that the concept of poverty changes according to the society in which you live, and also the period of time in which you live. With regard to current government policy, those in poverty are those whose income is below 60 per cent of the median average income.

Try it out

Look at Table 11.9 and identify the groups at risk from poverty.

Poverty can be transmitted from one generation to another. Those children born into poor families are likely to remain in poverty themselves, because they are considered to be in a 'poverty trap' from which it is difficult to escape. The factors that keep people in poverty include:

* low-paid workers may find if they have a pay rise that it will reduce their benefits and they are actually worse off

* because of low disposable income, poor households cannot buy goods in larger, more

UNITED KINGDOM/GREAT BRITAIN				PERCENTAGES
	1991–92	1996/97	2001/02	2002/03
Income before deduction of housing costs				
Pensioner couple	26	19	22	21
Single pensioner	23	23	22	21
Couple with children	20	19	16	15
Couple without children	9	9	9	9
Single with children	46	37	31	31
Single without children	22	16	16	17
All individuals	21	18	17	17
Income after deduction of housing costs				
Pensioner couple	25	22	22	23
Single pensioner	30	33	22	20
Couple with children	24	23	20	19
Couple without children	11	11	11	11
Single with children	59	62	53	51
Single without children	28	25	22	24
All individuals	25	25	22	22

TABLE 11.9 *Individuals in households with incomes below 60 per cent of median disposable income by family type. Figures for 1991–92 for UK. Figures for 1996 on for Great Britain.*

Source: Households Below Average Income, Department for Work and Pensions

economic quantities, so they spend a higher proportion of income on necessities such as food

* access to transport is also restricted so that poor households cannot use cheaper out-of-town supermarkets, which again means they may spend more of their income on food

* low-income households are more likely to incur debt, and may be able to access credit only at very high rates of interest

* poverty often leads to ill-health so it is difficult to find and keep employment.

In 2005 the Department for Work and Pensions published a report based on the findings from the 2003 *Families and Children Study* (FACS). The annual FACS study began in 1999 with a representative sample of all lone parents and low/moderate-income couple families. From 2001 a representative sample of lone parents and all couples with dependent children were interviewed. The sample was drawn from a national register of child benefit recipients. The same 7,883 families were interviewed on a yearly basis and there was an 80 per cent response rate.

This FACS study examines the living standards of families with children who receive child benefit, and analyses the level of material deprivation they experience. This is measured as the ability to buy essential goods and to participate in leisure activities. Families were asked whether they possessed or took part in each of the following 34 items or activities, and if not whether this was because they could not afford to or because they did not want or need to.

Food and meat
Main meal every day
Meat/fish every other day
Roast meat every week
Vegetables most days
Fruit most days
Cakes/biscuits most days
Brand name food most days

Clothing and shoes
Waterproof coat for each adult
Waterproof coat for each child
Two pairs of shoes for each adult
Two pairs of shoes for each child
New clothes when needed
Best outfit for each child
Brand clothing/shoes for each child

Consumer durable items
Colour TV
Cable/satellite TV
Refrigerator
Separate deep freeze
Washing machine
Tumble drier
Telephone (including mobile)
Dishwasher
Video recorder
Central heating
Microwave
Car or van
Music system
Home computer

GREAT BRITAIN					PERCENTAGES
	NONE	1–2 ITEMS	3–5 ITEMS	6–10 ITEMS	11 OR MORE ITEMS
Lone-parent families					
1 or 2 children	12	17	22	28	22
3 or more children	7	8	21	30	35
Couple families with children					
1 or 2 children	38	21	17	13	11
3 or more children	24	14	18	25	19
All families with children	22	17	19	23	19

TABLE 11.10 *Families unable to afford items*

Source: Family and Children Study, Department for Work and Pensions

Leisure activities

Celebrations with presents on special occasions
Toys/sports gear for each child
Money for trips/outings/gifts to parties
One-week holidays (not staying with relatives)
Night out once a month
Friends/relatives for a meal once a month

The data was used to calculate the total number of all items on the list a family would like but could not afford. Around a fifth of low-income families with children could afford to buy all the items on the list, but a further one-fifth could not afford 11 or more of them (see Table 11.10). Lone parents were more likely to experience material deprivation than two-parent families. The group experiencing the most deprivation were lone-parent families with three or more children; more than a third of these were unable to afford 11 or more items. One in ten families could not afford new clothes when needed and almost one in five could not afford one night out a month.

Other findings from the study

Around one in five children lived in a household where no one worked. Around a quarter of the children lived in a one-parent family. Family income, partnership and work status were related to children's leisure activities. Children from lone-parent, workless and low-income families were less likely to have access to a computer, to have been on holiday in the past year or to have participated in organised activities.

Families of children with disabilities

This is another group likely to experience poverty. The Child Poverty Accord is a commitment by the Department for Work and Pensions, the Department for Education and Skills, HM Treasury, HM Revenue and Customs, and the Local Government Association to meet regularly to discuss child poverty. On 11 July 2005 Margaret Hodge (the Minister of State for Employment and Welfare Reform) gave a pledge to break the cycle of poverty for disabled children. Mothers of disabled children are less likely to be able to get back to work because of the problems with suitable child care. In Section 11.4 we will look at some of the government initiatives to try to reduce poverty.

Ageing society

In the UK the number of people over 65 is increasing compared to the total population. This is due to increased life expectancy and to a fall in the birth rate. In 2005, 16 per cent of the UK population was 65 and over. By 2021 there will be more people who are 65 and over (about 12.5 million) than children under 16 (11.5 million). By 2031 it is predicted that almost a quarter of the population will be over 65. There are many implications for this changing pattern which were covered in section 11.1.

From an economic perspective, there will be an increase in the economically inactive or dependent population and a smaller economically active population, so social policy will have to develop to support older people through state benefits and pensions.

Although an ageing society can be seen in a negative light, with increased demands on health and social care services, we should remember that older people's health has improved in the last 100 years, and it is only the over-75 age group that are likely to need additional support. Many older people are able to lead fit and active lives, working part-time in paid employment, or as volunteers, and helping younger members of the family. Many grandparents are actively involved in caring for grandchildren while the children's parents work. Many older people return to studying; the Open University has many students in their 70s and 80s.

Mental illness and suicide

Mental health problems

Mental health problems are common, and affect many of us at some time. Most people who suffer from mental distress and who receive care from the health service do so in the community, either through their GP or through the community mental health team. The numbers of consultations for mental distress account for a high proportion

	SINGLE	MARRIED/ COHABITING	WIDOWED, DIVORCED OR SEPARATED	ALL
Males				
Mixed anxiety and depressive disorder	4.8	7.2	9.6	6.8
Generalised anxiety disorder	3.2	4.0	10.3	4.3
Depressive episode	2.0	2.0	6.3	2.3
All phobias	2.0	0.9	3.1	1.3
Obsessive compulsive disorder	1.3	0.5	2.6	0.9
Panic disorder	0.7	0.7	0.6	0.7
Any neurotic disorder	11.1	13.1	24.2	13.5
Females				
Mixed anxiety and depressive disorder	13.2	10.1	10.7	10.8
Generalised anxiety disorder	2.7	4.3	8.1	4.6
Depressive episode	3.0	2.3	4.9	2.8
All phobias	2.4	1.6	4.3	2.2
Obsessive compulsive disorder	1.6	1.1	2.0	1.3
Panic disorder	0.6	0.7	1.1	0.7
Any neurotic disorder	20.5	17.9	24.6	19.4

TABLE 11.11 *The prevalence of mental disorders by sex and marital status*

Source: Psychiatric Morbidity Survey, Office for National Statistics

of GP appointments: only respiratory conditions are more common.

Try it out

Look at Table 11.11 carefully. Can you think of reasons why marital status may be a factor affecting a person's mental health?

Definitions of mental health

There are three broad approaches to the definition of mental health.

1. The first defines mental health as the absence of signs and symptoms of mental illness.

2. The second approach adopts a 'foundations of health' model, seeing mental health as a component of the physical, psychological and social foundations that constitute good health or overall well-being.

3. The third approach focuses upon positive mental health, based upon self-esteem, self-regard, competence and social integration.

The medical model of health tends to focus on the first definition, but increasingly professionals are focusing on the importance of social factors, such as poverty, which can affect a person's mental health.

The MINI index (or mental health needs index) calculates the relative mental health service needs between populations, and is based on 1991 census data. The MINI index scores are computed, and from these it is possible to identify the geographical areas where mental health problems are most likely to occur. For example, the areas where individuals are most at risk from mental health problems in London are Tower Hamlets, Hackney, Camden and Islington. The scores are based on variables which are known to be associated with mental illness rates, including aspects such as social isolation, poverty, unemployment, sickness, and quality of housing. Figure 11.17 shows the importance of social factors on mental health.

Mental health problems can affect people throughout their life course.

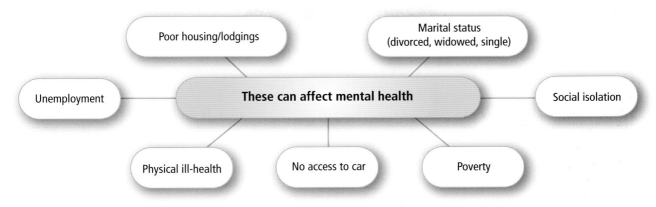

FIGURE 11.17 *Variables affecting mental health in adults*

Try it out

Can you think why people who are unemployed, permanently sick or divorced or widowed are more likely to become mentally ill? Conversely, why are people with mental health problems more likely to become unemployed or divorced?

Mental health problems in children

According to numerous research studies, child and adolescent mental health problems are increasing. In 1999 the Mental Health Foundation reported that 20 per cent of children were found to have mental health problems. Suicide and self-harm in adolescents has increased. In the National Suicide Prevention Strategy young people are seen as a vulnerable group. Eating disorders have increased among young people, with anorexia and bulimia rates increasing. It is estimated that at least 5 per cent of all female secondary school children have bulimia. Drug and alcohol use is increasing among young people, with increasing numbers smoking cannabis and binge drinking. Young people are more likely to use illegal drugs than older people. In 2002–03, 28 per cent of young people in England and Wales had used drugs. Thirty-two per cent of young men and 21 per cent of young women had used cannabis, an increase on previous years. Research studies show there is a link between regular cannabis use and mental health problems. In 2003–04, 37 per cent of young men aged 16–24 had drunk more than eight units on at least one day in the previous week. Of young women of the same age, 26 per cent had drunk more than six units on one day the previous week. Just as there is a problem with suicide statistics, there is also a problem with accurately recording the level of drug and alcohol misuse, so the real figure may be higher.

Figure 11.18 shows possible factors affecting mental health in children and young people.

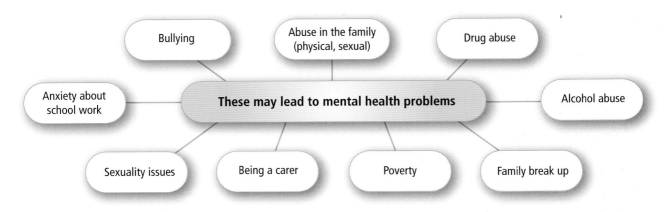

FIGURE 11.18 *Variables affecting mental health in children and young people*

Government response to mental health problems in children and adolescents

A range of approaches is currently in place, including:

* 'healthy schools' programmes giving pupils information and support

* mental health awareness training for teachers

* availability of counselling and rapid access to psychiatric services.

Mental health problems in adults

In a GP surgery every third or fourth person seen has some kind of mental disorder. In the last 30 years the numbers of hospital beds for people with mental health problems has decreased, while the work of psychiatrists, psychologists, community psychiatric nurses (CPNs) and GPs has increased. Primary care is increasingly taking on responsibility for mental health. Voluntary groups, self-help groups, friends and family are also supporting people with mental health problems.

Depression and anxiety are common conditions and can be treated effectively in the community. People with more serious mental illnesses, such as schizophrenic and psychotic disorders, may need a period in hospital for assessment and then will be treated in hospital or in the community.

Mental illness in older people

As people live longer, certain mental illnesses may affect them. The two main categories of mental health problems in older people are *functional disorders* (anxiety, depression and schizophrenia) and *organic disorders* (vascular dementia, and Alzheimer's disease, which is also caused by changes in the brain). It is estimated that at least 15 per cent of people over 65 suffer from depressive illness.

Key concept

Functional disorders: these cause the person to have problems living a 'normal life' because of anxiety or other problems.

Organic disorders: these are caused by biological changes to the brain such as a diminished blood supply.

FIGURE 11.19 *Factors affecting depression in older people*

Dementia

The incidence of dementia increases with age, with about one person in 20 over the age of 65 affected, rising to one in five of the over-80s. Early dementia may be difficult to diagnose.

National Service Framework for Mental Health

The National Service Framework (NSF) for Mental Health was drawn up in 1999.

The NSF has seven standards:

1. Promoting mental health and well-being and reducing discrimination and social exclusion experienced by people with mental health problems.

2. Delivering better primary mental health care to everyone with mental health problems, including those with severe mental illness.

3. Providing an effective out-of-hours service for people with mental health problems (including the use of NHS Direct).

4. Delivering effective services for people who have severe mental illness so that prompt treatment is available, in a hospital bed if required.

5. Delivering hospital services when required, and devising a care plan on discharge from hospital.

Stan's story

'I have been a carer for my wife, May, for seven years now. I didn't realise anything was wrong at first. She was 76 when I first noticed she had problems remembering things, but I didn't take much notice until one day we went to the supermarket and she was putting all these things in the trolley we didn't need. I said to her we didn't need them but she said we did, so we went home and put everything away in the cupboards. In the evening she said to me, "Who has bought all this stuff we don't need?" and she accused me of buying it all.

'I realised then she had a problem and we went to see the GP who gave us this drug Aricept, which seemed to help slow the process down.

'We went to see the psychiatrist and after a lot of tests it was confirmed that May had Alzheimer's. It was a terrible shock for both of us. I felt we had worked hard all our lives and we should now be enjoying life. Instead I have had to see my wife deteriorate. We can no longer have conversations about anything. She is sleeping a lot during the day but tends to be awake at night and sometimes she wanders out of the house so I am always on duty.

'Apart from all the shopping, I have had to learn new skills. I never knew how to do the washing, ironing and cooking, but I have had to learn. I also have to help May get dressed and washed as she gets in a muddle. The thing I find really hard to cope with is the repeated questions. She asks me the same thing twenty times because she cannot remember anything. I have the support of the local Alzheimer's Society, which has really helped me, as they arrange outings for carers so we can have a break.'

Support for carers like Stan is essential if people with mental disorders are to be looked after in the community.

Try it out

What kind of support would help Stan? What agencies could provide this help?

As life expectancy increases the incidence of dementia will increase and this will impact on the provision of health and welfare services.

6. Ensuring that the needs of carers are assessed on an annual basis.

7. Reducing the suicide rate by at least one-fifth by 2010.

Although parts of the NSF have been completed successfully, the suicide rate is still causing concern.

Suicide

Around 5,000 people take their own lives in England every year. In the last 20 years suicide rates have fallen in older men and women but have risen in young men.

Deaths from suicide and undetermined injury, England 2000

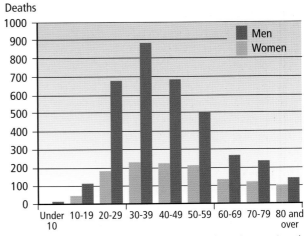

FIGURE 11.20 *Deaths from suicide and undetermined injury, England 2000*

Source: ONS

The majority of suicides now occur in young adult males. In men under 35, suicide is the most common cause of death (ONS 2000).

Problems with suicide statistics

Suicide statistics are based on coroners' verdicts in inquests. Coroners may take certain factors into account when deciding on a verdict of suicide, including whether there was a suicide note and whether it could have been an accident, and sometimes it is not clear if the person intended to take their own life. For this reason the true suicide rate is probably not reflected in the official figures, and the real figure is probably much higher.

The following factors imply a higher risk of suicide:

* male
* living alone
* unemployment
* alcohol or drug misuse
* mental illness.

Suicide rates are related to social class with the highest rates of suicide in social class V.

The National Suicide Prevention Strategy for England was published in 2005 and sets out how it will support the *Our Healthier Nation* target

(1998) of reducing the death rate from suicide by at least 10 per cent by 2010. The strategy will be delivered and evaluated jointly by the Department of Health and NIMHE (the National Institute for Mental Health in England). The strategy has six goals:

1. to reduce risk in key high-risk groups
2. to promote mental health well-being in the wider population
3. to reduce the availability and lethality of suicide methods
4. to improve the reporting of suicidal behaviour in the media
5. to promote research on suicide and suicide prevention
6. to improve monitoring of progress towards the target for reducing suicide rates.

Suicide prevention is seen to be the responsibility of everyone. Although people with a mental illness are at high risk, and mental health services support many people who have suicidal tendencies, around 75 per cent of people who commit suicide are not in contact with mental health services.

Disability and dysfunction

The Disability Rights Movement developed in the 1970s and 1980s, and challenged traditional ideas about disabled people. Before the 1970s, disabled people tended to be seen in the media as 'poor helpless victims' or 'brave people coping with adversity'. Disabled people lobbied for equal rights and for anti-discrimination legislation that had already been passed for women and ethnic minorities.

The Disability Discrimination Act was passed in 1995. This Act gave disabled people rights in the areas of employment, access to goods and services, and buying or renting land or property. These rights came into force in December 1996 and in 1999. In 1999 the Disability Rights Commission was set up. In 2004 the 1995 Act was further extended (see Figure 11.22) to include a duty for the providers of goods and services to make adequate provision to allow for people

Social class differences in suicide: men aged 20–64, England 1997

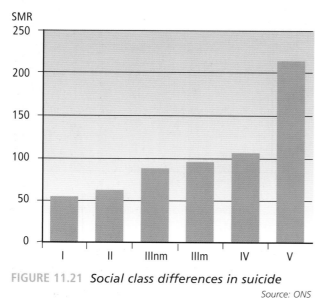

FIGURE 11.21 *Social class differences in suicide*

Source: ONS

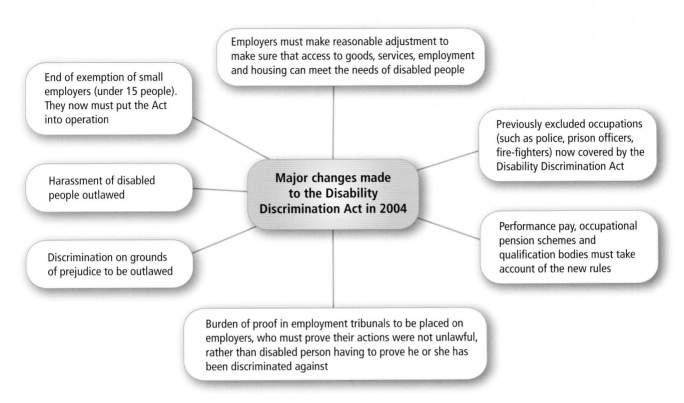

The following are the major changes made to the Disability Discrimination Act in 2004:

- Employers must make reasonable adjustment to make sure that access to goods, services, employment and housing can meet the needs of disabled people
- End of exemption of small employers (under 15 people). They now must put the Act into operation
- Previously excluded occupations (such as police, prison officers, fire-fighters) now covered by the Disability Discrimination Act
- Harassment of disabled people outlawed
- **Major changes made to the Disability Discrimination Act in 2004**
- Performance pay, occupational pension schemes and qualification bodies must take account of the new rules
- Discrimination on grounds of prejudice to be outlawed
- Burden of proof in employment tribunals to be placed on employers, who must prove their actions were not unlawful, rather than disabled person having to prove he or she has been discriminated against

FIGURE 11.22 *Changes implemented in the Disability Discrimination Act in 2004*

with disabilities. It also meant that employers would be unable to discriminate against disabled job applicants on the basis of their disability. Employers would not be able to sack people diagnosed with serious conditions such as cancer or multiple sclerosis.

According to the census of 2001, there are ten million disabled people in the UK. Although around 3.5 million people with disabilities have full-time jobs, many are unemployed and claiming incapacity and other benefits. It is estimated that that about one million disabled people want to work but are unable to do so as they lack the appropriate support. The disability living allowance (DLA) is a benefit for people who are disabled and have personal care and/or mobility needs. DLA accounted for over half of benefit expenditure on disabled people in the UK in 2003–04 (see Figure 11.23).

Try it out

Look at Figure 11.23 and describe the patterns you see.

Recipients of disability living allowance (DLA): by sex and age, 2004[1]

United Kingdom

Rate per 1,000 population [2]

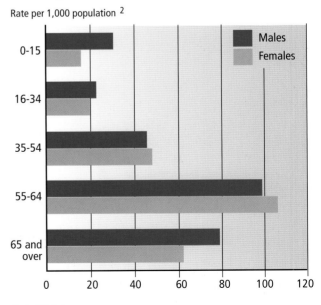

1 At 28 February
2 Rate calculated using mid-2003 population estimates.

FIGURE 11.23 *Recipients of disability living allowance*

Source: Department for Work and Pensions: Northern Ireland Statistics and Reseaerch Agency

Long-term sickness and disability was the most common reason given for economic inactivity by men of working age in 2004.

The government has a 20-year plan for getting disabled people into work, **Improving the Life Chances of Disabled People**. This plan was published by the prime minister's strategy unit. It states that rehabilitation should be work-focused and employers and health services should work together to provide a package of care that is work-related. GPs tend to focus on the person's disability or impairment (using the medical model of disability), but now they will need to take a more holistic approach. GPs are concerned about whether they will have the time to do this and also they have ethical concerns about policing patients and encouraging them back to work when it may not be in the best interest of the patient.

Lack of educational opportunities has often meant that disabled people have limited access to employment. The Learning and Skills Council is carrying out a review of training available for people with disabilities. The Department for Work and Pensions has developed a New Deal programme for disabled people.

SCENARIO

Margaret

Margaret has been claiming incapacity benefit for ten years, and despite being partially blind and having diabetes she was keen to get back to work. She contacted her local job centre plus office and a work-focused interview was set up for her with one of the incapacity benefit personal assistants, Joyce. In this interview Joyce discussed the various options that would help Margaret get back to work, including the benefits she was entitled to:

* return to work credit
* adviser discretionary fund
* job grant working tax credit.

Margaret would be entitled to all of these if she returned to work. Joyce helped Margaret in her job search. She applied for a job as a catering assistant and returned to work. Margaret is better off in work than she was when claiming incapacity benefit.

1. **If Margaret is back in work, how does this help Margaret?**
2. **How does it help society and the government?**

Summary of Section 11.3

- Income and wealth distribution
- Unemployment
- Poverty
- Ageing society
- Disability and dysfunction
- Mental illness and suicide

Social issues in context

Hussein is 25 years old. He came to this country from Pakistan when he was a child, as his family decided they would have more opportunities in the UK. Hussein worked hard at school but found the work difficult. He enjoyed helping his uncle in his shop and when he left school he hoped to continue to do this. When Hussein was 18 he was diagnosed with schizophrenia and admitted to hospital. His family were devastated as they had high hopes for him. Hussein wasn't in hospital long and medication seemed to be effective, although he still became anxious at times. He found that people were frightened of him when they found out he had a mental health problem. He stayed at home most of the time and rarely went out. The community psychiatric nurse visited him and suggested that he could do some voluntary work and then perhaps look for a job once his confidence improved.

Using concepts, can you identify?

1. What factors have affected Hussein's position in society?

Go further – Can you analyse the issues using theory?

2. Explain why certain groups are more likely to experience disadvantages in society?

Go further – Can you evaluate using a range of theories?

3. Using concepts covered in this section, discuss why certain groups are more likely to experience poverty in UK society?

11.4 Government responses to social issues and welfare needs

Government policy depends on a number of factors, including the political ideology of the party in power. Different governments have different ideas about the role of the state in providing welfare services, and since 1998 there has been an increasing reliance on a mixed economy of provision with a range of statutory, private and voluntary agencies providing services and support. Many former state agencies providing housing and other community services have been replaced by independent agencies. The Benefits Agency and the Child Support Agency are further examples of independent bodies now providing services that were directly provided by government departments in the past.

Section 11.1 looked at the influences on social policy in the UK. Many government responses may appear to be in response to pressure from the media or interest groups, but very often the link between influence and outcome is difficult to identify. For example, many government responses are influenced primarily by economic factors. The Child Support Agency was set up to reduce benefits being paid by the state to single parents by putting responsibility for supporting children back on their parents. Various 'Back to Work' schemes could be seen to be driven by a need to reduce spending on benefits. Furthermore, people who return to work will pay tax and National Insurance and contribute more directly to the economy.

Examples of government responses to social issues and welfare needs

Social protection is the term used to cover support given by the government to assist the most vulnerable groups in society. Social protection is also known as social security or income maintenance and is usually in the form of pensions and other benefits, paid to individuals by the state. Figure 11.24 (A) and (B) on page 260 shows government income and expenditure.

Try it out

Look at Figure 11.24 (A) and (B) on page 260 and identify the key patterns shown.

Poverty is a key issue in the UK, and certain groups are more likely to experience it. These include older people, workless people, single parents and some ethnic minorities. Policies to

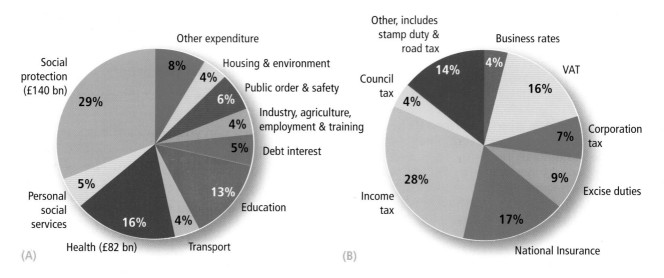

(A)

(B)

FIGURE 11.24 (A) *Government spending on social security and other areas of welfare and support 2004–05 (£485 billion)*
(B) *Government income from taxes 2004–05 (£451 billion)*

Source: HM Treasury, 2004–05 figures

deal with poverty reflect the ideas and values of the government in power at the time. Some political parties have believed that too much reliance on state benefits encourages dependency, whereas others see the role of the state as directly providing support for all members of society. Since 1997 there have been several initiatives taken by the New Labour government to reduce poverty, and these are summarised in Figure 11.25.

Examples of recent welfare government policy related to poverty			
Health	**Low income**	**Education/Employment**	**Support and community regeneration**
NHS plan (2000) Reform of NHS	Working families tax credit to support families	Extra funding for education and lifelong learning	Sure Start programmes increased
NSF's National Service Frameworks for mental health, older people, diabetes, children's services	Sure Start maternity grant – for pregnant and nursing mothers	Payments for 16–18-year-olds who stay in education	Neighbourhood renewal programmes in poor communities
Choosing Health (2004) Improving the nation's health	Minimum income guarantee for pensioners	New Deal programme for single parents and disabled people	Affordable housing programmes
PCTs identify health needs and put in appropriate services	Income support increases for families		Healthy living centres developed in poor areas
Multi-agency with health, social care and education working together	Children's trust £250 for each child born from September 2002		
	National minimum wage increased		
	Fuel payments for older people		

FIGURE 11.25 *Recent government policy related to poverty*

Poverty

Various reports on health inequalities in the UK showed that poverty was still a key issue and affected many groups. Poverty needs to be tackled from birth, and to this end various government policies came into effect from 2001 onwards.

In the government paper *Tackling Health Inequalities* (Department of Health 2001) six key themes were identified for future policy:

1. ensuring a sure foundation for life through a healthy pregnancy and childhood

2. improving opportunities for children and young people

3. improving NHS primary care services for all groups of people

4. tackling the major killers – coronary heart disease and cancer

5. strengthening disadvantaged communities

6. tackling the wider causes of health inequalities.

Health inequalities tend to reflect social inequalities in society; by focusing on improving the health and life chances of disadvantaged groups it is hoped that the numbers of people in poverty and the inequalities in society will decrease.

Children in poverty

The number of children in poverty has increased compared to other groups. In the mid-1990s about one in four people in the UK were living in poverty, but among children the figure was one in three.

The Acheson report (1998) also influenced social policy related to poverty. It recommended the following changes to policy:

1. an increase in benefit levels for women of child-bearing age, expectant mothers, young children and older people

2. increased funding for schools, in deprived areas, with better nutrition in schools, and healthy schools programmes

3. parenting and relationship programmes should be developed and information on substance abuse and sex education should take place in schools

4. easier access to affordable fresh food would help poorer families to improve their diets

5. poorer people are more likely to smoke and this affects their health and mortality rates (as well as their disposable income); stop-smoking programmes should be aimed at deprived groups.

Many of these recommendations have been put into place. Benefits have increased. Sure Start programmes support mothers and young children and provide child care, enabling mothers to return to work. Health professionals are working closely with teachers and social workers to promote health advice and support, through strategies such as the healthy schools programme. Regeneration programmes are supporting deprived individuals and groups and developing programmes to improve their quality of life.

A Ten-Year Strategy for Child Care

Since 1997 the government has increased early years services and support, including Sure Start programmes which have been based in areas of most deprivation. However, too many parents have difficulty accessing the child care they need. The ten-year strategy aims for early years and child care services to become a permanent core strand of the welfare state. The strategy aims to provide a child care guarantee for parents through a range of providers.

The four key strands of the ten-year strategy are:

1. Choice and flexibility

Greater choice for parents balancing work and family, to include:

* extension of paid maternity leave to nine months with a further goal of 12 months

* giving mothers the right to transfer some of their maternity entitlement to fathers, encouraging fathers to be more involved in their child's development

* giving all families easy access to integrated services through a Sure Start children's centre in their local area, including early learning, child care, health and family support.

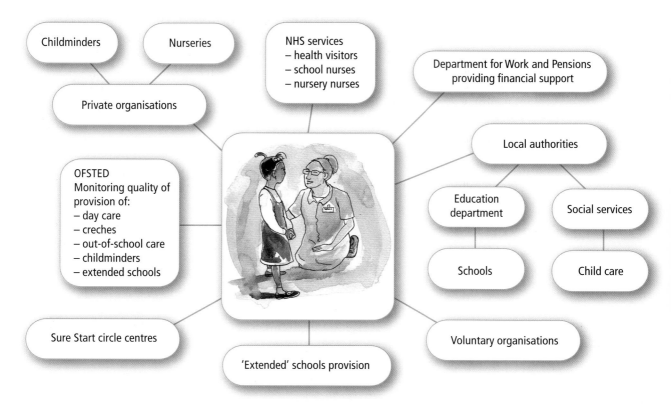

FIGURE 11.26 *The range of partners involved in the child care strategy*

2. Availability

Affordable, flexible, high-quality child care for all families with children up to the age of 14, including:

* a goal that all 3- and 4-year-olds will have access to 20 hours a week of free, high-quality early learning for 38 weeks of the year by 2010

* a child care place for all 3–14-year-olds between the hours of 8 am to 6 pm each weekday by 2010

* by 2010 all parents with children aged 5–11 will be offered affordable, school-based child care on weekdays between 8 am and 6 pm all year round

* by 2010, all secondary schools will open on weekdays between 8 am and 6 pm all year round, offering a range of activities such as music and sport.

3. Quality

High-quality provision with a highly-skilled child care and early years workforce, including:

* all full-day care settings will be professionally-led

* the child care workforce will develop with a new qualification and career structure in 2005.

4. Affordability

Families need to be able to afford flexible, high-quality child care that is suited to their needs. This will be paid for by the increase in the working tax credit from April 2005 and the maximum proportion of child care costs that can be claimed has risen from 70 per cent to 80 per cent. All benefits are reviewed on an annual basis.

Poverty and older people

According to current projections, by 2007 the number of people over state pension age will be greater than the number of children 16 and under. As previously mentioned, there are clear economic implications, since the numbers of people in work and paying taxes may well be insufficient to cover the cost of pensions.

However, many people aged over 50 are interested in working up to the age of 65 or beyond. As people live longer, they want to remain active and maintain their income levels. There is no official state retirement age at the moment although people have the right to claim their state pension at a certain age. The government has made changes to the age when men and women can collect their pensions. At the moment women can claim the state pension at 60 and men at 65. In the future the age will be 65 for both. The government is considering proposals to increase the age at which people can access their state pensions still further – perhaps to 70. People retiring now could expect to spend a further 20 years in retirement; this has implications for health and welfare policy and service provision.

Legislation related to the employment of older people

Age discrimination in employment will be unlawful from 2006. The EU *Directive on Equal Treatment* requires all member states to introduce legislation prohibiting direct and indirect discrimination at work on the grounds of age, sexual orientation, religion, belief, or disability. As a result of this legislation, it will be unlawful for employers to impose a retirement age below 65. Workers will have the right to request the opportunity to work beyond 65 and employers will have a duty to consider this. The employment legislation will be reviewed in 2011. The Department for Work and Pensions (DWP) ran a national campaign in 2005 to encourage all employers to adopt a non-ageist approach to retirement to support the recruitment and retention of older workers. The DWP has set a target for increasing the employment rate of people between the ages of 50 and 69 by 2008.

Unemployment

Unemployment is one of the factors that can lead to poverty. The government has introduced a range of New Deal programmes aimed at reducing unemployment among long-term unemployed people and younger people who have found it difficult to access work. New Deal programmes are also aimed at lone parents who may find it hard to access child care.

Unemployment and ethnic minorities

Ethnic minorities make up about 8 per cent of the UK population. They tend to be a younger population and between 1999 and 2009 they will account for half the growth in the adult working population. There is a wide variation in the labour market for different ethnic groups. Pakistanis, Bangladeshis and Black Caribbeans tend to experience higher unemployment levels and lower earnings than Whites. In addition to the anti-discrimination legislation already in place the government has put forward specific policy proposals to improve the employment opportunities for ethnic minorities.

The **Ethnic Minority Task Force** was set up in 2004 to develop a range of policies and programmes to ensure that people from ethnic minorities achieve their potential at school and have access to training and employment. Representatives from the CBI (Confederation of British Industry), the TUC (Trades Union Congress) and the CRE (Commission for Racial Equality) are part of the task force, which works across different government departments, including the Department for Work and Pensions, the Department of Trade and Industry, the Department for Education and Skills, and the Home Office.

Avoiding poverty throughout life

Childhood experiences, educational achievements and employment opportunities are greatly affected by poverty. In 2005 the government produced a five-year strategy called *Opportunity and Security throughout Life*.

This strategy identifies an ageing society as a major challenge facing the welfare state. The strategy is aimed at tackling deprivation across generations.

* Parents out of work for long periods leads to poverty for their children.
* Childhood poverty can lead to adult unemployment.
* Retirement income is determined by lifetime patterns of working and saving.

Central to the strategy is the aim to have an employment rate of 80 per cent in the working-age population. This would mean there would be 2.5 million more people in work by 2010. This would reduce the number of benefit claimants, especially those claiming incapacity benefits and lone parents on benefit. *Pathways to Work* programmes have focused on people with ill-health and disabilities, including people with mental health problems. They are encouraged to undertake work-related activity.

The strategy will reform the benefit system and opportunities for work, but it will also focus on:

* healthier and safer workplaces so there are fewer accidents, less occupational ill-health and less sickness absence
* a more active role for employers in assisting staff to return to work after illness
* more back-to-work support from GPs and the NHS

SCENARIO 1

A group of people with mental health problems have been working as volunteers for a gardening scheme in a London borough. They all have severe mental illness and are on incapacity benefit. Because of their volunteering role, they have received letters from the Benefits Agency inviting them to discuss their return to employment. As a result of these letters, two clients have been readmitted to hospital with a severe relapse of their mental condition, which means they are unable to do the volunteer work which was seen as essential rehabilitation.

SCENARIO 2

A member of staff at a college in London had severe depression. Although he was not admitted to hospital he was referred to a psychiatrist and was on medication. When it became clear he would be absent from work for several months, the occupational health adviser at the college saw him to discuss his return to work once he was feeling better, with the agreement of the psychiatrist. After four months he began to feel better and it was agreed he would attend the college for a few hours each week and then gradually build up to full-time work, with time off for hospital appointments. After a year he is still on medication and still having treatment from the hospital but he has returned to work.

Look at the two scenarios. What are the problems for the people and organisations in each scenario? If the person in the second scenario had been employed by a small company what problems might there have been in helping him return to work in this way?

* extended employment advice and support
* ongoing development of disability rights.

Think it over

Why do you think the government has decided to implement this strategy?

Summary of Section 11.4

In this section we have looked at examples of responses made by government to social issues and welfare needs. Policies are continually changing, reflecting the changes in society. They also may reflect external pressures from EU legislation, the needs of the economy and the influence of media and pressure groups. Many of the continuing changes in the organisation of health services can be seen to be a response to media pressure. One example of this is the reorganisation of child protection services after the Laming Report into the death of Victoria Climbie, which focused on the inadequacy of health and social services in preventing and recording abuse in young children. The report was commissioned as a result of sustained media pressure.

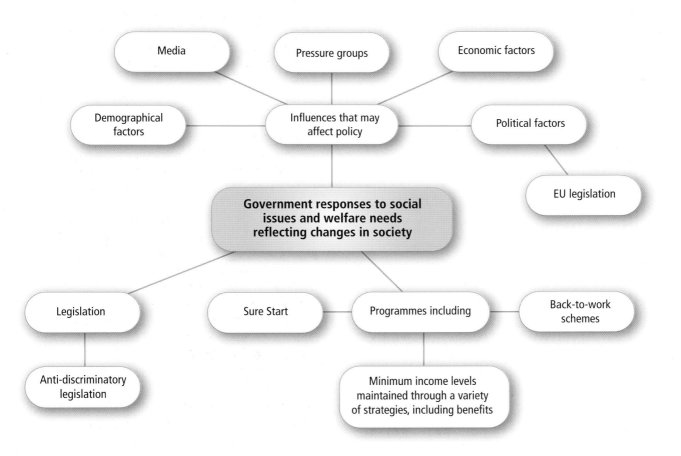

You are the cabinet minister with responsibility for the Department for Work and Pensions. Following a detailed review of government spending, you have been told to devise policies to reflect the needs of the population, but at the same time you need to encourage people back to work in order to save money on benefits and increase the government's income through taxation. The population profile reflects an ageing society; life expectancy is increasing so people are drawing their pensions for at least 20 years after retirement. At the same time the birth rate has declined, and unemployment among young people is slowly increasing.

Using concepts, can you identify?

1. What approaches would reduce government spending?

2. What approaches would increase the amount of taxation of different kinds?

Go further – Can you analyse the issues using theory?

3. Analyse government policy to explain why different political ideas may be reflected in different policies (you may need to review section 11.1 for this).

Go further – Can you evaluate using a range of theories?

4. Using examples from this unit, evaluate the impact of legislation and social policy on the individual.

UNIT 11 ASSESSMENT

How you will be assessed

In order to achieve the unit, you must produce a report on a social issue or a welfare need of interest to you. Your report must focus on either people who are ill, young children, older people or people with special needs. You will be given instructions regarding the structure of the report but your report will need to include evidence for each of the following assessment objectives:

A01 Origins of social and welfare issues
A02 Demographic change and social and welfare issues
A03 Social issues in context
A04 Government responses to social issues and welfare needs.

Assessment guidance

In the introduction to the unit it was suggested that you prepare a file of information on the topic you have chosen. You can add to it throughout your course.

A01 Origins of social and welfare issues

In order to achieve the highest grade you need to show that you have an in-depth knowledge and understanding of the origins of a social issue or welfare need. Your report needs to demonstrate excellent skills in obtaining information and that the information you use is drawn from a wide range of sources. Your report needs to be full and accurate.

A02 Demographic change and social and welfare issues

To achieve the highest grade you need to show that you can thoroughly apply your knowledge and understanding of social issues and welfare needs. You must be able to provide full explanations of how at least three of the demographic factors have affected the social issues or welfare needs you have chosen to investigate. Specialist vocabulary needs to be used in an accurate report.

A03 Social issues in context

To achieve the highest grade you need to demonstrate excellent skills of knowledge and understanding of the contemporary issues or welfare need through detailed research. You need to demonstrate independent thinking when analysing work-related issues and problems. Information needs to be drawn from at least four sources of evidence of different types.

A04 Government responses

To achieve the highest grade you need to show a high level of knowledge and understanding of at least three of the government's responses to the social issue or welfare need chosen. At this level you need to show a high level of evaluative skills from which you are able to draw well reasoned and detailed conclusions which are valid and supported by evidence.

Unit test

1. Name four social factors that can affect a person's position in society.

2. Define the following terms:

   stereotyping   marginalisation   labelling   discrimination.

3. Social change occurs because of the influence of a variety of factors. Identify two factors and evaluate their influence on social change.

4. Policy related to welfare has changed a great deal over the last years. Compare and contrast the approaches of the traditional Labour Party in the period beginning 1945 and the New Labour government since 1997. (You may need to refer back to section 11.1 here.)

5. Demography is of particular interest to service providers because planning of service provision in the future is based on data relating to the present time. If the population is getting older and the birth rate is lower, what are the implications for service providers? What services will they need to develop, and what services may they reduce?

6. Migration figures are included in the study of a population. What is the definition of:

   immigration?   emigration?

7. The infant mortality rate is often used as an indicator of the health of a population. What factors could affect the infant mortality rate?

8. Poverty is seen as a problem in the UK at the moment. What are the two main ways of defining poverty and how is each measured?

9. Suicide among young men is still causing concern. What factors may put young men at risk from suicide?

10. Unemployment is seen as a social problem. What is the problem for:

    the government   the family   the individual?

References and further reading

Acheson, D. (1998) *Independent Inquiry into Inequalities in Health* (London: HMSO)

Aslangul, S., Meggitt, C. (2002) *Further Studies in Social Care*, 2nd Edn (Hodder and Stoughton: London)

Department for Work and Pensions (2005) *A Five Year Strategy* (London: HMSO)

Department for Work and Pensions (2005) *Touchbase* (London: HMSO)

Department of Health (1999) *National Service Framework for Mental Health* (London: HMSO)

Department of Health (2000) *National Service Framework for Older People* (London: HMSO)

HM Government (1998) *Saving Lives: Our Healthier Nation* (London: HMSO)

HM Government (2004) *Choosing Health – Making Healthier Choices Easier* (London: HMSO)

Housing and Black and Ethnic Minorities (2003) Office of the Deputy Prime Minister (London: HMSO)

Moonie, N. (2000) *Advanced Health and Social Care* (Oxford: Heinemann)

Moonie, N. (2005) *AS Level in Health and Social Care Single Award* (Oxford: Heinemann)

Moore, S. (2002) *Social Welfare Alive*, 3rd Edn (Cheltenham: Nelson Thornes)

Social Exclusion Unit (2005) *Multiple Exclusion and Quality of Life amongst Excluded Older People in Disadvantaged Neighbourhoods* (London: HMSO)

Social Trends 35 (2005) (London: HMSO)

Useful websites

Commission for Racial Equality
www.cre.gov.uk

Department of Health
www.dh.gov.uk

Department of Trade and Industry
www. dti.gov.uk

Department for Work and Pensions
www.dwp.gov.uk

Home Office
www.homeoffice.gov.uk

National Assembly for Wales
www.wales.gov.uk

Office for National Statistics
www.statistics.gov.uk

Office of the Deputy Prime Minister
www.odpm.gov.uk

Social Exclusion Unit
www.socialexclusion.gov.uk

Teenage Pregnancy Unit
www. teenagepregnancyunit.gov.uk.

Understanding human behaviour

This unit covers the following sections:

Introduction

All health and social care workers have to be able to understand the people that they work with. This unit is designed to explore some of the influences on human behaviour and some of the ways in which people are affected by social issues. The unit explores the way in which behavioural approaches, cognitive approaches, humanistic approaches and psychodynamic approaches interpret human experience. The unit also stresses the importance of care values when working with service users.

How you will be assessed

This unit is externally assessed through a written examination.

12.1 Influences on behaviour and their effects

SCENARIO

Jackie's story

Jackie is 32 years old and was referred to a counsellor by her GP. Jackie is a single parent with a six-year-old son who presents some behavioural difficulties at school. Jackie has recently left her job because of poor health and stress.

When Jackie first met the counsellor she was very nervous and distressed. Some of the things she said to the counsellor included: 'I just feel tired and exhausted, I can't sleep at night. I feel tense and nervous all day and I just can't cope any more.'

The counsellor asked Jackie to tell her a little about her past life. Jackie's life story includes the following:

'We used to live in a rented house, dad was in and out of work, and sometimes we didn't have enough money to pay the bills. I remember my parents arguing over money. I suppose I was very close to my mother. I remember my early childhood as happy. I don't remember much about my father, only at mealtimes. My older sister, Mum and I all had to be quiet, and dad would talk the whole time – we weren't allowed to interrupt. My father was a very strict man; he ordered us all about – he wouldn't let my sister bring her boyfriend into the house because he didn't like him. I remember him shouting and hitting my sister because he was angry. In the end my sister moved out – that's when I was 14.

'That was the same year that my mum died of cancer. That was terrible. You probably think I'm mad but I thought that Mum's death was my fault. I thought that if I had been a better person these things wouldn't have happened to me. I don't want to talk about it any more – it makes me cry when I remember it.

'After Mum died, dad took up with another woman, and I hated her and she hated me – in the end I had to leave like my sister did. So I met up with this man and we lived together and I had Jake. It all changed after I had Jake – he left me and went off with someone else. Now I just think you can't trust anybody, everyone is out for themselves and no one cares about anyone else. You only listen to me because it is your job.

'The school I went to was a "dump". Most of my friends didn't care about lessons and the teachers couldn't keep order. I couldn't read till I was nine and I've never been able to write or spell properly. Perhaps I had dyslexia, you hear a lot about that now, but no one had ever heard of it in my school and they just said I was lazy. My mum and dad didn't care because they said I didn't need to be good at school, I just had to be pretty in order to meet the right man.

'When I think about the future I only think about Jake. I don't think my life is worth living but I have to be around to look after him. That's why I came here, so that you lot don't take him away from me. I don't see a future apart from him.'

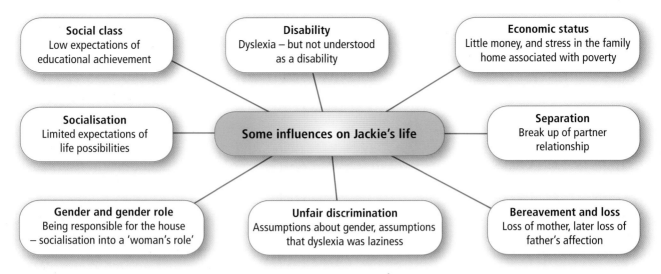

FIGURE 12.1 *Influences on Jackie's life*

Most people experience some stressful life events during their lives. Many people can describe some form of disadvantage in their lives. For Jackie, a whole range of things has come together to make her feel negative about herself, about others and about the future. Jackie has become depressed because of her life experience and because of the current influences creating a great deal of stress for her. The effects of negative influences might be summarised as shown in Figure 12.2.

Although Jackie's story appears very depressing when we look at influences and effects, it is important to remember that there are a number of positive things even within her own statements. Jackie may have enjoyed a loving relationship with her mother at the beginning of her life, and she now lives for her son. These two positive influences may provide a starting point that may help Jackie to 'discover the inner resources' needed to think positively and find a way of coping with her situation.

Effects of negative influences

Negative self-concept

Self-concept is the understanding that we have of ourselves. It is a learned idea of how we are distinct from other people. Self-concept includes our level of self-esteem. Self-esteem is the degree to which we value ourselves. Low self-esteem may result in low self-confidence when we mix with other people.

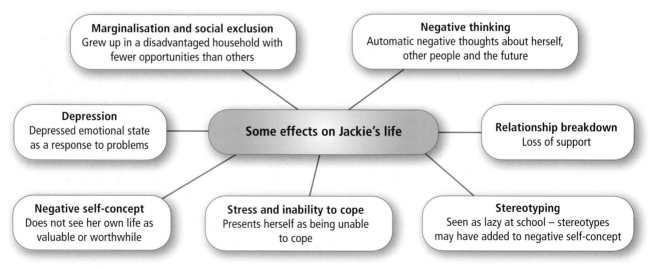

FIGURE 12.2 *Effects on Jackie's life*

The humanistic approach stresses the importance of having a positive attitude that you are a valuable and worthwhile person. Many people develop a negative view of who they are. Jackie was told that schoolwork didn't matter – but that she had to 'meet the right man'. Her relationship failed though – and now she is a lone parent. The conditions of worth that were placed on her may lead her to evaluate herself negatively. She might think this way – not because of what people say to her now, but rather because this is what her father and mother said many years ago. She may have 'internalised' or taken in the belief that she must be successful at relationships in order to be a worthwhile person. She might also have taken in some of the social stereotypes about lone parents. She then damages herself because she cannot see through the conditions of worth that other people have created for her. See humanistic approaches (page 298) for more detail on this issue.

Stress and inability to cope

Stress has been an important health concept since Hans Selye wrote about the issue back in 1946. Selye explained stress in terms of three stages (see Table 12.1).

Stress results in physical exhaustion. Jackie no longer has the energy to go to work; she states that she feels exhausted, anxious, unable to sleep and 'can't cope any more'. It may be that Jackie has become exhausted because of the operation of her physiological stress response. Jackie may need rest and relaxation in order to recover. But the problem is that something is making her feel threatened. If she begins to recover, the threat might set the stress response going again and she will simply end up exhausted once more. Counselling might aim to remove the feeling of being threatened – and so enable Jackie's stress response to switch off.

Depression

Most people experience times when they 'feel low' and lack the emotional drive to get on with work or social activities. Many people have to organise their life so that they have a range of sporting or social activities that boosts their emotions so that they can enjoy life. Clinical depression means that a person has a more serious illness where the day-to-day stimulation that normally enables us to function is insufficient to keep us going emotionally. People who are seriously depressed may experience feelings of hopelessness, anxiety, suicidal thoughts, and physical symptoms such as aches and pains, slowed movement, weight loss or gain.

NHS Direct states that 'most of the 4,000 suicides committed each year in England are linked to depression'. The NHS Direct *Health Encyclopaedia* estimates that 'about 15 per cent of people will have a bout of major depression at some point in their lives and it is the fourth most common cause of disability worldwide'.

Stage one – feeling threatened	A person experiences a shock – or a situation that makes him or her feel threatened.
Stage two – trying to cope with the threat	A biological stress response is triggered. This 'stress response' involves a range of physiological changes that might provide a person with more energy to struggle with a physical problem. The stress response may have evolved in order to help us to run or fight if we feel threatened.
Stage three – exhaustion and giving up	If the problem does not end, if we cannot find a way to feel better about the shock or the bad situation that we have encountered, then we become physically exhausted. Our body cannot provide us with extra energy for ever. This exhaustion is not just emotional. Exhaustion is a physical situation where our body no longer has the resources to cope.

TABLE 12.1 *The stages of stress*

Jackie may be one of the 15 per cent of people who no longer have the emotional resources to 'pull herself together' and 'snap-out' of their negative feelings. Jackie will need help if she is to recover from the situation that she is in.

Negative thinking

Jackie says that her life isn't worth living, she doesn't have a future, 'you can't trust anybody' and counsellors only listen to people in order to make money out of it. Negative thinking can be seen as a symptom of depression, but cognitive psychologists such as Aaron Beck argue that negative thinking may cause depression. Learning to think positively may provide a way for individuals to recover from depression. Cognitive approaches (see page 292) might provide a way in which people can immunise themselves against stress, anxiety and depression, and also a way in which people can escape from the 'prison' of their depression. It is possible that people who experience positive relationships and happy, contented early lives often learn to think positively about life. Not surprisingly, some disadvantaged people may learn to think more negatively.

Relationship breakdown

Roughly one in three marriages ends in divorce. In 2003–04, National Statistics reported that one in six adults aged 16 and over lived alone in Great Britain. The general household survey in 2002 reported that 38 per cent of women aged 18 to 49 were single, compared with 49 per cent who were married. In 2004, 24 per cent of children lived in lone-parent families. It is likely that the majority of people will experience a disrupted emotional relationship with a partner and for many people the ideal of a lifelong partnership will not be a reality.

Historically, many people have been socialised into the idea that a successful life involves successful relationships. Jackie may have grown up with expectations that have proved to be wrong. She may have had a secure emotional relationship with her mother in early childhood, but since her early childhood Jackie has experienced many losses. Her mother died when she was 14. Jackie's sister left home after arguments with her father. She experienced her father as rejecting her after he found a new partner. Jackie found a partner and had a child, but her partner left her. Jackie has concluded that you can't trust people – but she is closely attached to her son. Possibly she is mirroring the love and affection that she received as a child from her mother.

Marginalisation and social exclusion

Marginalisation describes a social process where people are pushed to the margins of society. They are metaphorically almost 'off the page' and irrelevant as far as most people are concerned. Marginalised groups are groups of people whom the majority of society prefer to ignore. An example of a marginalised group might be 'lone parents '. Some people may label lone parents as a problem group who use up benefits without contributing to the country's economy.

The term social exclusion is used by the government to identify people who are excluded from opportunities that the majority of UK citizens enjoy.

Issues identified in the government publication *Opportunity for All* (1999) that may result in the reduction of life opportunities are shown in Figure 12.3.

Jackie appears to have experienced a range of disadvantage in her early life. It may not be fair to state that social exclusion caused her current difficulties. But it may be true that she was at greater risk of depression than more advantaged people, because of reduced opportunities in her life.

Labelling and stereotyping

Labelling and stereotyping are fixed ways of thinking. Labelling involves using a category as

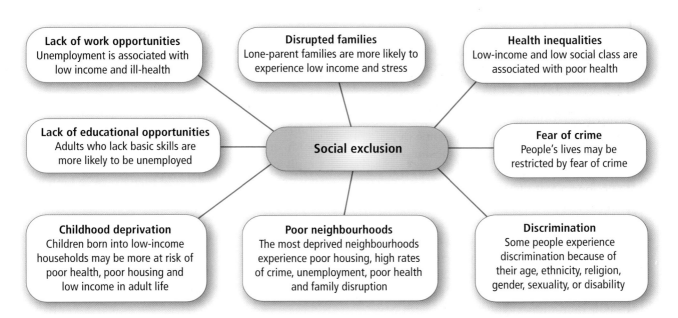

FIGURE 12.3 *Issues contributing to social exclusion*

an explanation for a person's behaviour. 'Lone parent' might become a label associated with the idea of being poor, needy, and unable to cope. A stereotype is a fixed way of thinking involving generalisations and expectations about people. Lone parents are often stereotyped as people with a range of social problems. Health and social care texts always point out the danger involved in labelling and stereotyping others. Labelling and stereotyping are probably most dangerous when a person labels and stereotypes themself. In the scenario about Jackie, the real risk is that she may start to label or stereotype herself as a 'no hoper'. This kind of negative thinking may intensify depression. See cognitive approaches (page 292) for further information on this issue.

Early low self-esteem

Young children do not have the intellectual ability to discuss their self-concept and self-esteem. 'Self' is an abstract idea that most people learn to describe during adolescence. The fundamental feelings that we have about ourselves may come about long before we can use language to describe self-concept and self-esteem. Our deeper emotions about ourselves may be influenced by the quality of attachment to carers in our early years. If we experience secure attachment and love we may develop a positive sense of security that may later influence our levels of self-esteem. Infants who do not develop secure attachments may be seriously emotionally disadvantaged in life (see psychodynamic approaches on page 304). The quality of our emotional attachment might be associated with the idea of early influences on self-esteem.

Jackie's story involves secure attachment – she was not fundamentally disadvantaged during her early years. Because of this Jackie still has the inner resources to want to live – for her son. The early love that Jackie experienced still protects her from complete emotional collapse.

Addiction

Drugs that influence mental processes and emotions are called psychoactive drugs. Some psychoactive drugs, such as cocaine and heroin, create physiological and psychological dependence in the people who use them. Addiction happens when a person requires a drug in order to function; painful withdrawal symptoms may occur if the drug is not available. The term 'drug dependency' is a wider term that can indicate a degree of physical or psychological dependence on a drug.

It might be a mistake to assume that drug dependency is purely a physiological issue.

The social availability of addictive drugs and cultural assumptions about taking drugs will play a part in determining whether a person becomes dependent on drugs or not.

In Jackie's story she has not become dependent on drugs or on legally available substances such as alcohol. The reason that she has not become dependent may have a lot to do with her socialisation, and the attitudes that she has learned towards drugs and alcohol. She may have seen herself as a person who does not experiment with drink and drugs. Equally she may have been born with a biology that is less inclined to drug dependency – so that alcohol and perhaps other drugs she might have experimented with have not resulted in a physiological desire to keep repeating the experience.

Some people are less fortunate than Jackie, and they may experience alcohol or an illegal drug such as heroin as providing temporary relief from emotional problems and stress. The problem with using substance abuse as a way of coping with emotional difficulty is that there is a range of physical side-effects and social disadvantages associated with addiction and dependency. For some people drug dependency may become the principal problem disrupting their life.

Some influences on behaviour

John (see John's story below) has good mental health, and he does not have a problem that can simply be put right with some advice or with some practical help. Like so many people John is struggling to be happy and fulfilled. Counselling and psychological therapy is not just about problems or about people who might be thought of as being ill. Many people become involved with psychological approaches because they are interested in exploring their own personality and

Did you know?

Sigmund Freud was once asked what mental health is. His reply was that mental health is the ability to love and to work. Perhaps everyone has some degree of difficulty figuring out how to live their life. Perhaps if you can make loving relationships and get on with other people well enough to hold down a job, that's as good as mental health gets.

SCENARIO

John's story

John is 50 years old and works as a manager; he has started to attend person-centred counselling sessions in order, in his words, 'to get more out of life'. Some excerpts from the first session are reported below.

'Well, I wanted to explore my thoughts and feelings. I don't have a problem to tell you about, I mean I've got a steady job, nice house, enough money to live on – other people would say my life is just great; but I don't feel it's enough. I feel that there has to be something more – I mean I spend most of my time working to pay the mortgage off, but I feel I should be doing something more.

'You see when I was young, my family were very religious, well that is my relatives were – my father wasn't, but I was sent to Sunday school and I came to think that everything in this world has a purpose – God has given it a purpose – and I still feel that this is true – but I don't know what my purpose is. At one time I was focused on my kids, I was making money – in my head I thought I was making it for them. But they've grown up and they've got their own lives now. I got divorced, but I'm still friends with my ex. I don't go to church now – and I don't really know what I believe any more. I think well, I'm well into the second part of my life and what have I done with it – I think I need to change but I don't know how to change or what I ought to be doing.'

how they may achieve greater satisfaction from life. John's story provides a way of understanding some influences on behaviour.

Early socialisation

Our first, or primary, socialisation involves learning from our carers and from the people that we live with at home. Early socialisation therefore involves our learning from parents and within our family.

Key concept

Socialisation: Giddens (1997) explains socialisation as 'the process whereby the helpless infant gradually becomes a self-aware, knowledgeable person, skilled in the ways of the culture into which he or she is born'. Socialisation involves learning the social norms of the culture that you grow up in.

As well as learning 'the ways of the culture' into which we are born, our early learning will also involve learning to make emotional bonds with a carer or with a small number of carers. Our first experience of relationships will be based on our first attachment to others. This attachment may influence the development of an 'internal working model' of human relationships (see psychodynamics on page 304). Positive experiences involving love during infancy may provide a positive basis for relationships in life. Deprivation of a loving bond in early life may result in difficulties with forming intimate adult relationships later in life.

Many of our assumptions about our self will be influenced by primary socialisation. The attitudes and beliefs of our parents or carers provide a foundation for our own attitudes and beliefs. Our views about the significance of

John's story

John explains his early assumptions about life – life has to have a purpose – and this idea was something he may have learned during his early socialisation.

educational and career success or the significance of personal relationships may be influenced by early socialisation.

Social roles

Actors take on 'a role' when they act out a character in a film or play. A social role is the act that you put on in order to meet other people's expectations. The actor wants the audience to temporarily believe that they are the character they are acting. In social situations we also want to be seen as living up to other people's expectations. For example, it is important to wear the right clothes for the role that you are undertaking; a senior executive could not turn up for work in gardening clothes. There is an act that has to be lived up to – you have to look the part. Social roles go well beyond the way we dress.

Key concept

Social roles: these involve behaving appropriately in order to meet the expectations that other people have of the role.

John's story

John took on the social role of being a male 'provider': he worked to get the money for the household. He didn't say it, but his wife took on the gender role of looking after the home and the children.

Social class and economic status

Social status is formally classified using the National Statistics Socio-economic Classification. The eight analytic classes in Table 12.2 provide an outline system for interpreting the social class of different occupations.

Key concept

Social class: the status given to different types of occupation or work. Social class is currently defined by the National Statistics Socio-economic Classification system.

1	Higher managerial and professional occupations: large employers and higher managerial occupations higher professional occupations
2	Lower managerial and professional occupations
3	Intermediate occupations
4	Small employers and own account workers
5	Lower supervisory and technical occupations
6	Semi-routine occupations
7	Routine occupations
8	Never worked and long-term unemployed

TABLE 12.2 *Social status classification*

The work role that a person performs is likely to have a major influence on his or her self-concept. People who manage others, people with high status roles, or people who are very highly paid are likely to achieve a high degree of self-esteem from their work. People in high-status jobs are likely to receive respect and even admiration from others. People who see their job as routine, boring or something that anyone could do, are unlikely to receive the same respect and admiration, and may gain little in the way of self-esteem from their job.

Wealth may also contribute to social status and self-esteem. The term 'retail therapy' is used in a semi-humorous way to describe how some people boost their self-esteem by spending money on things like designer clothes, cars, jewellery and so on. Low economic status – being poor – may create low self-esteem, in some people within UK society.

Separation

During the first years of life infants build a close attachment with one or more carers. If a child is separated for any length of time this may have an impact on the security of their attachment. It is possible that children who experience separation may have great difficulty feeling secure in relationships in later life. A secure attachment in early life not damaged by separation may help an individual to cope with grief and loss in later life.

Key concept

Separation: this is being parted from someone that you are emotionally attached to. The psychodynamic theory argues that separation in infancy can influence the ability to make secure relationships in later life.

John's story

John probably experienced secure attachment in his earlier life.

SCENARIO
Martha's story

Martha is 86 years old; she grew up in the Caribbean and lost her husband six years ago. Martha lives in a care home and she is thought to have Alzheimer's disease, although a formal diagnosis has not been made. Martha often looks anxious and afraid; she says things like 'please forgive me, please forgive me' in a repetitive way to the care staff who work with her. She also pleads with the staff to let her leave the home so that she can 'get the shopping so that the children can have their tea'. The staff ignore Martha's behaviour, explaining

John's story

John has high self-esteem – he is a manager, this is partly why he has the courage to undertake counselling. Despite having high self-esteem he still has difficulty in feeling satisfied with his life. Poverty and low socio-economic status may create disadvantage for people, but wealth and status do not in themselves guarantee a problem-free life.

that she is confused and doesn't know what she's saying. Sometimes the staff will play along and say things like 'bless you my child – you are forgiven,' and then laugh. Martha usually looks more distressed when she is treated this way.

Martha is not receiving a good quality of service – she is distressed and she is not receiving support. Martha is Black, she is a woman, and she has a cognitive disability. Martha's religion and culture may be different from other people's religion and culture. Martha may be receiving a poorer quality of service because of discrimination.

* Martha is being excluded – she is not treated as if she belongs in the society of ordinary people because she is confused.

* Martha's self-esteem and confidence are being challenged because others laugh at her.

* Martha is not being treated with respect – no one is interested in exploring her needs, including why she wants to be 'forgiven'. What is really happening is that Martha is experiencing a high degree of stress and she has associated this with childhood experiences of being punished. Martha is religious and so she talks about forgiveness. She is desperately seeking emotional support as she doesn't understand what is happening to her.

Unfair discrimination

The word discrimination originally meant 'to tell things apart'. Obviously there is nothing wrong with 'telling things apart'. Unfair discrimination refers to providing a worse quality of service to certain categories of people compared with others.

Key concept

Unfair discrimination: this means treating some types of people less well than others. People are often discriminated against because of their ethnicity, culture, gender, religion, sexuality or age.

FOCUS OF DISCRIMINATION	EXAMPLES OF RISK OF DISCRIMINATION
Ethnicity	People might not be included in activities, spoken to with respect or chosen as friends, because they are seen as 'not like us' – 'not to be trusted'.
Religious belief	Assumptions are made that everybody follows the same cultural traditions. For example, Christmas is celebrated, but other religions' festivals are not.
Gender	Certain work activities and job roles may be seen as only right for certain genders. There may be prejudice against men who undertake child care roles, as this is labelled as a woman's role.
Disability	People with a disability might be thought of as being defective or damaged people who deserve pity because they are not 'normal'. Disabled people may be seen as being problems or 'cases' rather than people.
Culture	People may make assumptions about customs, ways of dressing or other behaviour that is different from their own 'norms'. Different religious customs may form a focus for prejudice.
Sexuality	People might be avoided, or excluded from activities perhaps because others are threatened by difference or because people have prejudiced attitudes and beliefs.

TABLE 12.3 *Unfair discrimination*

Discrimination may damage a person's physical or mental health because it may cause:

* loss of confidence in your own abilities or a failure to develop confidence

* anger and frustration

* vulnerable and unsafe feelings

* low self-esteem – belief that you are inferior to others

* stress and poor mental health

* exclusion – feeling that you do not belong with others

* depression and anxiety

* withdrawal from other people.

Gender

Males and females have different chromosome structures that result in different biological features. Biological differences are referred to as differences in sex. The term gender is used to explore the social assumptions associated with a person's sex. It is possible for a person to choose to change his or her gender, but a person cannot change their chromosome structure.

Key concept

Gender: the differences between males and females based on cultural or social expectations.

Historically there were strong assumptions that men and women should do different jobs and lead very different lives. It was assumed that women should look after children, do housework, or light manual or clerical work that fitted in with household responsibilities. Men were assumed to do the more valuable administrative, management or heavy labouring jobs. Whilst there have been great changes in assumptions over the last 40 years, assumptions still exist about gender roles. Men who work in child care may be discriminated against with statements such as: 'there must be something wrong with them, wanting to do women's work'. A gender pay gap exists and results in women in full-time work being paid on average just 82 per cent of men's earnings, according to the Office for National Statistics in 2004. According to research reported in *Social Trends* (2004), men still undertake the majority of maintenance and repair work in most homes, whilst women undertake the majority of laundry, shopping and household cleaning tasks.

Assumptions based on gender can result in women being discriminated against as being less important or of lower status than men.

Martha's story

Could gender play any kind of role in the way Martha is being treated? Compare Martha's story with the two anecdotes below:

William is an 86-year-old ex-army captain with Alzheimer's disease; his key worker quickly learned that William was easy to get on with providing he was called 'Sir' and always treated with respect.

Sid was in care, and he was an ex-boxer who had Alzheimer's disease. The staff were very careful to speak to him in a respectful and gentle voice because they were afraid of what might happen if he became aggressive.

These two male residents were treated with respect because of their perceived power. Ex-army officers and strong men still retain their social status. Martha was not treated with respect, perhaps partly because many women are not perceived to have a high social status.

Ethnicity

A person's race or ethnicity is often central to his or her identity and self-concept. Ethnicity can become a basis for unfair discrimination where people who belong to one ethnic group fail to understand, respect or value differences associated with ethnic group membership.

> **Key concept**
>
> *Ethnicity:* the racial group that a person belongs to. The national census uses the following broad ethnic group categories: White, Asian or Asian British, Black or Black British, mixed, Chinese and other. Sub-categories of ethnic origin are grouped under these broad classifications.

National statistics suggest that ethnicity can influence the quality of life or 'life chances' that a person may have in the United Kingdom. For example, the 2001 UK census found that Pakistani and Bangladeshi people reported higher rates of poor health and limiting long-term illness than White people. People of Chinese ethnicity reported the lowest rates of ill-health. The Office for National Statistics (2004) states that: 'minority ethnic groups have lower levels of household income than the White population'. The 2001 census reports the risk of being a victim of a racially-motivated crime as 4.2 per cent for Pakistani and Bangladeshi people, 3.6 per cent for Indian people, 2.2 per cent for Black people and just 0.3 per cent for White people.

> **Martha's story**
>
> The care staff did not understand Martha's need for security – they did not talk to her about her family or children. Part of the reason might possibly be that care staff might feel awkward, or unable to engage with her life experiences. Discrimination does not always involve active prejudice, sometimes discrimination might result in being ignored.

Culture

Culture refers to the traditions, beliefs, values and ideas that are passed on within a group of people. Culture will be a major factor influencing the way a person develops their identity or self-concept. Different geographical, ethnic, and religious groups may belong to different cultures. The way a person makes sense of life experience will be influenced by their socialisation into a system of assumptions, beliefs and values.

> **Key concept**
>
> *Culture:* the collection of values, norms, customs and behaviours that make one group of people distinct from others. A person's culture will influence the development of their self-concept.

Culture includes a very wide range of issues including religion, music, art, architecture, literature, language, including non-verbal language, as well as customs and beliefs. Care workers could not possibly understand the full cultural background of every service user that they might encounter. Care workers could ideally build a supportive relationship with service users that might involve learning a little of the service user's cultural background. Being willing to learn a little of a service user's culture might demonstrate respect and value for them.

> **Martha's story**
>
> Care staff did not listen to Martha's anxious statements – her statements about forgiveness and children could have led to building an understanding about her past culture and life. Instead she was just seen as another person with Alzheimer's disease and her behaviour was understood as 'illness' rather than clues as to how her life was experienced.

Disability

The Disability Discrimination Act defined a disability as 'a physical or mental impairment which has a substantial and long-term adverse affect on a person's ability to carry out normal day-to-day activities'. Impairment means a loss of function, perhaps caused by damage to a body system. The degree to which an impairment disrupts day-to-day living depends on the social responses and resources available to the person with impairment. For example, if you have short sight you may be unable to drive. As soon as you can get a pair of glasses the disability disappears. The impairment stays the same but the disability is removed because of the services of an optician. If you have to use a wheelchair many places with steps cannot be reached independently. In the past people might have pitied you because of your disability. A more useful alternative is to build ramps – so that you do not experience the same level of disability. Many people do experience limitations on their ability to carry out 'normal day-to-day activities' because of disability.

Social Trends (2001) estimates that there were 6.8 million people of working age with long-term or work-limiting disabilities in the United Kingdom in the spring of 2001. Disabled people were 'much more likely to be economically inactive than non-disabled people'.

Statistics for Wales based on the 2001 census suggests that almost a quarter of the population (23 per cent) had a limiting or long-term illness or disability that restricted their daily activities.

The Department of Health quote 157,000 people on the register of blind people in England at March 2003, with 155,000 people on the register of partly-sighted people. In March 2001, 50,282 people were registered deaf, with 194,840 people registered as deaf or hard of hearing in England.

Bereavement or loss

Many people build their sense of self-esteem around a personal relationship. Some other people include career success or material possessions as part of their understanding of self. When people lose a partner who has been central to their life, this loss can disrupt a person's sense of who they are. For some people a loss of health or a loss of social status can also result in a threat to self-esteem and self-confidence. The process of coming to terms with a major loss can take some time. While people struggle to cope with a major loss they may experience feelings of shock and numbness, a tendency to deny the seriousness of the loss, feelings of self-blame or anger before they can rebuild their sense of self.

Martha's story

Martha lost her partner some years before she developed Alzheimer's disease. It is likely that she has not fully recovered from the stress of her loss. She may feel that she is indeed being punished because life is so unpleasant now. Part of Martha's distress may be associated with loss and grief. If Martha had the opportunity to talk about her life it might be that talking could help to reduce some of the stress that she is experiencing. She is not seen as having a need to talk because she is labelled as 'confused'.

Martha's story

Martha may not have been seen as a person – rather she was an 'Alzheimer's case'. Martha's behaviour (asking for forgiveness) was seen as a symptom of Alzheimer's disease. No further attention was paid to the significance of this behaviour for understanding her past life experience and culture. People with disabilities are often treated as if they are problems rather than people – the 'does he take sugar' discriminatory approach to disability.

SCENARIO
Michael's story

Michael is 23 years old and explains that he finds it difficult to make friends or develop relationships. 'I don't know if I've always been shy, the thing is at school I used to get bullied, there was this small gang and they used to go after me – call me names, demand money, push me about. I tried telling my dad – but he just told me to stick up for myself – but there were five or six of them, so I couldn't. I tried telling the teachers but they didn't do anything. So I just hated going to school and I felt useless and worthless and now I just haven't got any confidence. I just think there is something wrong with me, that's why they picked on me, and when I meet new people I think – that they will think – that I'm not right. I just go to pieces inside and I can't speak to them and I guess I'm not right because I go to pieces.'

The experience of being put down, pushed around and victimised has become part of Michael's self-concept. Michael now has negative thoughts about 'not being right' and these thoughts are preventing him from developing an effective social life and partnerships.

Try it out

These bad experiences had happened in Michael's past. What kind of help could Michael get now to help him overcome the effects of these bad experiences?

Violence and bullying

Discrimination may result in bullying. Like discrimination, bullying may undermine a person's self-confidence and self-esteem, and create stress, depression and anxiety. Bullying is when an individual or group of people intimidate or harass others. Bullying might involve:

* physical violence or assault
* theft of property
* receiving abusive messages such as text messages

* verbal insults
* false stories being shared about you
* exclusion – being avoided or left out
* interfering with personal possessions such as school work
* receiving constant criticisms or 'put downs'.

Many children experience bullying at school, but adults also engage in bullying. The Protection from Harassment Act 1997 makes it a criminal offence to harass another person. It is possible for an adult to sue an employer if harassment or bullying has taken place at work. Because bullying can threaten a person's self-confidence, victims sometimes keep quiet about their experience. The Department for Education and Skills stresses the importance of telling others – talking about the problem and getting support – in order to cope with and prevent bullying within an educational context.

Did you know?

The biggest number of calls to ChildLine in April 2003 to March 2004 were about bullying – a total of 22 per cent of calls. In August 2004 ChildLine said that they had experienced a 42 per cent rise in the total number of children seeking counselling because of bullying.

Why do people bully others? Some people may want other people to be afraid of them; fear can create a basis for having power over other people. Some people want to control other people because they believe control gives them a higher social status and makes them feel important. Some people just want to control other people because they feel threatened and controlling others makes them feel safer. Some people learn to bully other people because they have been abused themselves and they are copying things that have been done to them. Some people might just imitate behaviours that they see other people doing.

Summary of Section 12.1

Who you are can be influenced by:

Early socialisation
Social roles
Social class
Economic status
Separation
Bereavement and loss
Unfair discrimination
Gender
Ethnicity
Culture
Disability
Violence and bullying

You may become vulnerable to:

Early low self-esteem
Negative self-concept
Stress and inability to cope
Depression
Negative thinking
Relationship breakdown
Marginalisation and social exclusion
Labelling
Stereotyping
Addiction

Consider this

Adi is a 55-year-old Black man who lives alone in an under-heated flat near the city centre. Adi is unable to work because of poor physical health involving heart disease and respiratory problems. Adi sought asylum in the United Kingdom after members of his family were killed in conflict abroad. Adi is afraid to leave his flat after dark because of crime and intimidation in the area. He has difficulty managing his benefits and sometimes goes without food because he has no money. His social worker reports that Adi often appears to be withdrawn and depressed. Adi says that he enjoys talking to his social worker because his social worker is of the same gender and ethnicity, and his social worker really understands his situation.

Using concepts, can you identify?

1. What are some of the influences that may have impacted on Adi's life circumstances and physical and mental health?

2. What are some of the negative effects in Adi's story?

Go further – Can you analyse issues using theory?

3. Explain how the influences that you have identified may have made Adi vulnerable to stress and depression.

Go further – Can you evaluate using a range of theories?

4. Explain the way in which different influences may have combined together in order to create a situation where Adi can no longer cope with daily life.

12.2 Theories of human behaviour

Behavioural approaches

Behaviourism focuses on how we learn from experience and tries to understand people in terms of the way experience moulds and shapes behaviour. Behaviourists use a relatively limited range of concepts to explain human learning. The Russian physiologist, Ivan Pavlov (1849–1936) and American psychologists Edward Thorndike (1874–1949), John Watson (1878–1958) and Burrhus F. Skinner (1904–90) all worked to develop behaviourist theories of learning.

Observation

Edward Thorndike studied the way that animals learn by observing their responses in controlled conditions. He noticed that animals would often learn by trial and error. For example, a hungry cat would experiment with ways of escaping from a cage in order to receive a reward of food. When the cat discovered actions that helped it to escape, it would remember those actions. Thorndike believed that any action that produced a good effect would become stamped into the mind of the animal. In 1898 Thorndike wrote an article in which he explained 'the law of effect'. The 'law of effect' means that actions are governed by their consequences. Animals and humans will learn to repeat actions which produce good effects and to avoid repeating actions which have bad outcomes. This theory provided a foundation for the development of behaviourism. Behaviourists believed that theories of conditioning and reinforcement could explain all human behaviour.

Conditioning

In 1906 Pavlov published his work on conditioned learning in dogs. Pavlov had intended to study digestion in dogs, but his work ran into difficulties because his animals anticipated when their food was due to arrive.

Pavlov was able to demonstrate that dogs would salivate (or dribble) whenever they heard a noise, such as a bell ringing, if the noise always came just before the food arrived. The dogs had learned to 'connect' or associate the sound of the bell with the presentation of food. It was as if the bell replaced the food; the dogs' mouths began to water to the sound of the bell. The dogs associated sounds with food. This learning by association was called conditioning.

The first time that Pavlov rang a bell, the stimulus of the bell would have been *neutral*. This means that the dog had not learned to associate anything with it. Once the bell is associated with the arrival of food it has become a *conditioned stimulus* causing the conditioned response of dribbling.

> ### Did you know?
> When Pavlov's research was reported in Britain Oscar Wilde (a famous author of the time) is reported to have said, 'Doesn't every intelligent dog owner know that?'

In the first half of the last century many people believed that all learned behaviour could be explained using the concept of conditioning.

Conditioning and behavioural therapy

Some people develop anxiety states, or irrational fears called phobias. In order to train people to learn to control their behaviour, psychologists may train people in relaxation techniques. A person learns how to create a physical sensation of relaxation through using deep breathing and muscle-relaxing exercises. Once a person has learned this skill they can condition the sensation to a word that they say to themselves. The person simply says 'relax' as they breathe out and the word 'relax' becomes a conditioned stimulus associated with the nice feeling of relaxation. Once a person has conditioned a word to a feeling they can use this learning to help them cope with fears. Someone who experiences fear and panic in crowds can say or even just think the word 'relax' and their conditioning will induce the relaxed feeling.

FIGURE 12.4 *The power of conditioning*

Conditioned learning can be used in a step-by-step way in order to help someone unlearn anxiety or fear. A person who is afraid of crowds might start by going out to only slightly difficult settings and practising their conditioned relaxation skills. Following a step-by-step approach the person may be able to face a really crowded situation. This approach is called systematic desensitisation.

Skinner's theories of conditioning

Like Thorndike, Skinner argued that learning is caused by the consequences of our actions. This means that people learn to associate actions with the pleasure or discomfort that follows. For example, if a child puts some yoghurt in their mouth and it tastes nice, they will associate the yoghurt with pleasure. In future they will repeat the action of eating yoghurt. On the other hand, if the yoghurt does not taste good they may avoid it in future. This principle is similar to the law of effect – behaviour is controlled by past results associated with actions.

Skinner developed a new set of terminology to explain learning by association. Behaviour operates on the environment to create outcomes. Pleasant outcomes are likely to reinforce the occurrence of the behaviours that created them. Behaviour operates on the world and so Skinner used the word 'operant' to describe behaviours which create learned outcomes. The term *operant conditioning* is used to describe learning through the consequences of action.

> **Key concept**
>
> *Classical conditioning (Pavlovian conditioning):* learning to make an association between different events. A stimulus results in a conditioned response.
>
> *Operant conditioning (Skinnerian conditioning):* learning to repeat actions which have a reinforcing or strengthening outcome. In other words, people learn to repeat actions which have previously felt good or are associated with 'feeling better'.

Reinforcement

Skinner developed Thorndike's work on the 'law of effect' using the idea of reinforcement to explain how a behaviour is learned. Reinforcement means to make something stronger. For example, reinforced concrete is stronger than ordinary concrete. A reinforcer is anything that makes a behaviour stronger.

SCENARIO
Reinforcement at work

Amita is an infant who is eating while sitting in a highchair. Amita accidentally drops the spoon she is eating with. Amita reacts with surprise that the spoon has gone. Her mother picks the spoon up and gives it back to Amita, smiling and making eye contact as she does so. This makes Amita feel good. Amita's mother goes back to her own dinner and stops looking at Amita. By accident Amita drops the spoon again. Once again her mother gives Amita attention and the spoon is returned. Once again Amita feels good. Half a minute later Amita drops the spoon on purpose – dropping the spoon has become reinforced. The consequences or outcomes of dropping the spoon feel nice – it is followed by attention.

Without understanding human behaviour, parents might think that the child is being difficult, or that she is playing a game. What is happening is that Amita's behaviour of dropping the spoon is being 'reinforced' by her mother. Her mother is teaching her to drop the spoon although she doesn't realise what she is doing. Reinforcement is happening because Amita is getting a 'nice feeling' each time she drops the spoon and her mother gives it back.

It is important to remember that life experiences cause conditioning. Most conditioning happens without anyone planning or intending it. Reinforcement and punishment frequently take place in educational and social care settings. They happen whether or not anyone intended reinforcement or punishment to happen.

Positive and negative reinforcement

Reinforcement always involves things getting better for the individual who receives it. Both positive and negative reinforcement make behaviour stronger. The term *positive reinforcement* is used to identify pleasurable outcomes for the individual who is reinforced. The term *negative reinforcement* is used to identify a situation where something which is unpleasant ceases. For example, a child at school may be bored during their lesson. Poking the child next to them with a pencil may relieve the boredom. The child

FIGURE 12.5 *Reinforcing behaviour*

may receive negative reinforcement that makes them feel better, as a result of their disruptive behaviour. The reinforcement is 'negative' because an unpleasant state of boredom has ended. Negative reinforcement is an important distinction, which is very useful when explaining problems like phobias and anxiety states.

The opposite of reinforcement is punishment; punishment has the result of blocking behaviour whilst reinforcement always strengthens it.

> **Key concept**
>
> *Positive reinforcement:* this involves *feeling good*. A 'nice' outcome that creates pleasure will strengthen your behaviour.
>
> *Negative reinforcement:* this involves a bad situation coming to an end – so that you feel better. Behaviour that results in an outcome of *feeling better* will be strengthened or reinforced.
>
> *Punishment:* this involves *feeling bad*. Your behaviour results in an outcome that is experienced as being unpleasant. Unpleasant outcomes may inhibit or block a response. Punishment is the opposite of reinforcement; punishing outcomes will inhibit or weaken a behaviour.

The concepts of conditioning and reinforcement offer some useful tools for understanding the ways in which life experience can influence human behaviour. They may not explain the whole complexity of human experience, though.

Modelling

Albert Bandura (born 1925) argues that conditioning only partly explains what is happening when people learn. He argues that people also learn from what they see and hear, and that people often imitate or copy others without direct reinforcement or conditioned association taking place. It is enough to see other people being rewarded for us to choose to copy the behaviour that seems to be rewarded. This is called 'vicarious reinforcement'.

> **Key concept**
>
> *Vicarious reinforcement:* we imagine that another person is receiving a pleasurable outcome and the imagination of reinforcement is sufficient to cause us to copy his or her behaviour. Perceiving others as being rewarded can change our behaviour. Bandura was able to demonstrate that children will copy the behaviour that they see adults perform. People copy or model themselves on people they associate as like themselves, but who seem successful.
>
> *Modelling:* other peoples' behaviour can create a model. We will copy what we see other people doing if they appear to receive reinforcement. People learn by imitating behaviours that appear to be rewarded. It is not necessary to receive direct reinforcement in order to learn new behaviours.

If people imitate what they see others rewarded for, how might the following life experiences influence a person?

* Seeing an elder brother or sister praised for school achievement.
* Seeing a friend being praised and looked up to because of violent behaviour.
* Seeing a neighbour do well from trading shares on the Internet.
* Seeing a person gain respect and being looked up to because they deal in drugs.
* Seeing a person being praised and thanked for caring for a relative.

Behaviour modification

Behavioural therapies always take a positive problem-solving approach to changing behaviour. Behavioural therapies do not involve too much talking or reasoning. If you have a problem it is because of conditioning. A behavioural therapist will design new learning experiences for you that can change your past learning. On a simple level parents and carers might use behavioural theory to influence children's behaviour.

A six-year-old boy becomes angry and aggressive when asked to clean his teeth at night. How might behavioural approaches work?

Modelling – the boy's parents might praise and give attention to his sister when she cleans her teeth without protest. Vicarious reinforcement of teeth-cleaning behaviour might influence the boy.

1. *Make teeth cleaning more reinforcing.* The parents could try buying flavoured toothpaste that the child would enjoy. If the experience becomes pleasurable it may be strengthened or reinforced.
2. *Analyse the child's behaviour – and analyse the parents' response.* The child's behaviour may be being reinforced by the parents' response. It may seem odd, but if the parents are becoming angry it is possible that their attention is actually reinforcing avoidance of teeth cleaning.
3. *Use behaviour modification.* Having analysed the behaviour it may be possible to use praise and other social reinforcers in order to reinforce teeth cleaning, perhaps involving a step-by-step approach.

Modifying behaviour – what not to do

Behaviourists argue that behavioural techniques should never involve bribery, punishment or emotional reactions such as anger.

✱ *Never bribe:* bribery is when a deal is negotiated, for example 'If you brush your teeth we will give you five pounds.' Bribery involves thinking – it is not a behavioural approach. Bribery puts the child in control – and eventually the child will be able to name their price for brushing their teeth.

✱ *Never punish:* punishment can block behaviour, but punishment does not guide a child into an alternative behaviour pattern.

✱ *Never become angry:* parents should never loose emotional control and become angry or start shouting. Anger and abuse are unlikely to result in the desired behaviour. Children are likely to imitate angry and abusive behaviour that they experience. Children may also be emotionally damaged by abuse.

Jason is a 23-year-old man with learning difficulty. He attends a day centre where he regularly lies across the main entrance to the centre. Staff become very concerned when Jason does this, and there is usually a lot of commotion involved in persuading Jason to stand up and leave the entrance.

Behaviourists would assume that Jason has learned this behaviour; the attention that he receives may be positively reinforcing his behaviour of lying in the doorway. Jason may also feel bored; lying in the doorway may relieve this boredom. Lying in the doorway may feel better than the alternatives – if this is the case then his behaviour is being negatively reinforced.

In order to modify Jason's behaviour, behaviourists would seek to reinforce an alternative behaviour. If Jason looked bored staff might try to involve him in conversation. If Jason responds staff might try to be particularly attentive and supportive. Staff attention might act to reinforce conversational behaviour.

Staff might try to gradually encourage Jason to talk to them rather than lie in the doorway. Staff might try to minimise the attention they give when he lies in the doorway but be very responsive and reinforcing towards communication.

Staff would not ignore lying in the doorway because it would be unsafe to do this. Staff would not punish Jason – this would be unethical – but it would also fail to encourage an alternative behaviour. If Jason does not lie in the doorway, perhaps he will set the fire alarms off instead! Behaviourism stresses the importance of reinforcing a new 'desirable' behaviour pattern to replace 'less desirable' behaviour.

Token economy

Different people find different things reinforcing. Within a controlled social environment, such as a psychiatric hospital or prison, access to sweets, cigarettes, TV or social privileges such as visits may be limited. Tokens might be traded for a range of different things that people find reinforcing. The idea is that the tokens become reinforcing in their own right. Ayllon and Azrin (1965) used tokens that could be traded in order to try and influence the behaviour of psychiatric patients. If, for example, there was a target behaviour that an inmate should talk more, that person would receive tokens in order to reinforce talking. Reinforcement could then be gradually stepped down as the person improved their social skills.

Token economies are not widely used because they require highly detailed analysis and total control of a closed social setting (i.e. a setting closed to outside influences). The use of token economies has to be carefully considered in relation to ethics and care values. Most social care settings are not closed institutions, and the use of token economies might be incompatible with the care values of choice, independence and empowerment.

Social skills training

The quality of an individual person's social interaction skills can be analysed and new skills can be taught. Social skills training will often involve the demonstration of a particular skill and an invitation to imagine using the skill. Role-play and similar techniques provide an opportunity for new performance to be reinforced. An example of social skills training might be assertiveness training – widely taught to people within the social care field. Anger management courses are used in prison and probation settings. Social skills training is also used with isolated young children. In these situations children might be encouraged to learn new social responses in the context of play, perhaps play involving just one other younger child.

Systematic desensitisation

Behaviourists regard people who have developed an irrational fear (phobia) as people who have learned their fear usually through negative reinforcement. For instance, a person might feel tense in a small dark place; they may withdraw from this place and then they will feel better. Feeling better involves negative reinforcement. Over time a person who backs away from something that frightens them is reinforcing (strengthening) their fear. Behaviourists might treat claustrophobia (fear of enclosed places) using systematic desensitisation.

To begin with it would be important to assess each individual person's fear. One way of doing this might be to ask the person about their most feared, partly feared and least feared situations. The person would then learn relaxation techniques. Systematic desensitisation would start with the least feared situations. The person would attempt to relax whilst in a mildly stressful situation. If the conditioned learning can be unlearned in easy situations, the programme of desensitisation can progress to learn to relax in moderately stressful situations. Eventually, systematic desensitisation will be successful when the person can relax in their most feared situation – perhaps going into a small dark cupboard in the case of someone with claustrophobia!

Family therapy

Caring approaches to personal problems often emphasise the need to understand the social circumstances that surround an individual. Family therapy applies 'systems theory' to the interpretation of individual behaviour. Family therapy sees a family as a system; it is not possible to understand why a particular family member behaves the way that they do unless the dynamics of the entire family can be understood. Families and other groups build their own private belief systems; we can only help people if we understand the private systems of thinking that surround them.

For example, perhaps a child will develop an eating problem. As well as assessing the behaviour a family therapist would want to know what the significance of the eating problem might be within the child's family. Perhaps the mother and father are close to splitting up their relationship, but because of the child's problem they stay together, focusing their attention on the child's needs. If the child was to be well perhaps the parents would stop putting aside their differences and perhaps the relationship would break up. As long as the child has a problem, the child can keep mother and father together.

The child is unlikely to have thought this strategy through on a conscious level, but the family system has created the environment where the child needs to remain ill. The family therapy approach would argue that the more traditional behaviourist and cognitive approaches often misinterpret individual motivation. A great deal of human behaviour can only be understood in terms of the significance of that behaviour within a system of group or family dynamics.

The strengths and weaknesses of behavioural approaches

Strengths

A highly focused approach
Behavioural therapy may be very effective for clients who have a specific definable goal such as overcoming a fear of heights, stopping smoking or becoming more assertive. Behaviour modification also provides a positive way of managing some challenging behaviours.

A highly structured problem-solving approach
Behaviour therapy and social skills training involve careful assessment and analysis of difficulties. A structured, often step-by-step training programme can then be designed to reinforce the development of new behaviours or skills.

The approach is often suitable for 'brief therapy'
Because behavioural approaches are highly focused and directive it may be suitable for people who are looking for a 'quick fix' for a problem in their life. Approaches that use systems theory (family therapy) may be more complex. Focused therapy may be cheaper than approaches which review wider life and personality issues.

An educational approach
Some behavioural approaches, such as social skills training, may be empowering and may help service users/clients to feel that they have greater control over their lives.

Can be combined with cognitive techniques
Nowadays a great deal of behavioural therapy is cognitive-behavioural therapy. Cognitive-behavioural approaches combine a focus on thinking with a focus on practical learning techniques such as desensitisation. A combination of cognitive and behavioural approaches is often found to be very effective at helping people to cope with problems such as phobias or managing body weight.

Weaknesses

A narrow focus
Some therapists would argue that simply trying to change your behaviour is often a waste of time. Claustrophobia might be caused by deep unconscious tensions, or perhaps result from a distorted sense of self. Just enabling people to go into small enclosed spaces does not get at the root of the problem. Some therapists argue that the service user or client will simply develop new problems to replace the claustrophobia.

A management approach, but only a mechanistic explanation of human need
Behavioural approaches offer a range of techniques for teaching people to learn new ways of coping with practical situations. Behavioural approaches generally assume that people may be thought of as mechanisms. Many service users and practitioners may find this assumption difficult to accept. Many people who seek counselling or therapy may expect a more in-depth exploration of personality issues.

Risks not complying with care values
Some techniques, such as behaviour modification, can easily result in abuse of service users if used by inexpert workers. McLeod (2003) notes that the technique of 'timeout' has been misunderstood by care workers in the past. The idea of 'timeout' is that an aggressive child experiences a neutral

situation where their aggression is not reinforced. Historically, care workers have used timeout as a punishing or unpleasant experience. There is always the risk that behavioural approaches look straightforward, but that staff with only limited training may misinterpret some of the techniques, with the outcome of breaching professional codes of practice.

Cognitive approaches

Cognitive approaches argue that it is not what actually happens to us that makes us happy or anxious or depressed, rather it is the way we think about life events that results in happiness or misery. Some people believe that what goes on inside their head is an accurate representation of reality. In other words, if you feel bad and you think that you might be a bit of a failure – well, these thoughts must be true – you must be a failure! Some people may have a dysfunctional belief that if you have a thought, the thought must be an accurate representation of reality.

Research into perception and memory suggests that what we see and what we hear and what we remember usually involve some bias and some distortion. Learning to challenge our thinking because our thoughts may not be true is an important skill – one that might be vital for human happiness.

Information processing

According to Gregory (1966), when information comes to our eyes or ears we have to build (or construct) our own inner mental interpretation of what we are seeing. What we think we see always involves an act of interpretation. People from different cultures may perceive the world differently.

Human memory is also selective in that only some details of events seem to be remembered. Human memory often appears to distort what was experienced. One theory is that memory, like perception, involves a reconstruction of what was experienced. What we remember depends on the way we have learnt to think.

Schema theory

A schema is a mental organisation for something. If you were told a story about going shopping, you would already have a lot of knowledge about the way shops are organised: how goods are paid for; conversations with shop assistants and so on. It appears that when we hear complex information we store the information associated with schemas that already exist in our thinking. When we come to recall information, we partly recall what we were told, and partly recall the associations that were made with our pre-existing knowledge. We can take in a great deal of new information linked to pre-existing schemas but our memories can become distorted in the process.

In order to be able to remember something you have to be able to connect what you hear and see with what you already know. The importance of schema theory for care work is that it explains how people's thoughts and understanding can become distorted. If you work with someone with different life experiences and different schemas from your own, you may not be able to accurately recall what they have told you. Zimbardo writes:

'People from other cultures, who do not share our cultural truisms, may "see" objects or events differently. Because as we have said before, in everyday life "seeing is believing" these differences lie at the basis of misunderstanding, miscommunication and mistrust between people from different cultures.'

Source: Zimbardo et al. (1995)

Biases in information processing

When we experience other people's behaviour we will create an internal memory or internal representation of what we experienced. We are likely to bias our memories to fit with our normal way of thinking. Or in more technical language we reconstruct what we think we saw and heard in terms of our pre-existing schemata ('schemata' is the plural of 'schema').

Try it out

Describe Figure 12.6 in words.

FIGURE 12.6 *What do you think?*

What did you think? Did you think the child is drawing a circle? This would be natural – you have completed the circle in your mind to make it simple and meaningful. It is a good guess but it is an assumption. We bias what we interpret so that things fit easily with the concepts that we use.

What else did you think? Did you assume that the woman was a teacher and that the child is drawing at school? You need to make complete sense of what you see so this kind of assumption helps to create a meaningful picture. Naturally there are many other possibilities – all we know for sure is that an adult woman is interacting with a child who has so far drawn a curved line on a piece of paper.

Human thinking is always open to bias. Social workers need considerable skill in order to be able to report objectively on the detail of what they have experienced when, for example, they assess people's needs. It is so easy for social workers to be biased by assumptions that appear to make things more understandable.

Mental set

Another kind of bias is 'set' or rigid thinking. For example, a care worker might watch a colleague coping with demanding service users by using firm authoritative commands. Perhaps the care worker tries this behaviour on a couple of occasions and it seems to work. After a while the care worker might develop a 'set' pattern of behaviour where any difficult service user is met by a firm authoritative response. The care worker might receive abuse and might be advised by their supervisor to try to be more flexible and yet 'set' thinking might block their ability to adapt their behaviour.

Confirmation bias

Confirmation bias involves searching for information to confirm the assumptions that you have made. An example of this might be a health care worker who has come to the conclusion that people with tattoos are more likely to be aggressive than other people. Instead of encountering people with an open mind the care worker will interpret what they see in terms of their beliefs. For example, the care worker could think: 'This person has a tattoo and waves their arms about, doesn't that confirm that they are aggressive?'

In many ways looking for evidence that fits your thinking will result in a self-fulfilling prophecy. If you treat people with suspicion because they have tattoos you might provoke more aggressive behaviour from them – but this will only prove to you that your ideas were correct after all.

Cognitive primacy

A study by a psychologist called Luchins in 1957 showed that people will interpret information differently depending on what information they have previously been given. People can be primed with information and this information will then go on to bias the way they interpret later experiences (see Figure 12.7).

Stereotyping

There are many ways in which the way we perceive and remember can distort our interpretation of people and events. Stereotyping is a type of fixed or set thinking that can result in cognitive primacy biases, or result in confirmation bias, or create mental schemas that we use in order to interpret experience. Many care workers use the concept of stereotyping in order to draw attention to the risks of bias inherent in our cognitive processes.

FIGURE 12.7 *Cognitive primacy biases interpretation*

Functional and dysfunctional beliefs

Human perception and memory involve bias and distortion. We are quite capable of having thoughts and memories that are inaccurate, biased, stereotyped, distorted and sometimes 'downright daft'. A more functional approach to understanding ourselves is to accept that we often need to challenge and question our ideas and beliefs.

Cognitive therapy

Cognitive therapy developed in the 1960s and is often associated with the work of Aaron Beck and Albert Ellis. Beck initially worked with depressed patients who appeared to experience 'automatic negative thoughts'. These automatic thoughts involved negative ideas about self, negative ideas about the world and negative ideas about the future. For example, negative thoughts about:

✳ *self:* there is nothing that I am good at. I will never be able to get qualifications. I am not an attractive or likeable person. I am a bad person

✳ *the world:* people do not care about others, people are cruel, life is full of suffering and then you die

✳ *the future:* things are getting worse in the world. It will be more difficult to get good jobs in the future. I have nothing to look forward to. If it's bad now it will be three times as bad next year.

Beck believed that these negative thoughts resulted in negative emotional states and that the combination of negative thought and emotion might result in people becoming anxious and depressed. Negative thoughts 'just happen'; they are not necessarily brought about because of terrible life experiences. People often experience distorted thought (or cognitive) processes.

For example:

Student: There is nothing that I am good at – I will never be able to get qualifications.

Counsellor: Why do you think that?

Student: Well it's just hopeless. I failed my last test – I can never do anything right.

Counsellor: When you said you failed, how low was your mark then?

Student: Well, it wasn't the mark I wanted, okay.

Counsellor: But you've been very successful in the past.

Student: Yes, but that was then – it's hopeless now. I just can't get anything right now.

Counsellor: So let me get this right – you didn't do as well as you wanted to on one test – and so you have concluded that you can't cope and nothing will go right.

Student: Well, nobody understands; people don't care; it's terrible, I just know that I can't cope any more.

In the example above the student is being overwhelmed by all three types of negative thinking, and is experiencing very unpleasant emotions. But the reality of the situation is just that one test didn't work out well. The cognitive approach would argue that it is not the reality of what happens to us that creates happiness or depression; rather it is the way that we think about events that creates positive or negative emotion. In the example above the student's thinking is distorted by over-generalisation.

Some types of cognitive distortion that might be associated with depression:

✳ *over-generalisation:* one experience that is emotionally received as being bad is taken as evidence that the whole of your life, other people, and the future will also turn out bad

✳ *polarised thinking:* experiences, self, other people and the future are seen in terms of being wholly bad or wholly good – people think in terms of fixed categories rather than in degrees of good and bad

✳ *personalisation:* the world is seen as focusing on you, for example 'Those traffic lights went red just to get at me', or, 'I bet my partner is unhappy because I'm not good enough'. Everything that happens is seen as connected with you.

Automatic negative thinking and distorted thinking may involve biases in information processing. Over-generalisation and polarised thinking are thought processes that are involved in stereotyped judgements. Confirmation bias may be involved in negative thinking. Rigidity and set thinking may contribute to some people's depression.

It is very important to understand that people do not choose to have negative thoughts, any more than people choose to fall downstairs. Automatic negative thoughts happen because people do not understand what is going on in their thinking. Distorted thinking is rather like falling downstairs; both of these accidents can happen if you don't understand what you're doing, or your attention is not on what is going on. Can you challenge the quality of your thinking? Some people do not challenge what is happening in their thoughts and they become depressed.

Self-talk

Cognitive therapy seeks to help people understand some of the processes happening within their own thinking. The goal is that people will learn to identify and check their own 'self-talk' – the thoughts that are going on in their head. For example, in 'validity testing' a person may be asked to test the validity of a thought process. You have broken up with a partner and you feel bad; but what evidence is there that you are a bad person, or that your life will always be like this or that other people are out to get you? If you can learn to identify how your own thinking works then you can control your own thinking. The cognitive approach argues that if you can control your own thinking then your thinking can result in positive emotions. The cognitive

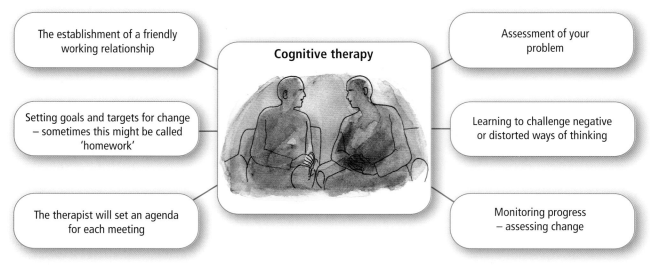

Cognitive therapy

- The establishment of a friendly working relationship
- Setting goals and targets for change – sometimes this might be called 'homework'
- The therapist will set an agenda for each meeting
- Assessment of your problem
- Learning to challenge negative or distorted ways of thinking
- Monitoring progress – assessing change

FIGURE 12.8 *Other factors that may be involved in cognitive therapy*

approach involves learning to challenge and manipulate your own thoughts and emotions.

McLeod (2003) explains that cognitive therapy involves the development of metacognitive knowledge. Meta means beyond or higher. Metacognitive means higher knowledge, or knowledge of how your own thinking works. One goal of education is to help people gain insight into their own thought processes – the cognitive therapist is in many ways acting as a teacher to help people to develop metacognitive knowledge and understand some of the risks involved in thinking. That is, to understand that just because you think something it does not mean that your thoughts are an accurate representation of reality. Skilful people can challenge the 'self-talk' that goes on in their heads.

Different responses to life events

Compare these two scenarios. Both men have experienced the loss of a partner and yet there is a completely different quality to their response.

SCENARIO 1
Max – partner died four months ago

You won't understand what it feels like; nobody does. I'm just living in a dark pit of despair. We had a life together and now it's gone and no one and nothing can ever replace her. I am finished now – I don't have a future. I just want to be dead. What's the point of doing anything, nothing matters anymore, and social workers, counsellors – they are useless – the future is just pain and misery. I can't go on, it's all just too terrible to think about and talking about it only makes it worse.

SCENARIO 2
Bill – partner died four months ago

Oh, it's been a terrible experience. I haven't got over her you know. Sometimes at night I just go into a deep depression; it's like I'm in a pit and there's no way out. But then – and I bet you'll think I'm weird – but then I start laughing. You see I remember our time together and I know that she would have wanted me to be OK. And sometimes I feel she's with me still and then I start laughing at the thoughts I'm having. I think sometimes I enjoy the feeling of despair – but I know I can snap out of it. I think of all the good things and I think to myself – well has it gone? In one sense it has – she's dead – but in another sense no one can ever take her away from me. We are still together in my mind and this thought gives me the strength to carry on with my life. So am I depressed or not? You tell me!

Both these people feel emotional pain and loss. Max is drowning in his suffering; he feels he is 'finished', helpers are 'useless' and the future is all bad. Max is experiencing the full range of automatic negative thoughts and has become seriously emotionally depressed. Bill has experienced exactly the same distress, but he has the ability to challenge his own mental experience. Bill does not believe that because he's 'in the pit', it has to be that way. Bill can burst out laughing! He can think flexibly and remember lots of positive issues that can alter the way he thinks and feels. Bill uses his thinking skills to challenge the negative thoughts and emotions that he experiences. So Bill can think his way out of his depressed emotions – so is he depressed? No, he's made up his mind not to be depressed.

The difference is not that Max has experienced a worse loss. The difference is that Max cannot access the thinking skills necessary to challenge the negative thoughts and emotions that come to him. Cognitive therapy might enable him to do what Bill can do – that is, challenge his own thoughts and construct positive ideas.

The strengths and weaknesses of the cognitive approach

Strengths

Can be combined with behavioural techniques
Nowadays a great deal of cognitive therapy is cognitive-behavioural therapy. Cognitive-behavioural approaches combine the focus on thinking with a focus on practical learning techniques such as desensitisation. A combination of cognitive and behavioural approaches is often found to be very effective at helping people to cope with specific problems.

A highly focused approach
Cognitive and cognitive-behavioural therapy may be very effective for clients who have a specific definable goal such as stopping smoking, becoming more assertive, becoming less anxious, coping with depression, or overcoming an alcohol or drugs problem.

A highly structured approach
Many people who are depressed or anxious may have difficulty making sense of their problems. Cognitive therapy is directive – the therapist will organise an agenda for each session and may design practical tasks (sometimes called 'homework') that the client needs to undertake.

The approach is often suitable for 'brief therapy'
Because cognitive therapy is usually highly focused and directive it may be suitable for people who are looking for a 'quick fix' for a problem in their life. People may feel that they have been helped towards coping with a problem with perhaps just four or five sessions. Focused therapy may therefore be cheaper than approaches which review wider life and personality issues.

An educational approach
Cognitive therapy aims to help people learn to understand and manage their own thought processes. Many people may experience this learning as empowering – it will empower them to cope with life in new ways. If cognitive therapy is successful then the client will become their own cognitive therapist – independently challenging dysfunctional thought processes.

Weaknesses

The cognitive approach may be too focused for some people.
Some people seek therapy for global life issues. People may wish to explore issues such as 'I don't know what I should be doing with my life' or 'There is something about me that prevents me from falling in love'. If a person needs to explore wider personality issues that cannot be focused on changing thoughts or behaviour then psychodynamic or person-centred therapy may be more appropriate.

People have to be able to explore their thoughts
Cognitive approaches involve learning to identify and challenge your own thinking processes. People will need some degree of language and thinking ability in order to take this approach on. Cognitive therapy may not be appropriate for

some people with learning difficulties. Cognitive therapy may also be inappropriate where people have more serious mental health problems that disrupt thought processes.

People have to be willing to accept direction

The cognitive therapist will seek to develop a friendly relationship, but they will expect to set the agenda for meetings and to guide and challenge the thoughts of the people they are working with. In many ways the cognitive therapist takes on the role of a teacher. Some people may be threatened by the balance of power involved in this kind of help. These people may resist the action-orientated approaches associated with cognitive-behavioural therapy. Some people may not co-operate with the idea of 'homework' to control their emotions.

Cognitive therapy might be criticised as a surface approach

Some psychodynamic therapists argue that simply addressing thoughts, emotions and behaviour is superficial. Psychodynamic therapists would argue that depression, anxiety, phobias and so on come about because of deeper unconscious conflicts. Psychodynamic therapists might argue that cognitive therapy doesn't really get to the underlying issues involved in mental health problems and that dealing with symptoms might only result in changing one set of symptoms for a new set of symptoms.

Humanistic approaches

Humanistic theory stresses the importance of each individual person's subjective reality. Humanistic theory stresses the idea that each person experiences life differently. People are not seen as being mechanisms that can be categorised, analysed and modified. There are no experts who can diagnose what is wrong with another person. Each person is the expert on themselves – and not on anyone else.

One of the major humanistic approaches is person-centred theory, developed by Carl Rogers (1902–87). Person-centred theory emphasises the importance of respect for the value of each individual person. It is the relationship between the counsellor and his or her client that enables the client to make progress and find a way of coping with problems. Carl Rogers argued that the counsellor needed to be able to step into the world of another person and understand their feelings and thoughts. This involves the establishment of empathy – a deep understanding and involvement in another person's life.

An overview of person-centred theory

Every human being has an inbuilt tendency to explore, grow and develop. This inbuilt tendency is called the actualising tendency. In an ideal world people can draw on the inner strength of the actualising tendency in order to develop a positive and effective self-concept that would enable them to live a secure and contented life. Unfortunately we live in a society full of power struggles. Children are taught that they must conform to other people's expectation if they are to be valued. Conditions of worth (see page 300) end up distorting many people's concepts of themselves. When people live with a distorted sense of who they are they may cease to value themselves, and in this state people are capable of harming themselves and others. People living with a distorted sense of self are likely to experience a wide range of psychological difficulties.

Helping people involves using relationship skills in order to enable them to explore their interpretation of self. The therapist will seek to enable a client to experience their own inner actualising and valuing tendency. Once a person is in touch with their own inner resources they may be able to escape from a distorted sense of self.

> ## SCENARIO
> ## Interview with Sean
> 'I live for the day you know – I may be 75 but there are a lot of things I want to do with my life. I think that life is what you make it, isn't it? I learned to stop worrying about trivial things like money and jobs a long time ago. I enjoy my life and I think positively about every opportunity I get. I've always been a craftsperson, I make wooden furniture – it might not be your thing

> – but I get a nice feeling out of designing and creating things. Many years ago, I worked as a cabinet maker for a furniture company, in the end it got me down. I was told to do things cheaply rather than do them properly – so I left. I think if you're not enjoying your work then something is wrong. I was unemployed for a while but I didn't mind, I knew I would get by. What really matters in life is being able to look back on life and feel proud and pleased with what I've done. There is no one else I would have liked to have been. I've lived my life as I wanted.'

Sean radiates a sense of contentment and happiness; he is not wealthy but he is happy. Sean has taken responsibility for his own life, he has found a source of inner strength and he doesn't worry about other people's evaluation of him. He knows what he enjoys – furniture – and he doesn't care if this isn't cool as far as other people are concerned. Sean has found a 'way of being' that has made his life psychologically comfortable. Within person-centred theory he might be described as self-actualising, or in touch with his actualising tendency.

Humanistic approaches to understanding people developed in the 1950s. Carl Rogers and Abraham Maslow are two of the best-known theorists associated with the humanistic approach, but these two authors held different views about self-actualisation.

Self-actualisation and the actualising tendency

In Carl Rogers' theory the *actualising tendency* is an inner biological need to grow and develop both physically and psychologically. The actualising tendency can give a person the power to develop, change and grow in order to direct their own life. Many people lose touch with their actualising tendency because social pressures result in a distorted and limiting self-concept.

In Abraham Maslow's theory self-actualisation represents a very high level of psychological

development. The majority of people in Western society will not achieve self-actualisation because needs such as self-esteem and safety have to be sorted out before a person can progress towards achieving self-actualisation.

The self-actualising tendency

Every human being is born with an inner creative drive to grow and develop. Understanding this actualising tendency lies at the heart of person-centred therapy. If a client can recognise their own inner value and worth they may be able to take control of the problems that they face in life.

Try it out

Do we really have an actualising tendency?

Sceptic: I don't think I've ever experienced any actualising tendency in my life!

Person-centred counsellor: Well, can you think of any time when your life has been at risk and what happened then?

Sceptic: Yes – for a dare I once tried to swim around a headland in the North Sea in winter; while I was some distance from the shore I developed cramp and couldn't use one leg. I realised that I was likely to drown, and it seemed so comfortable and easy just to give up and die. Then something hit me – a powerful feeling that I couldn't give up – I had to live, I don't know how I did it but I did make it into the shore, and I lived because of that instinct to survive.

Counsellor: Well, you might call it a survival instinct, but we would call it your actualising tendency. The actualising tendency is part of our biological makeup. It doesn't just work when life is in danger, it can work in every area of our lives to motivate us to cope with stress and unhappiness. The same inner biological force that saved your life might enable someone with social problems to be able to take control of their situation rather than go under and give into depression.

Conditions of worth

According to Carl Rogers we are born with an inner tendency to grow and develop, but many people fail to develop self-esteem and to lead a happy joyful life. A key problem is that our natural potential for growth and development is distorted by conditions of worth. Many children will learn that they will only be valued by their family if they meet the conditions or demands that their family make of them. For example, some children are told that they will be rewarded – perhaps with a new bicycle – if they do well at school. Such children also get the message that if they don't do well they will be looked down on and perhaps experience some emotional rejection. Many children grow up believing that they must fulfil their parents' expectations for them; for example, that they must follow the career that their parents expect, or adopt the lifestyle – perhaps early marriage and children – that their parents expect. Children may come to believe that they will only be a worthwhile and valuable person if they are successful in becoming what is expected. This is called *conditional positive regard*.

Person-centred therapists believe that every individual person is intrinsically valuable and worthy of respect. A therapist will respect and value the people that they work with regardless of their client's life stories.

Person-centred theory argues that parents should show *unconditional positive regard* towards children. Unconditional positive regard does not mean that parents have to praise or tolerate everything their children do. It is important that parents are honest with their feelings. Unconditional positive regard simply means that the bond between parents and children is not conditional on the child's performance of parental demands.

Organismic self

The word 'organismic' reminds us that each person is a biological organism. Within our biology are inner resources that we can draw on in order to constantly grow and develop into a more complete person. It is difficult to explain inner experience using language. Experience is fluid and constantly changing. Words tend to fossilise emotions and thoughts so that when we define who we are, we have a list of lifeless categories which we have analysed ourselves into. Our 'organismic' experience is much more than the words with which we try to capture it.

Self-concept

During childhood we begin to form an idea of ourselves as an individual. We are powerfully influenced by family, friends and the community in which we live. Our idea of self is constantly changing, and our idea of self can be strongly influenced by conditions of worth. As well as a self-concept we may also have a 'self that I would like to be' – an 'ideal self' that describes the person we would like to become. As long as our self-concept fits with our inner experience we will develop in a healthy way towards becoming a fully functioning person.

For many people conditions of worth result in distorted beliefs about self – perhaps beliefs that we are what our families want us to be. These distorted beliefs can result in mental defences and in negative and destructive behaviours. Sometimes conditions of worth result in individuals developing low self-esteem when they fail to live up to other people's demands.

Congruence

Congruence and incongruence are terms Carl Rogers borrowed from geometry. In modern language congruence means 'keeping it real'. Many people have to put on an act when they are at work. A receptionist may have to smile at a service user and say things like 'I am pleased to help you.' Deep down, the receptionist might be thinking 'I am tired, I can't cope with any more people with problems.' Carl Rogers would have said that the receptionist's behaviour is 'incongruent' with the feelings that he has.

Person-centred therapy stresses that counsellors must not put on an act. Counsellors must build an understanding of their clients. This understanding might lead to the development of empathy – the ability to enter the world of another person. Counsellors must also understand their own emotions and thoughts as they work with other people. What counsellors say to clients should always be genuine, or in other words what is said should be congruent with the counsellor's real inner feelings. A counsellor may feel anxious or threatened by what a client is saying. The counsellor must make a decision as to whether to share his or her feelings with the client, but the counsellor must never counterfeit their emotions or lie about their feelings.

FIGURE 12.9 *The goat can move only within the range that the rope and post allow*

Locus of control

A locus is the range of freedom of movement that you have. In the 1950s the concept of 'locus' was taught to junior school children. In Figure 12.9 the locus of movement of the goat is controlled by the length of rope attached to the post.

Carl Rogers used this idea of locus to explain the difference between being free to respond to our own inner actualising tendency, or being restricted by the views and beliefs of others. People with an internal locus of evaluation are controlled by their own personal values. People with an external locus of evaluation are controlled by a desire to live up to the expectations of other people. People with an external locus of evaluation will be very concerned to 'look good' or be approved of by important people. An external locus of evaluation means that the extent to which you value your self depends on how well you are fulfilling other people's expectations of you.

Locus of evaluation (control): an *external* locus of evaluation means that the person may develop a distorted sense of self. A person may only see their life as being worthwhile if they are fulfilling the expectations of other people – such as employers, family and friends. An *internal* locus of evaluation means that a person's self-concept is not distorted by the demands of other people.

'The person-centred point of view, however, places high value on the experience of the individual human being and on the importance of his or her subjective reality. It also challenges each person to accept responsibility for his or her own life and trust in the inner resources which are available to all those who are prepared to set out along the path of self-awareness and self-acceptance.'

Source: Mearns and Thorne (1999).

Consider this

Low self-esteem

'I guess I was just never as good as my sister; she was more attractive, she was better at everything. She won prizes, she went to university. My parents always told me, "Why can't you be like your sister," "Oh you're so clumsy," "How come she can do it and you can't". I used to get the blame for everything – she never did anything wrong, it was always me. And I wasn't good at school. I couldn't understand everything – I used to get told off. I wasn't in the "in" group with the other girls in my year. Some girls wouldn't talk to me. I used to get picked on. I don't know why; I guess I'm the sort of person with a sign on their head saying "Pick on me".

'Yes, my boyfriend knocks me about, I get hit and it hurts. You might say that I should leave him but you don't understand – at least I've got a boyfriend – if I lose him then I have nobody who cares.'

What has this person told you?

How might conditions of worth have influenced this person's views?

Why is she prepared to tolerate abuse and let her boyfriend have power over her?

How might a person-centred counsellor help this person?

A person-centred counsellor would take time to listen. The person-centred counsellor would come to understand how the world is experienced by this girl. During lengthy conversation the counsellor might begin to discover some of the strengths and positive factors in the girl's life. It might be possible for the girl to begin to sense her own actualising tendency. Because of the quality of the counselling relationship, involving sincerity (congruence), understanding (empathy) and emotional warmth (unconditional positive regard), the girl might begin to change the way she thinks about herself. Just because she had bad experiences in the past does not mean that she is now a worthless person. She might begin to increase her self-esteem and believe that she is a valuable person.

If you believe that your life is important and valuable you may find the inner resources to take control and not to allow other people to exploit you. A person-centred counsellor would use the quality of the counselling relationship to try to enable the client to take control and sort out their own life difficulties. A person-centred counsellor would not make demands on the girl – demands such as 'You must leave your boyfriend.' The girl would make her own decision based on being in touch with her own actualising tendency and her own 'locus of control'. Person-centred counsellors never tell you what to do. They would try to support the people that they work with to experience an inner sense of power and self-worth.

FIGURE 12.10 (A) *The emotional security of this person is dependent on the views of other people*
(B) *The emotional security of this person is founded on an internal understanding of self*

The strengths and weaknesses of humanistic approaches

Strengths

A 'way of being'

Carl Rogers explained person-centred theory as offering what amounts to a life philosophy. If you see through the conditions of worth that other people impose on you; if you develop an internal locus of evaluation; and if you have a positive concept of yourself drawing on an actualising tendency, you will have a high degree of emotional security. You may be able to face the struggles and threats of life with a high degree of self-confidence.

A philosophy relevant to modern society

The person-centred approach stresses that every individual person has the right to be respected and valued. This value system may be seen as a general principle essential for interpersonal relationships within a multicultural, multi-faith, multiracial democratic society. Respect and value for individuality is a value system embedded in much current government policy and in the GSCC code of practice for social care workers.

Empowerment

The person-centred approach aims to enable service users and clients to develop their own inner resources and have the power to address their own problems. The therapist does not have power over the people they are trying to help. The therapist does not 'treat' the people they work with. The therapist does not find causes, or offer cures for people's problems.

Weaknesses

Therapy takes time

Person-centred counsellors use the quality of their relationship, over time, to help people gain new insights into their life stories. This kind of work may not always be practical if a 'quick fix' is needed. For example, if a person needs help to give up smoking, a more problem-focused approach may get results after just a few sessions. Person-centred work may achieve more fundamental change in the way a person lives their life, but this may involve more time and therefore more expense.

There may be barriers to empowerment

Some people live their life with an assumption that 'experts can put things right'. These people will expect their emotional problems to be assessed in terms of causes, and will then expect the therapist to put things right. People who think this way may become frustrated if they have to work with a non-directive counsellor who does not provide explanations and treatments.

Person-centred theory cannot always be used on its own within health and social work settings

Although it is important for health care workers to understand person-centred approaches, there may be occasions when a doctor or nurse does need to be directive in order to minimise physical risks. Similarly, social workers often have duties to implement legal procedures, for example in order to prevent child abuse. It may be argued that whilst counselling can be purely person-centred, neither social work nor health care work can operate solely from the person-centred perspective.

Psychodynamic approaches

Sigmund Freud (1856–1939) developed a theory of the human mind that emphasised the interaction of biological drives with the social environment. Freud's theory emphasises the power of early experience to influence the adult personality.

Freud's theories are called *psychodynamic theories*. 'Psycho' means mind or spirit and 'dynamic' means energy or the expression of energy. Freud believed that people were born with a dynamic 'life energy' or 'libido' which initially motivates a baby to feed and grow and later motivates sexual reproduction. Freud's theory explains that people are born with biological instincts in much the same way that animals

such as dogs or cats are. Our instincts exist in the unconscious mind but we don't usually understand our unconscious. As we grow we have to learn to control our 'instincts' in order to be accepted and fit in with other people.

Conscious and unconscious mind: Freud's mental mechanisms

Freud believed that we were born with an 'id' a part of our unconscious mind that is hidden from conscious understanding. The 'id' is like a dynamo that generates mental energy. This energy motivates human action and behaviour.

When a young child learns to control their own body during toilet training, the 'ego' develops. The 'ego' is a mental system which contains personal learning about physical and social reality. The 'ego' has the job of deciding how to channel drive energy from the unconscious into behaviour which will produce satisfactory outcomes in the real world. The 'ego' is both unconscious (unknown to self) and conscious (a person can understand some of their own actions and motivation).

The 'super ego' develops from the ego when the child gives up their opposite-sex parent as a 'love object'. The 'super ego' contains the social and moral values of the parent that has been 'lost' as a potential partner.

Unconscious motivation

The essence of psychodynamic theory is that people are controlled by inner forces, but that people do not understand and cannot explain what is happening to them. For example, throughout adult life a person has to find a way to release drive energy that is compatible with the demands of society and with the demands of the super ego. Sometimes people may feel sandwiched between the demands of their biology and social pressures. Typically, today's world often creates pressure to 'achieve a good career' and please parents by 'doing well'. For some people the desire to enjoy their sexuality and perhaps have children may conflict with the pressure to achieve. The way people cope with these pressures will be strongly influenced by childhood experiences according to Freudian theory.

Freudian mental mechanisms

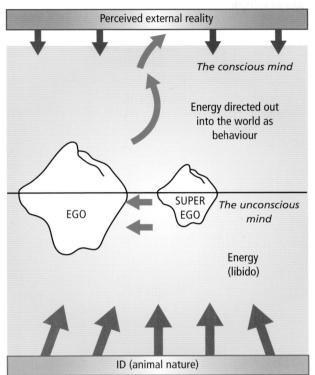

FIGURE 12.11 *Freudian mental mechanisms*

In order to understand behaviour a therapist needs to be able to understand what is happening in that person's unconscious mind. Therapists and counsellors cannot begin to understand the unconscious mind of an individual by asking direct questions. In order to understand how early experience has influenced the unconscious mind therapists might explore an individual's dreams. Alternatively, a therapist might ask a client to make up a story about a picture (the Thematic Apperception test) or ask them what they see in an ink blot (the Rorschach test).

These indirect conversations are a way of learning about another person's unconscious mind. Freud originally used the method of 'free association' to access the unconscious mind of his patients. This 'talking cure' involves getting the client to relax on a couch and just explain whatever comes into their mind in response to words that the therapist says.

Defence mechanisms

The ego is the decision-making part of our mind. The ego has to work out how to get on with other people whilst also coping with our unconscious animal instincts, and unconscious memories. The ego is under attack from the pressures of the real world and the pressures of the unconscious. If a person is to remain in good mental health their ego has to find a way of coping with all these pressures. Ego defences are ways in which people can make themselves feel safer and protect themselves from pressures.

> **Key concept**
>
> *Ego defence mechanisms:* the ways in which people distort their understanding and memory in order to protect their ego.

Examples of defence mechanisms include:

* *denial:* involves blocking threatening information or thoughts from awareness

* *repression:* forcing memories out of consciousness into the unconscious mind, it is a kind of motivated forgetting of unpleasant thoughts or memories

* *rationalisation:* reinterpreting events or memories in order to make them safer for the ego

* *displacement*: finding a different outlet for feelings such as transferring anger towards a parent to an 'out-group'

* *projection:* projecting forbidden emotions onto others; that is, what we see in others is sometimes in ourselves

* *sublimation:* a change of state in the way mental energy is directed; for example, sexual drive is directed away from partners and into activities such as collecting things

* *reaction formation:* changing an emotion into its overemphasised opposite; for example, changing love to hatred or hatred into aggressively expressed praise.

Possible defence mechanisms at work in the scenarios above:

1. Arnold may be using *sublimation* to redirect mental energy away from aspects of life which become threatening and into a much safer activity of collecting things.

2. Arnold may be using *rationalisation* to avoid recognising the real reasons for collecting so many old newspapers.

3. Andrea may be using *denial* to block out awareness of the seriousness of her illness.

4. Andrea may be *repressing* memory of past ill-health in order to make the situation feel safer for her.

5. Andrea may feel distressed and angry about the situation and about the care she is receiving, but she is using *reaction formation* in order to change her emotions into an 'over-emphasised opposite'. Reaction formation prevents her from being fully aware of her situation and feelings.

6. Andrea may be *displacing* her anger and distress on to the manager and defending her ego against full awareness of her motivation by using the defence of *projection* to claim that he dislikes her – it's his fault, he started it!

Some features of psychodynamic therapy

When a client discusses their concerns with a psychodynamic counsellor, the counsellor will be aware that what is said comes only from the client's conscious mind. Most problems that people experience will involve difficulties at an unconscious level. The psychodynamic counsellor has to find ways to access the client's unconscious motivations and needs which go beyond the surface level of the client's conversation.

Our unconscious minds are full of tensions. Individuals develop mental defence mechanisms to prevent their unconscious tensions from controlling their conscious life. For example, people can deny or repress memories that are unpleasant. Bad experiences in early life may be deliberately forgotten and locked away in a person's unconscious mind. A client may tell their counsellor that they had a happy childhood – although in reality they may have experienced abuse. The memory of abuse is repressed in a person's unconscious mind and no longer available to the conscious mind because of mental defences. Psychodynamic counsellors believe that what a client says is only part of the story that they need to find out.

The aim of psychodynamic counselling is to enable clients to become more able to control their emotional life and free individuals from being controlled by the forces of their unconscious mind. The ego needs to be able to control the id. Clients can achieve insight into their own mental conflicts through the skilled interpretation offered by a therapist.

McLeod (1998) lists the following characteristics of psychodynamic methods:

Free association

Free association is where the client says whatever comes into their head. Unconscious issues may slip out during this process.

Discussion of dreams and fantasies

Dreams and other products of a person's imagination may provide the counsellor with an insight into the workings of the client's unconscious mind.

Identifying defences

The counsellor will seek to identify the defences that the client uses in order to cope with their emotional situation.

Use of the counselling relationship

McLeod notes that psychodynamic counsellors 'tend to behave towards their clients in a slightly reserved, detached, neutral or formal manner. The reason for this is that the counsellor is attempting to present himself or herself as a blank screen on which the client may project his or her fantasies or deeply held assumptions about close relationships' (page 37). Psychodynamic counsellors expect clients to transfer their assumptions about relationships into the counselling relationship. So, for example, a person who was used to being dominated might behave submissively towards their counsellor. This sort of behaviour is known as transference.

Interpretation

The counsellor will seek to interpret the meaning of the client's statements and behaviour. Interpretation is a difficult skill which takes extensive training and practice to develop.

Projective techniques

Counsellors will sometimes use artwork or images to prompt communication. Children might be observed while they play to assist the counsellor in interpreting fears or worries.

Early relationships and their influence on adult relationships

Attachment theory

John Bowlby (1953) states, 'What occurs in the earliest months and years of life can have deep and long-lasting effects.' Bowlby studied mothers and babies in the mid-1940s, just after the end of the Second World War. Bowlby had noticed that some baby animals would make very fixed emotional bonds with their parents. For example, baby ducklings would attach themselves to, and follow, whomever they presumed to be their mother.

Bowlby's studies of infants led him to the conclusion that there was a biological need for mothers and babies to be together, and that there was a sensitive or critical period for mothers and babies to form this attachment, which is known as bonding. Bowlby stated, 'The absolute need of infants and toddlers for the continuous care of their mothers will be borne in on all who read this book.'

If the bond of love between a baby and its mother was broken through separation, Bowlby believed that lasting psychological damage would be done to the child. If a mother left her infant to go to work every day, or just once to go into hospital, there might be a risk of damage. Bowlby believed that children who suffered separation might grow up to be unable to love or show affection. Separated children might not care about other people. Separated children might also fail to learn properly at school, and might be more likely to turn to crime when they grew up. This theory that children who are separated from their mother would grow up to be emotionally damaged is known as *maternal deprivation*.

Some other researchers working outside of the psychodynamic perspective have doubted that babies are really affected so seriously by separation. Michael Rutter (1981) found evidence that suggests that it is the quality of emotional attachment between a carer and the infant that matters. Not being able to make an attachment may damage a child emotionally. But it is the making of a bond of love between the baby and a carer that matters, not whether temporary separations happen.

There is research that suggests that babies can and do make bonds with their fathers and with their brothers, sisters, or other carers. In one study (Schaffer and Emerson, 1964) almost a third of 18-month-old infants had made their main attachment to their fathers. It seems that babies give their love to the person or persons who give them the best quality affection and time.

Internal working model

John Bowlby believed that the quality of early attachment would set an emotional pattern that would influence adult relationships. Children who were deprived of appropriate attachment or children who experience separation – perhaps because of divorce – might be less able to form loving relationships during adulthood. A young child cannot understand what is happening if they are separated; and this may result in a deep unconscious fear that will influence or limit his or her ability to form an intimate loving relationship with an adult partner.

Bowlby believed that each person develops an internal working model of the way social relationships work. An internal working model develops from our biological need to form attachments with carers during infancy. The way our carers behave will influence the development of our internal model of human relationships.

Key concept

Internal working model: an internalised set of assumptions about the way in which we relate to other people. This internal working model develops from our attachments to other people from early years onwards.

Anxious, avoidant and secure attachment

Mary Ainsworth undertook research with infants using a 'strange situation' approach. This involved mother and infant being in a playroom. A stranger would enter the room and talk to the mother. The mother would leave the room, and then return. The child's behaviour in these different strange situations and when the mother returns could be observed. Ainsworth categorised children's behaviour into four types (see Table 12.4).

The different types of attachment are thought to lead to different internal working models of relationship in adult life. Mary Main quoted in McLeod (2003) undertook a range of research with adults. She concluded that people who had experienced secure attachment as a child were able to present a clear story of their past and of relationships – they appeared to develop an effective internal working model. This working model enabled them to think back and reflect on their life and evaluate the quality of emotional relationships. People who had experienced insecure attachment might be more likely to have confused or 'multiple' internal working models. It is possible that people who have not experienced secure attachment in early life may be less able to make sense of their relationships with other people.

Secure attachment	Securely attached children are upset when the mother leaves but accept comfort and return to playing when the mother returns.
Insecure ambivalent (anxious) attachment	Insecure ambivalent children become upset and anxious but cannot be comforted when the mother returns. They may want to be comforted but resist the approaches of the mother.
Insecure avoidant attachment	Insecure avoidant children may ignore the mother on return, avoiding contact perhaps as a way of protecting themselves from emotional disappointment.
Insecurely attached – disorganised	These children appear confused when the mother returns and may show a range of contradictory behaviours.

TABLE 12.4 *Ainsworth's four types of attachment*

Suppose you heard people say the following things:

1. 'Well I guess I must just be very lucky – I never really had to think about relationships, I mean I met my partner when I was 17 and it just worked, I mean we're very happy. Sure we argue, but I never think about it, we just belong together, and we give and take and everything works out.'

2. 'I think if you've been with a person for more than three days then it's too long. I don't trust anyone – they always let you down in the end. The only person I can trust is me. I live for going out and meeting people, I enjoy sex, but I don't get involved with other people – it is always more trouble than it's worth.'

What kind of internal working model about attachments do you think each of these two people have developed? How do you think early experiences of secure or insecure attachment may have influenced each of these people?

Why someone might find it difficult to develop trust in a close relationship

Early experience may provide some people with a sense of security and confidence that enables them to feel confident with other people and naturally able to develop an intimate loving relationship. People who experience insecure attachment may be less automatically able to attach; there is also the possibility that insecure attachment may result in a lack of confidence and trust towards other people.

Peter Marris (1996) believes that adult emotional security and quality of life depend on attachment. The quality of our early attachment directly influences our ability to make sense of other people. People who enjoy secure attachments are argued to have an advantage in life because they have the inner resources to cope with uncertainty in life. Life can be full of transition and change: new jobs; different ways of working; moving to new areas;

making new friends, and so on. People who were securely attached as children are more likely to develop an inner working model that enables them to cope emotionally. So success and happiness in life may be influenced by the degree to which you have experienced love during early childhood.

Transactional analysis

Transactional analysis is a way of understanding human interaction that developed out of the psychodynamic model of human mind. The approach was developed by Eric Berne who wrote a book called *The Games People Play* in 1964. Berne used the word 'transaction' for any exchange of communication between people. Transactional analysis analyses what happens when people communicate.

Berne believed that there were three ego states within each person. During our first five years of life we learn to remember the emotions and behaviours associated with parent behaviour. We internalise what could be called a PARENT voice. We carry an internal parent 'state of being' within our mind for the rest of our lives. We can recall the emotions and thoughts we had as a child. We carry an internal CHILD 'state of being' with us for the rest of our lives. From childhood on we learn to evaluate information and this rational ability develops into our ADULT ego state.

When two people communicate, one person will begin the exchange from one of the three ego states, and the second person will respond from one of their three ego states (see Figure 12.12).

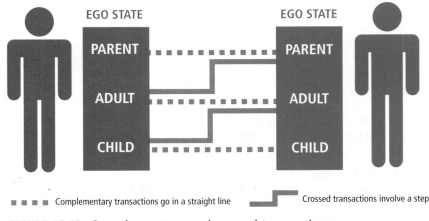

■ ■ ■ ■ Complementary transactions go in a straight line   Crossed transactions involve a step

FIGURE 12.12 *Complementary and crossed transactions*

Complementary transactions

When people's ego states fit each other then a normal healthy complementary transaction has taken place that enables good communication.

For example, in a care home, a service user might say: 'Oh, could I have a cup of tea please?' This is an ADULT ego state request. If the care worker responds with 'Of course; I'll bring you one in the next five minutes,' this would be an ADULT ego state response. A reasoned adult question has been met with a reasoned adult reply – the transaction is complementary.

Crossed transactions

A crossed transaction doesn't go in a straight line such as adult to adult. A crossed transaction is when the respondent comes back on a level that is different from that expected. For example:

Service user: 'Oh, could I have a cup of tea please?' (ADULT ego state).

Care worker: 'Well, just this once – I expect you are very thirsty – I'm very busy but I'll get it for you.' (PARENT ego state).

In this situation the service user might feel patronised, 'treated like a child', or that some kind of power game is being played. If the care worker had responded with the CHILD state ('Oh – you are naughty, aren't you?') the service user might have been equally offended. The service user starts the exchange at a certain level and if he or she is to receive respect then the care worker must respond on a complementary level.

If the service user had started in a CHILD ego state and had been responded to in an ADULT state, this would have also been a crossed transaction:

Service user: 'Can I be naughty and scrounge a cup of tea?'

Care worker: 'I'll bring you a cup of tea in the next five minutes.'

This response sounds dreadfully formal, unsupportive and perhaps unfriendly.

People may not be aware of the way in which ego states impact on their relationships with others. Transactional analysis provides a way in which therapists may be able to help people to improve their relationships with others. If people can identify ego states that influence their behaviour they may be able to learn how to offer complementary transactions and therefore 'get on better' with other people.

Berne's theories go much further than the simple analysis of ego states explained here. Berne is also famous for his analysis of the different power games that people use within relationships. More details of this theory can be found on the websites listed at the end of this unit.

The strengths and weaknesses of psychodynamic approaches

Strengths

An in-depth approach to personal problems

Psychodynamic approaches explore an individual's whole system of interpreting life – their internal working model of what is real. Psychodynamic therapists can access a complex range of theory in order to interpret the life stories of clients.

A comprehensive range of theory

Psychodynamic theory incorporates a complex range of theory that explains how early experience impacts on the unconscious mind and creates stresses and health problems for adults. Clients can explore possible causes of problems or disorders that they face within this theory.

Offers the possibility of psychological growth and development

Psychodynamic approaches may enable you to find new meaning within your life. Because psychodynamic approaches do not simply focus on behavioural problems (such as agoraphobia) there is time to explore an individual's emotion and thought in detail.

Weaknesses

Time-consuming

The psychodynamic approach is rarely quick and simple. Many people undertake psychoanalytic therapy for a number of years. One approach to therapy can involve three sessions a week for more than a year. This time-intensive approach may be expensive.

The theory base is not accepted by everyone
The theory of an unconscious mind and the central importance of early experience are not accepted as being beyond question by everyone. Some people may have difficulty working with a psychodynamic therapist if they do not believe the theory.

Authority
Some psychodynamic therapy involves the therapist explaining the client's life story. This kind of therapy is directive. Person-centred theorists argue that non-directive approaches may be better for many people.

Some strengths of transactional analysis

* Provides a way of analysing communication based on people's expectations.

* The theory of ego states may help care workers to provide more effective supportive communication.

* The full theory provides a way of understanding some of the hidden issues and motivations involved in human interaction.

Some weaknesses of transactional analysis

* The theory is not accepted by everyone.

* Amateur use of psychodynamic theory may be harmful. Freud emphasised that anyone using psychodynamic theory should undergo extensive analysis themselves. Without understanding yourself, you may misinterpret other people in order to defend your own ego. There may be a danger that some people will use TA to interpret other people's behaviour without analysing their own motivation.

Summary of Section 12.2

Approach	Focus	Advantages
Behaviourist	People's behaviour is learned and can be changed through conditioning, reinforcement and imitation learning.	Stresses the importance of new positive experiences in order to change. Therapy can be focused, quick and practical.
Cognitive	The way a person learns to think influences how he or she will behave.	Stresses the importance of understanding your own thinking processes. Therapy can be focused and relatively quick.
Humanistic	A person's understanding of themselves – self-concept – influences behaviour.	Stresses the importance of human relationships, valuing people and empowerment. Therapy may result in a new understanding of life.
Psychodynamic	A person's behaviour is influenced by his or her unconscious mind. The unconscious mind is influenced by early experience.	Stresses the complexity of human beings – and explains behaviour in terms of unconscious conflicts. Therapy works at an in-depth level of explanation.

12.3 Human behaviour and care values

Health and care practitioners

If you were to ask a range of health and social care workers about their job they might stress the importance of specific knowledge and skills. But all health and social care workers work with people, and have to make sense of people in order to be effective. See Table 12.5 for some examples of health and social care roles and their focus on people.

Our current knowledge and understanding of human behaviour

As the previous section demonstrates, there are different perspectives or views that are used to explain human behaviour. There are also many different theories that can be found within these perspectives. Examples of theories include Bowlby's theory of attachment, Skinner's theory of reinforcement, Beck's theory of negative thinking, Roger's theory of an 'actualising tendency'. These theories are not universally accepted or used by all health and social care practitioners. So what can be said in order to summarise current knowledge and understanding? Most health and social care practitioners are likely to accept the broad statements in Table 12.6.

Care values

All health and social care workers must respect and value the service users that they work with. The GSCC code of practice for social care workers identifies the following values within its code:

* respect for individuality
* promoting independence
* support for service users to control their own lives (similar to empowerment)
* promoting equal opportunities, challenging discrimination
* respecting diversity and different cultures
* respecting and maintaining dignity and privacy
* communicating appropriately
* respecting confidentiality
* understanding and using power appropriately
* recognising the right of service users to take risks – but minimising risks.

In order to show respect for individuality, promote independence and respect diversity care workers will need to listen to, understand and establish some degree of trust with service users. If a care worker can understand a little of another person's life story they are less likely to think about service users in a stereotyped way. Without care values health and care workers might fall back into the danger of labelling and stereotyping.

ROLE	KNOWLEDGE AND SKILLS MAY INCLUDE	FOCUS ON PEOPLE
Health professionals	Use of scientific knowledge and specialised skills in order to meet physical health needs.	Establishing confidence and trust, communicating effectively, maintaining a 'caring presence'. Respecting others and understanding individual perspectives on health needs.
Social workers	Working within legal frameworks in order to protect children or vulnerable adults and to assess social needs.	Establishing confidence and trust, building an understanding of individuals and their social context. Respecting others and understanding their interpretation of life.
Care workers	Meeting the physical, emotional, intellectual and social needs of service users.	Building a supportive relationship based on understanding of human need. Respecting others and understanding their identity as individuals.
Counsellors	Using psychological knowledge and advanced social skills in order to meet individual need.	Using a social relationship as a focus to provide support or enable a person to change.

TABLE 12.5 *Examples of health and social care roles*

INFLUENCE	DEFINITION
Individual biological differences	Some approaches have little to say about the importance of our physiology but most people will recognise that we are influenced by physical conditions. For example, low blood sugar levels influence a person's ability to concentrate. Being in pain will influence a person's emotions. Some aspects of personality – such as the degree to which we seek or avoid excitement – may also be influenced by physiology and physical health.
Past learning experiences	Behaviourists explain behaviour using concepts such as conditioning. The psychodynamic perspective stresses the importance of early learning. Humanistic theory stresses conditions of worth. Cognitive approaches stress the way we have learned to think.
The environment – including social context	The social context that surrounds us will be very significant in influencing our past learning experiences. Culture and social behaviour are likely to influence how others respond towards us. The degree to which we can build secure attachments, develop an internal locus of control, receive reinforcement, or learn to think positively will be influenced by the 'life chances' we are exposed to within our environment.
A person's own interpretation of themselves and events	Behaviourist approaches have little to say about the importance of a person's own story. Other approaches are highly focused on exploring the way in which a person builds their own assumptions about life. Psychodynamic approaches explore the 'internal working model'. Cognitive approaches explore thought processes. Humanistic approaches explore the ever-changing self-concept that each person builds for themselves.

TABLE 12.6 *Influences on human behaviour*

SCENARIO
Coping with difficult behaviour

Nicole is a social worker who recently interviewed a 78-year-old woman about her request for home care. Soon after Nicole had introduced herself the woman became very demanding and argumentative, and later, when Nicole explained that services were not free, the woman became verbally abusive.

Why was the woman difficult to talk with – and why might she have become abusive? Nicole should consider each of the following issues.

* To what extent might physical health problems, pain or frustration with physical inability to cope influence the service user's emotional reaction?

* To what extent might the service user have learned to be demanding – did Nicole reinforce this behaviour without realising it?

* Might the service user's behaviour have been the result of deeper insecurity?

* To what extent can the service user's behaviour be explained in terms of her learning to react to authority figures with anger? How far is demanding behaviour a result of the social context of the service user?

* To what extent might the service user have felt that her self-concept was being threatened?

Nicole will need to feel that she can produce an explanation for the service user's behaviour if she is to feel confident that she can work with this person. If you can't make sense of a person's behaviour you are likely to become anxious about having to work with them.

What Nicole will not do (providing she behaves professionally) is to label or stereotype the service user – perhaps, for example, as being 'mad or bad'. Nicole must use her understanding of human behaviour in order to avoid taking emotional revenge on a difficult service user. Nicole will use her understanding of people together with care values in order to cope with her own emotions.

SCENARIO
Errol

Errol has diabetes and very high blood pressure; he has been advised that he must stop smoking if he wants to live. Errol cannot cope with the idea of giving up smoking. In discussion he says: 'You don't understand how it feels – I have to smoke, I get awful feelings if I can't get a smoke. Sometimes I wonder what's the point of it all anyway, I mean when your number's up, its up, isn't it. We've all got to die – and what's the point of living – all the good times are gone. When you get older it's all downhill. Sometimes I think – yes, bring it on – there is nothing good in the future – I'm no use to anyone, so what!'

Discussion

It is easy not to respect and value Errol – he is a smoker – he can be stereotyped as 'irrational – a danger to himself and others'. He could be given the label 'depressed'. But these approaches will not help Errol. Taking an attitude of respect and value will involve listening to his life story. Errol's story involves the belief that later life involves illness and suffering. Errol does not believe that his life is important any more. This is a very sad story – but Errol is the person in charge of the story – only he can change it.

FIGURE 12.13 *If health and care workers can build an understanding of the people that they work with, they will be more likely to value individuality and respect the diversity of others*

How psychological approaches might help a care worker to understand Errol's story

The psychodynamic approach

Freud pointed out that people often fail to make logical decisions about their lives. Each person is full of unconscious pressures and conflicts – perhaps resulting from our early years. Some psychodynamic theorists might suspect that needing to place a cigarette in the mouth indicates a 'fixation', an unresolved issue that goes back to the oral stage of development in early life. Perhaps Errol has a deep insecurity about life because of events that he cannot consciously recall. Psychodynamic therapy might enable Errol to understand some of the issues that influence his emotions. He might then be able to take a more positive view of life.

FIGURE 12.14 *If health and care workers do not work from a value base, they may be more likely to label or stereotype service users*

The cognitive approach

Errol has a range of negative thoughts about himself and the future. These negative thoughts may create an emotional state where he loses the will to live – and engages in self-destructive behaviour. Cognitive therapy might enable Errol to understand his thought processes and develop more positive thoughts and emotions. He might then describe his situation differently.

The humanistic approach

Errol does not appear to value himself – perhaps this has something to do with the conditions of worth he applies to himself. Errol is not in touch with the actualising tendency – he sees no joy in living. Perhaps within an encounter that involves deep respect and empathy Errol will recover a sense of joy in being alive. Errol can then tell a much more positive story.

The behavioural approach

Errol experiences not smoking as a punishing experience. Smoking is reinforced with a pleasurable outcome. Perhaps a set of experiences could be designed so that Errol can experience pleasurable outcomes that he can substitute for smoking. New life experiences can result in changed behaviour and therefore new interpretations of life.

Social care workers do not design or deliver therapies. The reason that social care workers need to know about different approaches is that they have to understand behaviour. Rather than judging Errol as a self-destructive and perhaps worthless person, we can understand him as a person who is vulnerable to unconscious pressures, as a person who has a distorted sense of self, as a person who has not learned to understand his own thought processes. Errol may be able to use one or more of the approaches above in order to make sense of his situation. If Errol can create a more positive view of himself he may be able to take control of his life and find the inner resources to give up smoking.

Understanding the possibilities for interpreting behaviour may help social care workers to avoid labelling and taking judgemental attitudes towards service users.

Some people may need to work with a professional therapist in order to cope with personal problems. Many people can manage to take a positive approach to life just with the help and support that caring friends and relatives can provide. Being respected, being listened to and being able to talk through your own life story can provide a positive social context that may empower many people to manage their own life experience.

SCENARIO
Megan

Megan is 14 years old and has a history of self-harm involving cutting her hands and arms. At first she refused to talk to her social worker, so the social worker asked her if she enjoyed drawing. Megan nodded, so the social worker provided coloured pens and paper. Megan's social worker tries to communicate respect and value to Megan. She does this by using non-verbal communication involving eye contact and a gentle facial expression. Megan has had several sessions with the social worker where she draws abstract, very heavily coloured diagrams. The social worker hopes that by providing a 'caring presence' Megan will eventually feel safe enough to start talking about the abstract shapes that she has drawn. In time Megan may begin to explain some of the feelings and issues that lead her to self-harm.

The social worker will not try to 'cure' or 'control' Megan. All the social worker is trying to do is to enable Megan to begin to express her thoughts and feelings. If Megan can explain and understand her own feelings she may be able to change her own behaviour. Megan may need professional help, and the social worker could refer her to a therapist. The first step may be to create an emotionally safe setting where skilled communication and appropriate social care values enable the social worker to gain some insight into Megan's experience.

Summary of Section 12.3

Working within the system of values provides a starting point for empowering people to use their own inner resources to guide their lives.

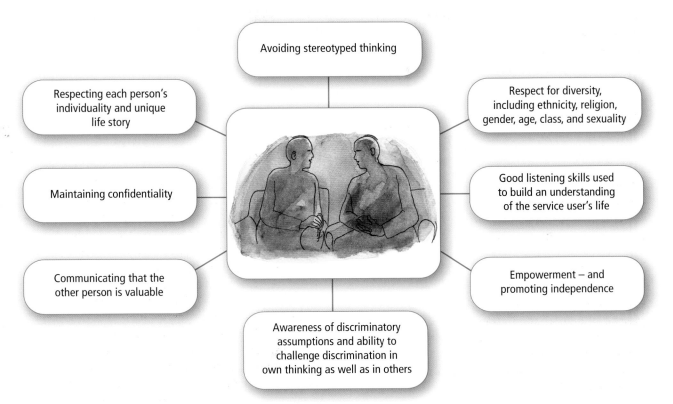

Avoiding stereotyped thinking

Respecting each person's individuality and unique life story

Respect for diversity, including ethnicity, religion, gender, age, class, and sexuality

Maintaining confidentiality

Good listening skills used to build an understanding of the service user's life

Communicating that the other person is valuable

Empowerment – and promoting independence

Awareness of discriminatory assumptions and ability to challenge discrimination in own thinking as well as in others

Consider this

With reference to the study of Adi in sections 12.1 and 12.2, Adi's social worker has built an understanding of the influences on Adi's life. Adi's social worker has been able to find community resources that are appropriate to Adi's identity needs. The social worker has never tried to impose therapy on Adi, and forms of help have been carefully discussed and agreed with Adi before any approaches have been undertaken.

Using concepts, can you identify?

1. Give examples of ways in which the care value base has guided the social worker's behaviour?

2. Give examples of respect and value shown towards Adi?

Go further – Can you analyse issues using theory?

3. Explain why Adi may not have felt safe working with a woman or a member of a different ethnic group, and why it was important that he had the opportunity to work with people he felt safe with.

Go further – Can you evaluate using a range of theories?

4. How might experiencing respect, value, and empowerment contribute towards Adi recovering from stress and depression? Can you explain how being treated with a lack of care values might contribute towards increased stress and depression?

UNIT 12 ASSESSMENT

How you will be assessed

This unit will be assessed through a $1\frac{1}{2}$-hour written examination. Some questions relevant to this unit are set out below.

Unit test

Health education workers undertake some interview research in order to gain a better understanding of why some young people deliberately exceed the safe limits on drinking alcohol. The following anonymous statements are recorded in the interview material:

✳ Person A: I just love drinking; it gives me a buzz – drinking makes me feel so good.

✳ Person B: It must be okay, I don't believe all that health education rubbish, my Dad drinks heavily and it's never done him any harm.

✳ Person C: All my friends drink heavily and I have to join in to be one of them.

1. Using your knowledge of behavioural approaches, explain the main process that might be causing person A to drink excessively. (2)

2. Explain two features of a behaviour modification approach aimed at reducing person A's drinking behaviour. (4)

3. Using your knowledge of cognitive approaches, describe one thought process that may be influencing person B's response. (2)

4. Explain what is meant by distorted cognition. (4)

5. Cognitive therapy is sometimes explained as taking an educational approach; can you explain what is meant by this? (4)

6. Using your knowledge of learning theories, explain why person C may have learned to drink heavily. (2)

7. Explain whether person C's response suggests an internal locus of control or an external locus of control? (2)

8. Explain what is meant by locus of control. (2)

Health education research with some adults who abuse alcohol includes these statements:

✳ Person D: I know I am killing myself with drink, but I can't stop. I suppose I am just a pig (meaning too greedy). I don't deserve to live.

✳ Person E: I feel better when I get drunk, you could say that I drink to forget things. There is nothing good in my life – my life is full of trouble and things go wrong – drinking takes all my problems away.

9. Person D may have a distorted sense of self. Describe a concept that humanistic approaches might apply in this situation. (2)

10. Using your knowledge of humanistic approaches, describe two possible reasons why person D may have developed a distorted sense of self. (4)

11. Person D might be referred for person-centred counselling. Explain three features of person-centred counselling that might distinguish this approach from cognitive or behavioural therapy. (6)

12. Explain two concepts that the psychodynamic perspective might use in order to interpret what Person E has said. (4)

13. Explain how attachment theory could be relevant to understanding the distress that person E is experiencing. (4)

14. Person E might be referred for psychodynamic counselling. Explain three features of psychodynamic counselling that might distinguish this approach from person-centred counselling. (6)

Person E above grew up in a poor family where his father and mother were often out of work. Most of his family and friends drank excessive amounts of alcohol as almost 'a way of life'.

15. Analyse two social influences that may have contributed to the use of alcohol as part of the lifestyle of person E. (6)

Tom is an 86-year-old member of a reminiscence group at a day centre. Tom is a happy person who feels in control of his life. During discussion Tom talks about his life explaining: 'Life was hard in them days, but everyone looked after everyone else. My family would go without things just so I could grow up fit and healthy. No one could want a better family, and all my life I've been lucky – I've been looked after by a wonderful wife and I have had a good life. I've never been rich but I always had enough to get by. Life is what you make it – I enjoy my life. I've got no time for people who moan and grumble – if something's not right in your life then do something about it – that's what I say.'

16. Explain some social influences that may have contributed to Tom's positive outlook on life. (6)

17. Using cognitive theory, evaluate possible explanations for Tom's ability to think positively about his life experience. (6)

18. Psychodynamic theory might explain that Tom's ego is able to balance the pressures within his mind. Explain what the ego is and explain some of the tensions that a person's ego may have to deal with. (6)

19. Using humanistic theory, evaluate possible explanations for Tom's positive self-esteem. (6)

20. Evaluate why the care worker who is leading the reminiscence group will be concerned to work within a system of care values. (4)

Ross is a five-year-old boy who has difficulty in attending to school work. Ross will often leave his seat to look for things on the floor or to talk to other children. Cathy is a classroom assistant who has the job of trying to help Ross to concentrate.

21. Cathy is calm and patient and never becomes angry with Ross. Using your knowledge of behavioural approaches, explain why Cathy does not try to control Ross' behaviour using punishment. (2)

22. Using your knowledge of care values, explain why Cathy would not use punishment in order to try to control Ross' behaviour. (2)

23. Cathy would never attempt to control Ross by using promises such as 'If you sit quietly I will give you some sweets.' Using your knowledge of behavioural approaches, explain why Cathy would not try to negotiate with Ross in this way. (2)

24. Cathy will try to reinforce Ross' attention using social reinforcement. Explain what social reinforcement might involve. (2)

25. Cathy knows that there are tensions between Ross' parents. Cathy thinks that some of the attention problems are connected with stress within the family. Explain the central assumptions involved in family therapy. Explain the difference between a family therapy approach and approaches that simply focus on Ross' behaviour. (6)

26 Ross' parents sometimes talk to Cathy in a slightly childish way and sometimes in a more formal adult way. Cathy is always careful to maintain a complementary transaction in her communication with the parents. Using your knowledge of transactional analysis, explain what is meant by a complementary transaction. (4)

References

Ainsworth, M. D. S., Blehar, M. C., Water, E., Wall, S. (1978) *Patterns of Attachment: A Psychological Study of the Strange Situation* (Hillsdale, New Jersey: Lawrence Erlbaum Associates Inc.)

Ayllon, T., Azrin, N. H. (1965) 'The measurement and reinforcement of behaviour of psychotics', *Journal of the Experimental Analysis of Behaviour*, 8, 357–83.

Bandura, A. (1977) *Social Learning Theory* (Englewood Cliffs, NJ: Prentice Hall)

Berne, E. (1964) *Games People Play* (New York: Grove Press)

Bowlby, J. (1953) *Child Care and the Growth of Love* (Harmondsworth: Penguin)

Clark, A. M., Clark, A. D. B. (eds) (1976) *Early Experience: Myth and Evidence* (Somerset: Open Books)

Giddens, A. (1997) *Sociology* 3rd edn (Cambridge: Polity Press)

Gregory R. L. (1966) *Eye and Brain* (London: Weidenfeld & Nicolson)

Herbert, M. (1981) *Behavioural Treatment of Problem Children* (London: Academic Press)

Luchins, A. S. (1957) 'Primacy-recency in impression formation' in C. Hovland (ed.) *The Order of Presentation in Persuasion* (New Haven, Connecticut: Yale University Press)

McLeod, J. (1998) *An Introduction to Counselling* 2nd edn (Buckingham: Open University Press)

McLeod, J. (2003) *An Introduction to Counselling* 3rd edn (Buckingham: Open University Press)

Marris P. (1996) *The Politics of Uncertainty* (London: Routledge)

Mearns, D., Thorne, B. (1999) *Person-centred Counselling in Action* 2nd edn (London, California, New Delhi: Sage)

Rutter, M. (1981) *Maternal Deprivation Reassessed* 2nd edn (Harmondsworth: Penguin)

Schaffer, H. R., Emerson, P. E. (1964) 'The development of social attainments in infancy', *Monographs of Social Research in Child Development* 29 (94)

Social Exclusion Unit (1999). 'Opportunity for All' (London: HMSO)

Social Trends, Vol. 32 (2002) (London: HMSO)

Social Trends, Vol. 33 (2003) (London: HMSO)

Social Trends, Vol. 34 (2004) (London: HMSO)

Tajfel, H. (ed.) (1978) *Differentiation Between Social Groups: Studies in the Social Psychology of Intergroup Relations* (London: Academic Press)

Tajfel, H. (1981) *Human Groups and Social Categories* (Cambridge: Cambridge University Press)

Zimbardo, P. G. et al. (1995) *Psychology: A European Text* (London: HarperCollins)

Useful websites

The following websites may provide a source of updated information:

Beck Institute for Cognitive Therapy and Research www.beckinstitute.org

Eric Berne www.ericberne.com

General Social Care Council www.gscc.org.uk

NHS Direct Encyclopaedia www.nhsdirect.nhs.uk

Office for National Statistics www.statistics.gov.uk

The International Transactional Analysis Association www.itaa-net.org

Anwers to assessments questions

UNIT 7

1.a) Range of professionals working together to assess and plan services in a co-ordinated way.

b) Any two of the following

Discharge care manager, occupational therapist, social worker, district nurse, members of the intermediate care team, physiotherapist, dietician, diabetic specialist nurse.

c) Based on the individual's needs, services provided based on need, the individual will be involved in decision-making and offered a choice, carer/family will be involved, flexible service provided.

d) Personal and social care needs; physical needs; cultural and religious needs; transport and access needs; financial needs; leisure needs.

A more detailed discussion of the needs will earn more marks.

e) Role of the advocate described and evaluated for the highest mark. Advocates support and speak up for client; help individuals understand their rights; help individuals develop skills to express their wishes; promote independence; empower individual; raise self-esteem; increase user participation.

f) Detailed discussion and analysis with evaluation will achieve the highest score. Empowerment gives Mrs Brown control over her affairs, increases her self-esteem, encourages independence and self-confidence. Mrs Brown needs support to manage the transition from hospital (a secure environment where she is a passive patient) to her own home where she makes her own decisions and has more control over day-to-day living.

g) The use of technology and staff to assist patients/clients to remain in their own home with supportive systems in place to monitor and intervene in the case of an emergency.

h) Monitoring, supporting, predicting functions defined and described.

i) Shopping, collecting prescriptions, dealing with bills, transport are some examples.

2.a) A key worker takes overall control of the assessment and care planning cycle to avoid duplication or omission of tasks.

b) Policies and procedures in place to reduce age discrimination. Monitoring of performance and complaints. Patient surveys including questions on discrimination. Quantitative data on medication, operations and treatment of older people.

3.a) GP or practice manager.

b) Patient focus groups, patient satisfaction questionnaires, clinical governance systems, monitoring complaints.

c) May provide a more user-centred practice, service users are central to the development and planning of services, service users should be consulted on a regular basis.

4.a) Independent sector: private or voluntary organisations, private hospitals, Mencap.

Public sector: statutory services set up by legislation (e.g. NHS/social services).

5.a) Services provided by statutory, voluntary and private organisations.

b) Advantages: flexible, cost-effective, meets service users' needs.

Disadvantages: service user not always clear who is providing service, cheaper service may not have quality.

6. Children's services working together to assess and plan to meet children's needs. Education, social care and health care working together. Child protection issues involve a range of agencies, including statutory, private and voluntary agencies

Services for older people developing a seamless service, single assessment and intermediate care using a range of service providers.

7.a) Two voluntary organisations need to be identified by name.

b) Evaluation of the contribution made by the voluntary sector to health and social care should include the following:

Provide services for minority groups as well as larger client groups.

Many volunteers are users of the service and understand the issues.

Clients feel more comfortable using the voluntary sector than the statutory sector.

Voluntary groups may find it easier to access hard to reach and marginalised groups, for example those with mental health problems.

Services may be more user-centred and adapted to meet the needs of users.

Voluntary groups are part of the community.

Need to evaluate – problem of the two roles of the voluntary sector – to lobby for certain groups and also depend on the statutory sector for funding.

Funding is always a problem for voluntary groups and sometimes services may be reduced or withdrawn if there is no money to meet the needs of clients.

UNIT 8

1. Health trend data shows changes in health over a period of time – usually years – whilst incident data shows the distribution of a condition at a point in time.

2. Morbidity data is information about ill-health as opposed to mortality data, which is information about deaths. Health-related behaviour data is more responsive than either of these two, being able to show changes in health behaviour which can be used to monitor the impact of health promotion activities more effectively then either of the other two since it will respond more rapidly.

3. For men: drinking between 3 and 4 units a day or less indicates no significant risk to health. Regularly drinking 4 or more units of alcohol a day indicates an increased risk to health.

For women: drinking between 2 and 3 units a day or less indicates no significant risk to health. Regularly drinking over 3 units a day signifies an increased risk to health.

Better education and communication.

Improving health and treatment services.

Combating alcohol-related crime and disorder.

Working with the alcohol industry.

4.

Model	Aim	Health promotion activity
Medical approach	To keep people free from diseases associated with inactivity, e.g. diabetes, obesity and heart diseases.	To encourage people to seek early detection and treatment of inactivity-related disorders, e.g. blood pressure and weight screening.
Behavioural change approach	To change people's activity behaviour.	Persuade people to start becoming more active.
Educational approach	To develop people's understanding of the effects of inactivity on health and their decision-making skills.	To give information to service users about the effects of inactivity. To develop their abilities to take up activity and maintain that pattern.
Service-user-centred approach	To ensure that activity advice is available BUT not to offer it unless the client actively seeks it.	The issue would only arise if the service user selected it. Any further discussion would depend on the service user's willingness to address the topic.
Societal change approach	To incorporate activity into everyday life, i.e. change the way in which society as a whole views activity.	Increasing the opportunities for activity, e.g. by reducing costs in leisure centres, improving cycleways and pedestrianising more areas.
Fear	To make the effects of inactivity so frightening as to encourage people to become more active.	For example, a campaign about heart disease which emphasises how young people can die of a heart attack and how activity can prevent this.

5. Who is this leaflet for?

Who produced the leaflet?

How long ago was it first produced, and is the information still relevant or accurate?

Is the language level used appropriate to the target audience?

Is it well designed?

Will it connect specifically with the target audience?

Are the key messages clearly identified or are there too many other distractions?

For the particular leaflet and target audience, where is the best place to display it?

6. Will the person be able to choose freely for themselves?

Will I be respecting their decision, whether or not I approve of it?

Will I be non-discriminatory – respecting all people equally?

Will I be serving the more basic needs before addressing other wants?

Will I be doing good and preventing harm?

Will I be telling the truth?

Will I be minimising harm in the long term?

Will I be able to honour promises and agreements I make?

7. **Normative need:** local data about the numbers of people who exceed the recommended safe drinking levels.

   Comparative need: lack of action to address alcohol concerns in this neighbourhood by comparison with a neighbouring area.

   Felt need: people's local concerns about the impact of alcohol on their local community.

   Expressed need: comments about the impact of alcohol on their local community, for example to local workers or at a public meeting or perhaps in the press.

8. SMART is:

   Specific
   Measurable
   Achievable
   Relevant
   Timed

9. *Summative* assessment is of what has happened; *formative* is an evaluation of *process*.

10. Changing behaviour; cost-effectiveness; disease reduction.

UNIT 9

1. 1C, 2D, 3B, 4A.

2. You should have circled rubella, athlete's foot, chicken pox, measles.

3. A clinical diagnosis points to one clear-cut medical name; a differential diagnosis consists of more than one condition with similar signs and symptoms.

4. a) a vector

   b) droplet inhalation

   c) food

   d) drinking water

   e) direct contact

   f) sexual contact

5. A sign is a feature observed by another person, usually a health professional, whereas a symptom is complained of by the patient.

6. a) A gene is the location of an inherited characteristic on a pair of chromosomes, whereas an allele is a characteristic on one chromosome only – like half a gene.

b) Dominant refers to an allele that shows itself in the individual, whereas a recessive allele does not unless in the presence of another recessive allele.

c) Autosomal refers to all chromosomal pairs (1-22 pairs) except the sex chromosomes. Sex-linked refers only to the sex chromosomes (23rd pair).

7. A patient who agrees to reduce and stop smoking after discussing the matter with the doctor is exhibiting patient–doctor concordance. A patient who uses nicotine patches provided on prescription by the doctor is showing patient compliance.

8. Facilities for diagnosis might be X-ray department, pathology laboratory, ultra-sound scanning and, from a specialist centre, magnetic resonance imaging (MRI).

9. Two local strategies to reduce lung cancer as a result of smoking might be:

Anti-smoking self-help groups

Removal of cigarette vending machines from public buildings.

Two national strategies might be:

Government ban on smoking in public places

Short clips on effects of smoking on TV at peak times.

10. 1C, 2D, 3A, 4B.

UNIT 10

1. Research can be used to: describe something; explain something; test a hypothesis; make generalisations.

2. In health and social care, topics might relate to: care-related situations and problems; testing or review of existing knowledge, treatments and practices; explaining relationships between factors affecting health and well-being; evaluating service interventions and policies.

3. Primary data is that collected by a researcher during the course of a study.

Secondary data is that which has been collected by someone else, other than the researcher of a given project, and is found in other published or Internet sources.

Quantitative data is expressed in numerical form, and can be presented as tables, bar charts, pie charts, graphs, etc.

Purely qualitative data cannot be expressed in terms of numbers. It is often concerned with people's values, attitudes and/or opinions.

4. Secondary research allows a study to be contextualised, and gives background information which can be helpful to a researcher working on a related topic.

Secondary data can be compared and contrasted with primary data; it may also lend support to data collected during a study.

5. Select four principles from:
obtaining consent
avoidance of deception
providing debriefing
enabling withdrawal from the investigation
maintaining confidentiality and the anonymity of participants
protecting participants from harm.

6. Structured data is usually quantifiable and may be presented in the form of tables, bar charts, etc. It is collected in the same way from every respondent, whether by self-completion questionnaire or one that is administered by the researcher.

   Unstructured data is not necessarily quantifiable and includes any topic that the respondent feels is relevant.

7. Unstructured interviews may be used to collect qualitative data; they are very useful at the pilot stage of a project.

8. Percentages alone can be misleading. It is important to give the size of the sample, together with numerical values for responses to each question. This is particularly important for small-scale studies.

9. Bias can result from: the desire of the respondent to please the interviewer; dislike of the interviewer by the respondent; lack of objectivity by the interviewer, including use of leading questions and inappropriate prompts. Leading questions or badly worded questions on a self-completion questionnaire may also lead to bias or may skew the results. Even if an interview involves the use of a structured questionnaire, biased answers may result from any of the factors listed above.

10. There may appear to be a correlation between two variables; however, researchers must test for the possible influence of other factors, and sometimes also seek confirmatory evidence from other studies, before a causal inference may be made.

UNIT 11

1. Gender, ethnicity, social class and age.

2. Stereotyping is using a fixed way of thinking that involves generalisations and expectations about a group of people.

   Marginalisation means being at the fringes of society.

   Labelling is linked to stereotyping. If you apply a negative label to someone, they may adopt certain behaviour as a result, and this is known as the self-fulfilling prophecy.

   Discrimination is treating a group or an individual differently/unfairly on the basis of a social characteristic, such as age, gender, or ethnicity.

3. Answers could include two of the following: technology, mass media, cultural change, political change, ideology, economic factors, cultural change. Students need to state how important these factors are in influencing social change. For example, Marx would say that all social change is caused by economic factors; others would say that other factors are equally or more important, for example the role of technology in developing new transport and communication systems. There are no right answers, but students need to defend their argument.

4. According to the traditional Labour party, welfare should be provided by the state 'from the cradle to the grave'. Universal provision of services will ensure everyone is treated fairly. Means testing is seen as stigmatising, bureaucratic and inefficient. Through state intervention, social stability is ensured.

   According to 'New Labour', welfare should be provided by a range of agencies, including the private and voluntary sector. Means testing is seen as an efficient way to target those most in need of support. Limited services must be carefully allocated – universal provision is wasteful.

5. Implications for service providers if there is an increasing older population: more support services needed to provide care for older people, especially related to problems affecting old age – e.g. chiropody, orthopaedics, physiotherapy, diabetes, support for eye problems. Care in the community will need to be expanded so that people can be looked after in their own homes, and hospital admissions reduced.

Implications for service providers if birth rate continues to decline: fewer services needed for babies and young children, and workers in these areas may need to be retrained. Fewer places in nurseries and hospitals will be needed for babies, children and young people.

6. Immigration relates to the numbers of people coming into a country – such as the UK – and intending to stay for at least one year.

   Emigration relates to the numbers of people leaving a country – such as the UK – and intending to remain away for at least one year.

7. Standard of living, disease levels, lack of clean water, lack of adequate nutrition, environmental factors, such as a smoky atmosphere, inherited conditions, lack of adequate care.

8. The absolute level of poverty is when the individual or family lacks sufficient resources to maintain a healthy existence. Relative levels of poverty are usually referred to current studies and this term is used when the individual or family has a low income (usually below 60 per cent of the median average income) and does not have access to material goods and activities that are seen as necessary to participate in everyday life.

   Absolute poverty could be measured by defining the basic income level required for subsistence (basic existence). Relative poverty could be measured by an instrument like the index used by the Department for Work and Pensions, to assess how far individuals and families are able to participate in everyday life.

9. It is difficult to say why young men are at risk, but factors that appear to be relevant include a lack of social support, unemployment, social exclusion, a history of mental illness, and the use of alcohol and/or drugs.

10. Unemployment is a problem:

    for the government as it means the government has to fund benefits for those who are unemployed, and if people are unemployed they are not paying tax and National Insurance which is an important part of the government's income.

    for families experiencing unemployment, as they tend to have a poorer standard of living, and are likely to experience poverty, especially if family members are disabled. Families from ethnic minorities tend also to suffer from social exclusion. Children in workless families are less healthy as well as experiencing poverty.

    for unemployed individuals, who may feel isolated and depressed, and lack self-esteem and motivation. They may experience poverty. Lone parents who are workless are likely to be in poverty. The individual's experience of unemployment will be affected by social factors such as age, social class, ethnicity and gender.

UNIT 12

1. Reinforcement: the behaviour of drinking alcohol is strengthened because of a pleasurable outcome. Conditioned learning: a conditioned association between pleasure and alcohol is also correct.

2. Behaviour modification would seek to strengthen (reinforce) alternative behaviours. Behaviour modification would involve assessment of behaviour and the design of a programme – possibly using a step-by-step approach, where positive reinforcement is used in order to encourage learned change. Behaviour modification involves learning through experience.

3. Over-generalisation, that is one example is enough to predict the future, polarised thinking – drinking must be good because otherwise it would have to be bad – there is no middle ground. The concept of stereotyping – i.e. fixed rigid categories – is also relevant.

4. Thinking that is distorted by processes such as cognitive primacy, automatic negative thoughts, set thinking, stereotyping, or other processes that prevent thought processes from being completely rational and reasonable. Emotion can play a role in distorting thought processes.

5. Cognitive therapy focuses on thinking skills. Service users may learn to analyse their own self-talk. Cognitive therapy involves developing thinking skills – sometimes called metacognitive skills. Learning to detect distorted and/or negative thinking processes involves learning about self. The skills of a therapist may be similar to the skills of the teacher.

6. Imitation: Bandura's theory of copying or modelling ourselves on other people. Person C may be copying his or her friends.

7. An external locus of control – Person C needs to be thought well of, and accepted by friends. Person C is trying to please and fit in with friends; their behaviour is not guided by their own inner needs.

8. Locus of control means how you evaluate yourself. Do you evaluate yourself in terms of other people's expectations of you; or do you evaluate yourself in terms of your own internal systems of belief and understanding.

9. Person D appears to have low self-esteem, or a negative self-concept.

10. Person D may have been influenced by the conditions of self-worth they experienced from others. Failure to achieve conditions of self-worth may turn into low self-esteem/negative self-concept. Person D has lost touch with their own self-actualising tendency – resulting in negative and self-destructive behaviour.

11. Person-centred counselling involves:

    Creation of an empathetic or understanding counselling relationship as the main focus for change.

    A non-directive approach where the therapist does not suggest solutions to the client's problems. The client finds their own solution using the support of the therapist.

    A focus on the actualising tendency that may enable a person to take control of their situation.

    Also relevant: self-concept, self-esteem, conditions of worth, the need for therapist congruence.

12. Unconscious conflicts – the need to suppress unconscious memories; loss of ego control, the use of alcohol as a defence against internal problems – possibly going back to childhood.

13. Insecure attachment in early life, might result in a range of problems associated with human relationships and adulthood.

14. Psychodynamic counselling involves:

    The therapist providing an analysis of the client's situation.

    An explanation of the client's experience with reference to the concept of the unconscious mind.

    The use of a complex range of theory with respect to dynamic mental processes and defences.

    The assumption that early experience is central to the development of mental mechanisms.

15. Social influences include socialisation into the use of alcohol as a social norm, economic status and poverty creating stress that is relieved through drinking, social class expectations. Imitating the social behaviour of others – referring to social learning theory is also correct.

16. Economic status – Tom did not experience stressful poverty, gender role – has worked positively for Tom, early attachment – possible evidence of secure attachment within the family. Social inclusion – Tom experienced a sense of belonging. Tom's positive attitude suggests a lack of negative effects from social influences.

17. Tom is able to evaluate his own thinking and challenge negative thoughts. Tom has metacognitive knowledge of his own thinking processes. Tom does not experience distorted cognition as a result of thought processes such as automatic negative thoughts, set thinking, stereotyping, or polarised thinking. Tom is able to prevent emotional reactions from controlling his thinking.

18. Ego represents the decision-making focus of the mind – ego represents 'self'. The role of the ego is to balance unconscious pressures, including the animal instincts of the id, with the external demands of society. A person's ego will have to balance the tensions between biological drives and social expectations. Unconscious memories of past experience must be balanced with current demands of human relationships.

19. Tom is in touch with his actualising tendency. He may evaluate the world using a positive locus of evaluation. Tom's self-concept is not distorted by conditions of worth. Tom has developed his potential to become a fully functioning person – free of the distortions that society may have pressured him into.

20. Care values emphasise respect, choice and empowerment; these values may help to promote positive self-esteem and to prevent stereotyping, stress, negative thinking and damage to an individual's self-concept.

21. Behavioural approaches stress the importance of strengthening behaviour; using positive reinforcement to achieve change. Punishment can block a response but it does not strengthen an alternative behaviour. Punishment is an inefficient way of influencing behaviour.

22. Care values stress choice, dignity and empowerment. Punishment may disempower service users, undermine dignity and the ability to make choices. Punishment may also damage the self-esteem and self-concept of a service user.

23. Negotiation involves thought processes – negotiation is not part of a behavioural approach. Bribery puts the person receiving the bribe in control of the situation. Cathy might lose control of the situation if she tries to bribe Ross to behave.

24. Social reinforcement is likely to involve praise, attention, non-verbal behaviour, such as smiling, positive emotional eye contact and possibly touch.

25. Family therapy uses a 'systems approach' in order to interpret behaviour. Ross' behaviour can only be understood in terms of its social significance to others – particularly his parents. Family therapy would explore the way parents respond to problem behaviour. A family therapy approach would not try to modify Ross' behaviour without developing an approach to work with the whole family group.

26. A complementary transaction is an appropriate type of communication that fits the ego state of the person who initiates the conversation, for example adult to adult. It is the opposite of a crossed transaction where communication is responded to with an inappropriate ego state, for example child to adult.

Glossary

Acheson report (1998) a major milestone report which outlined the current state of health inequalities in the country and set out a programme to address them which later influenced many areas of government policy.

action research a research style that focuses on a particular task or problem. A group of people works together to solve the problem, reviewing and monitoring their own actions as they proceed.

acute infection sudden onset and relatively short-term.

advocacy when someone speaks on the behalf of someone else who is unable to voice their views because of learning difficulties, mental health problems or other reasons. The advocate can be a professional, a volunteer or a relative.

ageing population a population in which the proportion of people over the age of 65 is increasing.

ageism negative feelings towards and discriminatory behaviour against a person on the basis of their age.

aggregation to aggregate data is to combine information collected at different times, and possibly from different sources.

aim the 'aim', or outcome, is the broad goal for a piece of work. Usually a project has only one or two aims.

allele half a gene, an inherited characteristic on one chromosome.

analgesic pain-relieving drug.

antibody blood immunoglobulin produced as a result of stimulation by antigens.

antigens proteins on the coats of micro-organisms that stimulate antibody formation.

arthrodesis fusion of a joint.

arthroplasty artificial joint.

assessment a formal method of identifying the health and social care needs of a person in order to set up a care plan.

attachment the emotional process that results in a loving relationship between people. John Bowlby emphasised the importance of attachment during the early years of a child's development.

attributable outcome an outcome which can be directly related to a piece of health promotion activity, that is the cause and effect can be linked.

autosomal refers to 'ordinary' pairs of chromosomes 1-22.

behaviour modification involves the use of reinforcement to strengthen a new alternative behaviour that has been designed to replace a previous undesirable behaviour.

bias distortion of the results of a piece of research, caused by the undue influence of a specific factor.

birth rate the number of live births per 1,000 of the population.

Black Report (1980) a milestone report which clearly described the health inequalities in Britain; viewed as too politically sensitive by the government of the day, the report was suppressed and its distribution strictly limited.

bonding the emotional tie between an infant and his or her mother.

cancer covers a wide variety of diseases caused by uncontrollable growth of a particular body tissue (e.g. lung, bones, etc.).

care plan the plan of treatment and care decided upon in partnership between the service user and carer and the named nurse or key worker.

case conference formal meeting of professionals, service users and family to plan future action.

case report a detailed descriptive study of one particular case. This could be an individual patient or service user.

causal inference a strong suggestion that one particular variable has a specified effect upon another (e.g. that smoking causes lung cancer).

census full-scale national survey undertaken every 10 years since 1801 (apart from 1941). Statistics from the census form the basis for planning social policy and welfare services.

charities non-profit-making organisations set up to support different groups; they may also lobby on behalf of these groups.

Child Support Agency established 1993 by the Conservative government to reduce the cost to the taxpayer of financial support for one-parent families. Absent parents (usually the father) are traced by the CSA and required to pay an appropriate amount of support.

chronic infection gradual onset and long-lasting.

citation the act of making reference to another piece of research.

clinical governance action taken by NHS Trusts to ensure that clinical standards are maintained in hospitals and in the community.

clinical nurse specialist a trained nurse who has had additional training in a specific area (e.g. asthma or dermatology) so that she/he can take responsibility for caring for patients.

clinical trial *see* Randomised Clinical Controlled Trial.

clinician any health professional who is directly involved in the treatment and care of patients (e.g. doctor, midwife).

closed question the kind of question that has a fixed set of answers.

code of conduct professional code of behaviour and practice drawn up by a professional body in order to set standards (e.g. those drawn up by the General Medical Council, or the Nursing and Midwifery Council).

cognitive primacy a person can be primed with information and this information will then go on to bias the way he or she interprets later experiences.

cohort study a systematic study of a specific group of people.

communicable diease infectious disease, passes from person to person.

community strategy a planning document led by the local authority and owned by key partner agencies locally, known as the local strategic partnership. The plan sets out the way in which the partnership will work together to improve the local community across all issues (health, environment, crime, transport, employment, housing, etc.).

comparative need identified from comparisons between similar groups of people, where one group is identified as having poorer health as a consequence of an identified difference.

complementary and alternative medicines (CAMs) a term used to refer to treatments and therapies not encompassed by conventional medicine.

compliance following advice or instructions.

concordance agreement, usually between patient and doctor.

conditional positive regard valuing a person only when they conform to your expectations. Conditional positive regard is a form of social control identified by Carl Rogers who worked within the humanistic perspective.

conditioned learning learning by association. Classical conditioning was described by Pavlov. Operant conditioning, where a behaviour is strengthened by reinforcement, was described by Skinner. Conditioned learning forms an important part of the behaviourist perspective.

congruence when your behaviour fits with your emotions and thoughts.

correlation a link between two data sets, or two (or more) variables within a data set. Correlation does not necessarily imply causality.

Council for Voluntary Services an umbrella organisation for a wide variety of local voluntary sector organisations.

council housing homes built for, and rented out by, the local council as a low-cost alternative to buying.

counselling a form of therapy which is based on an in-depth understanding of psychology together with advanced interpersonal communication skills.

culture the collection of values, norms, customs and behaviours that make one group of people distinct from others. A person's culture will influence the development of their self-concept.

death rate the death rate is expressed as the number of deaths per 1,000 of the live population.

deficit needs physiological needs, safety needs, belonging needs and self-esteem needs that represent the four deficit needs described in Maslow's hierarchy of needs.

demography study of population changes, including death and birth rates and migration rates.

dependency culture the New Right view that universal welfare provision encourages people to expect the state to provide for them.

dermatophyte fungal infection of the skin.

desensitisation a technique based on the theory of conditioned learning, which aims to help people to unlearn an association between the emotion of fear and some situation or object.

direct payment system system by which payments can be made directly to the service user in order to purchase care.

direct taxation income tax or inheritance tax directly levied on a person's income or wealth.

disability the consequence of impairment, or other individual difference. The disability a person experiences is determined by the way in which other people respond to that difference.

disproportionate random sampling a technique to make sure that small groups within a target population are adequately represented in the sample, where this is felt to be important.

distorted cognition ways of thinking that result in inappropriate assumptions about the world.

district nurse a qualified nurse who works closely with the GP and is employed by the PCT.

domiciliary services health and social care services that take place in the service user's home.

dominant an allelele that shows itself in an individual.

drug action team a local partnership responsible for planning the local delivery of the government's drugs strategy.

drug prevention initiatives a range of initiatives which aim to discourage people from using drugs.

drug reference group a local partnership which is tasked to deliver the DAT (drug action team) strategy.

ecologically-based family therapy a method of working with an individual, taking all aspects of his or her life into account.

ego a term used in psychodynamic theory to describe the decision-making component of the mind.

endemic an infection constantly present in a geographical area.

epidemic sudden spread of a disease in an area.

epidemiology study of the geographical incidence of disease in order to demonstrate potential causes (and cures).

equity the principle of social justice directing resources to those who need them most.

ethics to act ethically is to act in a principled manner.

ethnic group a group which shares a common origin, culture or language, as in black and minority ethnic groups.

ethnographic study study of aspects of human behaviour in a specified situation. This usually concerns large groups of people.

evaluation to judge the worth of something.

evidence-based practice to base practice on evidence of what works best.

exercise on prescription a supervised series of exercise sessions usually based in a leisure centre, provided to patients at a reduced rate or free in response to an identified condition such as high blood pressure or mild depression.

experiment a research style involving the comparison of two groups (in social research) or of the behaviour of a specific substance under different conditions.

expressed need a felt need which is voiced by a person or community.

family credit a social benefit in the UK which tops up the income of low-paid workers with children.

family therapy emphasises the need to understand the social circumstances that surround an individual. Family therapy applies 'systems theory' to the interpretation of behaviour.

felt need needs which people feel, that is things we want.

feminism the ideological perspective that examines society and events within society from the viewpoint of women.

food deserts populated urban areas where residents do not have access to affordable healthy food.

food safety the practice of storing and preparing food safely.

gene inherited characteristic located on a pair of chromosomes.

general practitioner the family doctor; they are independent contractors who are funded through the NHS but not employed by it.

generalisation the extent to which the findings of a study are applicable to a wider population.

gross national product (GNP) a measure of the value of the productivity of a country, and therefore its wealth.

health authorities an arm of the health service whose role is to monitor the performance of Primary Care Trusts, support public health practice and develop local health partnerships and networks.

health care assistant a health worker who is not a registered nurse but who may have achieved a Level 3 NVQ award. HCAs work in a variety of settings in hospital and in the community.

Health Development Agency (HDA) a national health agency set up in 2000 to provide information about what works in terms of health promotion activity to enable evidence-based practice in health promotion.

health education an aspect of health promotion which largely relates to educating people about good health and how to develop and support it.

Health Education Authority (HEA) a special health authority which existed to co-ordinate national campaigns and provide government with specific advice about health promoting activity. This was replaced by the Health Development Agency (HDA) in 2000.

health improvement programme a local health document for each Primary Care Trust which sets out plans for meeting both national and local health targets in partnership with other local agencies. Renamed the health improvement and modernisation plan as a result of the NHS Plan 2000.

health promotion outcome the result of a piece of health promotion work; a reduction in a particular disorder or an uptake in screening, for example.

health protection measures taken for a population to safeguard health, for example through legislation, financial or social means. This might include legislation to govern health and safety at work, or food hygiene, and using taxation policy to reduce smoking levels or car use by raising the price of cigarettes or petrol.

health visitors a branch of the nursing profession with a key public health role in local communities, working at a neighbourhood level to identify local health need and support community activity to address those needs.

home care services community team which provides social care for clients in their own home.

Human Immunodeficiency Virus (HIV) the virus which leads to the breakdown of the body's immune system leading to the syndrome known as AIDS.

hypha a fungal filament.

id a term used in psychodynamic theory to describe the 'powerhouse' of drive energy that motivates behaviour.

identity understanding of self which an individual needs to develop in order to cope with life in modern society.

ideology a systematic set of beliefs which explain society and its policies.

imitation learning learning to imitate or copy the behaviour of others.

immunisation process of making people immune to certain diseases, by challenging their immune system with a weak or inactivated version of the disease organism to stimulate the person to create antibodies to the disease.

immunity defence against disease.

incidence the rate of a disease at a given point in time.

income support a means-tested benefit for unemployed people, single parents and disabled people whose income has been assessed as inadequate.

incongruence when a person's behaviour does not fit with his or her beliefs and feelings.

Independent Complaints Advocacy Service (ICAS) a statutory service offering free, impartial and independent support to people who wish to complain about their health care or treatment. They are situated in all areas of the UK.

independent sector agencies that provide health and social care independently from statutory providers.

indirect taxation taxes that are levied on goods and services (VAT).

infant mortality rate the number of deaths of infants under one year old per 1,000 live births; an indicator of general prosperity.

informal care care (usually unpaid) that is given by friends, family or neighbours.

internal working model an internalised set of assumptions about the way in which we relate to other people. This internal working model develops from our attachments to other people from early years onwards.

intervention to take action in order to effect a change, for example to intervene by helping someone quit smoking.

joint commissioning where the NHS and social services co-ordinate services and share costs.

key worker a named person who ensures that the care plan is followed and care is given to the user. Now more likely to be termed the lead professional. The lead professional could be a nurse, a social care worker or a therapist.

life expectancy the average number of years a newborn baby can expect to live.

local authorities political bodies that control towns, cities and rural areas as distinct from national government. Responsible for environmental health, building control, leisure facilities, refuse collection, street cleaning.

locus of evaluation/control an external locus of evaluation means that a person may only see their life as being worthwhile if they are fulfilling the expectations of other people. An internal locus of evaluation means that a person's self-concept is not distorted by the demands of other people.

longitudinal study a piece of research conducted over a significant period of time, allowing the impact of a number of variables to be taken into account.

mammography the use of X-ray photographs of the breasts (a mammogram) to help discover possible cancers.

mass media an umbrella term for a range of media which convey information to the general population, including radio, television, newspapers and magazines.

mean a figure arrived at by adding all score values, and then dividing this by the total number of scores.

means tested benefits social benefits which are delivered only when the claimant is able to show need. Many older people in need tend not to apply for these benefits.

median the middle value in a set of figures.

medical model a model of health which adopts a scientific view of health and body functioning.

meta-analysis a comparison of all research into a specific topic.

metacognitive knowledge meta means beyond or higher. Metacognitive means higher knowledge, or knowledge of how your own thinking works.

milestones major points along the course of a project by which its progress can be monitored.

mixed economy the public, private and voluntary sectors all provide goods and services for service users (e.g. day centres, nursing homes).

MMR vaccine vaccination against measles, mumps and rubella.

mode the most frequently occurring score in any group.

modelling people often imitate or copy others without direct reinforcement or conditioned association taking place. Albert Bandura argues that it is enough to see other people being rewarded for us to choose to copy the behaviour that seems to be rewarded.

morbidity rates information related to the nature and extent of illness in a population.

mortality rates the number of deaths per 1,000 of the population per year.

mycelium mass or body of fungal hyphae.

mycosis any disease caused by a fungus.

national healthy school standard a national initiative which uses an organisational approach to health promotion to provide schools with a framework within which they can work to develop their health promoting capacity.

national service frameworks a mechanism for unifying standards of care within the NHS.

negative reinforcement an outcome which strengthens or reinforces behaviour. Negative reinforcement means that a bad situation improves or gets better and this improvement strengthens the behaviour associated with it.

NGMS the new contract negotiated by the government with family doctors to govern the delivery of general medical services.

NHS Direct a 24-hour telephone service that is staffed by nurses.

NHS Plan (2000) government document which outlines a ten-year plan for modernising the NHS.

NHS Trusts hospitals and PCTs which are statutory bodies and employ staff to deliver health care.

non-communicable disease disease that cannot be passed from one person to another.

normative need need identified by an expert or professional according to their own standards; where something falls short of this standard then a need is identified.

obesity a body mass index (BMI) in excess of 30.

objectives the specific goals to be achieved in delivering a stated aim or outcome.

Office for National Statistics (ONS) national body which compiles information on the UK population; responsible for carrying out the census every ten years.

official statistics statistical data provided by central and local government and government agencies on unemployment rates, crime rates, etc.

oncogene gene that causes cancer.

open question a question to which the respondent replies in his or her own words. Such questions cannot usually be answered by a simple 'yes' or 'no'.

operant conditioning conditioning caused by reinforcing outcomes which cause a behaviour to become strengthened.

opportunity sampling the use, by the researcher, of those people who are available and/or willing to take part in a study.

organismic self organismic stresses that each person is a biological organism. Within our biology are inner resources that we can draw on in order to constantly grow and develop into a more complete person.

outcome evaluation seeks to establish the worth of work when it has reached its conclusion.

outcome measures indicators of success for health-promotion activity.

palliative treatment of symptoms, not a cure.

PALS (Patient Advice and Liaison Service) departments within every trust that advise patients on the services available and deal with queries and complaints.

pandemic infection that affects a high proportion of the population in a large geographical area.

pathogen disease-causing micro-organism.

patriarchy used by feminists to describe society as organised by men for the benefit of men and the oppression of women.

PCTs Primary Care Trusts set up after 1999 to commission services from hospitals and other agencies to deliver care. They also employ staff to provide community services.

perception our experience of the world as filtered through our sense organs.

pharmacist qualified professional dispensing prescriptions and giving advice to patients.

phobia irrational or unreasonable fear which influences an individual's behaviour.

pilot study a 'dry run' to test out a new data collection tool; doing this allows for modifications and improvements to be made before the actual study begins.

placebo something that looks like a medical intervention, but which in fact does not contain any active treatment at all.

population as well as meaning the people who live in a particular area or country, this term is used in research methodology to indicate the total number of people who are being studied.

poverty a lack of sufficient resources to achieve a standard of living considered to be acceptable in that particular society.

PPI forums Patient and Public Involvement forums of patients and members of the public who have a special interest in the NHS. They are attached to PCTs and hospital trusts and they monitor services and represent the public.

prejudice a pre-judgement or fixed idea which may result in harm to others.

prevalence a measure of how many people are suffering from a particular condition or behaving in a particular way at any one time.

prevention reducing or avoiding the risks of diseases and ill-health primarily through medical interventions.

primary data information collected by a researcher during the course of a study.

primary health care setting usually refers to the GP surgery, health centre and community services.

primary prevention an attempt to eliminate the possibility of getting a disease.

privatisation government policy in which the public sector is reduced and services are transferred to private agencies (e.g. gas, water, electricity).

probability the likelihood of a set of data being obtained. A data set with a probability of 1 is inevitable; that with a probability of 0 is impossible.

progressive taxation direct taxation which increases dependent on the amount of income received. This measure is to achieve a greater equality of distribution of income and wealth in a society.

proportionate stratified sampling a technique to make sure that the subjects chosen for research represent the characteristics of the target population; thus, if 70 per cent of the target population is female, the gender split of subjects in the actual sample must be 70 per cent female, 30 per cent male.

psychodynamic a psychological perspective which interprets human behaviour in terms of a theory of the dynamics of the mind.

psychoneuroimmunology (PNI) a scientific discipline that specifically explores the relationships between the mind and the various systems within the body, in particular the immune and hormonal systems.

public health specialism workers with expertise in assessing the patterns of ill-health locally and identifying what types of health care provision and health promoting activities are required to improve health.

punishment behaviour results in an outcome that is experienced as being unpleasant. Unpleasant outcomes may inhibit or block a response. Punishment is the opposite of reinforcement; punishing outcomes will weaken a behaviour.

qualitative data cannot usually be expressed simply in terms of numbers. It is often concerned with people's values, attitudes and/or opinions.

quantitative data can be expressed in numerical form. It can also be presented in tables, bar charts, pie charts, graphs, etc.

quota sampling the selection of a specified number of subjects, who satisfy a number of predetermined criteria; often used by market researchers when stopping potential subjects in the street.

race a large group of people with common ancestry and inherited physical characteristics.

racism discrimination against a person on the basis of their racial background, usually based on the belief that some races are inherently superior to others.

random sampling selection of subjects at random from the sampling frame.

randomisation allocation of a group of selected subjects to either a treatment group or a control group. This can be done manually, or by computer.

Randomised Clinical Controlled Trial (RCCT) a research method involving more than one sample group. One group receives a specified treatment, the other doesn't (it either receives another treatment, a placebo or no treatment at all) and the results are compared.

recession deteriorating economic conditions when unemployment increases and productivity declines.

recessive an allele that does not show itself unless in the presence of another recessive allele.

redistribution when income and wealth are taken from the rich by progressive taxation and given to the poor in the form of benefits.

relatability the extent to which research findings may be applicable to other, similar population samples.

reliability the extent to which a set of results can be replicated by repetition of a test, experiment or survey.

reminiscence therapy a form of therapy where an individual uses the memory of their past to strengthen their current self-concept and self-esteem.

research a systematic enquiry that is designed to add to existing knowledge and/or to solve a particular problem.

respondent a person who takes part in a survey, and who 'responds' to the questions (either by self-completion of a questionnaire, or during an interview).

risk assessment procedure that assesses the risks in the environment to the service user (e.g. unsafe homes). It can also be applied to people with mental health problems when a doctor will decide whether they are a risk to themselves or to others.

rounding an adjustment made to a quantity so that it is expressed as a whole number (rather than as a fraction or as a decimal).

sampling the selection of a representative cross-section of the population being studied.

sampling frame a comprehensive list of the potential subjects for a study.

schema an organised pattern of thought.

school nurse a specialist branch of community nursing, historically with a key role in screening programmes within schools, but increasingly involved with other health promoting activity, such as drop-in sessions on school premises, offering advice about drug use, sexual health, etc.

screening identification of unrecognised disease or defect by the application of tests, examinations and other procedures which can be applied rapidly. Screening tests sort out apparently well persons who may have a disease from those who do not.

secondary data data collected by people other than the researcher of a given project, and found in other published or Internet sources.

secondary prevention activity to improve the health of those people identified as being in the early stages of a disease.

self-actualisation an important need identified by Maslow which explains that individuals need to fulfil their potential. Most people spend their life focused on deficit needs and do not achieve self-actualisation.

self-actualising tendency a natural tendency to develop and grow identified by Carl Rogers. According to Rogers everyone is capable of responding to their inner self-actualising tendency.

self-advocacy when the service user is encouraged to speak on their own behalf about the services they need.

self-concept the learned idea of self that an individual develops. This sense of self enables a person to understand themselves as separate and distinct from other people.

semi-structured data information collected about specific topics, but expressed in the respondents' own words.

settings-based approach a way of organising health promoting activity. A setting might be school, hospital, primary care, workplace, etc.

sex-linked an inherited condition located on the sex chromosomes pair 23 (mainly the X chromosome).

sexually-transmitted infection (STI) diseases which can only be passed by sexual activity.

sign a feature observed by the patient, doctor or carer.

SMART an acronym for effective objective setting. Objectives should be specific, measurable, achievable, realistic and time specific .

social class the status given to different types of occupation or work. Social class is currently defined by the Office for National Statistics socio-economic classification system.

Social Fund budget made available under the Department for Work and Pensions to provide interest-free loans and other payments to the recipients of social security benefits.

social role a set of expectations which guide an individual's behaviour in specific circumstances.

social security the system of welfare support provided by the state for its citizens.

social skills training training to use verbal and non-verbal behaviour to achieve the desired effect on others in social situations.

Social Trends annual digest of statistics produced by the Central Statistical Office.

socialisation involves learning the social norms of the culture that you grow up in.

societal change attempts to elicit health improvement by changing society (e.g. by reducing tolerance to drink driving).

specialist health promotion services a small specialised service which supports the development of the health promoting role of others, the development of new services and policies which can promote health locally.

statistical significance when figures satisfy certain statistical tests, they are said to have statistical significance.

strategic health authorities 24 health authorities responsible for assessing needs in their area, delivering services through the PCTs and trusts, and monitoring quality of service.

stress response the physiological processes which result from a mental perception of threat.

structured data data collected in a standardised way; such data can usually be quantified.

subject used in research methodology to indicate the person or people being studied.

summative evaluation an assessment of what has happened.

Sure Start/Sure Start Plus local programmes concentrated in neighbourhoods where a high proportion of children are living in poverty. The programmes work with parents and parents-to-be to improve children's life chances through better access to family support, advice on nurturing, health services and early learning.

survey a descriptive study which has a very broad scope. It involves the systematic collation and analysis of data from a target population.

symptom a feature complained about by the patient.

synoptic test a form of assessment that explores a student's knowledge gained from studying a range of units. The synoptic test will assess a student's general understanding of core health and social care issues.

systematic review a thorough and systematic comparison of RCCTs to produce convincing evidence for the effectiveness (or otherwise) of a particular drug or treatment.

Tackling Drugs Together first national drugs strategy launched in 1993.

target audience the group an activity is aimed at.

The Health of the Nation (1992) the country's first national health strategy.

transactional analysis the approach was developed by Eric Berne; a 'transaction' is any exchange of communication between people. Transactional analysis analyses what happens when people communicate.

transmission method of spread from one person to another.

triangulation comparison of data from different sources on the same subject.

unconscious mind within psychodynamic theory, the unconscious mind contains drives and memories that influence our behaviour. An individual is not conscious of these influences on their behaviour.

universalism an approach to welfare that maintains that all citizens have an equal right to free and accessible services provided by the state.

unstructured data data that is not tightly controlled by the interviewer, or by the questionnaire being completed. Such data is expressed in the respondents' own words.

vaccination challenges a person's immune system to produce antibodies by injecting a dead or weakened version of the disease organism.

validity relates to the quality of research results.

value judgements to judge someone or something from a standpoint based on your own values; for example, because I don't smoke and believe it to be bad for the health, I think that a person who smokes is a bad person.

variable something that can occur in different forms, that is it can vary in its characteristics.

vector intermediate carrier from one host to another.

vicarious reinforcement if we imagine that another person is receiving a pleasurable outcome and the imagination of reinforcement is sufficient to cause us to copy his or her behaviour.

victim blaming people frequently simplify health choices by blaming the person who chooses to adopt an unhealthy behaviour for making that choice. In reality things are rarely that simple, for example people cite lack of time due to work pressures as the major cause of taking too little exercise.

voluntary sector non-profit-making organisations that provide services and also act as pressure groups. Age Concern and Mencap are examples of voluntary organisations.

welfare pluralism provision of services from many different sources: private, public and voluntary.

welfare state areas of service provision that the government has a role in funding, planning and regulating. The key areas are health, education, income maintenance, housing and personal social services.

World Health Organization established on 7 April 1948, it was a response to an international desire for a world free from disease.

Index

Page numbers in italics refer to Figures and Tables